Kissing Consciousness

Inviting in a World Beyond Self-Judgement

The Handbook for The Movement

VOLUME I

Edited by Kylie Stedman
Illustrations by Mike Young Design

Kissing Consciousness Publishing
With thanks to La Maison, Edmonton, Canada

www.KissingConsciousness.com

Printed in the United Kingdom

First Printing, 2020

ISBN: 978-1-9162587-0-9 (Paperback)
ISBN: 978-1-9162587-1-6 (eBook)

Kissing Consciousness Publishing
Potten End, Berkhamsted, Hertfordshire, HP4

www.KissingConsciousness.com

Disclaimer

The information provided in this book is designed solely to provide a helpful perspective on the subjects discussed. This book is not meant to be used, nor should it be used, to diagnose or treat any medical or health condition, or to replace an appropriate health professional. For diagnosis or treatment of any medical problem, consult an appropriate health professional. References are provided for informational purposes and do not constitute endorsement of the source. Web addresses listed in this book may change.

Contents

Thanks

Thanks to Kylie Stedman, David Blacker, David Heard, Keith Pointon, Jon Freeman, Jan Day, John Christian, Mike Young, Daniel Harris, Fiona Cutts, Jim Lockard and Sam Pearce, and an extra special thank you to Angèle Beaudoin.

Introduction

"The map is not the territory." – Alfred Korzybski

Human beings evolved from animals, developing human thought in the process. Human thought is largely based on concepts. We can conceptualise life. Engineers can conceptualise the mechanics of bridges. We can conceptualise *ourselves.*

On the flip side, the arrival of conceptual human thought also brought the capacity to self-judge: To believe that there could conceivably be a difference between what we are, and what we *should* be. Animals don't run around beating themselves up about what they should have done last Thursday, or two years ago.

Looking at this from the perspective of the individual, we can also see how this capacity to think of ourselves conceptually usually develops early in childhood. When we're born we cannot distinguish ourselves from our mothers – physically, mentally or emotionally. We distinguish ourselves as individuals, first physically, then emotionally, and then as we distinguish ourselves mentally we develop the capacity to create a concept of ourselves. This begins what's known as the *Egocentric* stage of human development. Crucially, as our concept of ourselves develops, we also develop the capacity to believe that something is *wrong* with that concept. We judge ourselves: We're not good enough, or not allowed to relax as who we are. We should be better, different, whatever.

But even if we are pleased with our concept of ourselves, the concept is ultimately not us. It's not entirely who we are. It is only a concept. We can realise that the concept is not us because it did not exist when we were born. It came along later. If that concept of ourselves were truly and fully us, who were we before we were capable of developing concepts?! There was a Self before there was an Ego.

This is the point at which humanity confused its own Ego with its true nature. We did this both individually and collectively. Wisdom was lost.

And so humanity's greatest tool – its mind – has separated it from its very nature, its own identity and its natural way of being. This has led to a world that has dehumanised every single one of us. Our task, as humans, is to learn how to have minds and enjoy their benefits, without allowing them to constrict us in any way, or to hide our true selves from us. This is actually easy to do, just by noticing that this is the nature of the mind. After all, we enjoy the benefits of pocket calculators, but don't allow them to tell us what to do! As a human race, we are in the process of regaining our true identity. There's a deeper, more satisfying truth to our true identities, to who we are. We are human beings not 'human thinkings'. Thinking is merely a part of who we are.

The nature of human thought has given us the capacity for self-judgement. Furthermore, an entire buffet of rules and constraints has emerged, especially during recent centuries of political and religious power, which have prevented all of us from even being able to remember what it was like to be fully free to act naturally. This is no-one's fault. Humans evolved to this system – and are now thankfully evolving beyond it. Wisdom is being reclaimed.

Chapter One

The Simplicity and The Stupidity

The Simplicity

Your consciousness is like a light switch. At any given moment a light switch is either off or on. It cannot be both off and on at the same time. Nor can it be *neither* off nor on at the same time. It can only be in one of those two states. There aren't multiple options.

A light switch can be switched off or on at any given moment. It can remain on for hours, then remain off for hours, or it can be quickly switched off and on, on and off, several times a minute, or even several times a second. It is a moment to moment thing.

This is you! This is exactly how you operate. In any given moment you are either in a state of self-acceptance or a state of self-judgement. This state is what determines your relative happiness or misery in any given moment. People tend to think it's about what they've got. Or what they are doing. Not so. Happiness is primarily about a state of Consciousness.

You can try it! Try being happy whilst simultaneously judging yourself! You'll find it impossible. Try being discontent while being in a state of self-acceptance and self-love. It can't be done. You're either one or the other, "off" or "on", in any given moment. You can't have light when the switch is "off", and you can't have it dark when the light switch is "on."

Specific possessions and activities do have some relevance, as do feelings and emotions, but they're essentially 'secondary'. We'll come to this later.

This Thing Called 'Conscious'

So this is what 'Conscious' means: That you have no self-judgements operating on you in a given moment. It also means that you are operating from a position of genuine choice, and effectiveness and power, and a hundred (okay, about 30 or 40) other qualities that we'll come to later.

The opposite of 'Conscious' is 'Unconscious', meaning that you are operating under the influence of self-judgement(s). In a sense, when 'Unconscious' you'll only have the *illusion* of choice, rather than the reality of it. Of course, by the nature of these things, you will be at least somewhat unaware that these self-judgements are affecting you. Or if you are familiar with working with self-judgements you'll be at least somewhat unaware of exactly *how* the judgements are affecting you. We'll talk later about 'Unconscious Unhappiness'. As my friend David Heard says, "If you are doing it for other people's approval, how can it make you happy?!"

Self-judgements also masquerade as judgementalism of others, or of the world. We will talk about this later, too. For now, what we want to understand is how to achieve a full state of self-acceptance on an ongoing basis, without interruption by any 'Stuckness' caused by self-judgements …

Being 'In The Flow'

I'm sure you've heard about the notion of 'being in the flow'. When you are Conscious you are in the flow and everything is okay, you are at one with yourself and you have that smile on your face – you know the one I'm talking about! When everything you do has that golden quality to it.

And when you are Unconscious? This is when everything pisses you off. Even the things you're supposed to enjoy are not 'delivering' for you. You are at odds with yourself and everything you try is futile. This is because you are tripping yourself up. Your self-judgements are sabotaging you.

We all have moments of Flow and moments of Stuckness, to varying degrees. The amount of Stuckness we have is determined by the amount of self-judgements we take on board growing up, and throughout life – minus any proactive efforts we may have made to let go of them.

In this book I am going to teach you how to spot self-judgements, wherever they're hiding. I am going to teach you how to let go of them, first individually, then rapidly, thousands at a time, so that you can more likely fulfil your heart's desire in this life, regardless of how much of a psychological head start you *didn't* get.

So the key to life, the key to joy and happiness and success and maximising your prosperity, is prolonging the moments in which you are 'in the Flow' (of self-allowance) into nice long strings, and releasing the moments in which you are in 'Stuckness' (self-judgement), so that they rarely arise, and are quickly dealt with even when they do.

Let's say you have 10 moments, as different life contexts arise: Flow, Stuck, Flow, Stuck, Flow, Flow, Flow, Stuck, Stuck, Stuck. What causes us to go from a state of being in the Flow to a state of being in Stuckness? I mean, why on Earth would we ever choose to give that juiciness up?! Answer: We move into Stuckness when the situation changes into something which is not 'allowed', as a result of our self-judgements. The change in circumstances could be a change in our thoughts, a memory, an event, or someone entering the room, around whom we are not allowed to be ourselves.

Experiencing annoyance and frustration can be a good thing because it wakes us up to where we have a self-judgement acting upon us, which we can then choose to change. These self-judgements create our negative beliefs.

How do we change a self-judgement? Not directly – they change when we become Conscious of them. Self-judgements are always false, always lies, so illuminating them with our awareness gives them no place to hide. So the more Conscious we are, the more happy and successful we are. The two are hugely intertwined.

Conscious You, Conscious Body

Being in self-judgement causes stress. What happens to your body when you are in self-judgement? It is constricted, right? You feel tense, almost holding your breath. Of course you are tense – you have to watch your step, in case you do that thing your self-judgement prohibits.

What happens to your body when you are in a moment of total self-acceptance? You are relaxed, aren't you? So a totally unavoidable consequence of the off/on nature of your Consciousness is that you can also feel it in your body, good or bad. That is why I invite you to 'think' with your body, or rather *not* think. In other words, it's not so much about thinking, but attuning to your bodily information. Your body is the infallible guardian of your 'truth'. If you 'think' with your body, you are a genius. If you think only with your cognitive mind, you are shutting down many of your capacities and truths.

Kissing Consciousness

Whilst it sounds rather sexy, and there's no harm in that, the name Kissing Consciousness actually has nothing to do with lips.

K.I.S.S. is a business acronym which means "Keep It Simple, Stupid!" I have commandeered it for our use here, in our desire for Conscious Living (i.e. living without self-judgement). Therefore, 'Kissing Consciousness' means "Keeping the approach to Conscious Living simple."

'Kissing' in the context of Consciousness means following the simple principle of immediate knowing and awareness of what is, and nothing else. So I invite you to keep your approach to Consciousness simple. Whenever you don't, you are avoiding your own feelings and your power.

Recently, a friend asked me for my thoughts on a situation he was dealing with. After I'd helped him drop into his feelings of fear so that he could release them and get back into his power and choice (his Flow), he still had elements of feeling which he wasn't ready to face. In avoiding those feelings, he went back into all kinds of hurried thoughts and statements about what he could do about his situation. Then he smiled, realising he was 'doing it again' – avoiding himself and his own inner information. You can live at odds with yourself or you can live at one with yourself; it's entirely up to you. Being aware is simple. Being unaware leads to all kinds of ill-fated attempts to control what is usually the uncontrollable. When people start talking in complicated ways it's usually a sign that they are avoiding themselves and their feelings.

The last word of the K.I.S.S. acronym, 'Stupid', is also relevant to Conscious Living. 'Stupid' is another way of saying 'Unconscious', because it reflects the bizarre and stupid – *unaware* – things we think, do and say when we have Unconscious self-judgements influencing our thoughts and behaviour. Kissing Consciousness is all about letting go of the self-judgement that eradicated our full awareness and made us 'Stupid' (Unconscious) in the first place.

The Stupidity

When you were young you were told not to do something. This was something that represented the wholesome truth of who you were. But you weren't just told not to do it; this was communicated to you with an emphatic assertion and energy that made it clear to you that the part of you that was that way inclined was not even allowed to be acknowledged.

You've held on to that judgement until now. Would you like to let it go?

How can I know this about you? It's an experience common to every human being ever born. You probably had many such experiences, both remembered and forgotten. Thousands. Yet this is good news because it means that the opportunity for gain here is huge beyond belief.

This is what Kissing Consciousness does. It offers an insight and awareness that invites you to let go of self-judgements long Unconscious and buried, and thus regain the real, amazing, beautiful and wondrous parts of you that are also your way to real joy and happiness. You have so much to reclaim: The power, the trapped energy, the opportunity ... do you need a deep breath?

"Don't be sexual. Don't be confident. Don't be happy. Don't be popular. Don't be successful. Don't be healthy. Don't feel loved. Don't be free! Don't be you!" Oh my goodness, all that is heavy. But it is heavy only when it is held on to and avoided. Shall we let go of it all?

About This Book

This is a **physioactive** book, which means that it's likely going to have an effect on your body. It's not a mental-only, 'read a few theories that you agree with but nothing actually changes' book. It says things that may awaken places in your Consciousness, and in your body.

Imagine the taste of vinegar in your mouth. Notice that, just by thinking about vinegar, you may well have created a physical response in your body. If your Consciousness and your body are that intertwined, what else can you ask of your body, or of your Consciousness? What else can your Consciousness do? What else can your body do?

That's a dummy example of how the words of this book may affect your body, but let's have a real example. Imagine that that which you desire most, but are afraid to achieve, is given to you ... and as your pulse races and your mouth goes dry, your body reacting uncomfortably in fear … instead of avoiding the feelings and pushing them all back down into numbness (and the perpetuation of self-denial), imagine that you allow them to *be.*

Allow them to be. Allow them to be forever, for an eternity. Can you notice that you are still alive? That's an example of how we will use Consciousness and apply it to get real breakthroughs.

Chapter Two

The Power of Love

Welcome to a cold but clear Monday night in Malmö, Sweden. In this chapter you're going to get to hear and 'sit in on' a presentation called 'The Power of Love' that I gave at Mindfloor in November 2014. It's slightly edited down.

www.KissingConsciousness.com/PowerOfLove

James: Thank you, nice to see you all. And what was that question…?

Audience Member: How old are you?

James: How old am I?

Audience Member: Are you old enough to stand here? (we all laugh)

James: I would think so, I'm 41. You tell me if that's old enough. (smiles, more laughter)

(to all audience) How are you doing, you okay?

Audience: Yes.

James: Great. Me too.

Welcome to The Power of Love. I'm James Blacker, I'm a Wisdom Coach, and I'm also an Integral Philosopher, and this is my introduction presentation for the live, larger events that I do called 'Awaken Your True Potential', which is based on the Wisdom Course that I wrote about eight years ago. We've been teaching that as a live event for about a year, and yesterday we were doing it in Copenhagen, with a group of people like yourselves …

The whole point of this really is to change anything that we want to change, or get more of ourselves out of ourselves … probably the most important thing is to be true to ourselves. So this really is aimed at helping us to do that in a world which largely discourages it, and makes it at best a very difficult thing to do.

So how did you get on with the questions?

Audience Member: Good.

James: All good? Did you have any thoughts from them, has anybody got anything that they want to talk about before I start? Has anybody got anything that is urgent to raise, or that they'd like to achieve, or has been on their mind all day? ... You all look pretty [happy]!

Audience Member: It makes you think. You just read those questions, I mean, you have to use your mind, then you answer, then you get back to the questions and you answer something else, so I mean, very good.

James: So it makes you think? Great. Does anybody want to share any of their definitions? Would anyone like to share one of their definitions of what love is?

Audience Member: To me love is a lot. It's a love for my family, love for my friends. It's also passion. And energy. And love is not for ... I give a different part of all my heart to different people.

James: Lovely.

Audience Member: That is my answer. Top of my mind.

James: Okay. Thank you. Anyone have a definition of positive thinking they'd like to share?

Audience Member: Try to see opportunities instead of lack.

James: Thank you. And yours was?

Audience Member: Yes ... see anything as neutral and for growth.

James: See anything as neutral and for growth? Wow, I like that! What do you mean by 'neutral'? Neutral as in ...?

Audience Member: Is not good, is not bad. It is just growth through events, not good or bad. Anything is for growth. Anything that happens.

James: And that's positive thinking. Wow!

Realisation 1: Success

James: Cool. Okay, first thing I'd like to do is define two different versions of Success. So I'd like you to … go into your minds with your eyes closed, and … I want you to imagine a situation in which you've lived your life and you have a definition of what success is … maybe a few, three or four things, some 'tick boxes' that you need to tick in order to consider yourselves successful. And I'd like you to imagine that you've reached that, or you've achieved that, and then the feeling that you have does not fulfil you. Okay? … that you've got there but you don't feel fulfilled. So I'd like you to, if you can, to feel into the feeling of having done something, maybe even for a long time, maybe even for a year or a decade, decades … and then you have that feeling of not being fulfilled.

You look to me like you've pretty much been able to tune into that kind of feeling. Yeah.

There are two sayings of Success, two different wisdom quotes let's say, which are very similar. You've seen these kind of things … one is that "Success without fulfilment is failure." And the other is that "Success without fulfilment is nothing." So those two quotes are pretty much the same. Would you put your hand up if that feeling that you just had a moment ago is something that you'd like to have?

(nobody in the audience raises their hand)

Okay, that's good news … (laughter)

… because I'm going to define two different versions of success.

The first is … essentially, things you *should* be. So society has its definition of what success is, and maybe it's a house, a car, these kind of things. But these are really external things, so … all of us, when we get into the habit, the mindset of getting drawn into that kind of thing, we're essentially trying to achieve things maybe semi-consciously for other people, or what society thinks is success.

So the first definition of success is based on … essentially judgementalism. Or judgement … so something we *should be.*

Realisation 2: Our Inherent Perfection

James: So we have our basic nature, which is beautiful and wonderful, and is going to give us everything we want to fulfil ourselves. And then we have all these ideas of "I need to be this, I need to be that, my mum wants me to be this, my dad wants me to be that … there's something on the TV – oh, I shouldn't have grey hair … blah blah blah", so everywhere we are going we are getting pulled all over the place. So the first definition of success, which is what 80% or 90% of the people out there are all chasing for, is success based on self-judgement and judgementalism.

There's one alternative, of course, which is Success based on your true heart's desire, and what's true for you. So we're going to define those two, and having defined them, we're going to help ourselves to … me too, very much me too, everything we do is very relevant to my life, as well as – I'm sure – yours too.

So we have Success as love-based Success, and we have judgement-based success.

Realisation 3: Assessment or Judgementalism?

James: (writes the two definitions of success on the white board, pauses, looks at the scruffy writing) … that's terrible handwriting, isn't it!

Audience Member: Yes.

Audience Member: Judgement!

James: (smiles, audience laughs) It's an assessment. … That's a good place to go, okay, so we have a difference between assessment and judgement, and this is very important because in spirituality a lot of people say, "You can't make judgements, you mustn't make judgements." We have to keep our feet on the ground, so if I'm trying to park my car, that's six feet wide, in a space that's five feet wide, I need to make an assessment about whether it's going to fit. But at the same time, if somebody's saying, "by my age I should be in a relationship, I should have children, blah blah blah," that's not an assessment, that's judgement because the word 'should' is coming in …

Realisation 4: The Language of Love (and Non-Love)

James: We're in Sweden, so this is slightly difficult, but certainly for the people in England and America, etcetera … hopefully … do you have 'should'? Is the word 'should' in your language? So in English we have Future Tense, Present Tense and the Past Tense. We also have the Conditional Tense, which is, for example, "This is what you ***should*** have done!"

Audience Member: 'Ought to' is more … That you ought to have done …

James: Ought to, yes. So as a tense it's kind of got its own section in grammar. So it's quite interesting that we talk about Unconditional Love and Conditional Love. A lot of people say that the name for Unconditional Love is Love, and the name for Conditional Love is something else. … In English we have what's called the Conditional Tense. So it's quite easy once we learn, to actually see when people are talking to us in a way that is not based on them actually loving us – because they use the Conditional Tense. Three words that come in a lot are 'should', 'would' and 'could', and their reverses, which are 'shouldn't', 'wouldn't' and 'couldn't', which is just the same thing in reverse – if you 'should' be in a relationship you 'shouldn't' be single, for example.

Realisation 5: Judging Others

James: So that's a clue there. Often when people are judging us, the reason they're judging us is because they are judging themselves as well.

Audience: Yes.

James: So we're going to come on to that as well.

There was another point I had there, my brain goes here, there and everywhere! … Oh yes, okay, so yes Conditional Tense is "You should be this, and you should be that." Sometimes there's another part of grammar which comes with it, which is Imperative Grammar, which is, in other words, telling people what to do. So as a wisdom teacher, and hopefully as somebody who's committed to The Power of Love, I never tell people what to do. Very rarely. Maybe if a car's coming …

(audience laughs)

… but essentially I never … never, ever tell people what to do. … because, well for two reasons. The first is that it's not my place to tell them what to do. So if I need them to be something else … why do I need them to be something else?!

Audience Member: Yes.

James: … you know. It's like if you come here this evening, you either choose to come or you choose not to come. And if you choose that you don't come and I have a problem with it, that's not …

(acting, in a gruff voice) "Come here, you must come!" … that would reflect something self-judging in me!

But the other thing is, one of the principles of wisdom is, because you are being true to your heart you want to be what we call 'Self-Referral', in other words we make decisions from within. We get information from outside, but we make decisions based on … what's true for our heart, our gut instinct, what our senses are telling us, we trust our own awareness.

So the opposite of that is doing things that other people tell us to do, which is being what we call 'External Referral'. So in other words my reference for what I should do is coming from outside, which is kind of what I did at school … I was always – "What are you writing down there? I'll write the same!"

Audience Member: Yeah.

James: Yeah? Or if you have people who tell you what to do a lot, and that's again something that we were brought up to …

(acting, as James) "Right, I've got a career over here I'm going to…"
(acting, as Parent) "No you're not, you're going to be an accountant!"
(audience laughs)

Several years of non-fulfilment later! Yeah, so that feeling that we did at the start, remember that? I knew all about that there. Yeah, so where was I? So that's the language that we use, and that helps us pick up what's going on.

Okay, so what we've got there is we've got an idea, and rather than love being something that we've never thought about, we've focussed into the definition of Success that we want, that is based on love, and the definition that is illusory, and is based on the opposite of love, which is…?

(audience silence)

What's the opposite of love? Fear. We always think of love and fear as opposites.

Realisation 6: Defining Love

So we're going to talk about The Power of Love, so we're going to define love ... Do you have the story in Sweden about the Inuit ... there's a saying about them that they have 42 different names for snow?

Audience: Yes.

James: You're familiar with that? In England we have one name for snow, which is the white stuff. It comes down and we have to clear it off our driveways, and the kids love it and the adults hate it because it plays havoc with the car! But the Inuit, they of course have lots of different words for snow because they use different types to build their houses, etcetera, and if they don't understand what they're doing then their house falls down and nothing else works either. That's kind of where our society is with regards to love, because we've all heard the classic song, "What the world needs now is love, sweet love."

Realisation 7: Becoming Conscious

James: But nobody has defined love, and therefore nobody is really taking hold of it and leveraging it, to actually use it proactively with a Conscious Mind, and to bring Consciousness to that which is Unconscious. So that's what we're going to do here today.

We're only going to use one definition of love – ***the*** one definition. It's not that it's the only 'right' way but with all these different definitions there's one that is actually useful for us, helping to bring love to our own lives, and then anything that we want to achieve to fulfil our heart's desire.

The Power of Love can help us achieve anything our hearts desire. To an extent, it can help us achieve anything that our heart doesn't want as well, if we're in *Unconsciousness*. Sometimes we try and achieve things that are against our best interests, and sometimes we do actually manage it. But using love to do that is more of a struggle, so it's easier to become Conscious and then decide what it is that we really want. And then, as I imagine you guys have had to do, certainly I have had to do, is to clean up those bits which have been Unconscious.

Realisation 8: Free Will

When I was a child I had an idea of what I wanted to be, and I had a very strong sense of my own personality. But very quickly that was eroded, and I had an idea of what other people wanted me to be. So all of my relationships with people like my parents, grandparents, and all these kind of things, were all inauthentic, because I can't give you what you demand of me!

So before the opportunity arises, let's say with my relatives, in a natural experience of life I may have wanted to greet them, as in:

(acting, as James) "Ah great, how do you do?", say hello and that kind of thing. But people have so much fear that they fear … there's a social embarrassment … what if the grandkids don't want to talk to the grandparents or something?! So before we get to that situation we're going to tell them:

(acting, as parents) "You make sure you say hello, you kiss them on the cheek! Okay?" All these kind of things. So everything is not free, it's demanded. So what I've realised, which has been painful, but it's been okay, is to realise that a lot of my life has been based not on free will.

The author, Mick Quinn, wrote a spiritual book called 'The Uncommon Path', which was a double best-seller on Amazon, and he then used that wisdom in Guatemala where he and his wife run a charity. They teach Critical Thinking and Integral Philosophy to teens in Guatemala. In his book, Quinn defines two different types of free will. The first is Conceptual Free Will, because we think we have free will – we get born and we're told we have free will. So when I'm 18, I'm off to be an accountant, the idea is that I've chosen that by my free will, okay? But it's conceptual, it's slightly Unconscious.

Audience Member: Uh huh.

James: Yeah, you know it! So the opposite is Conscious Free Will. The opposite of Conceptual Free Will is Conscious Free Will. So the task is to bring the

Unconscious bits – you remember the feeling that we felt during the exercise at the start of the talk, which is unfulfilling? They come essentially from Unconsciousness, the motives and choices we make which are Unconscious. So it's about bringing those back into Conscious awareness.

Realisation 9: Mindfulness Alone is Not Enough

James: Conscious awareness is a similar thing to a word that you've probably heard, which is 'mindfulness'. So here I am, I'm going to get told to do mindfulness, and I've got some beliefs that I'm a really terrible person, or I'm useless and all that kind of thing. These thoughts are buried down, they're uncomfortable to think about. So these thoughts are buried down here. If I go to mindfulness with them, I'm going to go to mindfulness with these thoughts of "I'm a terrible person, I'm useless, blah blah blah." So there's not a lot I can do with that, so I'm going to kind of stay down here a bit …

So when we use mindfulness what we need to use it ***with*** is some kind of understanding, some kind of intellectual understanding of what I've been explaining in the last few minutes, to explain where this stuff comes from. Otherwise we're going to believe this [self-judging, negative] stuff when we get mindful of it. So it's important to start to define love. On the larger weekends I run we define wisdom as well, which makes it darn near impossible to believe in judgementalism. Really, when we talk about the wisdom principle, judgementalism has no place to go.

So it's becoming Conscious with one or two teachings for us to understand that what we call love is actually our pure, our basic nature, because it's just allowance and we go with what we want to do. It's kind of like a flower judging itself – a flower doesn't judge itself, it is what it is. So the human race has this problem with … the mind … and the fact that it makes judgements, so really the task is simply, anywhere we want to, we can choose just to come back to awareness of allowing ourselves to be in our pure being, which simply means letting go of that which doesn't work.

We're going to harness The Power of Love, so we need to define the type of love we're going to use to do that. I'm going to explain three different definitions of love, and then identify the one that is the basic principle for using love to change and heal anything.

Realisation 10: Self-Judgement in The Nervous System

James: It's quite an amazing thing. Over the weekend we were working with people who had 'stuff', had a lot of pain trapped in the body, maybe for two, three or four decades, because of things … they had taken on board, self-judgements that they "need to be this, must not be that", and that they were able to release from their bodies. The thing is, if you get a "need to be this, need to be that," if it happens at age 8, or 18, or 28, it stays there until Consciousness is brought to it, and in modern life there's no reason, other than what we're doing now, why Conscious Awareness would be brought to it. So what we've been seeing is that these things can be there for a decade, or several, and so when we actually bring Conscious Awareness to them this stuff is leaving the body, because … I don't know if you're aware, science now indicates that anything that we suppress down in what we call 'The Shadow' is stored in the physical body … in the nervous system …

Audience Member: Mm.

James: And the immune system is just a circulating nervous system, meaning that the state of our nervous systems influences our immune system, so this stuff is incredibly important for our health as well.

So let's get some definitions of love. Can we have a few more definitions of love, because I want to get three or four up on the board, and then …

Audience Member: Warm light.

James: Feel free to just shout stuff out.

Audience Member: Connection.

Audience Member: Freedom.

James: (referring to moving a pen, OCD style) Okay, so … did you see that? Everything has to be in order!

Audience Members: Yes.

James: I've had a lot of that conditioning, so I'm just letting it go. I've checked my passport about 28 times on this trip. It's a habit I'm getting away from.

Audience Member: With mindfulness! (laughing)

James: With mindfulness, yeah – even when I'm checking I know exactly … I'm going back 30 years to who told me to keep checking! Same with the handkerchief as well:

(acting, as parent) "Every day, you must check your handkerchief!"

Okay, so we've got warm light, we've got connection and we've got freedom.

Audience Member: Feelings that can't be rationalised.

James: Irrational feelings. Could you talk a bit more about that please?

Audience Member: Yeah, that you can't, when you're in love you do things that are irrational.

James: Why are they irrational? What might someone in love do that's irrational? Like jumping into a fountain? Shouting out "I love you!"?

Audience Member: Yeah, or just things that you wouldn't normally do, in your normal character maybe, you would do things that are uncharacteristic.

James: Uncharacteristic. Okay. That's interesting.

Audience Member: Or that you wouldn't necessarily do to anybody else.

James: Okay, so one specific person.

Audience Member: It might not be the person, it might not be romantic love, it might be love of … your job, or something.

James: Yeah! So love of job. What about a cheeseburger?

Audience Member: You might do anything to get a cheeseburger.

(audience laughs)

Audience Member: If someone is not following their heart, for me love can be to actually tell the person.

James: To help them wake up?

Audience Member: In a way that the person wakes up.

James: So with love – tough love, okay …

Audience Member: Yeah, I think it is with love, because I don't hurt any person and that can be love for me to really make someone wake up, and change their life.

James: And would your version of that, because I expect everyone would have their own, would your version of that allow them their own choice after that?

Audience Member: Yeah, absolutely. Absolutely. Absolutely.

James: Phew!

Audience Member: Yeah, yeah, yeah.

James: Just as well!

(audience laughs)

Audience Member: Just to show them the kind of way you're, I'm not hurtful, I'm not ... I have had situations where it would seem like it's hurtful, but people are coming back and say this is the best that has happened to me. And it was quite hurtful at the time, I really kicked their butts ...

James: I'm getting that.

Audience Member: For me it was love for the person, I see you hurt yourself and can we change this. So I'm not the fluffy love person. Perhaps it could be interesting to just have a different, slightly different definition of love.

James: Tough love. So essentially what you're doing, when we're talking about becoming Conscious from Unconscious, that's not so much doing it ourselves, that's kind of you're getting someone else to become Conscious of what they're doing, which is kind of what my job involves.

Audience Member 1: ... the feeling that you love that person is there, so it's like ...

Audience Member 2: I'm doing it from my love for the person. Absolutely.

Audience Member 1: It drives you, it's like a passion or something that you have inside that it makes you realise, you want to help that person, because you know that's going to be helpful for them.

Audience Member 3: I was just thinking that what she's talking about, actually for me contains honesty and compassion for this person. So it doesn't have to be fluffy.

James: No, it doesn't have to be fluffy. The honesty is interesting, honesty and compassion are different things, of course. So honesty can be love. Can honesty be hate, hurtful?

Audience Member: Yes.

James: It can. Okay. So we have to get rid of that then?

Audience Member: No, it's the combination between compassion and honesty.

James: Okay, using them together! Okay, so I would say that would equal service!? Service. Maybe that's part of compassion. Okay.

And yeah, I want to get back to … you were talking about you and your family – so you would have love for yourself but you would also have love for your family. You care about their wellbeing.

Audience Member: Yes. My own and them.

James: Yes.

What I like to make this about is one very simple principle, which is becoming Conscious. Incidentally, you might see me doing this (straightens body posture), sometimes I'll be like that (embodies bad posture) and then my self-awareness will say "notice this!", and I'll do that (straightens body posture).

(audience laughs)

One of the things when I was a kid, because of all that being pressed down kind of stuff I had to put up with, and the forced accountancy career, and all the stuff that went before that, I was kind of like down here (hunches shoulders, looks at the ground and mumbles). There was no way I was going to do public speaking in a room full of people like that, let alone go on the radio and talk to 80,000 people. So if I hadn't … if something hadn't changed I'd still be doing this (slumps shoulders, looking down at the ground), and I'd be probably the 15 stone plus that I was a couple of years ago, and all the rest of it that goes with it. I'm not saying that to show off, I just want to show an example of what we can do – with awareness plus a little bit of understanding of the principle of self-love.

Let's talk about your point, you made the point about love for yourself and love for your family, and that ties in with this here. Have you ever heard of people talking about 'depth'? People say "He's a deep person" or "They're shallow"? There's a kind of misguided rule in Spirituality that you're not allowed to say that one thing is deeper than another, otherwise you get told off for that ...

You can talk about 'deep' and 'shallow', that's the truth of it, but it has to be related to something. It's not as if in the Universe there's depth and then there's shallowness, but if you imagine depth and shallowness then you can imagine a line that would go up, relating to what the depth is *about*. For example, do you have degrees in Sweden? Do you do degrees?

Audience: Yes.

James: Okay. So you don't just do a degree, you do a degree *in something*, such as a degree in History, a degree in Physics, a degree in Art, Architecture, English, whatever it is. You get better and better at it, moving through levels of ability, deeper and deeper we might say, until you get a degree. It's the same with depth. We have stages of depth, different levels. But we also have lines of what we call development, and one of those is called 'The Line of Care', also known as 'The Line of Compassion'.

On The Line of Care, essentially it's the extent of "Who do you care about?" On the one hand you've got "Me." And as you were saying, you've got "I also care for my family." And the last study I heard, I think it was about 20% – 30% of people in society whose compassion extends to all human beings.

(draws a chart on the white board)

So this is The Line of Care, which is to deal with compassion. So care for "Me" only is **Egocentric**, and then care for "My family" [or tribe] is **Ethnocentric** – I care about both me and my family. Note also that it's a 'transcend and include' model, meaning that I retain the ability to care about myself when I progress to the next stage or level. I don't lose that capacity to care about myself when I start caring about my brother!

[Ethnocentric] might also include tribal love, so if you're Swedish, love for everybody in Sweden, for example.

And then we have "World", **Worldcentric**, meaning care for all the people in the world. And then if you really want to push the envelope – I said I was an Integral Philosopher, so this is from Integral Philosophy – we talk about '**Kosmocentric**', which essentially means care for all sentient beings, any person, animal or thing that can feel.

So this is The Line of Care, or Compassion.

(writes on the white board)

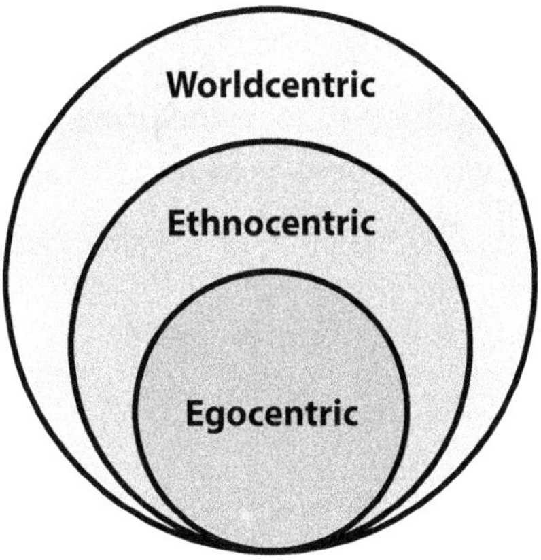

Figure 2.1: The Line of Care and Compassion

And we talked about attraction, liking cheeseburgers, but we can like men and women in the same way. The essence of that is that we like something, or we love it, or someone, it's an attraction or a fondness. Okay? So let's say a man is physically attracted to a woman. In and of itself, does that inherently mean that he cares about her, or might he just be Egocentric? He might not care about her! He might just be of the opinion …

(acting, as an Egocentric man) "She's physically attractive, I want! I like! I want to get this … what's that? You're suffering? I don't care!"

I'm just acting, of course. So there's a difference between love as compassion or care, and then love as attraction or liking.

So even that thing when we were talking about being irrational, I could irrationally be in love with somebody and still not care about them! An Egocentric person can do the irrational 'I've fallen in love' thing. They – perhaps – just think they care about the other person, but they don't really.

And then the third is … who said 'freedom'? So this is essentially freedom here. The words I use are the same kind of thing: Love as acceptance or allowance. And as you say, if you live like that, essentially what you've got is freedom.

The Three Main Definitions of Love:

1. Love as Compassion / Care
2. Love as Attraction / Liking
3. Love as Acceptance / Allowance

So these are our three main different types of love.

So in terms of The Power of Love, as in the principle of the phenomenon of love, there's one of these which allow us to actually leverage love, and actually become Conscious of it, and actually do something with it proactively, so that we can increase the amount of love in the world, and in our own lives. Everything we want to achieve … almost everything …

Audience Member: Number three?

James: It is, yes. The Power of Love [and Kissing Consciousness] is based on Love as Acceptance / Allowance. We might also call this 'Pure Consciousness'.

Realisation 11: Pure Consciousness

James: So we're going to work with love as acceptance and allowance of that which is. We were talking about Dr. Deepak Chopra earlier. One of the things I had been thinking about putting at the top of my new website is, "Pure Consciousness is the healing force of life", which is a saying of Dr. Chopra's. And that is essentially a pure experience of any moment that we're in, free from self-judgement.

Realisation 12: That Which Shuts Down Our Awareness

James: One of the reasons I had problems with my weight and such like was that I was eating from conclusion. So rather than eat something and have a pure experience of what I was doing, before I even do the thing there's a conclusion in my mind that says: Beer equals pleasure, chocolate equals pleasure. Okay? Sometimes chocolate equals pleasure. Sometimes I was doing it and I was making my kidneys hurt, I felt sick and I didn't want it anyway. And I kept doing it over and over again because the mind was in conclusion. The brain was saying "You like this!" So I was overriding the awareness of the fact that actually, if I'd been able to let go of all conclusion about it and experience it, sometimes it would have been a case of "Oh this is delicious", and sometimes it would have been "Oh, this sucks, this is horrible." So Pure Consciousness is the healing force of life, and this is the allowance that we're going to work with.

Before we go any further I think we'll take a five minute break and see if anyone wants to grab a glass of water. One thing I like to do is ... when we're judging ourselves or in a world of judgement, we kind of get into our minds a bit. The degree to which we do that is the degree to which we get out of our bodies. I encourage people to learn to think with their bodies, and become aware of them. So rather than sit here and get tired let's grab a glass of water or whatever we need to do.

So when we're working with Consciousness and we understand the principle of going from Unconscious to Conscious, we might be thinking about, "What can I shift?" "What 'Me' can I reclaim?" Some of the things we have desires around we don't even know about because they are so Unconscious. Apparently when I was two I used to charge around, and I was told to stop one day, and I did stop. And so I just assumed that I was quite quiet. So who knows?!

In one moment something might be a great idea and our awareness is saying to us, for example: "Right, we can do this, we can do that, and this is a good thing to do." So I might put that down in stone then and my brain, which doesn't love itself, needs to put that 'into the bank', intellectually speaking: "Right, I know that's working so I can love myself and I can forget about it. I'll shut off my awareness and stop living in the moment and that's okay." But if a week later that's no longer the right idea, my inflexibility might cause me to take a while to react to that.

So with this tour particularly it's been amazing that I've just learned not to do that, and so things have changed as I've gone along. And Wednesday was going to be about The Wisdom Diet. I have a programme which uses The Power of Love for weight management. There are five things that you can do with dieting that don't work: You deny yourself food, you force yourself to exercise, you can fail them, you can quit them, and they take time. [Do] you remember the two definitions of Success? That's kind of like the self-judgement version of trying to do conventional dieting, which is why it doesn't work. So that's what Wednesday was going to be, and so again, the thing about conclusion being a subtle form of non-self-love, I changed Wednesday from being a day for The Wisdom Diet, to being a day for the Awaken Your True Potential class.

Realisation 13: Confidence

James: … so I arrived in Copenhagen on the Thursday, and as usual I'm guilt-tripping myself, because I haven't intellectualised a whole list …

Audience Member: Why?!

James: Why what?

Audience Member: Why do we humans have a tendency of always feeling guilty? Because you've said that now so many times, you get the information and then you make it into some sort of guilt, because I think that's something that most of us do.

James: It's conditioned.

Audience Member: Why?

James: It's all conditioned.

Audience Member: It's stupid!

James: Yeah, we were saying a moment ago, our parents, and their parents, have come from the 80s and then the 60s, and then before that was the 50s which was really repressed, so it's total fear. And then before that we had wars. [In] the example I gave you, I was talking about my handkerchief. I've never once ever had a thought that I would forget my handkerchief. Or even that I need one. And yet I'm so in the habit of it because of continually hearing someone else's fearful message, "Take your handkerchief!" It's the reason I check my passport so much. It's just conditioning. As soon as one person shuts down their awareness in any moment, they're into belief systems, for example: "This belief system will keep me safe", "This belief system will do this for me" … Which is why people will stick with one job all their lifetime, and it's 'safety', even when there are better opportunities.

Realisation 14: Learning to 'Think' with The Body

James: I was saying I was guilt tripping myself. All day Friday my mind is saying, "Well you've got Friday now, you can darn well use all of Friday to write your notes." And my body – the last thing we're going to talk about is learning to make decisions and think with our body – all the time on Friday when my … actually not my guilt but my wrong interpretations! – were saying I need to do planning, my body was saying to me, "I don't want to do that. If you make me do that I'm going to feel uncomfortable and it won't work." So I just about grabbed it [noticed it in my awareness]. And it was saying to me, "Do Friday night from your spontaneity. Trust that it will work. Because if you're going to do this as a career or something you need to enjoy it. And you need to be at ease with yourself." And I'm like, "You're kidding?! Really, you want me to do it on the fly?"

(audience laughs)

And my body's reply – and my genuine wisdom's inner voice – is "Yeah, you know your stuff don't you?" I replied, "Yeah … I'd like to control it, though! And write things down." But because I'm now a good six months to a year into really solidly going with what my body says, I'm receptive to it. "Okay!" I agreed, and it just worked a treat! And it was the only way. So yeah, it's building up that trust. You see?

Confidence. If I write down the word 'confidence', which is a form of trust, isn't it? If you want to you can write down the word 'confidence'. And then if you underline it, with the exception of the last three letters, you'll get the key to what confidence is.

Audience Member: One more time?

James: If you underline it with the exception of the last three letters you'll get the key to what <u>confide</u>nce is. We ***confide***. Yes, so trust or confidence is about confiding in ourselves. Our Unconscious, that we think is beating us up, is actually waiting for us to stop interpreting things in that way, and regain the relationship of trust and confidence – confiding – between our awareness and our thoughts. And that's the best relationship we will ever have.

Realisation 15: You Can Always Feel Love Consciousness (or its Opposite, Non-Love) in The Body

James: When we understand the theory of The Power of Love as we covered in the first half of this evening's talk, that's fabulous. Then what I'm aiming to do next is to turn it into something such that I don't have to analyse every moment of my life, and I don't have to judge myself if I don't intellectually understand it. So I can just make decisions with my body. The brain still does things, for example it knows that 10 + 10 = 20, and if I get a thought to go down to a specific shop to buy a bag, or to phone a colleague to plan something then I will do it, but essentially I'm thinking with my body.

Realisation 16: Living in the Moment and Ease Ending Stress

The thing we were talking about with success – with the self-judgement-based success, and the love-based success – we have an equivalent thing in our bodies. Just about every aspect of life is subject to this, so we have the same thing with stress. If we're in judgement we'd be in stress. You see? If I'm not judging myself I'm living in the moment. If I am judging myself, part of me kind of thinks I'm living in the moment, and at the same time I need to try and control the future …

Audience Member: Mm.

James: … because you've got definitions of yourself that you need to be in order to be okay! So the living in the moment goes side by side with trying to control this outcome. So our attention, rather than being cotention and together as one focus, is actually ditention, so we're focussed in two different places and we're at odds with ourselves.

This is very similar to The Wisdom Diet's teachings, whereby we're trying to lose weight by denying food and the body is saying, "I'm hungry though, how's this going to work?!" So essentially wisdom – or love – is something we can feel in our bodies!

(stands up straight, relaxes shoulders and exhales loudly) "Jeepers, how much was I holding on to, with the presentation!" And you can see that there, some of that was how much I felt the need to be in control, as I've been judging myself, "What if the presentation doesn't go well?!"

One of the masters used to have a saying that "Turbulence always seeks peace, but peace seeks dynamic activity." If you're in judgement you're outside of yourself. That turbulence wants to be at peace! Once it is, when you get to Pure Consciousness, then you can do amazing things. And then you can go and do the thing that you'd do from wisdom when your inner guide is saying to you, and you're listening to your body and it's telling you the best thing you can do: When to speak, when to be silent.

So when I was working with people yesterday and I explained this to them, my body was saying to me, for example in a ten minute conversation when they're talking about stuff, my body might be sometimes saying "Speak", and sometimes in other moments as I'm about to start talking, the body is feeling in and telling me, "Shut up!" and I could feel it, it was like …

(mimics as if pushing words back into his mouth) … and I'd catch that back in.

Thank you very much, that was The Power of Love.

The full video recording of this talk is available at:

www.KissingConsciousness.com/PowerOfLove

Summary of Realisations

1. There are two definitions of Success: One based on self-love, the other based on self-judgement.
2. Our basic, inherent nature and who we are is already perfect. It is essentially love itself, because it is the absence of non-love.

3. Assessment forms of judgement are different to judgementalism. Assessment is based on truth or facts. Judgementalism is based on fear and is controlling or selfish opinion.

4. Non-love has its own language. **The Conditional Tense:** should, would, could, and its negatives, e.g. shouldn't, and **Imperative Grammar:** telling others what to do – are often examples of this.

5. Judging others is always a reflection of judging oneself, because the person being judgemental is Unconsciously motivated by the self-judgements they themselves have picked up which cause them internal dissatisfaction.

6. If we can define 'love' we can begin to leverage it to heal anything and achieve whatever's possible.

7. We may gain leverage on love by bringing Consciousness to that which was previously Unconscious.

8. Self-Sense Fear or ignorance, i.e. lack of love in society has inadvertently eroded our genuine (Conscious) free will.

9. Mindfulness is of no use until we *also* learn that we are not our negative thoughts, or self-image, and that those thoughts have been conditioned by the fear inherent in our society.

10. Science has now confirmed that everything that is stored in the Unconscious Mind, or 'Shadow', is also stored in the physical body and its nervous system, and therefore also influences the immune system.

11. Pure Consciousness is the healing force of life.

12. Shutting down our awareness or Consciousness in favour of a conclusion or a belief system is a very subtle expression of having shut down our love for ourselves, and is a refusal to accept all of the brilliance and divine glory of who we really are.

13. Love is the key to confidence because it allows us to confide in ourselves.

14. We can learn to 'think' best with our body. The body 'thinks' accurately true to yourself because it has not got the self-doubt

caused by inherited self-judgement that the mind has. It can then, therefore, also help the mind to re-align its own, true thinking.

15. Love Consciousness is something we can actually feel in our bodies. We can learn to 'think' with our bodies, and so *feel* non-love belief systems, and so we can learn to love ourselves unconditionally through awareness of what that actually feels like in the body.

16. Self-love is the key to living in the moment as we only have one point of focus brought about by one congruent knowing of what we truly want to do and be. It is also the way to end stress forever.

Chapter Three

The Binary Nature of Your Consciousness

Why 'Conscious'?

In this chapter we're going to explore some of the themes from the last chapter and address the question of what is so great about being 'Conscious'? We also define The Kissing Consciousness Structure, including The Kissing Consciousness Binary.

Why might we want to be 'Conscious'? Well, because it is true success, contentment, empowerment, relaxation, confidence, freedom and more, all rolled into one complete experience of that moment of life.

The alternative for that moment is self-denial and frustration, Unconscious Unhappiness, powerlessness, stress, lack of confidence, self-constriction and more, all rolled into that one experience of that moment of life.

The choice between Consciousness and Unconsciousness is the choice between self-respect and self-judgement, between self-honesty and self-delusion, between self-acceptance and self-rejection, between living creatively in the moment and living regretfully in the past or with neediness of the future, between living as the cause of your life or as the effect of judgementalism of it. It's the choice between being true to yourself and not being true to yourself.

'Conscious': What is Conscious (Living)?

But there's a further point, which is that all of the Unconscious stuff mentioned above is not entirely a choice. As we shall see more and more, choice is only really possible in the absence of self-judgement. Self-judgement influences your thinking in such a way that choice is compromised.

'Conscious Living' is the state of being free of self-judgement in a given moment and so living unselfconsciously. It includes awakening to recognise when self-judgement is having a destructive effect, since that recognition itself stops the destructive effect. (../conscious)

Throughout this book, I'll refer to various web pages on the Kissing Consciousness website, but instead of typing the web address in full each time, I'll use standard web notation to indicate that whatever follows the ../ comes after the .com/ of the full web address www.KissingConsciousness.com.

e.g. (../conscious) means go to www.KissingConsciousness.com/conscious

What is Love?

'Love' is a rather abstract term representing various expressions of Consciousness or thought, or frames of mind. In The Power of Love (Chapter Two), we defined three main types of love, which are:

- Love as Acceptance or Allowance
- Love as Compassion or Care
- Love as Attraction or Liking

We then identified the first of these, 'Love as Acceptance or Allowance', as the type of love which is useful for harnessing The Power of Love, or Consciousness. For simplicity, we shall now call this type of love **'Love Consciousness'**.

In Love Consciousness, we are in acceptance of ourselves. We are okay with reality being as it is, as it arises, without needing to judge it or resist it (which is, incidentally, a different thing from wishing to change it).

Given that it's also possible to ***not*** be okay with ourselves and the way reality arises, we shall call the opposite of Love Consciousness **'Fear Consciousness'**.

So we have:

Love Consciousness **Fear Consciousness**

... as our two primary states of life.

Now, remember our light switch analogy from the very start of the first chapter? In any given moment of life you are either in a state of Love Consciousness, or in a state of Fear Consciousness. You're either in a state of acceptance of yourself and life, or you're in a state of self-judgement.

What is Success?

In Chapter Two, we also distinguished two very different ways of defining success. The first type of success is based on other people's definitions and imposed upon us as a tyrannical prison. The second type of success is based on our own terms and what we'd like to choose for ourselves. Or, in other words, we have success based on self-judgement, or success based on self-love.

And now that we have defined our two primary states of Consciousness, we can make use of them by putting various expressions of them into a 'binary' table, like this:

Love Consciousness	Fear Consciousness
Success based on self-love	Success based on self-judgement

This results in the following, ever-present characteristics of Love Consciousness and Fear Consciousness:

Love Consciousness	Fear Consciousness
Success	Frustration

Love Consciousness-based Success is defined from the inside, based on internal truth. Another way of expressing this is in terms of whether or not we are being true to ourselves:

Love Consciousness	Fear Consciousness
Being true to yourself	Not being true to yourself

Later we will talk about how to *correctly* interpret failure with the benefit of this insight.

We can also use our Binary Table to show the basic distinction between self-acceptance and self-judgement:

Love Consciousness	Fear Consciousness
Self-Acceptance	Self-Judgement

What is Choice?

> "Choice is something that happens when you're not in your head." – James Blacker

Choice requires freedom of mind. If someone offers you a choice between Option A and Option B, but you're not 'allowed' to choose Option A because of a self-judgement, and you 'choose' Option B, that is not a choice!

It's perfectly possible that Choice – and I'm giving it a capital 'C' to mark it out as a specific and important phenomenon – is completely unfamiliar to you. You may well take all of these insights on board, let go of the judgements that caused you to live from the illusion of Choice, and then realise, "I have absolutely no idea what I really want!" or "I've lived much of my life choosing for other people!" This is normal and understandable, and in the absence of further judgement, this realisation may become an utterly divinely graceful state to be in, as you start to improve your life profoundly with the new arrival of *real* Choice. Even after three, four, five or more decades of adult life, this switch from self-judgement to Choice is perfectly natural and effective. (../choice)

Would You Like to Choose Choice?

You may consider it harsh to live for decades before realising what authentic free will Choice really is. On the other hand, you may also consider that in previous centuries, most people would have lived their whole lives and died without ever experiencing genuine free will Choice. Even in this century, so far only a few are waking up to their potential for authentic Choice. It sounds crazy, but it is humanity's current reality. Further, if we don't judge the pain of the lost decades, we can see the timing of this realisation as perfect.

Let's create a Consciousness Binary Table for the phenomenon of Choice:

Love Consciousness	Fear Consciousness
Choice	The illusion of Choice, no Choice

What is Confidence?

"Confidence is the ability to confide
in yourself." – James Blacker

Confide-nce

Confidence is inevitable when we are in self-acceptance (self-love) because in acceptance, there is nothing blocking the flow of information to and from our Conscious Mind's awareness. When we are in self-judgement, however, Confidence is impossible, because the flow of relevant information is blocked by that self-judgement – we are not *confiding in ourselves* about it.

When we don't confide in ourselves, our inner guidance or insight (or we could say our Conscious awareness of our true Choice) as to what is the best thing for us to do – and what we'd like to do – doesn't work properly.

If we want Confidence, therefore, the only thing we need to do is to release our relevant self-judgements. We shall be discussing how to do that in the next chapter on The Kissing Consciousness Tool.

Let's add Confidence to the Binary Table:

Love Consciousness	**Fear Consciousness**
Confidence	Lack of Confidence

What is Positive Thinking?

In The Power of Love chapter we saw that positive thinking is:

- truth-based thinking
- the absence of negative thinking

For now, let's focus on the first insight.

Imagine a person who is capable of jumping three metres telling themselves that they can jump over a five metre chasm! Positive thinking is identical to both Confidence and Choice, in that it starts with self-honesty, the ability to be clear with oneself about one's true choices, rather than being blocked by self-judgement. There's nothing 'positive' about pursuing something that isn't really your Choice or blocking your ability to be honest with yourself about what you can and cannot do. There are thoughts that let you be you, and then there are negative thoughts which don't.

Love Consciousness	**Fear Consciousness**
Positive Thinking	Negative Thinking

What is Stress?

In physics, stress, for example on a piece of wood, is not caused by a single force acting upon it, but by *two or more* forces or factors acting on it at the same time.

At some point during your school days you might have experimented with holding your ruler down firmly on a desk, with about half of it hanging over the edge, and then pushing down on it. If you had a 'shatterproof' ruler made of Perspex, the ruler made a 'twang' vibrating sound and movement. If your ruler was made of wood, the same treatment would probably break it.

The point at which the ruler overlapped the desk was the stress point of the system. This is how Stress works in us, too. When we have a trust of what is the single best action for us in a given situation, we experience no Stress in taking that action. It flows. But if we have self-judgement causing us to doubt ourselves or deny ourselves that flow of Choice and action, we have a *second* force acting upon us in a different direction – and we experience Stress!

"The solution to stress is to yield
… to self-love." – James Blacker

Stress is not the same thing as work, exhaustion or challenge. A person exhausting themselves down at the gym is not necessarily experiencing Stress. Work is not in itself Stress, either. People who love their jobs rarely have any difficulty working strongly, because they are in alignment with themselves. (../stress)

Love Consciousness	Fear Consciousness
Absence of Stress	Stress

What is Happiness?

"To thine own self be true." – William Shakespeare

The word 'happiness' is like the word 'love' – it's a somewhat abstract, vague term that's difficult to work with. So, rather than starting with attempts to define the word 'happiness', I suggest we start with our understanding of The Binary – of Love Consciousness and Fear Consciousness – and work backwards.

If self-acceptance engenders Success, Confidence and Choice, while self-judgement leads to Frustration, lack of Confidence and only the *Illusion* of Choice, then clearly Love Consciousness corresponds with Happiness, and Fear Consciousness with Unhappiness. So we can get a sense of Happiness as Love Consciousness, compared to Unhappiness as Fear Consciousness. Try being happy whilst operating under self-judgement! Try being unhappy in a moment of self-acceptance! Happiness – in a general sense – is the natural state of the absence of self-judgement.

Love Consciousness	**Fear Consciousness**
Happiness	Unhappiness

Unconscious Unhappiness

"Unhappiness comes from sitting on the
gifts that we have." – Dr Robert Holden

Moments we live in self-judgement are understandably accompanied by a sense of Unhappiness, which I call 'Unconscious Unhappiness'. The solution to Unconscious Unhappiness is not acquiring some 'thing', but rather, letting go of whatever self-judgement is causing the Unhappiness. If someone has a lot of Unhappiness, they're likely weighed down by a lot of self-judgement. This can be good news because it means there is so much good stuff available to regain!

Happiness as a Consciousness vs Happy Emotions

The second thing we need to do to understand Happiness is to recognise that there's a difference between Happiness as your state of Consciousness and happy emotions.

You can be in a state of self-acceptance and at the same time experiencing a sad feeling, for example if you're grieving, or acknowledging the dystopian state of the world or its effect upon you to date, or anything else, large or small. So we have two different 'levels' of Happiness:

- Happiness as a Consciousness (as the self-acceptance that Love Consciousness is)
- Happiness as happy or joyful emotions and feelings

… and the Consciousness level is *primary.* Happy feelings and emotions, or indeed any feelings and emotions, are *secondary* to our Consciousness, by which I mean that they are influenced by it. If our Consciousness changes, either from self-judgement to self-acceptance, or vice versa, then it's likely that what we feel or experience as emotions will change, too.

So that uncovers a crucial realisation: That it's possible to pursue – or even get – happy emotions or pleasurable experiences *at the expense of being true to yourself!* It's possible to pursue happy emotions, feelings, entertainments or pleasures at the expense of our Happiness Consciousness, to pursue False Happiness at the expense of True Happiness. Indeed, this pursuit is essentially *the* cause of people failing to manifest their own Happiness.

The irony – and tragedy – here is that when people favour the pursuit of happy emotions and feelings over their pursuit of Love Consciousness, they are almost certainly moving in the opposite direction of their truths, against their best chances of a happy life and the virtually permanent, ever-present Happiness they wish to have. And so in this book, when I refer to 'Happiness', I'm referring to Happiness *as a Consciousness.* The following table will help to clarify our awareness of Happiness, and its relationship to emotions and feelings …

Love Consciousness	Fear Consciousness
Feelings and emotions that emanate from Love Consciousness	Feelings and emotions that emanate from Fear Consciousness

There's no 'set of emotions' for each type of Consciousness, but emotions and feelings emanating from the two groups do tend to have a distinct feel to them. Feelings emanating from Fear Consciousness tend to be heavy and dominating. In Love Consciousness, feelings and emotions don't tend to 'stick' to us. We'll complete our exploration of Happiness in Chapter Five.

Paradise on Earth

There is another reason why being 'Conscious' is so beneficial. So far we have only considered it in terms of what it means for you, as an individual. In Volume II of Kissing Consciousness we explore the benefits to society as a whole, and they are even more phenomenal and profound. Virtually every problem that there is in the world is the result of Unconsciousness, of Unconscious motivation, i.e. it is caused by self-judgement in the collective sphere.

The Binary

Let's look at the characteristics of Love Consciousness and Fear Consciousness we've covered so far, combined into a single table:

Love Consciousness	**Fear Consciousness**
Self-Acceptance	Self-Judgement
Success	Frustration
Choice	The Illusion of Choice
Confidence	Lack of Confidence
Positive Thinking	Negative Thinking
Absence of Stress	Stress
Happiness	Unhappiness

The Three Levels of Helping People

Teaching people insights around The Binary has value in itself, but Kissing Consciousness sees this as only the first step to fulfilment. The second step involves helping people to actually shift Fear Consciousness to Love Consciousness, at seminars or in personal one to one sessions. A potential third step is to empower people to make these shifts by themselves, *in any moment.*

1. Teach people insights about Love Consciousness and Fear Consciousness
2. Help people to turn Fear Consciousness into Love Consciousness
3. Empower people to turn Fear Consciousness into Love Consciousness *by themselves*

In this chapter we'll comprehensively explore insights into The Binary, and then in the next chapter on 'The Kissing Consciousness Tool' we'll address how to turn Fear Consciousness into Love Consciousness.

What The Binary Isn't

You'll notice that the Binary Table doesn't include such things as 'being noisy vs being quiet', or 'liking adventure vs preferring to stay at home'. These are personal preferences. Labelling them as 'Conscious' or 'Unconscious' would be a self-judgement.

There's no need to learn all of these insights either. My purpose in mentioning them here is simply to help you recognise the two different states as they arise in life.

You Are The Key: Success is Already in You

It may seem strange to have Success and Happiness and the rest primarily based around a single state of being (Love Consciousness), but this is likely because up until now everything you have been taught about You has not been able to honour the fact that your inherent natural being is already perfect. You have – and already had – all the drives and potential abilities to be fully You already within you.

Personal development approaches – or other attempts to make life happier or more successful – which don't honour this truth are upside-down to your true nature. As such, they may have had you chasing your tail, and probably felt rather heavy and unfulfilling. Of course you can still enhance your potentials with growth and development, but even these drives come naturally from the real you when you are being true to yourself. The difference is whether it feels like you are driving yourself forward as per your Choice, or are being dragged forward by self-judgement and other people's judgement.

The following is the complete Binary Table for the concepts we'll cover in the rest of this chapter.

Love Consciousness	**Fear Consciousness**
Cause	Effect
In Your Being	'In Your Head'
Being True to Yourself	Not being True to Yourself
True Self	False Self
You	Not You
Permission Granted	Permission Denied
Living in the Flow	Stuckness
Behaviour Flows	Forced Behaviour
Maximised Quality of Life	Compromised Quality of Life
Self-Referral	External Referral
Awareness	Locked 'in Conclusion'
Possibility	Limitation
'Presence'	'Absence'
Healthy	Unhealthy
Honouring your Life Force	Dishonouring your Life Force
Inner Guidance	Ignored Inner Guidance
Embodied	Disembodied
Mind is your Servant	Mind is your Master
Conscience	False Conscience
Knowing	Doubting
Yielding	Justifying

Love Consciousness	Fear Consciousness
Softening	Defending
Genius	Second-Guessing Yourself
Skill (Grace)	Gracelessness
Unselfconscious	Self-Conscious
No Charge	Charge
Willingness	Unwillingness
Responsive	Reactive
Receiving	(Trying to) Control
Self-Embracing	Self-Fearing
In Your Power	Not In Your Power
Self-Sincerity	Self-Insincerity
Authenticity	Inauthenticity
Life is Real	Life is Fake
Freedom	Self-Constriction
Self-Kindness	Self-Unkindness
Self-Compassion	Lack of Self-Compassion
Self-Approval	Self-Criticism
Ease	Lack of Ease
At One with Yourself	At Odds with Yourself
Desire	False Desire
Welcome Emotions	Unwelcome Emotions
Living in the Moment	Living 'in Your Head'

Love Consciousness	**Fear Consciousness**
Peace	Turbulence
Timing	No Timing

The Primacy of Your Consciousness

When you are operating under self-judgement you are literally living your life as an *effect* of that self-judgement. Self-judgement drives your thoughts, dictating to you what you can and cannot do, which in turn drives your behaviour. In this way, in that moment, self-judgement prevents you from being the *cause* of your life.

In the absence of self-judgement we are free to be the cause and driving force of our choices, our behaviours, our life.

Love Consciousness	**Fear Consciousness**
Cause	Effect

Little wonder that Unhappiness accompanies self-judgement, if we aren't even allowed to be the cause and driving force of our own lives! In the absence of self-judgement, however, you are free to be, and are being you at the level of your 'Being', your inherent nature – that which you are before any judgements are (or were) dumped on top of you. (../primacy)

'Being'

"You didn't come into this world.
You came out of it." – Alan Watts

Almost from the moment we are born we are all fed a lie: That we have landed here and have to *become* something. We're not good enough – yet. We're not it – yet. We have to 'be' something we're not in order to prove ourselves worthy.

We start off with defaults of 'happy' and 'empowered', but then, very quickly, self-judgements are allowed to rain down on our Consciousnesses and seep into our bodies, compromising our immune systems, corrupting our minds, and denying our hearts. We forget that the default of 'happy' existed before, and we buy into the lie that we are *separate* from Success.

Our Being is that which we truly are, prior to any self-judgement, constrictions, labels, or controls – prior to being 'put into a box' in order to make who we are acceptable to the people and to the world around us.

Being is Ever-Present

Our Being is always present as our underlying nature. However, in moments of self-judgement we don't recognise this because we get caught 'in our heads'.

Love Consciousness	Fear Consciousness
In Your Being	'In Your Head'

Being True to Yourself

Four hundred years ago, Shakespeare wrote "To thine own self be true." Society today makes that very difficult for everyone. The commercial message is: "Conform to this image of success that we've created for you so we can make money out of you." The social message is: "Be like we want you to be and you'll get our approval." This context of self-judgement not only fails to support the individual in being true to themselves, but works actively against it, creating the web of entanglement that this work is here to help unravel. What's bizarre is that the pedallers of these two messages are themselves entranced by them.

Love Consciousness	Fear Consciousness
Being True to Yourself	Not being True to Yourself

Being true to self can mean anything from not displaying that ugly vase that someone gave you as a present on your mantle piece, to giving up one career in favour of another. It ranges from the huge things in life to the tiny, and we will cover them all in many ways over the remaining chapters.

The False Self

The opposite to being true to ourselves is being 'False Self'. In this state, we are playing a role, pretending to be someone we are not, because we have been taught that we are not allowed to be who we are. False Self started as a matter of safety – we had to pretend in order to survive and be safe in the environments we were in. Long after the original danger has passed, the False Self remains. The true personality can be reclaimed, but often it is long since forgotten, and the 'someone' you are playing the role of being might as well be an alien, given the degree to which it is not you.

Danger isn't necessarily physical. Even the slightest subtle hint that we might be ridiculed for something trivial, such as singing, or sharing a desire, can create a False Self aspect. We are all subject to these to one degree or another.

I know all about being False Self. I've pretended to like accountancy when I really wanted to study philosophy. I've had to pretend not to have much sexual nature or desire, and it took me forty years on the planet to acknowledge that I was a good dancer. I've pretended 'choosing' to eat junk food, because I wasn't Conscious enough to choose for my body. That's three big examples and one moderate example out of the thousands I could give. I'm sure you have yours, too.

If you have unhappy thoughts because you have to choose something that makes you unhappy just because it's 'who you are', then it's NOT who you are – that is just another part of the self-judgement lie. If it's not your true Choice then it's not who you are. Your true Choice will always make you happy, or at least happier.

Love Consciousness	**Fear Consciousness**
True Self (Fulfilled)	False Self (Unfulfilled)

Expressing this another way gives perhaps the most sobering Binary Table of all:

Love Consciousness	**Fear Consciousness**
You	Not You

In Chapter Seven, on Relationships, we'll talk about not taking people's False Self at face value.

Being is a Natural Default

In a sense, there is no 'art of Being', no set of skills or practices you have to – or even can! – undertake to make yourself authentically you. There simply is You. That is your Being. There's Being, and then there are self-judgements getting in the way of our ability to recognise and honour Being. So instead of having an 'art of Being', we have the art of releasing self-judgements and then appreciating that what remains, which is your Being, takes care of itself. Note that whenever we are reluctant to allow who we are to 'take care of itself', thinking instead that we have to force it or control it, this, too, is an effect of self-judgement.

You are like a river that flows all by itself. You don't need to manipulate positives to make you what you are, to make you great, or happy – they flow naturally. You just need to release the negatives that have gotten in the way, the self-judgements that have been conditioned into your mind and your body's nervous system.

Being and Direct, Real Experience of Life

> "Being: For people who want to have real lives, rather than conceptualised lives lived in their heads." – James Blacker

When we are in our Being we have a direct, real experience of life, and of reality. Conversely, when we are in our heads, we are not actually experiencing reality – we are thinking about a *concept* of what we are doing, rather than experiencing the actual moment itself. By adulthood, most of us have gotten into the habit of living in concepts and thought, and forgotten how to live the experience itself.

Love Consciousness	Fear Consciousness
Direct experience of yourself and reality	Conceptualised experience, and so only the possibility of 'conceptualised happiness'
Reality experienced as reality	Concepts experienced as reality; reality experienced as concepts

One might point out that we don't experience reality as it is fully anyway, due to the limitations of the five senses. While this is true, it's not particularly relevant to our quality of life. It's our nature to experience the five senses the way we do. Realising that you're unable to hear a dog whistle might bother you less than realising that you're missing out on a load of sexual pleasure because you're habitually in your head around sex – "I'm getting sex, so this must be a good thing!" – and gotten *out* of the habit of allowing yourself to be in the *Being* of sex. The same is true of food. Most people eat food 'in their heads', whilst filtering out the *experience* of everything beyond the first bite or two. That's largely why we have an obesity crisis.

This principle applies to ALL areas of experience of life, and has tremendous impact on our quality of life. (../being)

Human File Permissions

Love Consciousness	**Fear Consciousness**
You're Allowed	You're Not Allowed

You may know that every computer file has 'permissions'. If you right-click on any file and choose something like 'Properties', you'll see attributes like 'Read' and 'Write', which have check boxes that are either ticked or unticked. File permissions determine what you're allowed to do with the file.

Just like a computer file has file permissions, you also have 'Permissions' settings – to do with EVERYTHING, from money to love to health and body, right down to whether or not you're allowed to squeeze the toothpaste tube from the middle. In every case, you have a 'Human File Permission' set to either 'Yes' or 'No'. Kissing Consciousness calls these (your) 'Human File Permissions', or 'Permissions' for short.

Permissions set to 'Yes' don't require your attention at all. They manifest when the opportunity for them arises and you choose them.

Your Permissions are set to 'No' where you aren't allowed to honour something that's true about you because of Unconscious self-judgements. All self-judgements are non-permissions, 'No' Permissions.

Every single aspect of your Consciousness is set to either 'Yes' or 'No'. Where we have Permissions set to 'No' we may wish to release the self-judgements around them so that they become a 'Yes'. Once we release the self-judgement that caused a 'No' Permission it becomes a 'Yes' automatically, we don't have to do anything else.

You have Permissions around whether you're allowed to say you're angry. You have Permissions around asking questions in class, and around declining obligations you don't fancy. All of it. It's all Permissions. Let's look at a made up sample of a person's 'File Permissions':

Allowed to swear	Yes	
Allowed to have a mind at peace		No
Allowed to be healthy	Yes	
Allowed to choose own career	Yes	
Allowed to honour sexual energy fully		No
Allowed to earn more than £10,000 a year	Yes	
Allowed to earn more than £50,000 a year		No
Allowed to be in a relationship	Yes	
Allowed to be in a truly happy relationship		No
Allowed to feel good about it if single		No
Allowed to cry	Yes	
Allowed to cry in public		No
Allowed to leave awkward silences unfilled	Yes	
Allowed to fail at life		No

No matter what you do, a 'No' Permission will always prevent achievement of any goal.

So all we have to do to achieve something we want – and that's possible for us – is to slide the 'No' Permissions over to the 'Yes' column by releasing the false self-judgements. The rest happens automatically.

Note that if something literally isn't possible for us, the only reason we would still be contemplating it is self-judgement. If something is simply not possible for us, then it's not a self-judgement that's stopping us from having it, it's just reality.

Long before your Conscious Mind has been triggered into wanting something, your Subconscious Mind has sent a 'Permission Request' to itself to see if it is allowed.

Love Consciousness	Fear Consciousness
Permission Granted	Permission Denied

Being You and 'Getting You'

These aren't just Permissions around what you can get and have, but much more importantly, around you being allowed to *be* you; being allowed *you*, we might say. You can get all of You. That is a gift worth more than anything.

Every single Permission, each 'Yes' or 'No', is also a 'Yes' or 'No' to You. If you're not allowed a happy relationship, another way of understanding that is that you're not allowed to *be* that person whose choice is a happy relationship … or whose choice is a passionate vocation … or whose choice is to dance in the rain.

Love Consciousness	Fear Consciousness
You're allowed You	You're not allowed You

More graphically, imagine you made a 'Permission Request' to be You:

Love Consciousness	Fear Consciousness
Permission to be You Granted	Permission to be You Denied

Ultimately, your Permissions are really up to you. That is what becoming Conscious is all about. The moment you become aware of a 'No' Permission it can no longer stick. Why? Because it's based on a lie, and the awareness illuminates the lie.

The 'Default' Permission for Consciousness is 'Yes'

We aren't born with any 'No' Permissions.

At first, there is simply life and what is and isn't true and possible. Then self-judgements came in and some of our Permissions were switched to 'No'.

The Formula of Your Human Potential

The default nature of Permissions can be understood this way:

- There is what's possible for us
- But then self-judgements deny us some of that

Those two bullet points express the simple formula of human potential, which has been complicated in all manner of ways by judgementalism-based notions of Success and Ego-based teachings. As David Heard said in our 2004 recording on The Keys to Happiness:

> "It isn't the potential that someone else decides should be true for you – that you be the school captain or something like that. It's about an intrinsic internal." – David Heard

Love Consciousness	Fear Consciousness
Your human potential is automatically fulfilled	You misunderstand your human potential

If we take Unconditional Love to be the absence of judgement, then we can realise that:

> "Unconditional love for oneself is the same thing as fulfilling one's full potential." – James Blacker

If you have a self-judgement around something, all you can achieve with regard to that topic in that exact moment is to become Conscious of the influence of the self-judgement, and perhaps then let it go. And if you don't manage to let it go, then by definition it wasn't possible for you to do so at that point. Wow, doesn't that take the pressure off!

Permissions: Choice, Context and Availability

We each have 'Yes' Permissions around things that we aren't choosing right now or for which there's no immediate opportunity, particularly if other people need to be involved. Not having a dream relationship right now doesn't necessarily mean you have a 'No' Permission around it. Maybe there aren't any suitable candidates available. Or maybe there are, but they require a compromise which is not your true Choice. Not earning £50,000 a year doesn't mean you aren't allowed to earn that much. You may simply be choosing other priorities.

On the other hand, those who cry in public definitely have a 'Yes' Permission allowing them to cry in public. Those earning a million a year definitely have a 'Yes' around that. They couldn't be doing it if they had a 'No' Permission around it.

Here's the acid test: If it *bothers you* that you don't have something, you probably have a 'No' Permission around it and aren't doing what you can to achieve it. Or it may be that you aren't allowed *not* to have it, which would also cause the bother. If a person has a 'Yes' around something, and has chosen it, usually they are fine being patient because they know it is on its way.

Consciousness Accommodates All Permission Combinations

Consciousness accommodates all combinations of choices and Permissions. Imagine someone saying that their love partner is so accustomed to giving romantic gestures that they are unable to receive them. Essentially they're claiming that our Consciousness, our psyche, can't handle that combination of Permissions ... but this is simply not the case. What is really going on is that their love partner has a Permission around giving, but not around receiving, and they have come up with that other narrative because they are not ready to face the truth of their 'No' Permission:

Allowed to give romantically	Yes	
Allowed to receive romantically		No

A different person, or, crucially, the *same* person after they have released their self-judgement blocks around receiving romantic gestures, would have Permissions as follows:

Allowed to give romantically	Yes
Allowed to receive romantically	Yes

Their Consciousness would simply accommodate that combination of Permissions as a different experience of life.

The point here is for those of us who wish to understand ourselves and others to recognise such self-denying false narratives as 'Possibility Assuming'. They're prevalent in society across all possible topics. The main form 'Possibility Assuming' takes is: "Yeah, this was never going to happen, given that that happened." However, your Subconscious Mind will always elegantly find a way for your Permission combinations to manifest and play out in your life.

Sabotage

Sabotage isn't just a great song by the Beastie Boys, it's what we do to ourselves when we try to choose something that we have a Human File Permission set to 'No' around. You see a person you really like, you go up to them, you forget how to speak, you talk nonsense and start sweating … and they think you're an idiot. Simple! A classic example of self-sabotage.

Maybe a person has the opportunity and capacity to launch a fantastic project, but because they were told they had to "go into the family business" they don't even register their potential for the project in their Conscious Mind. That's a more subtle example of self-sabotage, but is exactly the same thing.

We unintentionally employ sabotage to make sure we don't allow ourselves to succeed in those areas where we have been taught we're not allowed to achieve. (../sabotage)

The Invincibility of Human File Permissions

The nature of Human File Permissions is such that if you have a 'No' Permission around something, it doesn't matter what positive actions you take to achieve that thing, all of your efforts will be in vain.

I actually find that reassuring – because I know I can't achieve anything by fighting against myself, I don't have to bother or worry about trying to fight myself.

Equally, if something is possible for you and you have a 'Yes' Permission around it, you don't really have to worry about how it comes about. You will do and/or be whatever is needed – and you will do and/or be so as part of your flow of Love Consciousness.

Just like computer file permissions, you can't cheat Human File Permissions. But you can change them.

Nature's NLP

> "I don't believe a human being needs to master NLP in order to be happy or true to themselves." – James Blacker

Neuro Linguistic Programming, or NLP for short, is "an approach to communication, personal development, and psychotherapy" (Wikipedia). As a young man at a personal development seminar, I was told I had to master visual, auditory, kinaesthetic, olfactory and gustatory (sight, sound, touch, smell and taste) representations in my mind. To make sure I had the right 'internal representations' in my head to achieve a goal, I was encouraged to pay attention to whether my 'mental image' was framed or panoramic, in colour or in black and white, up close or far away, etc. I remember feeling completely defeated and depressed as I thought to myself, "I have to learn and master this complicated stuff in order to lose my virginity?! I've got no chance!"

Nowadays I don't believe a human being needs to master NLP in order to be true to themselves. Young children are about the most dynamic, go-getting members of society, and they don't study NLP. I do believe that using our minds to get detailed views of our awareness can help us find our self-judgements, but that's not quite the same thing.

Children have an idea, and before you know it blankets and chairs have been used to make a tent in the lounge. They can achieve their visions without NLP training because taking action to achieve an aim is a natural process of life. If you have the ability to do something, wish to do it, and so choose to do it, and have no self-judgement blocks around it which may cause you to self-sabotage and prevent you from achieving it, it gets done. When was the last time you needed NLP to buy a train ticket?! I would suggest, as with all our favourable Love Consciousness characteristics (Confidence, Choice, positive thinking), that you don't need positive 'NLP style internal representations', you just need an *absence* of negative ones! If NLP works for you, great! But it is absolutely the Kissing Consciousness philosophy that NLP cannot override Human File Permissions ... and that with a 'Yes' Permission in place, no further NLP is necessary.

> **Proximate Causes and Distal Causes:** "A proximate cause is an event which is closest to, or immediately responsible for causing, some observed result. This exists in contrast to a higher-level ultimate cause (or distal cause) which is usually thought of as the "real" reason something occurred." – Wikipedia

I've noticed that when I let go of a self-judgement around something, an 'internal representation' (such as NLP seeks to achieve via manipulation) for achieving or honouring that thing *automatically* arises in my Consciousness, unbidden. So I now call this 'Nature's NLP'. When I 'do a release', I can 'see' and 'sense' the 'how to' of acquiring it, subject to patience for the right timing and opportunities. I've also become aware of how this Consciousness already exists where I already have 'Yes' Permissions. In fact, I would say the 'internal representation' is only a fleeting imagination, followed by the absence of any kind of internal representation at all. When it is gone, I'm left with the sense that I am simply free to go ahead with whatever it is I want to do.

Forcing one's mental internal representations is *not* the *distal* cause of change that everyone thinks it to be, but just the *proximate* cause of it, and is ultimately irrelevant in genuine change. I see the real (distal) cause as 'inner Permissions', as we have defined. If a person doesn't have inner Permission to achieve, for example if they've picked up a self-judgement that they aren't allowed to earn more money than their parents, have a happy love relationship, be slim, etc., then they'll never actually allow something like NLP to work for them anyway – unless it also happens to shift the self-judgement, either by intention or by accident. So the Kissing Consciousness view is that we might as well just focus on the Human File Permissions.

Programming

I'm not a 'flipping' robot! I'm not interested in being programmed! I'm interested in being me, I'm interested in *Being*. I prefer interacting with other people when they are being naturally themselves, too; not in their heads, not behaving like a programme. Imagine, the moment a baby is born, everyone welcoming it into the world by saying, "Hello! We're going to programme you!" Any observer would be quick to point out that this is sick. Of course it is sick! So why is it any less sick for an adult to ask it of themselves twenty or thirty years later?

De-programming vs Re-programming?

I'm not interested in programming. But I don't want to be left in my wounded, conditioned, self-judging, unwanted habit-doing, ineffective state, either – I do want to change that programming! … But not with *re*-programming, with *de*-programming. I don't want to jump out of one fire and into another. I trust that the natural, underlying me is true, and capable of being all I am. Why on earth wouldn't it be?! I believe the same for you, too. We all have natural programming anyway. This is what helps a flower be a flower, or a horse be a horse.

I suspect that the more self-judgements a person has, the more likely they are to think they want to replace negative conditioned programming with 'positive' programming. As people have fewer and fewer self-judgements, however, they are more likely to want to be free of programming altogether – so that they can simply enjoy being who they are. They trust the Being underneath.

'Being' Cannot Wear Off

Any programming or 'conditioning' of the mind can wear off, but your Being cannot. Your Being could be buried again, if you allowed more self-judgements in, and it may naturally change and evolve, as different things become important to you, but it cannot wear off. A tree never stops knowing how to be a tree. Being is the underlying reality. (../permissions)

Addressing Your Frustrations at Their Root!

Some personal development approaches promise to help you get to the *'root cause'* of your problems, but what exactly does 'root cause' mean in the context of healing, wounds, change, power, therapy, or achieving success? Essentially it means that we want to pull the 'lever' that's actually going to make the difference.

Behaviour (Is Not The 'Lever')

Now we've finished our detour into Being and gained some insights into how Human File Permissions work, we can apply them to our exploration of The Primacy of Consciousness, and the nature of cause and effect.

If Consciousness is ***primary***, (the cause), then behaviour is ***secondary*** (it only happens because the cause happens first). In other words, if we aren't in a state of Love Consciousness in a given moment, trying to exert influence at a behavioural level to get things 'back on track' is utterly futile.

We need to release the self-judgement at a Consciousness level, to allow the behaviour necessary for Success to flow towards achievement.

Forced Behaviour vs Flow Behaviour

It is always the quality of Consciousness – i.e. Love Consciousness or Fear Consciousness – driving a behaviour that determines whether that behaviour is forced, or happens 'in the flow'.

Love Consciousness	Fear Consciousness
Behaviour Flows	Forced Behaviour

And this leads to an experience of life which can be described thusly:

Love Consciousness	Fear Consciousness
Living in the Flow	Stuckness

As a corollary, a key principle of Conscious Living is that there's no behaviour which is inherently Conscious, and no behaviour which is inherently Unconscious.

Three Levels of Causation: Root Cause and Two Others

Do you know why getting socks or other naff presents for your birthday is disappointing? Because on your very first, actual birth day, you got the two most amazing presents possible – a body and a mind – and you haven't finished unwrapping either of them yet! We haven't even begun to imagine or understand what these two amazing gifts can do.

But for now, let's focus on what we do know. We know that the mind can determine what the body does. The body can influence the mind, too, particularly if we pop a pill, but we largely experience life by using our thoughts to decide what to do on a behavioural-physical-action-body level. We think "I want to make a drink" and then direct our bodies to make a drink. We think "I have to go to work", and then we drag our bodies there. The poor old body – it's largely subservient to the mind. We can represent this understanding with an ordered list, showing what causes what:

1. Mind
2. Body

Imagine a row of dominos lined up. If you tap the first one, it falls on the second one, which falls on the third one, and so on, creating a knock-on effect. The mind is like the domino that is knocked first, falling onto the 'body domino'. Whatever happens at the level of the mind determines what happens at the level of the body. If the mind decides to go and buy a newspaper, the body goes and buys a newspaper. If the mind decides to eat a pizza, the body invariably ends up eating a pizza. It doesn't happen the other way around; if the body wants a pizza or exercise, but the mind doesn't, it doesn't happen.

But we know from our Binary Table that the mind can be corrupted by self-judgement. If the mind has a self-judgement then our behaviours are not going to be effective. They are merely going to be an *expression* of that self-judgement.

We don't want our behaviours driven by the unhelpful thoughts of self-judgement. Where Consciousness is not present – when we are Unconscious, or unaware – our False Self thoughts dictate our behaviour, and thus our results – which is fine when our thoughts are our own, but when they are hijacked by the effects of self-judgement that's when it's important to become Conscious to them, and change the Consciousness that causes them.

Forced Behaviour: The Elastic Band Principle

What do people usually do when their behaviour isn't getting them the results that they want? Let's say they want to be slimmer, and so they want to eat less and maybe exercise ... what do they usually do? They force their behaviour.

And what happens? They force the diet or exercise against themselves for a while – and then when they can't sustain that forced behaviour any longer they snap back into their old ways, like an elastic band.

If you want one end of the 'elastic band' (for example, one's eating habits or working habits) to stay *sustainably* at a certain point, forever – i.e. after you've let it go – you have to move the other end of the elastic band, too. You have to move the entire elastic band as a whole, not stretch it. This means moving the Consciousness that causes the behaviour, so that the behaviour can come from Flow and Choice, and not from force, Stuckness and self-judgement. Otherwise, what are you going to do? Spend your whole life forcing your behaviour against yourself? That sounds like a whole load of no fun. It isn't sustainable anyway.

This Elastic Band Principle is the mainstay of my product, The Wisdom Diet, but the Elastic Band Principle itself applies to all areas of life.

"So We Can't Take Behavioural Actions?"

Yes, you can; of course you can. I'm just suggesting that you don't bother trying to force behaviours from Fear Consciousness. If you find that you really *want* to do something, then Love Consciousness is driving your desire to take that particular behavioural action. Remember, from Love Consciousness behaviour FLOWS! It's not so much that we want to save ourselves the bother of trying from Fear Consciousness, but that this endeavour distracts us from the real solution of shifting our Consciousness to release the blocks to Flow behaviour.

> "Effective behaviour flows with ease because your Ego is not the one trying to make it happen!" – James Blacker

Forced Thought-based Behaviour

In order to change our behaviours in a sustainable way, we need to change our habits of thought. And herein lies another trap.

Oftentimes, people will realise that their thoughts are negative or unhelpful – which is great – but then they'll try to force themselves to have positive thoughts instead. Forcing thoughts is just as ineffective and unsustainable as trying to force behaviours. You're still at war with yourself, still in a 'No' Permission situation.

Deepak Chopra recounts the story of a patient of his, a lady who always seemed cheerful and positive. One day he asked her about this, and she replied, "I'm terrified of having a negative thought!" As Chopra correctly pointed out, "Isn't being afraid of having a negative thought a negative thought?"

> "If you have thoughts which are caused by self-judgement you can't deal with them by forcing an opposite set of thoughts." – James Blacker

So mental activity can itself be a forced behaviour. And all forced thought-based behaviours are expressions of Fear Consciousness. If we have no self-judgements in a given moment of Consciousness, then we have no sense of any need to control or force our thoughts.

A further insight to note is that all forced thought-based behaviour inevitably leads to – causes – forced behaviour at the physical level. You get 'in your head', you get into forced behaviour! In fact, there's no forced behaviour without forced thought behaviour. So everything starts not with our thought, but with our Consciousness. By letting our *Awareness* change our *Consciousness*, different thoughts can arise, leading to different Flow behaviour. A healthy relationship to our thoughts is to let them come and go, without any fear of them, and of course that means without any judgement of them. When we have a moment of self-judgement we feel we have to control our thoughts. In the absence of self-judgement, we are happy to receive thoughts without attachment or resistance:

Love Consciousness	**Fear Consciousness**
Allows thoughts to flow, to come and go	Tries to force and control thoughts

'Consciousness Acts'

aka: Consciousness Actions, Awareness Actions, Acts of Awareness, Acts of Consciousness, etc.

> "Your Consciousness is primary because it is the cause of your thoughts, and by extension, the cause of your behaviour." – James Blacker

So what *is* the nature of our task when we wish to change something? You're looking to change your behaviour, but you're also looking to change your thinking which causes that behaviour – and without forcing your thinking. The way to do that is through an Act of Consciousness, or Awareness (same thing). The Act of Awareness changes the Permission, which changes the thinking, which in turn leads to altogether different (desirable) behaviours and actions.

We have behaviour (body) and we have thoughts (mind). But how do you know you have thoughts? How do you know you have physical experiences? Answer: Because you're *aware* of them, you're *Conscious* of them. So we actually have a third level in our ordered causation list:

1. Consciousness / Awareness
2. Mind
3. Body

And herein lies the key to change, 'healing', true Success and personal fulfilment. A simple moment of Awareness, of Consciousness – the briefest glimpse – of the false nature of our thoughts is all it takes to illuminate them and release their purpose.

'Mind, Body and Spirit'

In fact, if you have heard the term 'Mind, Body and Spirit' (and maybe even thought of it as new age fantasy), I would invite you to consider, for now at least, that this phrase is better expressed as 'Mind, Body and Awareness', or 'Mind, Body and Consciousness'. As part of that, I'd also invite you to consider your Awareness or your Consciousness as pretty much being equivalent to 'Spirit' in that phrase.

Consciousness is Not Thought

A distinction to note here is that Consciousness is not the same thing as thought. Consciousness is not thought. Thought isn't primary.

Choice is Not Thought

Let's consider the phenomenon of Choice, as we have already explored. We know that Choice is You being true to yourself, and key to your Success, Confidence, Happiness, and more …

As crazy as it might sound at first, Choice doesn't really happen at the level of our thoughts. When you know exactly what you want, you don't really have to think about it! Choice really comes from our Knowing. Zap, it's there, you know exactly what you want – it's just there! If you have to think long and hard about what you want, you probably aren't sure. If I've stared at a Chinese menu for more than a minute I know my mind is trying to talk my body into wanting something it doesn't really want.

Being is not thought. Success is not thought.

What 'Being' Looks Like

Now that we understand the 'secondary' nature of behaviour, we can explain what 'Being' looks like.

There is a nice – but troublesome – quote that "We are human beings, not human doings." The reason it's troublesome is that Being and doing something are *not* opposites. In fact, doing can be a valid expression of our Being.

As we already discussed with respect to Consciousness, Being has no set behavioural expression. Being cannot *automatically* be equated to:

- Sitting still
- Doing nothing
- Being silent
- Not using the cognitive brain

In any given moment, these things may be the expression of Love Consciousness, but they could also be the expression of Fear Consciousness. Again, they are behaviours, and so they are secondary.

The Three Levels of Personal Development/Success Approaches

Just as there are three levels of causation – Consciousness Acts, thought-based behaviour and regular (action-based) behaviour – so too there are three different approaches to what we might call 'self-help' or personal development:

- Behaviour-primary strategies and approaches
- Thought-primary strategies and approaches
- Consciousness-primary strategies and approaches

I would guess that of all the people who flounder with change to achieve Success, 90% do so because they buy into the notion of forcing behaviour, and most of the remaining 10% do so because they're trying to force positive thought. Either way, they flounder because they are trying to force change against their basic nature, their Being.

As we now know, a key principle of Conscious Living is that there is no behaviour that is inherently Conscious or Unconscious. It is the *motive*, the quality of Consciousness that causes a behaviour which determines whether or not that behaviour is Conscious. In Kissing Consciousness we therefore don't give any advice at a behavioural level, or judge any behavioural expression that a person may choose. To do so would be to lead people away from the freedom of being themselves and trusting their own knowing.

By working from the root cause, Kissing Consciousness has the power to change blocks incredibly effectively and quickly. Behaviour-primary and thought-primary approaches can take years to stumble across the required change in Awareness that a Consciousness-primary approach can zero in on in moments.

Love Consciousness is Even The Primary Form of Love

> "Without Love Consciousness none of the other forms of love are true, real, authentic or sincere." – James Blacker

We can now see that the other two forms of love which we identified in The Power of Love chapter are themselves *secondary* to Love Consciousness.

- Love as Compassion or Care
- Love as Attraction or Liking

On the face of it, Love as Compassion or Care might seem pretty primary. But if you think about it, you can 'do' compassion from self-judgement rather than from self-love – e.g. "I should go and work at the homeless shelter this Christmas" – and if done from self-judgement, it is not authentic. Authentic compassion is a secondary quality that flows from Love Consciousness.

The same applies to liking or loving things or people. If your liking or love is true then it comes from Love Consciousness anyway. If it is merely the expression of self-judgement, such as getting married for fear of being lonely, or liking a band because all your friends do, then it is coming from a place of Fear Consciousness.

The only way that pretending is authentic is if it's done to protect ourselves, e.g. from school bullies. If the things you like or love, or have compassion or care for, are things that you're only pretending about to yourself, or to others, they're not going to make you happy.

So Consciousness is the primary of ... pretty much everything.

Yes, everything. (../root)

The Paradox of Love Consciousness

Given all these amazing characteristics and outcomes of being in the state of Love Consciousness, it's understandable that people may get attached to being in it, and resist being in the state of Fear Consciousness. But this attachment and resistance is a trap. By wanting Love Consciousness, you're in Fear Consciousness.

The paradox of fearing and resisting being in the state of Fear Consciousness is that it puts us in it, while being willing to be in that state, and if need be releasing that resistance to it, puts us in the other state of Love Consciousness.

By definition, Love Consciousness is about allowing things to be the way they are, and accepting that they are the way they are, even if one of the things you're accepting is a thing you wish to change. Having an attachment to being in a state of Love Consciousness, or a resistance to being in a state of Fear Consciousness, therefore inevitably makes Love Consciousness impossible. It is impossible to 'fear' your way into a state of Love Consciousness. The only thing that releases you from the attachment-resistance trap is catching yourself in your Awareness and letting go of the attachment-resistance. And then, by virtue of having no attachment to the state you're in, you're back in the state of Love Consciousness.

So Love Consciousness isn't about being fearfully attached to being on one side of the line, it's about having a "care but don't mind" policy, a defiant and joyful willingness to be in Fear Consciousness, if that's your brain's mad desire. And in that, you're free.

"The moment you stop fearfully needing to jump across to the Love Consciousness path, it moves itself underneath you." – James Blacker

By needing to be in Love Consciousness, we automatically put ourselves in Fear Consciousness. Yet the moment we let go of that Neediness, Love Consciousness itself jumps underneath our very feet.

The structure of The Kissing Consciousness Binary now provides the basis for us to see the insight of The Paradox of Love Consciousness – and give it a name – so that we can use it more formally. This makes it infinitely casicr for us all to work with.

Here's your approach or relationship to whether you're in a state of Love Consciousness in any given moment:

Love Consciousness	**Fear Consciousness**
Not minding whether you're in a state of Love Consciousness or Fear Consciousness	Having attachment to being in a state of Love Consciousness and resistance to being in a state of Fear Consciousness

Defining The Paradox of Love Consciousness this way helps us see that letting go of the need to be in a state of Love Consciousness is a step in the right direction.

The Paradox of Love Consciousness applies not only to attachment-resistance about the state one is in, but also to fear of having a negative thought (like Deepak Chopra's patient) and of everything else: Fear of lacking Confidence, fear of lacking self-love, fear of not achieving our desires, fear of not having Choice, Being, Success, Awareness, Happiness, the lot. Every single aspect of Love Consciousness and Fear Consciousness is at the mercy of this paradox. (../paradox)

Tools to Help You Transcend The 'Secondaryness' of Behaviour and Beliefs

To further help you grasp that behaviours and the beliefs which lead to them are 'secondary' – neither inherently Conscious, nor inherently Unconscious – Kissing Consciousness has created three insightful concepts:

- The Illusion of Identical Experiences
- Consciousness-Behaviour (Banana) Splits
- Conscious 'Negatives' and Judgemental 'Positives'

This is basically me playing and having fun with Consciousness insights – but for a purpose. Each of these insights can help you shine further light on where you might have self-judgements causing you to live from Unconscious behaviours and unhelpful beliefs, rather than trusting your Awareness that a different choice may be true for you. Playful and fun as these insights may be, they could conceivably also be the difference between life and death – and are certainly the difference between Happiness and Unhappiness.

The Illusion of Identical Experiences

Understanding The Illusion of Identical Experiences will help you further distinguish between Conscious and Unconscious activities, and help you get out of the habit and self-deception of behaviour-primary strategies and thought primary strategies, and into the fun, effectiveness and freedom of a Consciousness-primary strategy, living from Awareness.

We're going to consider a behaviour that's driven by Love Consciousness (Choice, Awareness, etc.), versus *the exact same behaviour* when it's driven by Fear Consciousness (self-judgement, lack of Confidence, etc.). Since there's no such thing as a behaviour that is inherently Conscious or Unconscious, there are essentially two possible versions of each behaviour and activity in life, based on whether that behaviour or activity is flowing from our Being and Choice (from Love Consciousness), or is a forced behaviour motivated by self-judgement (Fear Consciousness).

This is what Kissing Consciousness calls **The Illusion of Identical Experiences**. These are displayed in Binary Tables by using the exact same wording in each column – so that only the different headings at the top of each column provide any indication as to the distinction between them.

Love Consciousness	**Fear Consciousness**
Drinking Water	Drinking Water

In this instance, we might imagine that drinking water from Choice, perhaps enjoying quenching our thirst, is a totally fulfilling experience compared to, say, drinking water when we don't actually want to, and our body doesn't actually need any water, but because we have a nagging, self-judging voice in our head saying we *should* "drink 8 glasses of water per day."

The Invisible Veil of All Experience

This isn't about having to be an expert on hydration – or whatever the topic may be – but about self-trust, about trusting our own knowing, and declining to do anything from a place of self-judgement because we now know and realise that this always means going against ourselves and our best interests. I invite you to become aware of the fact that every moment and every action, and therefore every experience of your life, is characterised by one of these two qualities.

We can put a whole raft of activities into the same Binary Table to give a broader example of this insight, as shown in the Binary Table opposite. If done from Love Consciousness they are a 'Flow Behaviour' (behaviour flows naturally), and if done from Fear Consciousness they are a Forced Behaviour.

Love Consciousness	**Fear Consciousness**
Art	Art
Being in Nature	Being in Nature
Celebrating	Celebrating
Drinking a Coffee	Drinking a Coffee
Exercising	Exercising
Fasting	Fasting
Feasting	Feasting
Going for a Walk	Going for a Walk
Hedonism	Hedonism
Introspecting	Introspecting
Luxuriating	Luxuriating
Meditating	Meditating
Masturbating	Masturbating
Partying	Partying
Playing	Playing
Praying	Praying
Relaxing	Relaxing
Resting	Resting
Saving Money	Saving Money
Sex	Sex
Sleeping	Sleeping
Stillness	Stillness

Love Consciousness	Fear Consciousness
Talking	Talking
Watching TV	Watching TV
Working	Working

A complete list would contain everything it's humanly possible to think, feel or do in life.

Although all these are different activities, yielding inherently different experiences to each other, ALL of the Love Consciousness experiences will tend to be enjoyable, fulfilling and effective, while the corresponding Fear Consciousness experiences will not be.

The Tint or Shadow of All Experience

As we go down each item in the list we can get a sense of what each activity would be like if we did it from our Being, from self-acceptance and Flow, at one with ourselves, compared to what it would be like doing that same activity from a place of self-judgement, being at odds with ourselves, going against our inner knowing, 'in our heads', with the nagging thought (truth) that actually this isn't what we really want to be doing right now.

Whenever we are doing something from self-judgement, there is always a nagging dissatisfaction at the back of – or even near the front of! – our minds, as we're left semi-consciously thinking about how we're not feeling good or right about this, or about what we'd rather be doing, or how we'd prefer things to be. We're sentient enough to feel unhappy, uncomfortable and pissed off, but not Conscious enough to wake up to the realisation that we can choose something different.

You might rest for ten minutes because you need a rest, but then carry on resting even after you get bored and have an urge to do something else, perhaps because you have an Unconscious self-judgement that you're not allowed to do whatever the 'something else' is. Just like that the experience of resting changes! It was congruent resting, and now it's incongruent resting.

Maybe last night you feasted, and it was fantastic, and you hope that if you feast again tonight you will get the same level of joy in the experience. But you don't get the same quality of experience, because where last night your feasting was spontaneous and responsive, tonight you are trying to make it flow even though you know it's not Flow. It's not the same experience – even though the activity is the same!

So this is the 'Veil' of All Experience, an invisible curtain that imbues all experience with either the 'tint' of light of pure Being, or the 'shadow' of Unconscious Unhappiness and self-judgement.

Understanding this isn't so much about defining each individual example or moment as it is about understanding the whole tapestry of a way of being in which we attune to living in the light and flow of Love Consciousness, and not in the darkness and shadow of Fear Consciousness. (../illusion)

"My favourite thing to do is not a
What. It's a How." – Josh Levin

Consciousness-Behaviour (Banana) Splits and Behavioural Banana Skins

If you are whimsically inclined you might like to use the word 'banana' as part of the term 'Consciousness-Behaviour (Banana) Splits' when referring to this concept. The full, literal description of the concept is something like the much less catchy, 'words which have different meanings as a Consciousness than they do as a behaviour'. Whichever name helps you understand it best, and maybe also communicate it to others, is great. This Kissing Consciousness concept didn't really lend itself to a nice neat name! Anyway, you'll see why I went with Consciousness-Behaviour Splits, and 'Behavioural Banana Skins' for its associated term … it is indeed a case of people tripping themselves up when considering a meaning at the level of behaviour, instead of at the level of Consciousness. Now, on with the bananas …

Consciousness-Behaviour (Banana) Splits

First of all, let's see how this looks on a Binary Table. Not allowing ourselves to appreciate the difference between the Conscious expression of a concept and that concept's expression as a behaviour is a self-judgement, because we have to shut down our Awareness to our actual Choice in order to do a behaviour that goes against ourselves and doesn't actually serve us.

Love Consciousness	Fear Consciousness
Allowing ourselves to appreciate the meaning and value of the concept	Getting into our heads about a concept and so locking ourselves into a fear-based behaviour

Let's look at some examples.

Compromise: Compromise is a classic example of a Consciousness-Behaviour Split.

If I were married with children, and on the first day of a family holiday we did exactly what I wanted, on the second day I might well choose to allow someone else to decide what activity we might all do. This is compromise at a behavioural level, but assuming it's my Choice to compromise, perhaps because giving everyone a say is important to me, I'm acting from Love Consciousness rather than Fear Consciousness. The important thing to note is that I am *not* compromising who I am at a Consciousness level. That's exactly what I want.

That scenario is totally different to a person compromising their truth by pretending to be happy to compromise on something when they're not. Compromising one's truth at a Consciousness level is typically Fear Consciousness.

Nurturing (Self-Nurturing): Picture a young lady who's returned home from a rewarding but emotionally challenging seminar or retreat. All her friends say to her, "Nurture yourself when you get home." Assuming she does want to nurture herself, not just do as her friends said (remember our insights on being Self-Referral), she might 'translate' the concept of self-nurturing into a checklist of clichéd behaviours: Have a long bubble bath with a glass of wine, then dress in soft clothes and curl up on the sofa. But for her, today, this behavioural level checklist doesn't feel like self-nurturing – it feels stressful and uncomfortable.

At a Consciousness level, perhaps what she really wants to do to nurture herself is to go for a run, because that's what her body wants to do. Or maybe she wants to complete a work task ready for the morning, because she knows it will only prey on her mind if she doesn't; to do it is more 'nurturing' than not to do it.

If you've ever tried to do self-nurturing from self-judgement, you may have noticed that it actually feels pretty anticlimactic. What could be less nurturing than forcing oneself to do something out of self-judgement?! Using the Kissing Consciousness approach, we might reasonably choose to have *every single moment* of our lives be of a self-nurturing Consciousness and nature. And if you're starting to wonder how you might achieve all of this – never compromising, always nurturing – remember, we're talking about all things coming from a Consciousness level, so all we have to do is be willing to decline self-judgement as it arises. There are no guarantees about how life will unfold itself for us, but it's not about that. It's about allowing the maximum possible outcomes and experience of life for ourselves by declining self-judgement.

Stillness: Stillness as a Consciousness may mean that the behaviour of your body or mind is anything but still in a given moment. But so what? Maybe there's a good reason for the mind to be turbulent, or the body active. Maybe they are processing. Stillness as a Consciousness is a different thing to stillness as a behaviour.

Loving Someone: How many of us haven't seen people go through the activities of 'loving someone' at a behavioural level – buying flowers maybe, or saying "I love you" – even as we know, instinctively that they're not actually loving that person at a Consciousness level? The behaviour that society might associate with loving someone doesn't necessarily guarantee the *Consciousness* of loving someone. Can we see *beyond* the behaviour, to see the underlying Consciousness? This explains why one person can spend more on Valentine's Day, but perhaps with a resentful attitude, and get less of a positive reaction than his mate who approaches it with a 'Romance Consciousness'.

Laughter: On the outside a person may be laughing, but inside something completely different may be going on for them. The history of Robin Williams comes to mind.

Meditation and Prayer: If you pray, the quality of your Consciousness is the most relevant factor, rather than the physical or verbal activity which people associate with prayer, such as putting one's hands together, or even the sentences we use out loud, or in our head. And whilst humanity continues to debate whether there is a God who's listening, whether your Subconscious Mind is listening isn't debatable: It is.

The same Consciousness-Behaviour Split principle applies to Meditation. You're not necessarily meditating *as an actual Consciousness* just because you're sitting with your eyes closed and legs crossed in the lotus position. And just because you aren't sitting like that, or your eyes are open, doesn't mean you *aren't* meditating. It is the state of Consciousness, of self-witnessing, which makes meditation the real deal.

I'm running out of page space in this book, so you can see more examples – including Accuracy, Hedonism, (Relationship) Freedom, Self-Discipline and Being Outcome-Oriented – on the Kissing Consciousness website, at:

www.KissingConsciousness.com/splits

Behavioural Banana Skins

Any behaviour that isn't done from Awareness is a forced behaviour. The approach of Conscious Living is essentially to use the Act of Awareness to decline a Behavioural (or thought-based behavioural) Banana Skin.

Conscious 'Negatives' and Unconscious 'Positives'

Although there are no activities or behaviours that are inherently Conscious or Unconscious, society certainly judges various behaviours as either desirable or undesirable, 'positive' or 'negative'. These are therefore further potential 'Banana Skins'.

We might think of exercise as a being a 'positive', for example, and consider it a 'negative' to spend all our money. But in any moment, our Awareness may be that spending all our money is the right thing to do, and exercising is not. Societal notions are all secondary; our Awareness is primary.

Conscious 'Negatives' and Unconscious 'Positives' demonstrate that the assumptions and conclusions we make about desirable and undesirable activities and actions are actually false limitations for us. Please note that the inverted commas around the words 'Negatives' and 'Positives' translate as 'so called'.

Love Consciousness	Fear Consciousness
Trusting our own Awareness, we are not limited or bound by any notions of what is considered positive or negative	Self-judgement causes us to doubt our own Awareness and be a prisoner of what is considered positive and negative

Conscious 'Negatives'

Conscious 'Negatives' are things we may think of as negatives, but they're not inherently negative because it is the Consciousness that motivates them which determines their value. They may actually be positive for us if our

Awareness says they are our actual Choice and truth in a given moment and context. Let's look at some examples.

Aimlessness: Aimlessness is often half-way between allowing yourself to not do something you don't want to do, and not quite yet doing something you do want to do.

> "By being willing to not judge what was arising, I got an experience and information which was only available *because* I was willing to not judge my aimlessness that was arising. Aimlessness is the 'waiting room' of the True Self." – James Blacker

Apart from there simply being nothing inherently wrong with aimlessness, it can also be seen to be the Choice not to act from self-judgement when we haven't yet worked out exactly what we *do* want to do, or haven't yet fully let go of the False Self Consciousness. 'Aimless', 'clueless' or 'vague' teenagers, for example, may simply be those whose true personalities have been most repressed. Their aimlessness is a step in the right direction.

Cowardice: Awareness, including the genuine Choice that comes with it, is always primary. Being true to yourself is being true to yourself, whatever that looks like. It would be a sad affair if a person had an inner guidance to go one way, but ignored it because a voice of self-judgement in their head said they shouldn't take that choice because it was cowardly.

Quitting: The same is true for quitting. Quitting might be seen as a 'negative', but if you are Conscious to your motives and truth, there may be good reasons for you wanting to do it.

Again, you can read more examples at (../CN)

Unconscious 'Positives'

Unconscious 'Positives' are things we may think of as positives, but they're not inherently positive. Again, it is the Consciousness that motivates them which determines their validity. They may actually be negative for us if our Awareness says they aren't our actual Choice and truth; it may actually be 'positive' for us to decline them.

Exercise: "I'm going to do some exercise!" is always met with a chorus of, "Ah, well done you!" But what if your body doesn't want to exercise in that moment? What if it's not the right thing to do? When we exercise against the body's wisdom because we are being driven by Fear Consciousness and self-judgement, perhaps because we're judging what our body looks like prior to the Summer season, we are probably going to be doing it damage, rather than doing it any good.

Proactivity: Proactivity is fine, but despite its positive gloss it is still not necessarily the most desirable approach in any given moment.

Preparation: Preparation is generally considered a positive, but it might not be. What if your self-judgement is driving you to prepare in detail, when your Awareness is that you can trust the way things will go? From an Unconscious place of Fear Consciousness, preparation might even be the result of fear controlling your natural ability to trust your flow, or to trust your own knowing. It might be stifling your spontaneity and innate talent. Hard Work is another potential Unconscious 'Positive', which I address in Volume II in 'A Consciousness Ethic'. (../UP)

Judgemental 'Positives' and Judgemental 'Negatives'

So far our exploration of Conscious 'Negatives' and Unconscious 'Positives' has only focussed on what we might experience solely within ourselves and our own Consciousness. As we consider the potential effect of other people being judgemental of us, however, we uncover a whole second layer of these dynamics, which we'll call Judgemental 'Positives' and Judgemental 'Negatives'.

In these instances, people use either the positive or negative connotations inherent in cultural biases as ways to control, manipulate or even abuse others. In fact, at the lower end of what we might call the 'abuse spectrum', all of these are abusive because there's an attempt to psychologically control, maybe even belittle, or worse. We'll use examples that assume that the judgementalism is intentional; however, it could also be unintentional.

Judgemental 'Positives'

Judgemental 'Positives' are things which frequently have a positive association in a culture, but may not necessarily be positive, and are used to lead others against their own free will, Choice and Awareness by asserting that people not doing them are not following a positive choice.

Duty: What if the instruction "Do your duty!" is an unintentional or even intentionally manipulative translation of "Surrender your Choice to me so that I can control you!"? If duty is anything other than secondary to Choice (i.e. you choose to do something that *happens* to also coincide with that notion of duty), then as a denial of someone's free will how can it be anything other than control? If you're talking about the role of the best man at a wedding, and pointing out that traditionally, one of the duties of the best man is to give a speech, then maybe it's fine and coming from a loving place. Even then, though, consent and Choice are still relevant.

Looking Ladylike, Pretty or Smart and Being 'Manly': If given for a genuine reason, compliments such as "You look very ladylike" or "You look very pretty" (or smart, or fashionable, etc.) or "You have a nice and 'manly' vibe" are healthy, innocent and loving moments of everyday life; mere expressions of a person's appreciation. If the intent behind them is control, however, often there is a latent judgement of you for those moments when you choose the opposite of what they are complimenting. And please remember that behind the Projection, they're actually judging themselves, so there's no need for you to take it personally. It's *their* self-judgement.

Judgement and approval always go together. If a judgemental person compliments you on looking like a lady, then it's quite possibly a control statement because they don't want you to look like a tomboy or however you might choose to look if left to your own devices. Compliments about 'manliness' might hide a judgement about men not being strong enough, being 'wimps', even homophobia. This, again, reflects their own Unconscious self-judgements. The compliment seeks to keep you on the track laid out by their Unconscious self-judgement, so that you don't threaten their False Self. A truly secure person is never judgemental under any circumstances.

The acid test is always "Oh, I don't want to be that, actually", or "I don't mind either way about that", and if that's met with total acceptance, or with resistance. As the saying goes, "A friend is someone you can be yourself with."

"Oh to hell with dignity, I'll go
when the job's done!" – M, Skyfall

Dignity: People may seek to control others psychologically by accusing them of having no dignity, but where is dignity if other people are dictating your 'choice' to you? Again, there is nothing inherently wrong with wishing to have dignity, or to do something with dignity, but at the same time, there's no obligation, either. It's just a choice.

Further examples, including 'Doing Good for Others (Charity Work)', at (../JP)

Judgemental 'Negatives'

Judgemental 'Negatives' are things which often have a negative association in a culture, but may not necessarily be negative, and which are used to lead others against their own free will, Choice and Awareness by asserting that people are following a negative choice by doing them.

"Don't Rock The Boat": It's not difficult to imagine this being said to someone who is threatening to speak out about injustice or abuse or some other need for change, by those who don't want justice or truth to surface. It can happen in business, for example where most members of a Board are in their Awareness about the need to take a leap forward, and one or two others are in fear based resistance to change. It may be in a family situation instead. Maybe a relationship has run its course and one or more people are ready to face up to that and one or two others aren't. Or it may be something smaller: sometimes, things just need to be said. So again there's nothing inherently desirable or undesirable about 'rocking the boat' – it all depends on context, Choice, and what's true for you. But that doesn't mean people can't use it judgementally, and/or with the intention of controlling others' behaviour.

Wasting Time: People who are not allowed to be in their Being or take time for themselves may wish to stop others enjoying free time because it triggers them (it rubs them up the wrong way). Those who don't take responsibility for their choices and boundaries may also resent seeing others enjoying free time. But consider: Doing something from Fear Consciousness does nothing to honour anything that's true anyway, so could be said to *always* be a waste of time.

Further Examples: Another example of a Judgemental 'Positive' is, "Stay positive and keep doing what you're doing." Sounds good, but again it's encouraging someone to be External Referral. External Referral commands which aren't 'flagged up' by the recipient's Awareness put people in a *reactive* state. Another example of a Judgemental 'Negative' is, "Don't take (something) for granted." Take here, TV journalist, Jon Snow's words; "I've witnessed people literally dying for their right to vote, so **don't take it for granted**." It's fantastic that he wants to appreciate such a valuable life insight, but doing it in a way that puts people 'under instruction', as it were, does nothing to help people's process of appreciating such things from their own free will. Yet we have all been brought up with this way of speaking, of giving advice *as instruction*, without realising that it actually *inhibits* people's development and empowerment and growth. We need an entirely new way of being that releases us from this 'second nature' way of being in our heads, and returns us to our first nature of living from Awareness and Choice – and that requires freedom of mind. If people don't have the *freedom* to take something for granted, they don't have the *genuine opportunity* to *choose* to appreciate and value it. As Wayne Dyer says, "I can't give you what you demand of me." Further examples at (../JN)

Further Clues and Insights

Judgemental 'Positives' tend to express in Imperative Grammar – i.e. telling people what to do – which, as we've mentioned, goes against the Love Consciousness principle of being Self-Referral. Judgemental 'Negatives' are also expressed with Imperative Grammar, telling people what *not* to do. These will often be accompanied by other non-love language, the conditional tense – i.e. should and shouldn't – "You should do your duty", "You shouldn't rock the boat."

With regular Conscious 'Negatives' and Unconscious 'Positives', where you're the only person involved, you're likely saying these things to *yourself*:

"I shouldn't be aimless", "I shouldn't be a coward", "I should exercise", "I should prepare."

Forget all of that self-judgement-based decision-making; what does your Awareness say? We can now put the typical effect of Imperative Grammar into our Binary:

Love Consciousness	**Fear Consciousness**
Self-Referral	External Referral

There's a difference between being External Referral and asking for help. When in Fear Consciousness around this issue, we are unwilling to ask for help due to the mistaken belief that it means being powerless, or External Referral. Ironically, that belief itself is powerless – and caused by *external* judgements.

Love Consciousness	**Fear Consciousness**
Being willing to ask for help	Being unwilling to ask for help due to the mistaken belief that it means being powerless or External Referral

Examples Are Not Justifications: Awareness and Choice Never Needs Justifying

Your Awareness doesn't need to be justified with beliefs and conclusions; it wouldn't be Awareness if it did!

Love Consciousness	Fear Consciousness
Accepting your Awareness of when a 'Positive' is really a judgement, or when a 'Negative' is really a Choice without needing to see a reason to justify it first	Judging your Awareness of when a 'Positive' is really a judgement, or when a 'Negative' is really a Choice and feeling the need to justify it in some way

The Elephant in The Room

So far we have looked at all these examples of Judgemental 'Positives' and Judgemental 'Negatives' from the perspective of being on the receiving end of others' judgements. We may also wish to see if we are holding onto any self-judgements ourselves which may have led us to try to control or limit other people. Rather than try to control others, we may find more joy in releasing the self-judgement, and thus allowing ourselves to have what we had previously been denying ourselves.

Love Consciousness	Fear Consciousness
Without self-judgements we have no need to seek to control others	The self-judgements which cause us to seek to control other people actually hide the truth that we are denying ourselves

"Everyone has got a story that will break your heart." – Terry Patten

Self-judgement is violence against oneself, and I say that not to be harshly judgemental of you, or to imply that you should be judgemental of yourself, but to help you to become fully aware of exactly how profound and considerable the effects of self-judgement are. Responding to our self-judgements without judging them demonstrates yet another aspect of the Love Consciousness state, that we are treating ourselves with kindness and compassion.

Love Consciousness	Fear Consciousness
Self-Kindness	Self-Unkindness
Self-Compassion	Lack of Self-Compassion
Self-Approval	Self-Criticism

True Desire

"Inherent in having the desire is the mechanics for its spontaneous fulfilment." – Dr. Deepak Chopra

When control and judgementalism from others causes self-judgement in us we essentially replace our true desires with false desires, which we sometimes also allow ourselves to believe are our true desires. The Mastery of Desire is the Awareness of this effect, such that we can respond and prevent it dominating our lives any time we sense things are not quite on song for us. In any moment, you're either allowing yourself to honour your true desire in that moment, or you're not.

A Big 'Eureka!' Moment

Sin

Understanding the real notion of sin may set you free. Some commentators observe an original Pagan meaning of 'sin', which translates as: "To pick up your bow and miss your target." According to Wikipedia, "The English Biblical terms translated as 'sin' or 'syn' from the Biblical Greek and Jewish terms sometimes originate from words in the latter languages denoting the act or state of missing the mark; the original sense of New Testament Greek ἁμαρτία hamartia 'sin', is failure, being in error, missing the mark, especially in spear throwing..."

Whether spear throwing or archery, the common theme is missing the mark, or target. So to Sin, in the Consciousness or energetic sense, is to aim at a false desire, or to have self-judgements causing us to not be allowed to aim at (i.e. choose) our true desire. That is another way of saying to "not be at one with our very own Being." Returning to our Binary Table, in Love Consciousness a certain quality of genuine Desire (the truth of our Being) is always present, while the effect of self-judgement is to override this and thus deny it:

Love Consciousness	**Fear Consciousness**
Desire	False Desire, or Sin

This gives us a more user-friendly, empowering, and helpful understanding of the concept of Sin. If you say 'Yes' to a proposal of marriage, but really meant 'No', that's a 'sin' against yourself.

Consider the following words of Father Thomas Keating, O.C.S.O, which also identify the 'sin' of False Self Desires: "So at one hand you have the basic oneness of everything, that is in its source, and the basic issue of separating ourselves from that oneness, which then means we're separating ourselves from our True Self, and from everybody else, and from the Kosmos, in varying degrees in which we sin, the meaning being 'miss the mark'. To miss the mark is to fail to recognise the truth of the situation." (../sin)

De-sire

Desire doesn't always mean something as obvious as getting a new car, or a splendid feast, or bars of gold. A wider understanding of desire is any way we truly are in a given moment. That *encompasses* all the big things, the small things, the subtle details, and even simply resting, as appropriate.

The etymology of desire is from the Latin 'desiderare', meaning 'to long for or wish for'. A further Latin interpretation has been suggested: 'of the father', with 'de-' meaning 'of', and 'sire' meaning 'father'. Correct or not, this interpretation nicely expresses the relationship between ourselves, our desires, and our Being. We started this section with a pertinent quote from Deepak Chopra: "Inherent in having the desire is the mechanics for its spontaneous fulfilment." Colin Turner also eloquently explains the nature of desire: "The importance of desire is such that with its power you already have the capacity to manifest, or attract, whatever you want in your life. The very fact that you have a 'desire', the Latin root of which translates as 'of the father', means that you have the God-given ability to achieve it. In other words, you would be incapable of holding a desire unless you had the capability to create its reality. Although most of what we are taught to believe conflicts with this, your desires are the very tools that assist you in expressing your purpose. It is because of false indoctrination, however well-meaning, that the art of manifesting our desires for positive benefit has been forgotten."

All of this is why Kissing Consciousness is a "moment-to-moment, and every moment" approach to personal development, rather than a behavioural-level (behaviour-primary) approach that focuses *primarily* on our activities. Love Consciousness is the gateway to our Desire. (../desire)

"What you want, wants you." – Peter Ragnar

Why "What you want, wants you" Might Annoy You

The phrase "what you want, wants you" might irritate you if you are taking "what you want" to mean or include your False Self, as we have discussed. It's important to realise that the phrase refers to the real, authentic "you", and so doesn't include the needy or false aspects of your wanting. If we (think we) want a love partner or a company car to raise our self-esteem, but this is not our true desire, our Ego is "missing the mark"! Hence The Mastery of Desire, for all that it may sound profound and out of reach to us mere mortals, really just means the same as usual – being in a state of Love Consciousness and using our Awareness to first notice, and then decline, self-judgement.

Desire vs Wanting (False Desire or Craven Desire)

When teaching The Mastery of Desire, I tend to use the word 'desire' for a choice that comes from self-acceptance, and the word 'want' for an illusion of choice which is motivated by self-judgement. The word 'want' can potentially be used by people in a positive way, however, I find that when used in society, it typically feels imbued with a different energy – a False Desire, or, as David Heard described it in our 'Happiness' audio recording, a 'Craven Desire'. This usage also ties in with the notion of 'wanting *for* something', and to want *for* something is to *lack* it, or to be without it, to *need* it. 'Want' also means 'scarcity'. It doesn't matter what words you use, though; what matters is getting a sense of the two different energies.

Desire can be actioned, and enjoyed for itself, in the moment. Wanting can be neither enjoyed for itself in the moment, nor effectively moved towards in the moment. As it is a self-judgement, the only useful thing we can do with it is to release it, and let our genuine, empowered Desire re-arise in its place. Letting go of the judgements around not getting it, and not being allowed it, frees you at the Consciousness level; you're free to either receive the thing, or re-set and recognise what it is that you truly desire. Most importantly, you're free to simply *Be.*

"Can you sense the self-judgement that's typically inherent in the energy of 'wanting'?" – James Blacker

The notion that we *need* a desired outcome is itself also usually a self-judgement. Essentially, what we're talking about here is Neediness. If you cannot be at peace whilst goals are unfulfilled, your goals own you. Fulfilment of goals which own you doesn't bring peace, either, because achieving goals is behaviour based (secondary), not Consciousness based (primary). When you have no goals that own you, you live in the moment, and are free. It doesn't mean you don't have goals, or don't achieve them. In fact, quite the opposite. It means that you're not dependent upon them or their outcomes for your sense of okayness or self-esteem, and therefore the fear of not achieving them cannot interrupt your Flow.

Love Consciousness	Fear Consciousness
Your goals and desires serve you	Your goals and desires own you; they are your prison

Approval

"Here's my truth; make it yours!" – Approval Tyrants

The underlying message in approval is: "Here's my truth, or even my Unconscious will, make it yours!" Whether we acquired a given self-judgement through an individual insisting that we meet their approval, or through the collective culture insisting that we meet its approval, the need to gain approval is always at the heart of a blockage. The threat itself may have long since gone, leaving only the historical Unconscious fear remaining. Often, after decades of the original fear being buried, we aren't even aware that our motivation for doing things is seeking the approval of others.

"If you're doing it for other people's approval, how can it make you happy? Answer: It can't." – David Heard

Approval is always a two-sided coin. The 'false positive' sense of warmth from someone's approval when we make ourselves a clone of them is matched on the other side of the coin by the cold pain of not feeling allowed to be ourselves, and the disapproving reaction we get when we try to choose the opposite way of being.

"Approval giveth, and approval taketh away." – James Blacker

An emotionally secure person – whether friend or parent – has no interest in asking another person to gain their approval. Requiring another to gain our approval is always a False Self expression. (../approval)

Authenticity, Freedom and Sincerity

Authenticity is another characteristic of Love Consciousness. We've seen that Love Consciousness is authentically who you are, and that Fear Consciousness is a False Self. Here are a few other ways in which this manifests, first in terms of how we are with ourselves:

Love Consciousness	Fear Consciousness
Self-Sincerity	Self-Insincerity
Authenticity	Inauthenticity
Life is Real	Life is Fake

And in terms of interaction with others:

Love Consciousness	Fear Consciousness
Authentic Connection with Others is Possible	Authentic Connection with Others is Impossible
Speaking Your Truth (including Silence)	Not Speaking Your Truth (including Silence)
The *Option* of Sincerity with Others	The *Certainty* of Unintentional Insincerity with Others

Freedom is a prerequisite of sincerity. Sincerity is only possible where there is freedom to be so – again, per Wayne Dyer, "I cannot give you what you demand of me." Physical slavery has mostly died out, however, mental slavery remains. Mental slavery is the current 'imprisonment' of humankind and society which Kissing Consciousness and many other movements, projects, teachings, etc., are releasing. Freedom is also a classic example of one of our Consciousness-Behaviour Banana Splits.

Love Consciousness	**Fear Consciousness**
Freedom	Self-Constriction

Success

"Success isn't something you find, it's something you ARE." – James Blacker

A gold star if you noticed that our two definitions of Success are a form of Consciousness-Behaviour Split. Success is a classic example of the principle, if not *the* classic example of it. Many aspects of what we might have thought of as success may instead be Unconscious 'Positives' or Judgemental 'Positives'.

Love Consciousness	**Fear Consciousness**
Honouring the Primacy of Success as a state of Consciousness in any given moment	Shutting out Awareness of our truth, getting caught in assumptions and judgements of what Success looks like at a behavioural level

What Success Looks Like

"We judge the quality of people's lives from the outside and that really gives us a misleading picture." – James Blacker

Just as we might not want to get caught into doing compromise at a Consciousness level, so too we might not want to get caught in the trap of pursuing success as defined at the behavioural level. Maybe we join the golf club or put children into boarding school or have a certain style 'look', not because it's fulfilling to us, but because that's what we've been told 'success' looks like, or because we think that's "what successful people do." Buying into a New Age community's idea of what 'success' looks like can be equally unfulfilling – Frustrating (Frustration of your True Self) – if done for the approval of that group. To avoid this Banana Skin we want our behaviour to emanate *from* Love Consciousness, from our Choice.

A notion of quality of life that is based on self-judgement has no real bearing on reality. It's a shame that so many people live lives of concepts, rather than of direct, real experiences. Starting from my mid-teens, I got into this trap myself for twenty years, and it had to be turned around and released. People who live with concepts of success, rather than making Success choices which are truly enjoyable in the way that actual experiential joy and life is enjoyable, are limiting – possibly even destroying – their own quality of life.

Just as with Confidence, or Being, or any of the other qualities of the expression of Love Consciousness, and contrary to the world's assumptions, there really is no set visible pattern or physical manifestation of what Success is. Success is what each individual chooses as true for themselves. Whether Success is about being on the cover of magazines, or having loads of money or status, or achieving things like exams or promotions, is all just personal Choice. A person enjoying a genuine sense of Success may be notable due to their energy, their demeanour, a sense of being at peace with themselves. They may emanate a genuine deep-seated sense of contentment, rather than a surface display.

Failure

What is failure? Is there such a thing? I once saw a man leading a seminar state that there is no such thing as failure. His audience challenged him, arguing that surely there is: for example, losing a boxing match, or a business going bust, or a political party losing an election, failing an exam, dating someone who ultimately chose someone else, losing a business contract to a rival company, all kinds of things. The speaker got into a mess because he didn't really understand the concept he was trying to convey. He had a nice-sounding 'meme', but hadn't thought it through. In fact, before we go any further, just as an interesting exercise I'll do a *Specific* Binary Table (relating to a specific context) as to why he got into trouble:

Love Consciousness	**Fear Consciousness**
Sufficient self-honesty to only claim to know, or try to present, things you know you understand	Self-judgement(s) of who or how you should be, leading you to try to present a concept you don't understand

He hadn't distinguished between failure at the behavioural level and failure at the Consciousness level.

Is there such a thing as failure? It depends in what sense we mean. At a behavioural (activity) level there absolutely is such a thing as failure, and acknowledging the truth of this enhances our psychological strength. (This fluffy new notion of schools not wanting to have any winners or losers only weakens students, because the children instinctively know deep down it's not true. False praise is damaging. The way to avoid raising insecure children is to not judge them for their level of achievement, whatever it happens to be.) Any aim or goal, *by definition*, brings with it the possibility of failure. There is no possibility of success in a venture without the possibility of failure as well. Then we have the notion that we can view all failure as 'feedback'. Provided the goal in question wasn't a final chance, such as a last chance at a sports world championship before retirement, or a destroyed ecosystem ending all human life, then indeed, we can use feedback from the failure to inform the next attempt. But this, too, is still at the behaviour level. And at the behavioural level there's no guarantee that any amount of feedback or any number of subsequent attempts would bring success in a specific goal or aim anyway.

Frustration, Misunderstanding, Rather Than Failure

> "If you fail at something, why do you think you were 'meant' to succeed at it?" – James Blacker

To really get to a notion of there being no such thing as failure, we have to look beyond the behavioural level. We need to understand why we *think* there is a *separation* between who we are, and Success. It is self-judgement that creates this sense of the possibility of failure *as a person*, or even failure at a behavioural/outcome level *taken personally* at a Consciousness level. To think we could have done any better than we actually did is a misunderstanding. We might say, or think to ourselves, "I should have done this differently", or "I should have been better equipped to succeed by now" – but notice the presence of the judgemental word 'should' in those sentences. Try expressing such a notion without the word 'should'. It can't be done. We just end up realising that was the best we could do, to the best of our Awareness and capacities. At a Consciousness level, any notion of failure can only be a judgement, and therefore not real.

It's *impossible* that You are a failure, or that you could ever fail to achieve something true to yourself that is or was or will be possible for you. *Even at the behavioural level*, it's impossible for us to fail at a goal that we could have succeeded in. And so, once people get their false self-judgements cleared, and realise the reality of the situation, failure at a behavioural level essentially loses all of its Egoic sting. It just becomes life. (../success)

The Achievement of Goals

Once we accept this fundamental truth of our inherent Success, and that it's impossible to not be who we are, and thus we stop judging ourselves for 'failures' and mistakes, we become powerful at achieving from that point on into the future, because we can respond to feedback, rather than react to it. We can see what we might do differently *from now on*, what we might choose, and what self-judgements we might become aware of – and release.

Relationship to 'Failure' and Mistakes

Far from being a passive response to failure, this is actually *the* springboard to achieving the things you wish to achieve. In Love Consciousness, we acknowledge that because our failures and mistakes are in the past, there is nothing we can do to change that past now, and so we don't let thoughts of those mistakes and failures bother us or inhibit us, even if they only happened a split-second ago. This is no complicated or high-level thing, merely self-compassion and self-honesty and reality-based thinking. How on earth can you possibly change the past?! You can go into drama and Ego if you want to, as most people do, or you can respond.

Love Consciousness	Fear Consciousness
Feedback	Drama
We accept that we can't change the past, so we don't let thoughts of it hold us back from what we wish to do now	We judge ourselves for mistakes, slowing down the process of moving on to the next moment

When our past performance in life is not judged, the feedback – and state of Consciousness – this provides becomes the insight and awareness we require to fuel a more informed and better equipped re-attempt to achieve something if we still want it. If we don't see something as a failure that's separate to our Being, and therefore don't judge ourselves for it, we can move on to the next thing immediately. This lets us move quickly through learning curves, through 'healing curves', and through achievement in life. And therefore, whilst we can't control such things as global economics, or even what talents we were born with, this (Love Consciousness) is the key to achieving in life based on what is in our hands.

We can actually 'unpack' this insight further. As we know, Love Consciousness is our true nature, and Fear Consciousness is actually our False Self, not our true personality. So not only is the quality of Love Consciousness as defined in the table above about your relationship to 'failure' and mistakes, it's also your *true* relationship to 'failure' and mistakes. In other words, it's your true personality to not beat yourself up or judge yourself for 'failure' or for making mistakes. This allows us to progress and advance through life at the speed of truth. Failure *as an identity – on any level whatsoever* – is False Self.

Love Consciousness	Fear Consciousness
'Failure' as feedback – information about who we really are	Failure as an Identity: "I'm a Failure!"

The Relationship between Success Consciousness and Achieving Goals

So what's the relationship between Success as Love Consciousness in the moment, and success in terms of achieving goals? Well ... because of The Primacy of Consciousness, 'Success Consciousness' (Success *as a Consciousness*) is also primary. Behaviour level activity – including achieving goals – is secondary.

We are better off if we prioritise our Consciousness in each and every moment, getting into an effortless, consistent flow. You cannot fail to achieve a goal that is based on being true to yourself. There is no 'failure' involved when you don't achieve something that's not a true desire of yours, because the fact of not achieving it is merely providing feedback to your truth. And that truth was hidden behind unavoidable self-judgements which were necessary to keep you (as) safe and well (as possible).

Love Consciousness	Fear Consciousness
Success	Frustration
You Are Fulfilled	You Are Unfulfilled

The Fuel of Dynamic Action

I hear speakers talking about taking action as the key to success – huge or consistent actions. What do you think *causes* the ability to take such action with ease? Our Consciousness. When that is aligned, our ability to achieve our true goals and aims runs at the optimal level. Behaviour *flows* from Love Consciousness, remember. The Flow Behaviour seemingly makes the 'magic' happen, but the Love Consciousness underneath it is the real driver. We don't need to formally set goals in order to harness this power; we can trust that if we are in our Being, any formal goal setting that's called for will follow as a natural consequence.

Principle: Achieving our true goals is a *by-product* of Love Consciousness.

Conscious Goal Setting

Before any specific goals are set, the 'goal' of being in a state of Love Consciousness in any given moment is primary. When we're living Consciously, this informs both if and when we set any other goals, whether formally or informally. Formal goal setting is a behavioural level activity. It's possible that we *never* set goals formally. Let's show that in terms of **The Illusion of Identical Experiences**:

Love Consciousness	Fear Consciousness
Goal Setting	Goal Setting

A healthy degree of consistently achieving basic goals in life is typically as important as the ability to appreciate where we are and to 'live in the moment'. But with clear eyes we can see that these are not separate things. When operating from Love Consciousness we don't have to worry about goal setting; your 'Being' includes truth about what you'd like to do and achieve, including whether to formally set goals. ALL moments can be appreciated for their own experience in and of themselves, and being true to yourself in each moment also optimises your achievement of goals along the way.

The Difficulty of a Task is Largely Irrelevant

"Self-judgements are the only false limitations." – James Blacker

Hardly any of the tasks required to be successful in achieving beneficial outcomes in our lives are actually technically difficult. Consider for example: Speaking to people, going places, simple math, logic or practical activities, not doing things that are unhelpful or negative, following through on basic tasks. Very few of us have to jump through hoops James Bond style, understand rocket science, run to exhaustion, or balance on a high wire above the city to achieve what we want to achieve. The things which you are allowed to do (Permissions) you find incredibly easy and 'no big deal', and this is because they come from your Being. You want to do them, for genuine reasons. As long as there's no self-judgement, you're 'allowed' to do them, and so they happen. What you find easy, other people may find incredibly difficult; they will wonder how you do it, and may envy you for it. What you find impossible, or difficult, others may find easy – and this may irritate you. Unless they're extraordinary tasks, you probably find them 'impossible' because you're trying to do them *against* yourself, *against* your Permissions. The things we aren't allowed to be or do or have or receive tend to look impossible. Yet when we change that 'Human File Permission' to a 'Yes' and look back upon a dream achieved, we immediately see those things we once saw as impossible as 'no big deal'. There's possibly even a sense of anti-climax at having achieved them – which is another good reason not to get too hung up on not having achieved behaviour-level goals.

Ease vs Easy

Ease and things being easy are different matters entirely. When you are in a state of Love Consciousness, however difficult a task may be, however much it may challenge you, or however much of your energy, attitude and resources it may require of you, there will always be a certain quality of 'ease' present, because you are at one with yourself.

Love Consciousness	Fear Consciousness
Ease	Lack of Ease
At One with Yourself	At Odds with Yourself

'Effortless Effort' or Even 'Struggling with Ease'?

An English philosopher, Colin Turner, said of life's tasks that they "may require effort, but should never be a struggle." Peter Ragnar talked of 'Effortless Effort' and the notion of people 'efforting' when they weren't allowing things to flow from Source, from their Being, but were instead 'efforting' against their true nature. I could even conceive of a way that struggle may be effortless, if it were coming from a place of Awareness and Choice, namely, that the struggle would only be at the behavioural level, not the Consciousness level. There's a difference between struggling against ourselves, and a struggling which is inspired by inner guidance as the right thing to do, or simply our Conscious Choice. I wouldn't let a self-judgement dissuade me from anything, even the associations we have around the word 'struggle'.

I believe all three of us, Turner, Ragnar and I, are saying the same thing, using different words to express the same principle – primacy of Consciousness – that we want to act from our Being and not from our heads, to flow with ourselves. This ensures our action is congruent, and guided by inner wisdom, rather than incongruent and at odds with inner wisdom. So rather than worrying about which word to use, you can get a feel for the quality of the characteristic of Ease with oneself. You can notice both when it is present in you and when it is absent. Once we have that understanding, anything and everything in life can be characterised by the quality and phenomenon of Ease, even though the task might also be difficult, require hard work, involve the *activity* of struggle, or be exhausting. When I run from that place of Ease, I can run six miles without even noticing it's requiring any effort. If I run from the place of self-judgement, however, fighting against myself and my body, even getting to the end of the lane can be excruciatingly painful and unpleasant, kidneys screaming out, "I don't want to be doing this!"

The Law of Being (The Law of Non-Repulsion)

The concept of 'The Law of Attraction' is that your thoughts 'attract' what you'd like to have. There are a couple of aspects of 'The Law of Attraction' to consider:

- Psychology Aspect
- Quantum Physics Aspect

Turning first to the psychology aspect, I think that as a name 'The Law of Attraction' can potentially lead to misunderstanding, and prefer to think of it as 'The Law of Non-Repulsion', or the nicer-sounding 'The Law of Being'. 'Law of Attraction' suggests that there's something 'over there', in the sense that, "I'm here, the thing I want is there, so I have to *attract* it!", as well as implying that we aren't allowed to make proactive moves towards achieving/acquiring the thing, as if we are stuck in our boots in the mud. We have to stand still and 'attract' the thing to us. 'The Law of Non-Repulsion', on the other hand, indicates that you're not driven by self-judgements causing you to push away (sabotage) that which you're capable of, and that you'd really like to choose. On the surface of it, at a behavioural level, of course we are dealing with other people and external things. At a Consciousness level, however, there's nothing separate to you, separate to your Being, that is 'out there' that you're trying to reach. We're actually already *inside* the process. The key is not the actual event of getting things, but being free to choose things, which may then lead to 'getting things'.

You may find that serendipity and synchronistic events occur when you are in your Being.

We'll discuss whether there is any reality to the quantum physics aspect in Volume II of this book, in such sections as 'The Field of Information'.

Choice and Decision-Making

Realising that Love Consciousness, Choice and Success are the same thing makes it easier to recognise Love (Consciousness) as a pragmatic power.

Thinking of oneself as "no good at decision-making" or "not the decision-making type of person" is typically a self-judgement, or a consequence of multiple self-judgements. Making decisions is about living, and allowing ourselves to be true to ourselves. Releasing self-judgements around decision-making restores the natural capacity for it. It doesn't mean we have to make decisions about everything, even when we are clearly ill-equipped to do so. It just means we have no resistance to the general phenomenon of taking responsibility for our own choices and wishes.

Love Consciousness	Fear Consciousness
Acknowledging our natural decision-making capacity	Not acknowledging our natural decision-making capacity

Success and Happiness: Success is Always a Consciousness

Happiness is not *inherently* found in either achievements or the gaining of possessions (although these things may bring joyful emotions). The reason we think it is stems from the fact that when we are not allowing ourselves these things where they are possible (Permissions), we're in Fear Consciousness, and thus we're in Unconscious Unhappiness. So we – unsurprisingly, but incorrectly – assume that Happiness comes from gaining the outcomes or possessions themselves, whereas in reality we have to account for Fear Consciousness changing into Love Consciousness. How many times have we seen someone become a millionaire, or marry the husband or wife they wanted, and yet remain miserable? The fact that this is possible shows that Happiness and Success are not directly found in possessions or outcomes.

Love Consciousness is The Mastery of Desire, which means having no attachment to the outcome of goals and aims, which means we're able to enjoy each moment for its own sake in the moment, in our Being ... *and* also focus fully and effectively on the achievement of goals where appropriate. (../goals)

Awareness

"All I want for Christmas is an Awareness-based lifestyle." – James Blacker

Awareness vs Being in Conclusion

We've talked about being 'in your head', and how that is caused by the presence of self-judgement, and how when self-judgement is absent we are in our Being. Similarly, in Fear Consciousness we may be not just 'in our heads' around something, but also fixed in conclusion around it, *locked into* a particular belief. If you are 'in your head', with all kinds of thoughts going round which are influencing you, you're also going to be in conclusion about those things, with locked in ideas and internal representations, most typically judgements around what's possible – or rather what's *not* possible – and how things are going to turn out. Your perception of what's possible for you, and available to you, will be hidden from you to that degree. These expectations of how things will be or have to be, whether good or bad, close down the space for what's really possible to occur. This state of being in conclusion shuts out our Awareness of what's really true for us and what's possible.

Love Consciousness	Fear Consciousness
In Your Awareness	Locked in Conclusion
Thus your Awareness is available to you	Thus your Awareness is blocked and denied to you

What is Awareness?

Awareness is a relationship with yourself where, in a given moment, you allow your Conscious Mind to receive all the information being made available to it. The degree to which you are in conclusion around certain thoughts and beliefs is the degree to which you block your Subconscious Mind from being able to share with you any information or insights (Awareness) about those matters. Every moment you're alive is an opportunity to receive information via your Awareness. Every time you go into conclusion you close down your ability to acquire that moment's Awareness. Furthermore, because your Choice is dependent upon your Awareness of what's true for you, your Choice is also compromised and denied to you whenever you are in conclusion or locked in belief systems around something. In fact, the same applies to all of the Love Consciousness characteristics.

Let's consider how Awareness and Confidence are related. If you aren't in your Awareness then you can't be Confident because you aren't *confiding* in yourself about what's true and possible for you – you have no Awareness of what you're not telling yourself! You and your Subconscious instinctively know that you are at odds with each other in these moments. Your Subconscious has information you are shutting out, therefore your Subconscious can't confide in you, and you aren't confiding in it. In this sense, we can see that Awareness and Confidence are essentially the same thing.

Awareness is also the difference between possibility and limitation. So we can really gain (ourselves) by opening this relationship with Awareness up, and dropping the tightly held attachments we have to beliefs, and even to thought itself. (../awareness)

Love Consciousness	**Fear Consciousness**
Possibility	Limitation

Beliefs and Belief Systems

"What if you can trust You, but you can't trust belief systems?" – Rikka Zimmerman

The insight in this quote has profound implications for the way we approach beliefs and belief systems. Let's take a look at an example of the way in which belief systems compromise our Awareness. In every walk of life, in every moment of life, beliefs are fine – benign – as long as they don't shut out Awareness.

Imagine a couple go on holiday to the same coastal resort every year. At some point they learn that the village to the North is safe and peaceful, but the village to the South is not so safe, and so they always go to the Northern village. Now let's say one time, for whatever reason, the Northern village is not so safe, and the clues are in front of them. If they are in their Awareness they can receive all of the information that is available to them to let them know what is going on. However, if they have locked that belief system in as a conclusion – that the North village is "always safe", they will shut out their Awareness – and potentially put themselves in danger.

Maybe we are locked in conclusion that we are going to be brave and ask that person out, and we may assume that the nervous conflict going on in our head around this is our old self-doubt and self-judgement about not being bold enough! But maybe our thoughts are just trying to direct our attention to the other person's engagement ring or some other subtle sign that they're not available, and our conclusions are blocking out the possibility of us receiving the Awareness that it's not actually our Choice to ask them out in light of that.

This is the issue with valuing belief systems and conclusions over Awareness.

"No belief can ever be Awareness." – James Blacker

Beliefs as Self-Judgements

What we really need to do is differentiate between two ways of seeing and relating to our beliefs and thoughts. Our relationship to beliefs is either Conscious or Unconscious, depending on whether we hold on to them tightly, as locked in conclusions ('Conclusion Beliefs'), or loosely, receiving them as 'Awarenesses', and then letting them go ('Awareness Beliefs'). Conclusion-locked *thoughts and beliefs themselves* are self-judgement. They limit us because we are not allowed to be or know what is beyond them.

Love Consciousness	Fear Consciousness
Flexible 'Awareness Beliefs'	Fixed 'Conclusion Beliefs'
Beliefs are secondary, backdrops to our Awareness	Beliefs are allowed to override our Awareness

Understanding the power of belief is great when you're first learning that negative thoughts can be unhelpful. However, since the power of truth and reality is invincible and automatic, our next step is to realise that the ultimate power and freedom lies in surrendering our concepts of ourselves. Rather than having beliefs leading the way; ("This is what I believe, so I'll have to make it true"), observation of reality and who we are leads the way, and beliefs – as Awarenesses – follow, like the wake behind a boat. When beliefs lead the way, we're still effectively imprisoned in our heads.

Beliefs and Labelling Things as 'Security Blankets'

> "People seek, yearn for belief systems as if the truth of who they are wasn't on their side." – James Blacker

The map is not the territory, so the saying goes, and when people label things it's generally because they want to rely on the label as a kind of security blanket. Ironically, and tragically, they are protecting themselves from their own power, glory, joy and majesty. Beliefs tightly held in place are essentially thousands of mini labels about ourselves and what's (not) possible. There's often no real need for us to attach labels to reality at all.

"To not need anything to believe in is
to believe in yourself." – James Blacker

Being (Bored) in Conclusion

Most people repeat silent mantras all day long on a daily basis, about what's not possible and how things have to be because of this belief or that belief, not realising that often the reason they keep repeating them is to wake themselves up to the fact that the mantras are False Self beliefs that are limiting them and holding them down. If they actually *observed* themselves impartially when saying these things, then rather than identifying with the story they are telling themselves, they might realise that they are boring themselves rigid. I certainly did. Goodness me, I find it boring to live from belief systems! It was a relief to wake up and throw all that heaviness off.

I'll give you a quick example. I used to believe that having things in common with people was a great way to establish rapport. If someone had a story about a part of the world I'd been to, or shared a background or interest of mine, I had an automatic 'go to' response to tell them we had that thing in common. When I noticed I was doing this on auto-pilot, as a servant to my beliefs, the boredom that came from that Awareness led me to leave it all behind. We talked before about living from concepts rather than directly experiencing life. That's what I was doing – living from concepts, living in my head from pre-conclusion. Gee, it was boring.

To decide in advance of a moment or situation what you are going to do in that moment is being in conclusion. It shuts out Awareness and compromises Choice. It precludes Presence. You can't be present to an activity or another person if you've already decided how things will go.

Love Consciousness	Fear Consciousness
'Presence'	'Absence'

Chopra calls this pre-conclusion 'Premature Cognitive Commitments': We make a 'commitment' in our mind (cognition) about how a future moment will turn out, or has to happen, or how we have to be/behave in it. That 'commitment' makes us inflexible instead of responsive in the actual moment.

Love Consciousness	**Fear Consciousness**
No prior assumption as to how things have to unfold	Premature Cognitive Commitments about how things have to unfold

Here are some examples of leading people or ourselves into being in conclusion:

- "If you're not nervous you won't do a good show."
- "Relationships that start with passion and fireworks don't last."
- "You never get it right first draft."
- "We will all have to experience grief at some point, and it will be awful."

All of these things may have started out as Awarenesses, maybe even as great Awarenesses. But they have been taken too far, and turned into something they are not – conclusions, fixed ideas of reality – with the result that they can potentially do as much harm limiting people's sense of possibility as they can do good by leading people to insights.

How on earth is leading someone into conclusion a service to another human being? "You'll never get it right first draft"? Last year my inner self dragged me to my desk and spent the next hour dictating a poem to me, and once written it was finished. "If you're not nervous you won't do a good show"? My friend has just shared a video of how that very belief used to make him so nervous he couldn't act because he was so nervous about not being nervous enough!

Another name for this phenomenon is 'Self-Fulfilling Prophecy'. You buy into the conclusion that "People slow down after forty", and so that's what you experience as a result. You believe "There's no such thing as a 'free lunch'", and so the generosity of others who give without thought of return is completely invisible to you.

People who rely on belief systems cannot function at full effectiveness. The limitation of beliefs – even positive, 'wise', empowering ones – first occurred to me twenty years ago whilst watching the UK show, 'My Family'. Consider these two sayings: "Absence makes the heart grow fonder" and "Out of sight, out of mind." Or these two: "He who chases two rabbits catches neither!" and "Don't put all your eggs in one basket!" Such 'equal and opposite' pieces of wisdom show that belief systems cannot be relied upon; we have to live our lives from Awareness, and trust our own instincts as to which might be appropriate in a given moment.

The New Shape of Beliefs

In a similar vein, Jon Freeman and I recorded a short audio product about 'The New Shape of Beliefs' for his body of work, so that we can start to help people understand their relationship with beliefs, and live from Awareness rather than from fixed thoughts, beliefs and conclusions.

www.KissingConsciousness.com/shape

'Ego-Hijack'

> "The Ego says 'turn left'. Our Awareness guides us to turn right, and things work out very well, and the Ego says, 'That was a great idea of mine to turn right, wasn't it!'" – James Blacker

Whenever we act from pure Awareness, from pure Being, we find things work out for us as best they can. The mind is then tempted to attribute whatever we did in that moment as being the *cause* of the positive outcome – as a 'mini belief system'. However, the cause of the good outcome was the principle of Awareness, *not* the action that Awareness led to. This is how Awareness becomes locked in conclusions and fixed, inflexible belief systems – a process I sometimes call 'Ego-Hijack'. It happens all the time in Conscious Living. Let's say we decide to do 'intuitive eating', and that guides us to have a salad. By the next day we've 'translated' 'intuitive eating' into 'salad', and so when intuitive eating tells us to have a pie, we ignore that in favour of our *conclusion* and have another salad – and then wonder why we don't feel so good. Answer: Because the body didn't ask for another salad!

Are Beliefs a Total Waste of Time?

Beliefs which are aligned with what your Awareness already knows are irrelevant, because they're just confirming what you're already aware of as being true. Beliefs which are *not* in alignment with your Awareness and what's true can often block your Awareness, creating limitations and inner contradictions. In this sense, beliefs, even 'positive' beliefs, are essentially redundant.

If we rely on a *positive* belief, we're still 'in our head', not in our Awareness. We're not in our Being, not trusting ourselves. It takes longer to make the same decision we were going to make anyway, because instead of deciding directly from our Awareness, the decision has to be re-routed via our belief systems, via our self-doubt and via our second-guessing ourselves.

"Reality is that which, when you stop believing in it, doesn't go away." – Philip K. Dick

How often have your moments slipped away because you doubted your own knowing? Deep down we know, intuitively, that we wish to be natural, flowing, at ease with ourselves and trusting ourselves in our lives. We don't wish to be in our heads, having to justify everything we do with a belief system.

Love Consciousness	Fear Consciousness
Allowing ourselves to trust ourselves	Not allowing ourselves to trust ourselves; but having to have a decision 'approved' by a belief

Conscious Experts

Expertise in each field of human study or endeavour is of course, still possible and valid, however, a 'Conscious Expert' always leaves room for Awareness. The greatest, wisest, most rounded experts maintain flexibility around their conclusions which allows them to access their Awareness and perform from their source of strength. They don't have an immature, Ego-based resistance to acknowledging when something needs modifying. When people become 'Unconscious Experts', we often see them dissolve in their own fear-driven certainty and insecure need to be right.

From Human Thinking to Human Being

What I am inviting you to consider may be a big ask for you. Operating from originality and Presence rather than habitual pre-conclusion really pulls the legs out from under our previous way of relating to life. But then again, when we were six years old and the stabilisers were taken off our bicycle, that was a big thing, too. There's a choice to be made: Whether to step back into living from the false security of attaching to belief systems, or step into the exhilarating freedom of living from Awareness.

Conclusions About What's Really Possible

So what's your Awareness of what's really possible? Not your conclusions, your Awareness? Is it possible that you don't yet have all of your Awareness of what may be possible?

My Awareness is that I have hardly any of my Awareness. My colleagues and I have discussed this – we don't think we've even scratched the surface.

Conscious Personal Development

Personal development offerings abound, but here I'll give just one example.

Conscious Ayurveda: Deepak Chopra seems to be the best-known proponent of Ayurveda, and fortunately he himself has suggested that the quality of (what he calls) Pure Consciousness is primary. I say "fortunately" because I've observed the Frustration and Stress of people who have made the rules of Ayurveda their prison, as they have gotten locked into conclusion around various things, and therefore shut out their own knowing and Inner Guide. This is by no means unique to Ayurveda – across virtually all of the personal development and wellbeing modalities there is a risk that people will turn the insights that are shared with them into inflexible beliefs and rules, which they then put before their Awareness.

The personal development industry is rife with conclusions, such as: "Once you make a mental breakthrough you have to take action." Many presenters also use Imperative Grammar, so there's a fair bit to be aware of in order to have a 'liberated' experience in personal development.

Information

Do we trust our intuition? Do we even *have* intuition? Do we trust 'energy' – whatever the hell that is? Do we trust our instinct? Do we have gut feelings, and do we trust those? Are we even paying attention to what's going on, or being open with ourselves?

David Heard simplified this issue for me many years ago. We were talking about self-trust and the importance of going with your gut instinct. I was getting caught up in all the different words (like intuition and gut instinct and energy) and the meanings and judgements that each word carries, when he said to me, "It's about trusting the information being provided." Intuition, instinct, bodily sensations, intellect, energy, Consciousness, or even anything that is potentially explained by Quantum Physics, can all go under the umbrella term of 'information'.

Where information comes from is not so important. Whether that information can be trusted is a fair concern. But what really matters is whether you allow yourself to honour the fact that you trust that information – when you *do* trust it. It's about that relationship that you have with *you!* Allowing yourself to honour and acknowledge that you *don't* trust some piece of information also demonstrates self-trust and good self-communication. Our Consciousness determines whether or not we allow ourselves our 'true to self' Choice with regard to the way we interpret (trust or don't trust) information:

Love Consciousness	Fear Consciousness
We allow ourselves our true Choice of how we may wish to interpret any information	We don't allow ourselves our true Choice of how we may wish to interpret any information

You 'Get The Information'

When you let go of a self-judgement you gain an increase in Awareness and in information. This information gets you back in touch with the (more) real you. So we say that by becoming Conscious we 'get the information'. The information doesn't have to be received intellectually into your Conscious Mind. It may come through as inner knowing, Awareness, intuitive insight, feeling, bodily information and senses, and potentially in other ways, too.

Love Consciousness	Fear Consciousness
You get the information	You don't get the information

"Everything is Energy"

What matters most is that, in those moments that it's true for you to honour any information you feel is available, that you allow yourself to do so from self-acceptance, rather than preventing yourself from doing so as a result of self-judgement. So in the case of 'energy', the key issue is not whether energy exists, or even what it is, but whether you allow yourself to trust it should you feel you want to.

Love Consciousness	Fear Consciousness
Allowed to trust what the energy is telling you, should you want to	Not allowed to trust what the energy is telling you, even if you wanted to

This essentially involves letting go of the self-judgement that, "I can't honour these notions, *even though I want to,* because science hasn't yet proven them, or conventional society hasn't yet approved of them." You can honour all of yourself without having to wait for science or society to catch up.

"Actually the gut instinct is more reliable than the brain because the cells in your gut haven't yet evolved to the level of self-doubt." – Dr. Deepak Chopra

Is it possible to get a sense of whether someone's intention towards you is good or bad just from their energy? I would say it is, and I would also say it's a different thing to whether they say the right-sounding things, or look a certain way. The same with other choices and aspects of life. What's the energy, what's the Awareness, what's the feel of a certain decision over a different option?

Love Consciousness	Fear Consciousness
Healthy	Unhealthy
Honouring your Life Force	Dishonouring your Life Force
Fulfilling your Life Force	Destroying your Life Force

Simply being willing to 'go with the energy' is the reason why I've used capital letters for all of the concept terms in this book, such as Confidence, Life Force,

Choice, Success. My sense on this was that the overall understanding of the insights behind these terms would be greater than it would be otherwise.

Someone made the point on social media that they were now at the point that they were willing to unfriend people "On energy alone." Absolutely. The whole point of trusting energy is that you don't then need to wait for some other capacity to confirm it. If you do then you're *not* trusting the energy!

Taking Responsibility

There's a sense in which it doesn't matter what you do as long as you're willing to take responsibility for your actions. You want to skip a college class? You want to skip work? You want to have pizza for breakfast? The outcomes of your actions will be on you whether you choose to take responsibility or not. Taking responsibility and Choice go hand-in-hand. By not allowing our young people to grow up with their own Choice, we cause their capacity to take responsibility for their actions to atrophy. (../information)

The Subconscious Mind

> "Your Subconscious is your best and most trustworthy friend. Even if you don't realise it, everything 'negative' it ever had to do was done to keep you safe as best it could. It's not omnipotent in the face of aggressive or controlling others, but it is loyal." – James Blacker

Have you ever watched Sherlock Holmes? That Dr Watson follows him around everywhere, wherever he goes, without question or thought for himself. Always loyal, always ready to act for Holmes; trusted, resolute, unwavering. That's what your Subconscious Mind is for you.

The Subconscious Mind's job is to manage and process much, much greater quantities of information and activity than our Conscious Mind is able to. We can drive home and realise we haven't been paying attention for five minutes – the Subconscious Mind makes that possible. Even when we don't Consciously know whether we've spent enough money to have our card declined, our Subconscious Mind knows. And when we make an approach to a potential love interest, our Subconscious generally knows whether we are going to get a 'Yes' or a 'No'. It knows everything about us. If some theories of quantum physics are correct, it may know everything about everything, or at least be connected to the source that does.

As part of my wish to understand myself I have often set my Subconscious the task of making itself known to me, so I can understand its capacities and its relation to me. It puts a tune in my head, and makes me think "Oh yeah, I wanna play that, what is it?" So then I sing it through fully in my head and I work out that it's Kirsty MacColl's song, 'A New England', so then I realise it's giving me a reminder that the New England Patriots game is about to start soon. Clever! Clever, Subconscious! Coulda just told me that the game was on! But then I remember – my bad – that I did ask you (my Subconscious Mind) for signs of what you could do! In any moment of Love Consciousness we are inevitably at one with our Subconscious. In Fear Consciousness we are at odds with it, not listening to what it is trying to tell us in order to help us.

Love Consciousness	**Fear Consciousness**
A constructive relationship with your Subconscious	A 'shut down' relationship with your Subconscious

I hated my Subconscious for a long time, thinking of it as something that was 'against' me. After panic attacks hit me at the age of eleven, seemingly taking my body out of my own control, I wasn't particularly keen to trust it or like it. I was completely lost to myself. What I've gained since is an understanding that my Subconscious was doing the best it could to look after me in the circumstances. It knew what I didn't about my truth – that succeeding in an unhealthy social system wasn't in my best interests. It doesn't have biceps to fight off dangers. The only biceps it had power to influence at the time were mine, and the biceps of a child can't fight off many dangers, let alone entire Ego-driven economic-political-social systems.

Like the eternally loyal Dr Watson, the Subconscious does what it can to help us survive. One of the things it does is repress those characteristics, passions, interests and qualities we hold which are unacceptable to the world around us … with the possibility that the time may come when it's safe for us to reclaim them, and that we might awaken enough to do so. (../subconscious)

The Unconscious

When the mind represses aspects of our personality to protect us it creates what Kissing Consciousness calls the 'Unconscious'. It's also called 'The Shadow', a term of Carl Jung's, or our 'Shadow Baggage'. Given that we've all come into a world which has a taboo around sex, and has yet to stabilise a level of wisdom in humanity – leading to violence and economic stupidity among other things – it's not surprising that most everybody is carrying a fair amount of Unconscious self-limitation Shadow Baggage. Denying us parts of our personalities and greatness might not seem like a good idea, but if the consequences of not doing so were potentially worse, maybe it does make sense.

Like quarantined computer files, the Unconscious is a part of the Subconscious Mind which contains whatever was deemed unsafe for the Conscious Mind to have access to. This Unconscious material is also the sum cause of what we are calling Fear Consciousness. Some of it might now be safe to acknowledge, but it will remain Unconscious until it is acknowledged. The Conscious Mind and The Subconscious Mind work perfectly well together, as one unified, coherent 'Us' (You), except to the degree that Unconscious elements get in the way of that, either because they are not safe to be acknowledged *Consciously* or because they have yet to be reclaimed *by* the Conscious Mind. We can bridge that gap by realising what is going on, noticing when we are feeling at odds with ourselves (i.e. noticing the presence of Fear Consciousness), and reclaiming what aspects of ourselves and our true personalities are presently safe to reclaim. Having harmony between the Conscious Mind and the Subconscious Mind allows the experience that we might think of as Inner Guidance. (../unconscious)

The Inner Guide

Our Inner Guide is information about what's possible for us, what's true for us. It also holds Awareness of what our actual true heart's Choice is in any moment – which we sometimes Flow with, and sometimes have resistance to.

Love Consciousness	Fear Consciousness
Listening to your Inner Guide	Not listening to your Inner Guide

In a sense, young children don't have – or at least don't *perceive* – an Inner Guide because they haven't yet separated from it, i.e. from themselves. They have yet to learn to doubt or deny themselves. As adults, terms such as 'Inner Guide' help during the process of reclaiming ourselves. We can get back to that original way of living by reintegrating that voice and again becoming at one with ourselves, functioning fluently as one unified (personal) Consciousness, knowing instinctively what we want to do and letting ourselves do it.

When our relationship with our Inner Guide is working properly we don't notice any separation between us and it. There is just us, living and choosing effectively. When we don't listen, there are kind of two selves; there is us, and there is that voice in our head which we're not quite acknowledging. I usually work on the 'three times rule'. If my brain tells me to do something a third time after I've let go of the suggestion twice already, then it's generally an Inner Guidance that I'm ignoring, and so I follow it and do the thing. But you don't have to wait three times.

Love Consciousness	Fear Consciousness
Relationship between us and our Inner Guide is seamless and unnoticed	We are at odds with our Inner Guide, ignoring or doubting the voice of our truth

The Vast Power of The Subconscious Mind

We do naturally trust our Subconscious instincts and intuitions. An uninhibited person flows with the vast, vast wisdom and information that their Subconscious Mind has access to, probably without giving it a second thought. Without self-judgement causing us to deny this very natural phenomenon, the vast power of our Subconscious Mind is available to us.

Love Consciousness	Fear Consciousness
The Power of your Subconscious Mind is available to you	We deny ourselves the Power of our Subconscious Mind

Your Very Own 'Inner Secretary'

You can talk to, and make requests of your Inner Guide the way Iron Man talks to Jarvis, his personal computerized artificial intelligence 'butler', in the Iron Man movies. Seriously, I'm not kidding.

That might sound fantastical but the point is that you don't need computers or artificial intelligence for things like knowing when it's time to do something. Your Subconscious can do that for you! I gave an example of this in The Power of Love (Chapter Two), of being 'told' it was time to catch the train from Copenhagen. The tech giants are selling you 'software' you already own!

The advantage of Consciousness is that you don't have to type the details into it in the first place, or even ask it to tell you. (It does help to develop your Consciousness, rather than deplete it to the point where you become useless without your devices. As the saying goes, that which you use gets stronger, and those attributes which you don't use will atrophy.) App software can only advise you so far as your Conscious Mind has informed it. Your Subconscious can do all that, *and* advise you, with all information possibly available in nature, fully briefed, according to what's *definitely* in your best interests, according to a system of self-management thousands of times more sophisticated than your Conscious Mind.

Everything we've been talking about has been based around trusting your own knowing, developing your inner Awareness and Confidence. If a technological device helps you with that, great, but I sense it's worth asking the question: Do you wish to receive the full promise of the Consciousness capacities that you were born with? If an app causes you to move away from the capacity to trust your own Awareness, isn't that also going to move you away from your Success?

What else can your 'Inner Butler' do? What else can't it do! All that information is available to you, all that computer-like processing capacity, thousands of times more powerful than your Conscious Mind. All you have to do is ask … and sometimes you don't even have to ask! This has very much been part of how I've written this book. Sometimes I have to do the tasks because it's necessary to get my Conscious Mind's understanding around them; at other times I'm listening and receiving instruction or guidance on what to put where, regardless of whether I'm given any intellectual reason for doing so. But it all works, all has a good reason, whether I know it or not. Often, these instructions are about the most subtle or detailed things. I don't question them, I can trust the knowing, and the energy of it in my body – "This feels good here …" or "That doesn't feel right actually – change it back."

The Body as The Subconscious Mind

Interchangeable Terms: The Body, The Subconscious Mind, The Subconscious Bodymind

Kissing Consciousness considers the body and the Subconscious Mind to be essentially the same thing. There's a term, 'Bodymind', used to address the interrelated nature of the mind and body, and treat it as one single entity. Kissing Consciousness uses the term 'Subconscious Bodymind' to mean the 'Subconscious Mind' in a way that appreciates the interrelated nature of mind and body.

Embodiment

The relationship we have with our Awareness, involving our Subconscious Mind, of course, also manifests in whether or not we are **Embodied**. In this context, being Embodied means being in touch with our body, at one with how our body feels, with what it is feeling and what it might want. The opposite is being **Disembodied**, which is being out of touch with your body's feedback.

The phenomenon of people being Disembodied, as a result of self-judgement and lack of connection (self-intimacy) in this modern, commerce-driven, emotionally painful society, will surely have contributed significantly to the Degenerative Disease crisis we see. I would suggest that people are dying of such things as heart disease and Cancer in greater numbers than they need to because the population's capacity to be aware of what the body is really asking for has been compromised, and has not been nurtured. We'll talk about this in Chapter Six on 'Body and Health'.

Love Consciousness	**Fear Consciousness**
Embodied (in your body and Awareness)	Disembodied ('in your head')

Embodiment isn't about being an athlete or a sportsperson. It's possible to be 'in your head' when you're exercising, and it's possible to be Embodied ('in your body') when you're not exercising – again, because there's no behaviour that is inherently Conscious or Unconscious. Embodiment is the physical experience of a state of Conscious relationship with yourself.

When we are Disembodied, there is a separation with the body, which is an unpleasant, semi-conscious or Unconscious state to be in. Almost everyone will be Disembodied now and again, when we have that one extra slice of pie at Christmas we didn't want, when we're afraid to share our thoughts at a business meeting even though our truth is urging us to speak up. It is when this becomes more frequent, or even ever-present, that the symptoms of disease and serious discomfort may occur. And, of course, Unhappiness is present, as we're in that Unconscious, self-judgement, Fear Consciousness state. We can't *force* Embodiment through physical action, but we can notice when we are Disembodied, and that Awareness leads us to allow Embodiment to return naturally in the same moment as an automatic consequence of regaining that Awareness – which may *then* also manifest as a physical shift or action, often a very subtle one, like breathing more deeply, or shifting one's posture, and often a refocusing of the eyes on the room or scene as Awareness (and Choice) returns.

We can feel good in this particular sense any time we want, just by getting Conscious to our body. This is the physical feeling equivalent of what we call Happiness. The pursuit of Happiness is the pursuit of being Embodied and aware. We can process our limitations that way, too, by being unwilling to disembody when our 'No' Permissions arise. We hold Presence to that dynamic tension where Conscious meets Unconscious and we ask the 'No' to let go. (../embodiment)

"Just because you're doing physical things, it doesn't mean you're 'in your body'. Just because you're doing mental things, it doesn't mean you're 'in your head'." – James Blacker

The Silent Body

You can use your head without being (Stuck) 'in your head'. Equally, you can be using your body but in a Disembodied way, for example by forcing it to exercise. If we are not listening to any signals or information from our bodies, then we are not holding open a path for authentic communication with our Subconscious Mind.

'Embodied' doesn't always mean that your Conscious Mind's focus of attention is in your body, as the body could be happily supporting whatever cognitive or other activity you're engaged in. The body, being as one with the Subconscious Mind (the Subconscious Bodymind), knows everything that both the Conscious Mind and the Subconscious Mind knows. And so whilst it has its desires for food, water, rest, movement, warmth, coolness, comfortable postural positions, etc., it also integrates that with an understanding of what is in your best interests. So being Embodied doesn't require always being proactively attentive to the body. There will be many periods of time when the body is quiet, allowing you to get on with activity and tasks. In fact, in a healthy way of being, this will be most of the time.

Being Embodied does mean not being pushed beyond that, however, to the point you're 'in your head' – *that* is something the body will notice – it would be suffering as a result of being ignored and overruled by you. The very subtlest of body Awareness will show you how being in your head is also going against your body. It's not necessarily about going for a run, or exercising. Every moment is one in which the body's physiology is mirroring your Consciousness, in which the body is either at ease, or tense, as you metaphorically – or even literally – hold your breath. (../bodymind)

Love Consciousness	Fear Consciousness
Listening to the body, perhaps 'passively'	Not listening to the body, ignoring its pleas
Being at one with the body, a naturally pleasurable experience!	Experiencing separation and dissociation from the body – not nice!

Physiology

Noticing how you experience your body in each of the states of Love Consciousness and Fear Consciousness can help you get an innate grasp of the different qualities of those two states. It saves you from having to 'think' your way out of Fear Consciousness. You can instead feel your way into declining it. This is key because the Kissing Consciousness approach is to release self-judgements via our bodies, and via our Awareness. I invite you to get in touch with what the 'Physiology of Self-Acceptance' feels like, and then decline and release anything that doesn't feel like that.

Love Consciousness	Fear Consciousness
The Physiology of Self-Acceptance	The Physiology of Self-Judgement

"Life's A Drag"

Imagine that every moment of a day you experience some form of physical force acting against one part of your body or another, or against your body as a whole. This is the physical equivalent of holding one's body in a state of self-judgement: Walking, doing tasks, moving about the world whilst in one's head, rather than Embodied and living in the Flow. As the English

Philosopher, Alan Watts, points out, in this state you are literally dragging yourself and your body around all day long, so life will indeed feel like a drag!

The effects of this are devastating but also subtle and insidious, so people aren't aware of them. As a society, we don't yet have a clear example of the absence of this negative effect to compare it with. Seeing what our Life Force is capable of is not something we are familiar with, either in terms of our life span, or the natural state of an adult in a given moment. What really *is* the natural state of an adult human? Using our imagination, we can get an initial sense of it by looking at the forest animals, and considering what a human equivalent of this relaxed, natural state may be like – the gains in our physical quality of life and Life Force from living free of self-judgement can be enormous and profound. And given that most of us have a mixture of moments of Flow and Stuckness, what happens when the approach of letting go of self-judgements catches on in the wider culture, and we start to see a society of people who are flowing in self-acceptance?

Love Consciousness	**Fear Consciousness**
In a harmonious relationship with your body	In a turbulent relationship with your body

Because Choice, Success and The Mastery of Desire are all perspectives of the same quality of Love Consciousness, the experience of these in the body is the same as the Physiology of Self-Acceptance.

Knowing

"Trust your own knowing." – Zach Rehder

Knowing vs Knowledge

'Knowing' is a phenomenon that's quite the opposite to being in one's head. Knowing, and *trusting your own Knowing*, is a different thing to the possession of facts, or what we refer to as knowledge. Knowing is an immediate quality of understanding which exists prior to the intellect, based on our Awareness. We all have Knowing, but the undercurrent of self-judgement combined with a cultural bias towards intellectual and academic knowledge means that very few people in our culture actually trust their own Knowing to any significant degree. The healthy state of affairs is for intellect to be a servant of Knowing, of your Choice, of your Being, rather than your master. When we allow ourselves to trust our own Knowing, we are in full flight, blossoming and powerful. Self-judgement compromises this natural state of affairs.

Your Mind as Your Servant

"The mind: Wonderful servant, horrible master." – Ken Wilber

This is a Binary notion:

Love Consciousness	**Fear Consciousness**
Mind is your Servant	Mind is your Master

Once mind is calmed to the role of servant, we are free to trust and receive our own Knowing:

Love Consciousness	Fear Consciousness
Trusting your own Knowing	Doubting, avoiding, hiding from, obliviating, denying your own Knowing

Peter Ragnar poetically distinguishes Knowing from knowledge:

"Words are never what they attempt to describe. The spell of words spin our heads and dizzily we fall into contests and debates. Oh, how well I know this! Knowing has nothing to do with knowledge. My heart needs no instruction in order to beat nor do my lungs require a teacher. Once I realized all my knowledge was of the past, and it was my knowledge which kept me from knowing, my words tumbled and fell and a deep and familiar knowing arose. Suddenly everything that I thought was at odds with itself became settled in serenity. It's when I saw the autumn moon for the very first time."

Yielding vs Justifying

Justifying is when you hear your own Knowing around a Choice, but deny it and don't go along with it, and a conversation kicks off in your head to justify why not. Notice that justifying is merely one part of yourself having a dishonest conversation with another part of yourself which is speaking the truth. There's no-one else involved, no external third party telling you what to do! It's all you. So the key is to decide for yourself which parts are the voice of the False Self, and which parts are the voice of that which you'd actually like to choose, but don't feel okay choosing.

The opposite of Justifying is trusting your own Knowing – or *absence of Justifying*. But what's most interesting is what we do when we start to catch ourselves justifying: We either keep Justifying, or Yield to the emotion and Awareness that we were resisting. (../yielding)

Love Consciousness	Fear Consciousness
Yielding aka: Softening	Still Justifying aka: Defending

Softening

"It's time for the human race to put the 'often' into 'soften'." – James Blacker

Yielding is also called 'Softening', which is a strength, not a weakness, and as part of Consciousness Facilitation (of oneself or another) it is important to honour the bravery of the act. For both men and women it can be a challenging and profound shift in Consciousness, mind and body, with repressed emotion, identity and Life Force being faced, felt and allowed back in. The person who softens gets strength back, Life Force energy back, more Choice, Success and all that good stuff, but it's still an energetic thing to do. It's also one that requires our character to outdo our Ego, or we won't Yield.

We need to start Softening, men especially, or our society won't survive its cold, dissociated, 'false strength' edge. The more we can provide a non-judgemental, safe space for this, the better. If people think they can't save face, they probably won't Yield.

Shall We Judge Ourselves for Justifying?

Notice, if you're judging yourself for Justifying, that if you stop judging yourself you get Awareness into why exactly you felt the need to avoid facing your own truth. This is the key to being able to comfortably break the limitation down. Maybe you aren't feeling ready yet. Maybe you were holding onto a judgement that you aren't allowed to breathe deeply enough to face an emotion. When we don't judge our Justifying, we make it Conscious, and so can turn it into Awareness.

Lying to Oneself Pretending to Know

Although Knowing is infallible, our relationship with that Knowing in our own Conscious Mind is not. In Fear Consciousness we will inevitably be motivated to see things in a biased way, in favour of our hopes and in avoidance of our fears:

Love Consciousness	Fear Consciousness
We can approach Knowing objectively	There is a tendency to approach Knowing with a fear-driven bias

Not Knowing and Not Needing to Know

One thing that helps our relationship to our Knowing be accurate is not needing to know. Not feeling the need to know is the natural state of Being, when we are not under the influence of self-judgement. Once again we see how being without self-judgements supports our Awareness and Choice.

Length of Time is No Disqualifier: Knowing is Knowing

Time is no disqualifier to Knowing, neither is brevity or quantity. An example of this? If you have a connection with somebody that, prior to thought, you know exists, they may ask you, "How can you be sure, we've only known each other for a short while?" It doesn't matter. Knowing is not dependent upon the conventional thinking we're familiar with. The same is true if you feel uneasy about someone; the slightest moment can hold all the information and Knowing you might require. Very few people are as yet ready to accept Knowing at this level … and yet, if they had no self-judgement around a Knowing, they would allow it in and allow themselves that outcome.

Conscience and 'Conscious Conscience'

Goodness me, the Conscience gets a bad press – it must have a lousy PR agency! Yet people love the notion of having an 'Inner Guide'. They're the same bloody thing! (… He says with a smile.) Conscience is actually the same thing as Knowing.

Conscience, the etymology of which is pretty much 'with Knowing', or 'being privy to', is about what you truly know. However, the notion of Conscience has been bastardised by culture to be a false judgement, a 'toxic guilt and shame' around things like chocolate, or sex, or putting ourselves first sometimes. So if we're to have a Conscious relationship with our Conscience, we must let go of the judgements we have taken on around the notion of the Conscience, and see it for what it really, naturally is. The first thing to realise is that our Conscience is on our side! Conscience is our own Knowing of our true heart's desire and truth, our Love Consciousness itself.

True Conscience vs Conditioned Conscience

Yes, your very Conscience has been sabotaged by judgementalism and conditioned self-judgement … and not just by you, but by society, which has totally misunderstood it. Your Conscience *itself* hasn't been conditioned and adulterated, only your interpretation of it. You've been told you should feel guilty about things you needn't feel guilty about, and thus (very likely) misunderstood the nature of what your own Conscience actually is. … I can see the Conscience as a heart-shaped, fluffy, cartoon-style animal, with big sad eyes, saying "Please love me again!"

Love Consciousness	Fear Consciousness
Conscience	False Conscience

Where you have bought into self-judgement caused by others, your own *interpretation* of your Conscience is not fit for purpose. This is the case for everyone else, too … which means that virtually all of society, almost all of it, at least, is inauthentic and currently ill-informed as to how to have a healthy relationship with their own Conscience and inner dialogue. The whole world has, sadly, been hoodwinked by the lie of judgementalism. There's barely a person in a hundred who has realised that and fully broken out of the lie. (../conscience)

Knowing and Science

Over the last few years, I've been stunned by some reports of scientific studies – not by the results, but by the fact that people even felt it necessary to get scientific confirmation of much of what I always held as the most obvious and self-evident of things. One such study confirmed that eight hour days of office work aren't good for us. I'm reminded of Del Boy's sarcasm in TV's 'Only Fools and Horses': "And you had to use *ink* to come to that conclusion?" Why are we as a culture doubting our Knowing so much that we feel we have to prove everything in such strict, limited mind ways? It is setting us back twenty, forty years. My point isn't that there's no place for science. Of course there is. The point is to not go so far as to do ourselves a huge collective disservice with respect to our Awareness, our Knowing. Isn't the need for scientific or logical proof of what you already 'know that you know' the act of second-guessing yourself? It's self-disrespect to *genuinely* Know something, and yet say to yourself, "Oh, I'll just get validation before I trust that." Your Conscience is permanently inviting you to step into your truth! (../knowing)

Genius

"Genius is simply the absence of second-guessing yourself." – James Blacker

Genius is a faculty of Consciousness, and is therefore relevant to each and every moment of life in the same way. It is not a specific behaviour, either. It applies to everything we might do in life, from buying the weekly shopping to talking to our mother-in-law.

To understand what Genius is it may help to first unpick what it isn't. It's not intelligence (IQ), it's not knowledge of facts, it's not about being academic and it's not even about being smart. It's about the flow of our Consciousness, and our capacity for trusting our Knowing not being interrupted by thoughts of second-guessing ourselves. In any moment we are in a state of Love Consciousness we are also flowing with our creative Genius. We cannot not be. As such, therefore, Genius is also available to all of us, whoever we are … all the time.

It sounds strange only because we have such a narrow cultural definition of Genius. Whilst Genius is typically associated with obvious things such as musical composition, art, literature or sports, as a phenomenon its actual daily, moment to moment expression is in everything, from grand gestures and projects to the minutiae of life. Genius is all about that unassuming approach to the moment, and the quality of originality and of course the amazing results it can give rise to.

How do you 'do' Genius? You don't. When there's an absence of self-judgement it does itself. It's automatic, it's a default state of Being. So your Genius and your Conscience are the same thing. That puts a different spin on Conscience, doesn't it: Ignore your Conscience and you're also denying yourself your own Genius!

Love Consciousness	Fear Consciousness
Genius	Second-Guessing Yourself

Second-Guessing Yourself Leads to Second Thoughts

With Consciousness, at least, I've noticed that if you go with your second-best option or choice, there will always be second thoughts. Of course there will. Your Inner Guide is trying to tell you that you have short-changed yourself, that you haven't got what you can, and what your authentic Choice is. What a loyal servant it is.

"Is That a 'Why' Question?"

Back in the day, the question we used to ask whenever we doubted ourselves was, "Is that a 'why' question?" In other words, why are you asking 'Why?' about your Knowing, your Awareness, your Choice? 'Why' doesn't matter: If you know that you know then you know. You don't do 'Why' if you're doing Genius. In this sense, 'Why' is a judgement that a Choice isn't valid or trustworthy in its own right.

In the Online Wisdom Course that I wrote in 2008, there is a whole module and accompanying audio on Genius. And of course, once the penny drops as to the interchangeable nature of Love Consciousness characteristics, you'll see that this whole book is about Genius. (../genius)

Creativity

Narrow Creativity and Broad Creativity

Let's look at how creativity plays out in our moment to moment experience of life. For our needs here I'm defining 'Narrow Creativity' as limited to the things that people usually associate with creativity: Art, poetry, music, literature, dance, etc. The intent is in no way to put those pursuits down, but to allow room for a second concept of 'Broad Creativity', namely, creativity in a much broader, more fundamental sense, which is a characteristic of any moment of Love Consciousness. All moments of Love Consciousness have the same signature aspect of this creativity, even if it is so subtle we don't particularly notice it. But it's there and we certainly enjoy it, and you can sense it, particularly since it is the same quality of Consciousness that comes with genuine Choice in each moment.

All of life is a creative act, the nature of reality exploring itself. But all of Love Consciousness is a creative act in a different sense, in that a moment of Love Consciousness is a moment without self-judgement, where whatever you choose to do in that moment has an air of originality about it because it's coming from freedom of Consciousness. And it doesn't matter how banal or mundane the thing you do may be, even if it's going to a bar, making a comment in conversation, or deciding whether to have a cup of tea; it will still have that quality of originality because a Conscious moment comes from your Awareness and Choice, not from your head or conclusions about what you might do in a given moment. When you are in your head you are controlling and repressing your creativity because you're not allowed to be or choose whatever it is you would otherwise do if you had no self-judgements around it.

Love Consciousness	**Fear Consciousness**
Creativity	Self-Denied Creativity
Originality	Lack of Originality, repetition of a previous moment of life

Remember, as with all expressions of Consciousness, creativity doesn't look like anything and it doesn't *not* look like anything. Everything that you or I ever do that is true to ourselves has a certain quality of creativity to it, however subtle … but not in the Narrow Creativity sense of music and art, although it may involve those things. And, of course, there's no guarantee that if you do a Narrow Creativity activity that you're doing it from a creative energy (Love Consciousness), rather than from a self-judgement energy (Fear Consciousness). This is, of course, simply another expression of our new understanding of The Illusion of Identical Experience – activities such as music and art could be driven by either motive. So, if you do a Narrow Creativity activity and your energy is 'off' you need to look at your Broad Creativity 'energy', your Consciousness. (../creativity)

Love Consciousness	**Fear Consciousness**
Narrow Creativity: Art, poetry, music, dance	Narrow Creativity: Art, poetry, music, dance

Vulnerability (of Consciousness)

Underpinning Broad Creativity is one of the most misunderstood and underappreciated of positive characteristics: Vulnerability. We first need to clarify the distinction between Vulnerability at a Consciousness level and vulnerability at a physical (behavioural) level. The latter might mean the human equivalent of being a worm out in the open for a flock of birds to descend upon, and nobody wants that. So in terms of *defining* vulnerability, this is another example of a Consciousness-Behaviour Split. Again the English language is insufficient: We have one word for two different things, and we really need two separate words. I'll refer to them as 'Vulnerability of Consciousness' and 'physical vulnerability' (using a capital 'V' to indicate Vulnerability of Consciousness). Vulnerability is currently considered a weakness by most of society, whereas it is actually a strength, and in part, this is because the distinction we're talking about isn't made. If you ask someone out you risk them saying "No", but which is stronger: Being willing to take that risk, or not being willing? Getting up on stage, or not doing that? At a Consciousness level, refusing to be Vulnerable means Fear Consciousness is preventing us from stepping into and living from the truth and glory of our originality.

Love Consciousness	Fear Consciousness
Vulnerability (at a Consciousness level)	Defensiveness in our Consciousness; control and avoidance of original life

Vulnerability is our first nature. When people get accustomed to Vulnerability it is often much less of a concern. In fact, we may not even notice it, as the experience of Vulnerability simply morphs into the whole package of excitement around choosing something and being alive.

Love Consciousness	Fear Consciousness
Excited at being Vulnerable because it equates to being alive!	Afraid of being Vulnerable because we're not allowed to be energetically alive

Vulnerability means being willing to not judge ourselves for however things turn out when we choose something. This is a great way to appreciate how 'Permissions' exist in the body, since the nervous system of a person allowing Vulnerability is different to that of one who isn't. If we're not willing to risk a certain outcome, even though it's otherwise our Choice to risk it, we don't step into the possibility and reality of who we are … and if we don't trust our Knowing, we are not allowing our Vulnerability. You can get a sense of feeling the 'edge' of when you are and aren't stepping into Vulnerability, and you may also notice that when you do step into Vulnerability, you get an energetic 'high', an uplift. That 'buzz' you get is the new energy that is reclaimed when a self-judgement is released. (../vulnerability)

Playfulness

"Playfulness is the ability to see
reality the way it is." – James Blacker

Given that an authentic moment of our life has a quality of 'Broad Creativity' about it, it also has a quality of playfulness, in the sense that it's a creative moment which is motivated from a place of freedom, rather than from a place of 'have to'.

The 'have to' effect of self-judgement, which also takes us into attachment to outcome, prevents the creative, playful quality of a moment from being experienced. It prevents the moment from being enjoyed. Alan Watts observed: "… and one remembers how fascinating the most ordinary everyday things are to a child; because they see them all as marvellous, … in a way that is not related to survival and profit." Can we remember who we were before, when we saw life as "not related to survival and profit"? This is not about pretending that a lot of people's lives aren't tough, or that survival and profit aren't relevant. It's about realising that when there isn't self-judgement, there's no resistance or attachment, and we can engage effectively in the creative playfulness of the moment. (../playfulness)

To enjoy (en-joy) something is to bring joy to it, to *infuse it* with joy, which happens automatically when we approach things in a state of Love Consciousness.

Fear Consciousness is Always Boring

This is why Fear Consciousness is always boring. Interacting with someone who is resisting letting go of their resistance to their feelings is boring also. It's not that there are boring people, but it is boring when people express themselves through their Fear Consciousness. It would also be boring to themselves, were they able to assess the moment honestly.

Charisma is the opposite. It's often a dirty word in the personal development world, Unconsciously assumed to be manipulative and insincere, but the expression of self from Love Consciousness is a natural charisma. People flock to watch babies – "Coochy coo, you!" – because they radiate the energy of pure Love Consciousness. But this is due to the quality of Love Consciousness; it's not dependent upon the baby's age. You can also radiate that quality of Love Consciousness as an adult, if you release all your self-judgements. Fear Consciousness is always stagnant, boring and a turn off – except to other Fear Consciousness. Love Consciousness is always creative, charming and appealing. (../boring)

Skill

When my friends and I were kids we would shout "Skiiiiiill!" to proclaim our glory whenever we did something great. I had a sense of something that I didn't cognitively understand, but intuitively half-understood – a sense of being … I don't know … blessed, graced, at one with myself – or the divine? Before I understood what it was, I thought of that quality, my 'skill', as personal to me. Now I understand it to be something generic and inherent in all of us.

If we put the notion of skill as it relates to specific personal vocations and hobbies to one side for a minute, the 'skill' that remains is a universal, moment to moment quality, which we all have when we're in our Being as it flows through us. It's having the 'magic touch' at life itself, being in harmony and grace with all things around us. When we're at one with life, that's the 'skill' that feels 'God-given', because there's no 'us' involved. It's also closely associated with gracefulness. (../skill)

Love Consciousness	**Fear Consciousness**
Skill (Gracefulness)	Gracelessness

'Positive (Not) Thinking'

aka: Positive Non-Thinking

"Positive thinking is merely the absence of negative thinking." – James Blacker

There's nothing you can do to achieve positive thinking, other than to release self-judgements. Positive thinking is naturally present when self-judgement is absent.

Positive Thinking Isn't Really Thinking

Positive thinking is not an opposite form of thinking to negative thinking, but rather the absence of negative thinking. In truth, it is not primarily a form of thinking at all, but a spontaneous way of Being, including Awareness and the fleeting movement of thoughts, that has always been inherent to us, and flows of its own accord when free of self-judgement. We have negative thinking on the one hand, and free-flowing, spontaneous activity, peace, Being, self-expression on the other.

The confusion is that the gritted teeth "I can do this!" illusory form of outward expression is considered to be positive. In reality this is the suppression of any Consciousness which is trying to make the individual aware of their own lack of Confidence in the endeavour – caused again, of course, by conditioned and Unconscious self-judgement – and so is actually negative thinking. Positive thinking would be to be honest with ourselves if we lack Confidence, or doubt we can achieve something.

> "The 'how to' of positive thinking is merely the removal of the cause of negative thinking: Self-judgement." – James Blacker

Take, for example, three men at a party, each with the desire to ask the lady across the room to dance. The first man is giving himself negative self-talk: "I can't do this!" The second man is trying to give himself positive thinking by forcing it upon his mind without addressing his inner self-judgements: "I can do this!", he tells himself, with an air of incongruence that would, in any case, repel anyone Conscious enough to sense it. Despite his brave intentions, the second man is still at odds with himself. The third man is already across the room and talking to the lady. He has no fear that she may say no, and as he has no fear of the outcome of the conversation, his conversation flows. She may want to dance, she may not want to dance, but her choice is not his responsibility. He is only responsible for presenting himself and his invitation as he would wish. And he could only have a fear that the lady may say no (or even a fear of her saying yes!) if he had a self-judgement which made that *potential* reply a problem. Let's be clear: Positive thinking is in the Consciousness, not in the behaviour. You can't just charge across the room and expect that behaviour to compensate for the fact that the Consciousness is compromised.

For the second man, that deeper inner part of him which is tripping him up actually wants him to fail. It wants to wake him up to the fact that he is trying to operate under self-judgement, not from authentic, genuine Choice of his own, or even from anything that may vaguely resemble being a fun way for him to live his life. If you are doing something from self-judgement, then you are not doing it as a Choice of your own. You are doing it for the appeasement of other people via the fears they have given you of how you '*must*' be – whether you realise it or not.

> "Self-belief is ultimately not just something that happens in the mind, but also in the nervous system." – James Blacker

It's the same principle for business, or a true relationship with your body, or any other area of life. In the absence of self-judgement, the instantaneous stream of your Consciousness goes straight from (1) idea, desire, impulse, to (2) being however you may wish to be in the light of that impulse. There's no middle stage of interruption to block it. This is the way of true Success and of freedom of mind.

"Mind The Gap!"

On the London Underground many of the platforms have been built such that when the train stops the doorway doesn't reach the platform. Passengers have to hop to the platform to avoid having a leg fall down in between the train and the platform, and the loud speaker system famously instructs them to "Mind the gap!"

This metaphor is ideal for understanding how to achieve Positive (Not) Thinking. You must mind (be aware of) the gap. When you're 'in the Flow' there's no gap between (1) impulse and (2) action. But when you're 'in your head' (self-judgement) there's a gap (or self-doubt loop) after the impulse, *prior* to action, which prevents the subsequent action being carried out from your Being. Instead, after the delay, you try to take the action – but from your head, not from your Being.

And note that 'action' can simply mean being you in your Being, without taking any actual action.

Love Consciousness	**Fear Consciousness**
There is no gap between the impulse and the subsequent action: *This* is Positive (Not) Thinking	There is a gap between impulse and action, and self-judgement causes it, creating a self-doubt loop: This is Negative Thinking

'Not Thinking'

"What use is 'positive thinking' if it doesn't extend to the body's nervous system?!" – James Blacker

Former Australian rugby league captain, Brad Fittler, later became a coach for the Lebanese national team. As coach, he praised one of his players by saying: "It's great to see him not think", meaning it was great to see him play on instinct, without self-doubt, rather than have a (negative) thought get in there and turn the instant 'Being' into a laboured thinking.

Another example of this understanding comes from Jonny Wilkinson, always a fabulous commentator on psychology:

"With goal kicking … the key is always accelerating beyond the skill. What stops you from doing that is thinking too much. … So as long as he can maintain a mindset of excitement and passion, he'll be able to do his own thing, and he needs clarity in his mind for that. There's been a lot of stuff going on in the press, and when it becomes about 'me and my image and my self-reputation' … those thoughts come in which stops that just pure application to the technique. He's got a great kicking style, technique is really solid, mechanically his cause and effect is bang on, but obviously he's just got to make sure his head's clear today so he can let go and enjoy his moment." (../positive)

Love Consciousness	Fear Consciousness
Positive (Not) Thinking	Negative Thinking

How To 'Not Think'

We have an understandable desire to stop our negative thoughts. But how do you 'not think' when the very essence of an intention is seemingly to think about something?

In the same way that good health is invisible (whereas ill health is totally dominant), Positive (Not) Thinking happens so imperceptibly, so quickly, so naturally and automatically, that it could also be said to be invisible. The same principle applies whether it's health, Confidence or positive thinking – once we have an absence of the negative, the positive flows inherently. Few people have been able to learn how to harness the power of positive thinking because it's been so misunderstood, because it's not a thing that is acquired in any other way than by an absence of negative thinking – which is achieved by letting go of self-judgements from the mind and body (the support of which is the primary activity of Kissing Consciousness).

"You're not going to be able to think
your way out of thinking!" – Jon Freeman

… and you don't need to anyway. You will never be able to achieve a state of positive 'self-judgement style' thinking because you can't just layer positive mental chat on top of negative thinking and pretend the negative thinking isn't there. The task is to release the judgement. And the first call to action in this – as explained by The Paradox of Love Consciousness – is not to mind, to have no resistance to the fact that negative thought is arising. We'll discuss this further in the next chapter.

Love Consciousness	**Fear Consciousness**
Letting inner Flow determine what to focus on, releasing self- judgements when catching oneself trying to control that	Trying to control the focus of your thoughts to mentally 'avoid' (ignore) any negative thoughts which may be arising

Negative Thoughts Aren't Ours!

'Car Parks' for Others' Thoughts

If you buy a car park and allow people to park their cars in it you have no problem understanding that those cars in your car park belong to other people and are not yours. In the same way, it is perfectly possible for other people to park their 'cars' – their thoughts – in your head. Indeed, this is exactly what happens, and every negative thought you've ever had is actually someone else's thought, someone else's belief, given to you … parked in your head. So there's actually no such thing as *self*-judgement. Rather, there is the process of having other people's judgements of us taken on board for our own safety and survival, in such a way that we have to accept them as our own. Every negative thought you have ever had has actually been someone else's. Your mind has been made a 'car park' for the negative thoughts (i.e. self-judgements) of other people's 'cars'. You have never ever owned a negative thought! (../negative)

'The Wake Up Test'

There's another way that we can see that negative thoughts aren't ours. Did you ever wake up one day and think to yourself, "I'm going to choose negative thinking today!"? No? Did you ever think to yourself, "From this point onwards I've decided I will judge myself for … (xyz)"? No? Exactly. Of course you didn't. Every negative thought you've ever had is conditioning from other people. Every self-judgement thought or belief you've ever had was someone else's, given to you … if 'given' is the right word for it!

… imposed upon you.

… and they never chose it either!

So it begs the question: Where did negative thoughts come from in the first place?

Your Gifts

Not everyone is built for sports, but everyone is a natural at relationships, at listening to their body to maximise their health and vitality, at knowing what they like, at making decisions, at self-confidence, at Genius. If you think otherwise, I invite you to consider the degree to which you may not even be aware of how your perception of your personality and character have been influenced by conditioned self-judgements. When I first started doing 'Shadow Work' around the age of thirty, I was surprised to realise that I wasn't as 'fully' being me or in touch with all of who I really was as I had always thought. The good news is that on realising this, you get to start the process of regaining all your gifts.

> "Your task is not to seek for love, but merely to
> seek and find all the barriers within yourself
> that you have built against it." – Rumi

It's the same principle as our approach to positive and negative thinking, you see? Kissing Consciousness takes a radical but wholly aligned approach to this notion of Rumi's.

Conscious and Unconscious Use of The Intellect

There's no behaviour that is inherently Conscious or Unconscious, including behaviours that use a human brain, such as using your mind for thinking, analysis, etc. Your mind is a tool, and like any other tool, you could pick it up and use it out of either self-acceptance or self-judgement.

Love Consciousness	Fear Consciousness
Conscious thought-based activity might sometimes be hard or challenging, but it is always a fulfilling Choice	Forced thought-based activity is always the effect of self-judgement, and is never a fulfilling Choice

It's important to note that 'forced' thought-based activity is not the same as 'hard' or 'difficult' or even 'struggling' thought-based activity – so long as the energy underpinning whatever one means by that term 'struggling' is Love Consciousness rather than Fear Consciousness, Choice rather than self-judgement. There's nothing inherently wrong with critical thinking. This book is a testament to critical thinking, as well as to intuition and Awareness.

Love Consciousness	**Fear Consciousness**
Critical Thinking	Overthinking

In Love Consciousness, when we are not using our cognitive mind for a particular task, any thinking there may be is almost invisible, fleeting and unnoticed. It doesn't get in the way at all. And when we do engage our brains in an intellectual or cognitive capacity whilst in the state of Love Consciousness, that experience is at least fulfilling, creative and generative, and not overbearing or 'heavy'. As noted before, the mind is a wonderful servant but a horrible master. (../intellect)

Love Consciousness	**Fear Consciousness**
Your thinking is invisible and unnoticed, unless you're engaged in an intellectual exercise, in which case it is at least engaging and fulfilling, and even then not intrusive	Your thinking is dominant

Unselfconscious

This is my favourite word and quality to both be and experience. My preference for all of society and humanity, in every moment, is for it to be Unselfconscious.

Unselfconscious vs Self-Conscious

To be Self-Conscious is to be overly concerned with some aspect of our behaviour – words, actions, body language, appearance, how we come across to others – such that we are inhibiting ourselves and modifying ourselves unnaturally and awkwardly. This is caused by … you guessed it … self-judgement. It's the quality we're in when we self-sabotage, when we have a 'No' Permission around something, because even though we think we're trying hard to allow ourselves to be or have something, we're actually making sure that we don't allow that thing, because we're not allowed it.

So the opposite of that, the absence of being Self-Conscious, is the quality of being Unselfconscious, and in this state we have no worries about whether how we behave or come across meets the approval of our inner self-judgements, because there are none. We are totally being us, in our Being, and this is a wonderful state of experience. It's also our *natural* state, and the one that supports our wellbeing.

Love Consciousness	Fear Consciousness
Unselfconscious	Self-Conscious

The dictionary definition of self-consciousness is something like, "Undue awareness of oneself, one's appearance, or one's actions." It is a preoccupation with one's thoughts around certain matters which motivate an unnatural self-moderating activity of mind, and then of behaviour also, which is unhealthy, unhelpful and undesirable. We may wish to become aware of this state of being in ourselves, so that we can choose to let it go and experience the alternative. This is where a notion such as "Dance like nobody is watching" becomes "Do everything like nobody is watching." Or more accurately (and more safely), "Do everything as if you're not judging yourself, as if you have no need for approval from others (or even yourself) of your behaviour, speech, words, choices, mannerisms, body language ..."

> "Practice being as relaxed around other people as you are when you're by yourself." – Colin Turner

Of course, as we've seen, we can't force authentic and relaxed actions at a behavioural level, so for notions of "Dance like ..." or "Practice being as relaxed ..." we need to bear that in mind. Again this desirable state of being Unselfconscious is achieved by itself once we let go of the self-judgements which cause us to be Self-Conscious and feel the need to gain other people's approval. It's not just with other people that being Self-Conscious happens, either. When we are alone it can occur for anything we're not allowed to be, anything we have self-judgement around. Perhaps people with food issues have noticed being Self-Conscious around eating decisions, for example. Just because one is motivated by gaining other people's approval doesn't mean those people have to be in the room, or even still alive.

The Outward Appearance of Being Unselfconscious

It is also a mistake to assume that people who never appear Self-Conscious have all their mindsets in place. It may just be that they avoid anything which may make them feel this way, avoiding challenging their False Self aspects, never allowing themselves to acknowledge parts of themselves, or their abilities or potentials.

Being Unselfconscious and Being Conscious of One's Safety

Being Unselfconscious is NOT about turning our Awareness off to the possible threats of people who would harm us. That Awareness still functions as normal. Being Self-Conscious is about the *judgements* that *we* have about how we should be, not about behaving stupidly or carelessly around potentially dangerous people or situations. We are possibly choosing to break out of the need to maintain the safety of our Self-Conscious false Ego's identity, not risk our physical level safety. These are two totally different things.

Cultural and Societal Expectation Creates Self-Conscious Adults

Certain behaviour that's expected of an adult due to judgementalism at a social and cultural level leads to almost all adults in our society being Self-Conscious to ensure that they're seen to fit in with those expectations. It's an incredibly unhealthy state, to be (often constantly) Unconsciously self-moderating in this way. (../unself)

'Charge'

When we are Self-Conscious it is because we have what we call a 'Charge' around something. 'Charge' refers to the quality of your energy or Consciousness when you have self-judgement around a certain matter – rather than being at peace, there's an energetic charge making things all uncomfortable. We say "I have a Charge around" something, or "Do you have a Charge around that person?", or "She has a Charge around money", or "Mike has a Charge around their wedding day; something about it is not resolved for him", or "Joe has a Charge around food", or "Sue has a Charge around asking guys out." Charge is a nice easy word to work with in practice. It's easy to see all of the areas of your life where you have a Charge around something and then work at releasing them. Charge means you're coming from your False Self. Small wonder, then, that it doesn't feel like much fun.

Love Consciousness	Fear Consciousness
No Charge	Charge

Attachment and Resistance

Attachment and resistance (and also therefore Fear Consciousness and self-judgement) are also known as 'Charge'. For example, where we might say,

"She has resistance to being poor and attachment to having money", we might similarly say, "She has a Charge around money." And: "He has attachment to his relationship with Alice, and fear of losing her love (resistance to that)" might similarly be said as, "He has a Charge around Alice."

Note that 'unattached' doesn't mean cold, uncaring, dissociated or divorced from feeling. It's merely the healthy relationship to life and self; it means in fact that we're in touch with what we truly feel. Attachment and resistance are dissociated from what we truly feel underneath the Fear Consciousness.

Love Consciousness	**Fear Consciousness**
No Attachment or Resistance	Attachment and Resistance

Attachment and resistance are equal opposites. If you have attachment to being single you have resistance to being in a relationship. If you have attachment to being rich you have resistance to being poor. If you have attachment to being fat you have resistance to being slim. If you're attached to a good supplier in business, you're resistant to losing them. If you have attachment to people holding the opinion that you're cool, kind or successful you have resistance to people holding the opinion that you're uncool, unkind or unsuccessful. The reverse or opposite of all these examples are also true: If you have attachment to being single you have resistance to being in a relationship, and so on. So you can see that *everything* that isn't Consciousness is attachment to something and resistance to its opposite. Your basic nature is to live *without* attachment and resistance. You block your creativity and playfulness, and all the other Love Consciousness attributes when you're in attachment and resistance. (../attachment)

'Grasping' is Just Another Form of 'Avoiding'

Often people make the mistake of trying not to be in avoidance of a feeling by 'grasping' for it, in other words trying too hard to 'avoid avoiding' it. In so doing, they unwittingly begin to avoid their fear of not being in control of when the feelings arise for processing. Ironically, this fear becomes another feeling that's good to allow in and feel, and stop avoiding. 'Grasping' is a potential pitfall because it is a forced-thought level, behaviour level act, rather than a Consciousness Act of Awareness. To say it another way: If you're *resistant* to *avoiding* feelings then you're *attached* to *facing* them!

This 'grasping' can often start as a healthy Choice to face up to feelings, but as people learn to associate avoiding feelings with pain, and facing feelings with a sense of emotional safety or certainty or the pleasure of a good-feeling release of Fear Consciousness, they can unintentionally get into this habit of grasping to face things. This is another example of 'Ego-Hijack', where the Ego, the mind, thinks "I can control this feeling and be okay if I push forward and insist on facing it." But it's just another control mechanism to avoid feelings. I call this 'Inverted Avoidance' – see Chapter Four. (../charge)

The alternative to attachment and resistance is Willingness.

Willingness

Willingness is a curious and powerful characteristic of Love Consciousness that initially seems almost counter-intuitive: Why on earth would you be willing to be bored, broke, alone, uncomfortable, nervous, unhealthy?! So, before we define what Willingness is, let's start getting a sense of what it is *not*:

- 'Willing to' doesn't necessarily mean 'choosing to'
- 'Willing to be' doesn't necessarily mean 'being'
- It doesn't necessarily mean liking something … or someone

Willingness and Unconditional Self-Love

Unconditional Self-Love is the Willingness to accept yourself however or whatever you are, and however your world turns out, prior to any beliefs and conclusions about what you – or it – should or shouldn't be.

I say to people, "Are you willing to … xyz?"

They say, "I don't want to xyz…"

I say, "I know. That wasn't what I asked; I said are you *willing to* xyz...?"
They say, "But I don't want to..."
I say, "No, are you *WILLING TO...?*"

There's a difference between wanting to be bored and being Willing to be bored. Being bored is not something I'd seek out, but I'm certainly Willing to be bored if it's my truth and my Inner Guidance. Being Willing to be bored can achieve amazing things.

Willingness is best understood as the Willingness for something to be true for you; the Willingness to accept that it is true. Conversely, Unwillingness is the Unwillingness for something to be true for you.

Willingness is About Our Relationship with Ourselves

> "When you realise the difference between choosing something and being Willing for it to be true, you'll realise that Unwillingness is a self-judgement, and thus a self-limitation." – James Blacker

We can also see this from the perspective of the relationship we have with our Inner Guide, our Subconscious Mind. If we are Unwilling to be something, which includes being Unwilling to acknowledge the truth of something, then we are ignoring and shutting out our Inner Guide, our Knowing, our Awareness. So Unwillingness is caused by self-judgement. Unwillingness simply means that some part of your Conscious Awareness is shut out.

Love Consciousness	Fear Consciousness
Willingness	Unwillingness

Responding vs Reacting

"Responsibility means having a creative response to a situation." – Dr. Deepak Chopra

In the Love Consciousness state of self-acceptance, we Respond to the situation as it is in a given moment. In the self-judgement of Fear Consciousness, however, we React to the situation Unconsciously – and of course this also means we React without genuine Conscious Choice.

Love Consciousness	Fear Consciousness
Respond	React
Responsive	Reactive

You can imagine, for example, that a young man who grows up in a homophobic household might easily (Unconsciously) become Unwilling to be gay. Being Unwilling to be gay doesn't mean he's gay, and it doesn't mean he's straight. It means he's Unwilling to consider or entertain the possibility that he might be gay. Therefore, were he to engage in a relationship with a woman, it would not entirely be a (Conscious) Choice, but would in part be a Reaction against the notion of being gay. (../respond)

Unassumed Inquiry as to One's Truth, True Nature, and Therefore Genuine Choice

This principle can apply to anything and everything. Most people in Western culture have grown up with it having been taken for granted that relationships are monogamous, for example, such that we are only meant to love one person, or at least only one person at a time. The rare few individuals who have objectively looked at their true nature from a place of *unassumed inquiry*, and found their true nature in that moment to be that they wish to choose a monogamous relationship, are experiencing exactly that: A genuine Choice of that type of relationship. For everyone else, however, monogamous relationship is not so much a Conscious Choice as it is an assumption of how life is meant to be and an Unconscious Reaction to growing up in a culture that judges anything else. Essentially, such people are 'in conclusion' about who they are with regard to relationship type choices. For a person who is Unwilling to be anything other than monogamous, any information which arises about one's nature being anything other than monogamous is shut out. If you're British you go on holiday to Spain every summer – 'cos that's 'what you do'.

Unwillingness Denies Genuine Choice

This is the difference between happy people and those living with the assumption or conceptual notion of Happiness: It's not about what they're choosing, but the quality of the state of freedom of Consciousness from which they're choosing it. People who are Unwilling to be single will 'choose' any relationship simply to avoid being single. That cannot really be said to be genuine Choice. Again, it is merely a Reaction. Whenever we're in a moment of self-judgement we always React – at least initially, until we can get Awareness of it.

The 'Vacuum of Consciousness'

In order to be effective, we have to be aligned with our truth, and to know our truth we must first have a 'Vacuum of Consciousness'. We need to allow space in our Awareness for what's true for us to arise.

Are you Willing to be unhappy? Are you Willing to be emotionally uncomfortable? Are you Willing to be bored? In order to be unconditionally true to yourself, you have to be *Willing* to be … well, everything, including bored out of your mind. Otherwise you will judge, i.e. resist, i.e. reject, being bored out of your mind, and therefore not receive the information from your Awareness that would change that state for you in a way that is in your interests. You will fill the 'space' with something that's not true to yourself. Nature abhors a vacuum, and if you have no judgements about what a moment is meant to be, it will be filled with what is your truth. It's fine that The Vacuum of Consciousness gets filled – but it's not ideal that your Fear Consciousness does the filling!

Love Consciousness	Fear Consciousness
We allow whatever's true for us to arise out of the Vacuum of Consciousness	We fill the space of our Consciousness with a False Self

Are you Willing to be vague, lost, uncomfortable, heart-broken, poor, aimless, lazy, undecided? If you aren't, then when that arises as your truth – or rather, attempts to – you will fill that space with other, False Self activities – and then reap the consequences of those False Self activities.

Unwillingness is The Unwillingness to Risk That Thing

You can't win in love unless you're Willing to lose in love. Unwillingness is just another way of saying, "I won't accept myself if … xyz." Are you Willing to be fat? Are you Willing to be uncool? Are you Willing to fail in business? If you aren't Willing to risk failing in business, you'll never start a business. If you're Unwilling to be unhappy you'll fill the space of Unhappiness with a false, fake happiness, making it more difficult to achieve genuine Happiness. Are you Willing to be *successful* in business, or elsewhere? You also have to be Willing to be the desirable things in order to claim them.

If you're not Willing to have a lack of clarity then you'll force clarity for the wrong reasons. If you aren't Willing to do sex without emotional intimacy then you can't choose sex with emotional intimacy. Without Willingness there is no Choice; you're only *Reacting* to the notion of sex without intimacy. Again, this, ironically, compromises the quality of the experience. If you're *Willing* to do sex without emotional intimacy, then if you choose to do sex with emotional intimacy, you're in your Being, you're free of your mind – and that gives a different (authentic) experience entirely.

Unconditional Love and 'Conditional Like' and Yeses

Love Consciousness is unconditional; it is acceptance of things as they are. Liking things, however, is conditional; you either like something or you don't. It's either your truth to say 'Yes' to something, or it isn't. So we don't want to confuse unconditional love for ourselves as meaning we have to say 'Yes' to everything, or lie about our truth. Unconditional self-love is about honouring everything that's true for us.

Specific Unconditional Self-Love and Total Unconditional Self-Love

To be Willing to be a certain thing, or have that be true for you, is 'Specific Unconditional Self-Love'. To be Willing to be *anything*, or have *anything* be true for you, is 'Total Unconditional Self-Love' … which is to be totally unconditional with life, with the Universe …

Unwillingness Isn't a Stick to Beat Yourself With

So bearing in mind 'The Paradox of Love Consciousness', we can see that the primary basis of Willingness is the Willingness to be in a state of Fear Consciousness, which itself puts us in a state of Love Consciousness. Unwillingness isn't a stick to beat ourselves with. That would just create more self-judgement. Nor is it a suggestion to force behaviour. Finding compassion for our Unwillingness is the place to start. When we are ready to release our self-judgement, Willingness will return all on its own.

The Comfort Zone

Someone asked me once if my 'stuff' could help them with their life and happiness, but without them having to come out of their comfort zone, because they didn't want to do that, didn't like that approach.

Everybody thinks of going beyond one's comfort zone as being just one single phenomenon. But we have seen from our exploration of The Illusion of Identical Experiences that there are actually *two* different versions of every action or activity in life: One happening spontaneously from self-acceptance, the other happening unenjoyably and by force as a result of self-judgement.

Love Consciousness	Fear Consciousness
Going beyond a comfort zone	Going beyond a comfort zone

So what you have is one load of people who are happy to go beyond their comfort zones – and indeed, are enjoying doing so, because they're doing it from Love Consciousness anyway, from Choice, from their Being, with Confidence and with Flow and all that self-supporting stuff – telling another load of people who are *not* in that state, but instead are in a state of Fear Consciousness (largely because they are being told that they *"should"* go beyond their comfort zone), to do what *they think* is the same challenge, but is actually a completely different proposition entirely, with a totally different dynamic. For the latter group of people, going beyond their comfort zone would be based on lack of Confidence, lack of (Conscious) Choice. They'd be attempting something from entirely the wrong motivation and this can only lead to more confusion, misery, frustration and lack of Confidence. It's the difference between a bird taking off, and a bird continually being pushed just before it's about to jump.

Love Consciousness	Fear Consciousness
Going beyond a comfort zone from Flow, out of Choice and from your Being	Going beyond a comfort zone from Stuckness, from self-judgement, 'in your head' and no Choice

I would never ever choose to go beyond my comfort zone from a place of Fear Consciousness, because nothing good is ever created from Fear Consciousness. Does that mean I'm someone who never improves their life, never challenges themselves, never achieves personal change? Of course not. I go beyond my comfort zone from Love Consciousness. Forced behaviour that emanates from Fear Consciousness is actually self-abuse. That's never going to be a recipe for personal Success. It's a recipe for misunderstanding, sadness, confusion and Frustration.

Conscious Comfort Zones

I say to people, "Imagine your comfort zone is a box. You are in that box. Now imagine that box is set on fire. Do you still want to stay in that box?" The moment we become aware that life in the 'comfort zone' is actually more uncomfortable than it is comfortable, we uncover a natural motivation to move beyond it. So you see, you don't have to force any behaviour from a place of Fear Consciousness. All we have done here is increased our Awareness, and become Conscious, to acknowledge what is really true for us, and then we make choices accordingly. So I'd invite us to get Conscious to our comfort zones – are they actually comfortable or uncomfortable?

Uncomfortable 'Comfort Zones'

So let's say your comfort zone is eating chocolate of an evening. You think it would be uncomfortable to not eat chocolate, to go beyond that to the alternative experience. Well, all you have to do is become aware of how it truly is for you to continue eating chocolate. This comes back to our Binary of 'direct, real experience of life', Awareness of how something really feels, of whether it's *really* our Choice. And if, after you gain Awareness of what's true for you, you find that it's actually your genuine Choice to stay in the box, then just stay in the box, because in that instance the box is no longer a comfort zone anyway – it's become obvious that it's a Choice. What's the problem?! There's no problem! On the other hand, if you find that actually it's an unpleasant experience to continue in the box, then your renewed Awareness will lead you to choose something more comfortable, more enjoyable.

I just keep turning up the 'heat' of the Awareness until I get to what is my real Choice, what my body and I genuinely want to do.

Your 'Uncomfort Zone'

If we get really aware of our comfort zones, we can realise when it's more uncomfortable in them than it is out of them, which then makes it easy to decline being in them. In fact, the comfort zone becomes the 'Uncomfort Zone'. As we realise this and climb out without any effort and without even having to think about it, we automatically find ourselves in what was previously the space 'outside of the comfort zone' … only it's now become kinda comfortable. It's pleasant, but also in an 'alive' kind of way.

> "When you add Awareness, your comfort zone becomes either your Choice, or your 'Uncomfort Zone'." – James Blacker

Comfort Zones as Self-Judgements

We can now see that comfort zones are caused by self-judgement … that they *are* self-judgements. Releasing the self-judgement automatically takes care of the comfort zone issue. This notion ties in nicely with another we shall come to in the next chapter, addressing the nature of fear as 'excitement in disguise'. (../comfort)

Willingness and Comfort Zones

Finally, whilst you don't have to *choose* going beyond a comfort zone (if it's not what you wish to choose), you do have to be *Willing to*, which means choosing it if it happens to be that it *is* your truth. That Willingness is necessary for you to be able to recognise that it is your Choice. If accepting your truth means going beyond your comfort zone, and you're Unwilling to acknowledge that or choose for yourself – which means you're at least somewhat *Unconscious* to your truth – that's fine, but you won't get to 'receive' yourself or that desired outcome.

"Are you Willing to go beyond your comfort zone?" basically translates as "Are you Willing to honour your Choice, to love yourself, if it were your truth to go beyond your comfort zone?" This is exactly why we use Awareness as a tool and release self-judgements: To facilitate your Consciousness such that it flows with your Choice to 'move beyond' Stuckness, wherever that may be true for you. (../willingness)

Confidence

"Self-love is the key to Confidence, self-judgement its prevention." – James Blacker

I heard a tale of a friend of a friend who ran a social event, even though she didn't want to, as a part of some form of confidence training. Her Confidence, her *(self-)confiding*, was literally telling her she didn't want to run the event, yet she was talked into going through with it in order to 'build confidence'.

This comes back to the notion of being Self-Referral (trusting your inner Knowing), not External Referral (doing what other people tell you to do). Confidence is a Self-Referral quality. It's ridiculously futile – yet understandably commonplace – to believe that you can build Confidence by doing something that your inner wisdom is telling you that you don't want to do, or don't believe in. If Confidence is a Consciousness, not a behaviour, then practicing, building, developing, and mastering Confidence is also a Consciousness, not a behaviour. There may be value in activities which allow people to push beyond what they thought were their limitations, but even so, if they are helpful they all still lead from the Consciousness. Bear in mind also that we are not really talking about the development of skills here. We're talking about the core of what Confidence is: A self-confiding, which is automatic whenever there's an absence of self-judgement in one's mind, whenever we are not 'in our heads'.

Confidence is a Consciousness, Assertiveness is a Behaviour

What happens is this: You go into a situation thinking you 'must be assertive', which has you totally in your head and shut down to your Awareness. 'Shut down Awareness' is the very definition of lack of Confidence, because you shut down your ability to confide in yourself any Awareness that your Inner Guide may wish to relate to you, in favour of this or that belief system (in this example, a belief in assertive behaviour).

Does this mean I'm against assertive behaviour? No. It means I'm *for* Conscious Choice. I'm for behaviour being led by Awareness. If you prioritise (and trust!) your Awareness, and then the Choice to be assertive comes from that Awareness in any given moment, great! What that makes me 'in favour of', if I had to put it in this way, is *authentic* assertiveness – that assertiveness which arises naturally from your Being. I'm 'against' false, forced, *inauthentic* assertiveness that is motivated by Fear Consciousness.

This principle doesn't apply just to assertiveness. It applies to all behaviours. Anything that you think, feel, say or do. All helpful behaviours and actions are informed by your Consciousness.

Is it possible that this approach of living from Awareness and genuine Confidence, rather than relying on belief systems and conclusions, might be a rather profound and axis-shifting process for many people? Yeah, it is. Did your world unwittingly teach you a false notion of what Confidence is? I'd say so.

What Confidence Looks Like

Confidence has no guaranteed 'look' in behavioural terms such as "This person speaks loudly, or wears smart clothes, or always states their opinions upfront, therefore they must be confident." What we can look out for, perhaps, are the tell-tale signs in someone's eyes or mannerisms which betray a person at odds with themselves. What our society taught us about confidence was based on behaviour and an external notion of success, rather than our own internal relationships with ourselves, our Consciousness, our self-love, our *Choice*! It's time to build a new model of Confidence for society. If you want ultimate, total self-confidence, relying on belief systems and conclusions to provide some kind of 'safety net' of pre-determined ways to address the upcoming moments of life isn't the way to do it.

Confidence is a Different Thing to Competence

In order to have total self-confidence do you have to be competent at every task or activity there is in life? Of course not. Confidence has got nothing to do with competence. As long as I'm honest with myself – as long as I *confide* in myself – about what I can and cannot do, about what's my truth and what's not my truth, then I'm going to have Confidence. And so are you.

Declining The Temptation to Build Self-Confidence Externally

Part of building self-confidence is therefore declining the temptation of attempting to build self-confidence externally from the praise and approval of others. I say *'attempting'* because it is actually impossible to build self-confidence externally in this way. (../confidence)

Receiving

"I receive!"

Receiving is the acceptance of all things that you can have, be, do, get, give, experience, etc., that you would choose. Collectively, that is the acceptance of You. Fantastic!

Again, our old friend self-judgement – lack of Permissions – is what stops us from Receiving everything that we are. Where our Human File Permissions are set to 'No' we're unable to Receive, even though we may want to, as there's an Unconscious block working against us. We all Receive some of what is true for us – nobody could be in denial of every single thing that is true for them – but where blocks exist, releasing self-judgement allows us to Receive those truths again.

If you have no self-judgements you can be said to be "Fully Receiving You." Or if you have no self-judgements around a certain moment, you can be said to be fully Receiving You *in that moment.*

Love Consciousness	Fear Consciousness
Receiving	Self-Denying

What Receiving Looks Like

As Receiving is a quality of Consciousness, not a fixed behaviour or activity, it may take on any visible expression.

Imagine, for example, a female employee whose male boss wants to give her a hug at Christmas, however innocently. If she receives the hug physically she is not necessarily Receiving in the sense of the phenomenon of Consciousness and being true to herself, since that would depend on whether she wanted to be hugged. If she didn't and her truth was to decline, but self-judgement prevented her from saying so, then to accept the hug would be to *not* be Receiving her truth. If it was her truth to decline the hug – and she allowed herself to decline – *that* would be Receiving. If the male boss in our example was resistant to her not wanting to be hugged by him, he would not be Receiving his inner strength to be okay with that, either.

So we can see that Receiving (or not) is everywhere, because it is a Consciousness. Receiving applies the same way with respect to a gift, or invitation to join someone on a holiday, or meal, or business project. If we want to study biology but we get talked into studying art, that is not Receiving. If we are offered a snack food and we take it and eat it, but really we didn't want to, that is not Receiving ourselves. Receiving ourselves in that instance might be about allowing in the Life Force that would come with not habitually repressing ourselves with food. Another time we might genuinely want the snack. So again the quality of Love Consciousness shows itself as allowing what's true for us, not necessarily what 'getting something' looks like on the surface. (../receiving)

(Trying to) Control

"Life or the Universe can't give to you what you refuse to Receive." – James Blacker

The Ironic Self-Defeat of (Trying to) Control

When we are in self-judgement we take an approach in which we think we are controlling a situation, but really we are controlling nothing. Jon Freeman uses the analogy of a child sitting in the car with daddy, holding the toy steering wheel and thinking he is driving the car. If we aren't allowed to Receive then, inevitably, we are hopelessly trying to control. When we are trying to control from a place of Fear Consciousness the only thing we are controlling is our avoidance of the emotion which our Awareness around the matter would bring, because we're not ready to feel it.

Love Consciousness	Fear Consciousness
Receiving	(Trying to) Control
	Unwittingly refusing to Receive whilst believing we're choosing to

Refusing to Receive is an Unconscious motivator – we're not aware we're doing it. It's all part of the bizarre dynamic that while we're in Fear Consciousness we have to defend our False Self.

Forced Behaviour as Defending Against One's Own Brilliance

Forced behaviour and trying to control is not only trying to do something towards a goal or aim, it is also making sure you do something *against* that goal, because you aren't allowed that goal. We do this under the guise of trying to do something good towards the aim. Our actions and words have the surface appearance of trying to do something towards the aim, but our underlying motivation is compromised.

In defending our False Self we are inevitably also defending *against* our True Self. We put a lot of effort into defending against what's true for us, but that we're not allowed to be (i.e. 'No' Permissions).

The amount of effort that goes into preventing ourselves from being successful or happy is the most curious phenomenon – bizarre, maybe tragic – but very real and all too common. For most people, defending their False Selves is not just an everyday but almost an every-other-moment way of life.

Isn't that crazy? That we actually defend our False Selves and our non-Permissions?! It's crazy but it's true, because we have to defend against what we once thought – or rather knew – it was unsafe to be.

Love Consciousness	Fear Consciousness
Receiving	Defending our False Self, preventing our True Self

The Double-Whammy of Repressed Consciousness

Before we continue, here's another insight based on my interpretation of some of Ken Wilber's work, which I dubbed The Double-Whammy of Repressed Consciousness: The effect of a self-judgement in terms of reducing the amount of Life Force energy available to us is doubled, because we have to also defend our False Self. Let's say we have 30% self-judgement (70% self-acceptance), which means 30% of our Life Force energy, our Consciousness, is (currently) shut down to us. But additionally, we're having to spend a further 30% of our Life Force energy defending our False Self, making sure we don't 'accidentally' achieve that thing which we're not allowed (again, our 'No' Permissions). It seems ridiculous, but this is how the mechanism of shutting down our characteristics which were once unacceptable to the world around us works.

Self-Fear: Being Afraid of Who You Are

So this is all essentially Self-Fear. You fear yourself because you Unconsciously sense that who you are, whether that be powerful and empowered, sexually vibrant, financially successful, or whatever it is, isn't compatible with what you are, or were, allowed to be. It might now be safe to allow yourself to be something, but you are first going to have to 'update' your Awareness. People are afraid to be successful, you see! This may sound strange, but Self-Fear is an incredibly widespread phenomenon given that it is the consequence of every single self-judgement in the entire world.

Love Consciousness	Fear Consciousness
Self-Embracing	Self-Fearing

Ultimately, you being afraid of who you are is also a lie, because it's again based on self-judgements and self-judgements are illusions ... but we do allow ourselves to *believe*, Subconsciously, semi-consciously, that we're afraid of who we are.

Releasing can be done to uncover the reality and the truth, returning to us the ability to Receive.

'Trying' is Not Doing

Even the Star Wars franchise knows this one: "Do. Or do not. There is no try." Another way to perceive the Binary is to recognise that there are two different types of 'trying'. This can be explained as an example of The Illusion of Identical Experiences, whereby 'trying' from Fear Consciousness is a totally different experience to trying from Love Consciousness. (Notice that when I'm referring to 'trying' in a Fear Consciousness context I'm putting it in inverted commas).

We can also explain trying as a Consciousness-Behaviour Split: Are you trying at a behaviour level? There's nothing inherently wrong with trying as a behaviour from Love Consciousness, as it can simply be the exploration of a possibility, an earnest attempt at some endeavour. However, 'trying' as a behaviour from Fear Consciousness is attempting to be something you're not, or be something you're not allowed to be, which is futile.

Love Consciousness	**Fear Consciousness**
Trying from Love Consciousness manifests as reasonable endeavour to explore possibilities	'Trying' as a Fear Consciousness is just another characteristic of self-sabotage, and manifests as futile efforts at the behavioural level

The Lie That's a Truth That's a Lie

Now that we have some introduction to the bizarre dynamic of refusing to Receive, let's look at our next Kissing Consciousness concept: The Lie That's a Truth That's a Lie.

Here's how it works (and remember, this always happens, and only happens, under the influence of self-judgement):

1. It's a lie that you want the thing that you're trying to achieve, because Subconsciously you know you're not allowed it. So you're pretending to be going after it, but 'secretly', unwittingly, making sure you don't allow yourself to Receive it, because the last time you checked that was not safe.

2. But it's true that actually you do want the thing. You certainly have a compelling feel for wanting it; it's just that self-judgement which is stopping you from Receiving it.

3. But you are under the influence of self-judgement, so how can you know what you will want once the self-judgement is removed and your True Self is revealed? The only way to know is to remove the self-judgement and then find out what your desire is.

Let's say you're attempting to be a television presenter, but you have a 'No' Permission around being allowed to be a success at it.

1. You sabotage your efforts to be good at it (the lie – that you want it).
2. But even so you feel deep down underneath that you want to be good at it (that's a truth – that you want it).
3. But until you release the self-judgement you can't be sure whether you will still want to be a television presenter after it has cleared. (So the lie is, again, that you want it … because you simply don't know).

So trying to force the thing we want into existence is futile, and the smart (Conscious) way to address the Frustration is to seek to release the Fear Consciousness. This is addressing the cause, not the symptom. Unconscious people always try to force the thing into existence against their true nature. All we can do is remove the self-judgement and find out what's really true for us under those circumstances. Here's a Specific Binary Table for how people deal with and address self-sabotage:

Love Consciousness	**Fear Consciousness**
Becoming aware of the self-judgement	Trying to force what we want into existence
Addressing the cause	Addressing the symptom

It might be that you don't want to ask that guy or lady out after all, because the motivation was coming from a fear of being alone. Perhaps once you release the self-judgement you will shed a new light on who you really are, and what you really want. (../lie)

'Being' in Control

There is actually a valid sense in which you can be in control, which is why the notion of never being able to be in control may grate with you or irritate, if you've had the experience of being in control of yourself and life at one time or another, as everyone surely has, and felt it to be a healthy and natural state.

Kissing Consciousness suggests that 'being in control' has two possible meanings:

1. That you are being in control
2. Or that your *Being* is in control

So I'd invite you to consider that when you want to be in control but you aren't, that you surrender (Yield) and allow your *Being* to be in control. When you are in your Being you are in control, because your Being is in control (and your fearful mind-based, Fear Consciousness False Self isn't). And of course, this 'Being' in Control is the control which feels good, feels light and is also effective. All positive, true, self-loving things stem from your Being, not from your Controlling. So when you feel uncomfortably out of control of yourself, you can drop back into your Being. (../trying)

Love Consciousness	**Fear Consciousness**
'Being' in Control	Trying to be in control

Power

"Being in self-acceptance the gates of your power are open. Being in self-judgement the gates of your power are closed." – James Blacker

Love Consciousness	Fear Consciousness
In Your Power	Not In Your Power

Power is the self-allowance to honour what's true for you. This, by definition, includes what's possible for you, and what's truly your Choice out of that range of possibility. 'Power' is no more complicated than this.

Of course, we know which 'gremlin' makes us think or feel otherwise.

"The source of your power is before you've thought. It is *prior* to thought." – James Blacker

The source of your power is your simple ability to choose to do the things you can do which it is your Choice to do. If and when thought comes in to the equation, it either aligns with Awareness of that power – in which case nothing changes – or it is self-judgement-based thought which gets in the way of it. (../power)

Power vs Power Over

There's a difference between 'Power' and 'Power Over'. When people lack self-allowance and Power, sometimes they try to compensate for the feeling with *Power Over* others. This attempt to feel fulfilled will always be futile, with the added consequence that people get hurt, sometimes murdered.

This distinction is important because it allows us to understand what is going on when we see people who have vast financial or political resources which allow them *Power Over* others, yet are so dissociated from their own heart, feelings, truth and original motives that they lack any genuine Power whatsoever. (Remember, if there's no Love Consciousness there's no Power!) Society is largely uneducated regarding this distinction, and so often mistakenly sees these people as having genuine Power. These people are not Responding to their own genuine Choice, however, but are Reacting Unconsciously, totally unaware of what is actually motivating their behaviour. In some cases, they may have 'lost' themselves as early as the age of two, three, four. When someone is genuinely enjoying themselves there is no thought, or reason for any thought, of controlling others.

We also see some who *don't* have vast financial resources impose whatever degree of Power Over (sometimes physical or psychological) they do have upon others, whether those close to them – their partners or children, work colleagues, friends – or just people in public. So it's useful to see the distinction: Power is empowerment and Power Over is essentially the unhealthy expression, or rather lashing out, of buried emotional pain. When this basic psychological truth becomes a common cultural understanding, the ability for 'Power Over' brokers to not look weak and needy will be gone forever … and hopefully then they can all get some mental healthcare.

And just to clarify: We're really talking about Power Over *as a Consciousness*, the needy sense of a need to control others. Of course stopping your toddler running into the road isn't a Consciousness level interest in controlling others.

Power Over in Relationships and Sex

If we're seeking Power Over in our intimate romantic relationships, our family relationships, social or even work relationships, this is also a case of us *not* being in our power. Rather, we're in Neediness. This is covered in Chapter Seven on Relationships. (../over)

Living in the Moment

"A moment is a measurement of Consciousness, NOT a measurement of time." – James Blacker

A second is a measurement of time, and a tenth of a second is a measurement of time, but a moment is a phenomenon of Consciousness, not time. If you doubt this then try to time a moment on a stop watch! It's not a passage of time; it's a thought, a notion. It's Consciousness.

If you try to 'live in the moment' by addressing the phenomenon of time, it's not going to work. Living in the moment is achieved by a state of Consciousness. And as with all of our other characteristics of Love Consciousness, it's not – and can't be – achieved by forcing a positive thought. It is a natural default state which exists automatically if there is an absence of self-judgement.

It is, of course, impossible not to live in the present moment in the literal sense. So again we see that this notion of living in the moment has clearly got nothing to do with time. It is about what we are doing with our Consciousness. And we can now understand that 'living in the moment' is subject to yet another Consciousness-Behaviour Split. If in a given moment we are in a state of self-judgement, then what we are doing in that moment is not going to be our Choice, for as we have seen there's no Choice where there's self-judgement. Therefore, our *focus* is not going to be fully present to what we are doing. Our attention is going to be elsewhere – on what we Unconsciously pine for. If we're not allowed to be in our Choice now, then the subtle notion we'll inevitably hold in our head is that we hope that we can be in our Choice later on, at some point in the future, and we'll wait for that until we can be happy. We are living in our head!

Are we saying that we should not schedule events into the future, nor indulge in memories of the past? No. So what we're really talking about is not whether one is thinking about past, present or future, but whether one is doing so from Love Consciousness or from Fear Consciousness. This is the difference between 'living in the moment', and not doing so – "Postponing the act of living", as David Heard phrased it in our recording on 'Happiness'. In Fear Consciousness, we have guilt about the past and anxiety about the future, and *both* guilt and anxiety in the actual present moment.

Love Consciousness	Fear Consciousness
Living in the Moment	Living in our head

The value of living in the moment is that it is the quality of Love Consciousness – because actually, if it wasn't, why bother?! If not for quality of life, what would be the attraction to living in the moment? It's about appreciating the current moment and not judging it for being what it is. There's always something we can do as a creative Response in the moment. So we don't need to think about time at all.

The Point of Power

"The point of power is the present moment." – The Seth Material

How can we affect or influence things? The point of power is always in the present moment. If we are anxious about something which may happen in the future, we can't actually reach that future reality directly from the current point in time. What we can do is address whatever is causing us anxiety about that potential future *now*. If we are under the effect of self-judgement, though, we don't allow ourselves to.

Similarly, if we have fearful, guilty or painful thoughts of the past, we can't directly reach back to the past. What we can do is forgive ourselves in the present – now. We can take action to influence the future in the present – in the now. Or we can release self-judgements which are causing us anxiety about the future, in the present – now.

Love Consciousness	Fear Consciousness
Recognising that the power is in the present moment	Failing to recognise that the power is in the present moment

Love Consciousness	Fear Consciousness
Allowed to address what can be done now, even if that be releasing a self-judgement	Thinking nothing can be effected in the present moment

The 100 Metres Sprint vs The 110 Metres Hurdles

If we have judgements – attachment and resistance – as to how things should be that create notions of fixed future points in our mind, this stops us flowing in the moment, because whatever our Inner Guide says to do in the moment might not serve the aim of the event or outcome we have attachment to. I think of this as the difference between running a 100 metre sprint, in which one can get one's momentum up, compared to the 110 Metres Hurdles, in which every ten metres or so one has to slow down because there is an upcoming fixed point one needs to adjust to. If you're trying to control the future you can't 'sprint' (get your momentum going) in the present moment. Any attachment you have to a certain future outcome of an event causes you to not flow in the present moment. (../moment)

Timing

"Timin' is the thing it's true, Good timin' brought me to you." – Jimmy Jones' 1960s song, Good Timin'

Ahh, the classics! By the time – no pun intended – that a 'No' Permission has sabotaged our Success in a given moment, and that same moment is seen through the lens of the self-judgement, lack of Confidence, being in our head, the Stress effect of it, etc., the fact that our *Timing* is also off is perhaps seen less as a *cause* of the Frustration of that moment, than as an effect or just a 'garnish characteristic' of what happens in a moment of Fear Consciousness – part of the play of it, we might say.

Under self-judgement, there's never going to be a good sense of timing, because it's all about the relationship to one's own mind and thinking, and the presence of self-judgement means that we're not allowing ourselves to do or be what or how we really want to in this moment. Whatever else we *do* do is forced, and thus inevitably has the characteristic of lacking Timing. Sabotage also goes hand-in-hand with a lack of Timing. This insight provides yet another way to identify the characteristics of Love Consciousness and Fear Consciousness, and get to know them. You can't be 'in your head' and have Timing. Timing is also something you feel in your body, if you choose to pay attention to it. As is true of living in the moment, Timing also has nothing to do with time. Timing might sometimes *play out* as an event in time, but what it is, again, is a state of Consciousness. (../timing)

Love Consciousness	**Fear Consciousness**
Timing	No Timing

Emotions and Feelings

It's not always in your best interests for you to feel into your feelings, for various reasons (for example if nasty people around might attack you for doing so), or even be aware of them (for example if your Subconscious doesn't want to overload you with too many emotions to process all at once). Nonetheless, in the Love Consciousness state you will at least be *Willing* to feel into your emotions and feelings, if it's the right thing for you in that moment.

Love Consciousness	Fear Consciousness
You're Willing to feel your emotions and feelings	There's an emotion or feeling you're unwittingly Unwilling to feel
Letting the feeling in	Shutting the feeling out
Allowing ourselves to postpone feeling our feelings until our inner wisdom says it's wise to do so	Feeling feelings against our will because we judge that we're 'not living Consciously' if we don't feel them – again this is putting belief systems before Awareness

False Emotions

aka: False Self Emotions

When we are avoiding a feeling, what we're otherwise feeling in that moment is at least partly false, since we are actually experiencing the emotion of avoidance and Neediness (see Chapter Seven) as caused by an Unconscious self-judgement. This also creates anxiety, because the deeper, intuitive self knows that more real feelings are being avoided. It knows we're trying to control but are out of control. When we are allowing ourselves to directly experience an emotion, that is real. . (../feelings)

Love Consciousness	Fear Consciousness
The emotions we are experiencing are real	The emotions we are experiencing are at least partially false

The Anatomy of a Moment

There's an animated cartoon you may have heard of called Speedy Gonzales. 'Speedy' was "The Fastest Mouse in all Mexico." In one episode, Speedy made the mouth of the cat who was chasing him explode. It happened as if by magic, in a split second.

Then, in the cartoon, we were shown a slow-motion replay of exactly what had happened. The animators of the cartoon broke that split second down into a series of slower moments which showed Speedy Gonzales open the cat's mouth, place a bomb in it, close the mouth and then return to his original position, as if motionless.

Similarly, a televised sports action replay might show a tennis ball at first coming towards us at full speed, but then, just as it arrives, it slows down to barely moving, so that we, the viewer, can see the motion and activity in profound detail.

This is exactly what we are going to do here, not with a bomb or a tennis ball, but with a single moment of Consciousness. We'll look at it in tiny, 'microscopic', minute detail, so that you can see and feel exactly what it is. This moment is the basis and building block of You, and your life, of all your Success and Permissions, but also of your Frustrations and lack of Permissions.

The Interchangeable Nature of All Consciousness Polarities

> **Polarity (noun):** The state of having two opposite or contradictory tendencies, opinions, or aspects.

The Consciousness pair of 'Confidence' and 'Lack of Confidence' can be thought of as a polarity; they are polar opposites. We may consider, also, that Positive (Not) Thinking and Negative Thinking are polar opposites. But the pattern doesn't stop there, because we can *interchange* the various 'positive' (Love Consciousness) and 'negative' (Fear Consciousness) qualities: Confidence is the same thing as Positive (Not) Thinking; Lack of Confidence is the same thing as Negative Thinking.

We can also interchange the pairs of polarities. Confidence is the opposite of Negative Thinking. Similarly, Positive (Not) Thinking is the opposite of Lack of Confidence.

This principle applies for ALL Consciousness polarities. If we wanted to, we could focus on any of the expressions of Love Consciousness as a way to focus on, and achieve Success, for example, with some rather bizarre sounding – but true – phrases:

- Awareness your way to Success
- Be ('Being') your way to Success
- Choose your way to Success
- Confide your way to Success
- Receive your way to Success
- Etc.

Hang on a second … we probably want to be using the wording 'as Success' rather than 'to Success', to show that real Success is something that happens in the moment. You just have to look at Success with clear, original eyes. And let's use some different examples:

- 'Presence' your way as Success
- Genius your way as Success
- Willingness your way as Success
- Yield and Soften your way as Success

And this doesn't just relate to Success, we can approach *any* of the other Love Consciousness qualities in this way, for example:

- Flow your way as Confidence
- 'Not Think' your way as Confidence
- Self-Love your way as Confidence

You see?

Now, remember that we don't achieve these positives by forcing positives but by releasing the negatives, so declining the Unconscious self-judgements is the way to achieve the positives:

- Decline Self-Judgement your way as Success
- Decline Self-Non-Confiding your way as Success
- Decline Forced Behaviour your way as Success
- Decline (Trying to) Control your way as Success

- Decline Second-Guessing Yourself your way as Success
- Decline Defensiveness your way as Success
- Decline being Self-Conscious your way as Success

And to save you feeling you have to learn any of that, it can all be summed up with just seven words – "Release self-judgement if you feel Stuck." All of this is here to help your insights come more easily.

An Increase in Love Consciousness (Self-Acceptance) Raises All of These Qualities

As they say, 'a rising tide raises all boats'. That analogy holds up here, with a rising tide representing your increase in Love Consciousness, or Conscious Awareness – 'Yes' Permissions – and the 'boats' representing all of the qualities of Love Consciousness.

You can't have an increase in Confidence (say, from 41% to 57%) without an increase in Receiving, also. If you increase your Confidence, your *self-confiding*, you *automatically and inevitably* increase your Receiving also, to the same extent, because they're the same thing, and they happen at the same time (in the same way that a spoke of a bicycle wheel can't go round without all of the other spokes going round also). All of the characteristics of Love Consciousness are the same thing looked at in slightly different ways, which means you can't have an increase in one characteristic of Love Consciousness without an increase in everything else that's of Love Consciousness, for example:

- Being
- Choice
- Ease
- Embodiment
- Freedom
- Genius
- Happiness
- Knowing
- Life Force Energy
- Peace
- Power
- Self-Kindness
- Unselfconscious
- Etc.

PAUDI: Passive, Automatic, Unnoticed, Default Invisibles

All of the characteristics of the one quality of Love Consciousness have the same kind of nature to them; that of being what we might call 'automatic', 'default', 'invisible', 'unnoticed', and even 'passive' in the sense that we don't have to do anything in terms of forced thinking for them to be present. Nothing is required. As we've seen, these 'positives' take care of themselves in the absence of any 'negatives' of self-judgement. And yet, their effect is always dynamic.

- **Awareness** is an automatic, unnoticed, almost invisible quality
- **Being** is an automatic, unnoticed, almost invisible quality
- **Choice** is an automatic, unnoticed, almost invisible quality
- **Confidence** is …
- **The Mastery of Desire** is …
- **Ease** is …
- **Embodiment** is …
- **Creativity** is …
- **Positive (Not) Thinking** is …
- **Being Unselfconscious** is …

'Dominant and Intrusive'

And conversely, all of the characteristics of Fear Consciousness are intrusive, oppressive, dominant, manufactured frustrations.

- **Being in Conclusion** is an intrusive, oppressive, dominant quality
- **Forced Behaviour** is an intrusive, oppressive, dominant quality
- **The Illusion of Choice** is an intrusive, oppressive, dominant quality
- **Lack of Confidence** is …
- **False Desire** is …
- **Stress** is …
- **Disembodiment** is …
- **Negative Thinking** is …
- **Second-Guessing Yourself** is …
- **Being Self-Conscious** is …

The Sub-Paradoxes of Love Consciousness

Remembering the principle of **The Paradox of Love Consciousness**, now that we understand the interchangeable nature of all the characteristics of Love Consciousness, we can see that all the aspects or perspectives of Love Consciousness are Sub-Paradoxes of Love Consciousness. In the moments you *need* Confidence – in a Fear Consciousness sense – then you won't have it, since clearly you aren't confiding in yourself about something! That's The Paradox of Confidence. In the moments when you *need* Choice then you won't have it: The Paradox of Choice. This applies across all the characteristics, and the insight will particularly come in handy when we revisit Happiness in Chapter Five.

We now have intricate and intimate knowledge and understanding of the makeup of any moment of life at the level of our personal Consciousness. Having these insights into the two contrasting qualities should help you get a good feel for them in a really short space of time.

The only caveat I would add to all of this is that in the moment of change, when we are transmuting a Fear Consciousness into a Love Consciousness, what we observe and experience may feel like a mixture of each. In that momentary process state what we feel may flip very quickly from the one state to the other, back and forth. (../anatomy)

No Grey Areas: The Illusion of 'Grey' Consciousness

Have you ever walked up to a person in a grey shirt or skirt, and when you got closer you realised it was a black and white striped shirt or skirt? This is because of the illusion of black and white lines close together looking grey. The same principle applies with moments of our Consciousness. There are only ever aspects of Love Consciousness and Fear Consciousness, but we may have to 'zoom in' to look at each aspect in turn, like the slow-motion tennis ball, to kind of mentally 'stretch out' the 'grey' in our Awareness until we can see each individual aspect of our Consciousness as a black or white line – something that's true for us, or something that's not our truth.

We may have many aspects of both Love Consciousness and Fear Consciousness around a given question, choice, issue or topic. Lots of Awareness of what's true for you, mixed in with lots of conditioned self-judgement, can give the appearance of what we might call 'Grey' Consciousness. But by tuning into each individual aspect – either Awareness of what's true, or a lie – we can see which ones are which. A 'grey area' in terms of what's true for you, is just a load of black and white 'areas' that you've yet to zoom into (or stretch apart) for a close-up look at each individual aspect in turn. We address how to do this in the next chapter.

The Confusion of Self-Acceptance

Self-acceptance is a quality of Love Consciousness, always. Many people seem to have gotten into confusion around this, however, since it relates to the desire to change something about ourselves and the notion that this desire to change is a bad thing because it's a self-rejection: "Why don't you just accept yourself / love yourself the way you are?" A classic example is if we are overweight: Do we accept ourselves for this, or admit to ourselves that actually we don't wish to be this way? A particularly graphic question of Peter Ragnar's which I remember was, "Do you really love the fact that you've got that 'tyre' around your waist?!"

Love Consciousness	Fear Consciousness
Self-Acceptance	Self-Rejection

Desire for Change as a Subset of Total Self-Acceptance

If we wish to change something about ourselves, or even about the world, then honouring that fact is merely a subset of self-acceptance. We accept everything about ourselves, and *as part of that*, one of the things which we wish to accept is that we wish to change something about ourselves.

Anger is another example. We are often taught that it's wrong (or worse, that it's Unconscious – as in unspiritual) to get angry. It's not. A part of accepting ourselves is accepting our anger, or any other emotion.

A Perfect Example of The Illusion of 'Grey' Consciousness

There's also an example of The Illusion of 'Grey' Consciousness here. Regarding the notion of being overweight, the matter of "Do we accept ourselves for this, or admit to ourselves that actually we don't wish to be this way?" is not one aspect of Consciousness, but two. There are two things here to be either accepted or rejected:

1. The fact that we are overweight
2. The fact that we wish to change our weight

And if, for example, we believed that having to accept everything about ourselves meant it was wrong to want to change things, and so judged ourselves for our desire to be slimmer, our relevant 'Permissions' would look like this:

Allowed to be overweight	Yes	
Allowed to want to change our weight		No

In this instance, we simply wouldn't allow ourselves to address our weight. And if we were in total rejection of ourselves for being overweight, and honouring only the fact that we wanted to change this and be slimmer, our Permissions would look like this:

Allowed to be overweight		No
Allowed to want to change our weight	Yes	

This isn't any better than the first combination of Permissions. From this second state of affairs we would try to change our weight – but we likely wouldn't get very far because we would be coming from a place of Reaction, of being in our heads around it, not in our Being; not at one with our Inner Guide but at odds with it. If we were to allow both to be true, we could allow our *Being* to address the fact that we wished to be slimmer. This is the effective state of affairs:

Allowed to be overweight	Yes
Allowed to want to change our weight	Yes

So there we have an example of *both* The Confusion of Self-Acceptance, *and* The Illusion of Grey Consciousness.

Incidentally, there's also a Permission here around being allowed to *not* want to change our weight. Because of the principle that genuine Choice requires freedom of mind, if we're not allowed to *not* want to change our weight, then we're not truly allowed to *want* to change our weight, either.

In the next chapter, 'Clarifying Grey Consciousness' explains how to turn The Illusion of Grey Consciousness into clear 'black and white' Awareness of all that's true for you, and all that's not. (../grey)

The Palate of Consciousness

Like the restaurant connoisseur of fine dining who has a sorbet between meals to clean the palate and approach the next dish with a neutral, and thus unadulterated perception, a person in a Conscious moment approaches the moment with a neutral, and thus unadulterated perception, so their truth arises unimpeded.

I said earlier that "All I want for Christmas is an Awareness-based lifestyle." The Palate of Consciousness defines the basis of the way in which one acquires that. (../palate)

Achieving The Palate of Consciousness Now vs Achieving Things or Outcomes in The Future

The conventional approach to Success is to prioritise achievements which are based on things, behaviours and outcomes, usually in the future. The way of 'Conscious' is to prioritise releasing anything that doesn't allow us to *be* as we are, unadulterated, and let behaviour and outcomes flow from there, because we understand and therefore trust that this is the way of true Success. Sometimes this will include resolving an Unconscious issue around how you will allow yourself to Receive a certain truth in the future.

Love Consciousness	Fear Consciousness
Seeing the wisdom in desiring a clear Palate of Consciousness around the issue now	Concern over how and if we will achieve a certain outcome in the future

Your Boundaries Are Supported!

Given that this principle is about returning to Choice, rather than denying Choice, The Palate of Consciousness aligns us perfectly with our boundaries. It is not about destroying or inhibiting healthy behaviour; it encourages and supports it. Indeed, it is where we *haven't* got Surrender (as a Consciousness) that we compromise our boundaries.

Surrender

Surrender is the key to Success in those areas where we have self-judgements and 'No' Permissions operating, and particularly to the total and complete level of Success that The Palate of Consciousness invites, but the notion of Surrender is largely misunderstood, partly because the word itself doesn't sound so proactive or 'kick-ass'. It actually *is* proactive. Surrender has nothing to do with running away or giving up – quite the opposite. Emphatically so, in fact. It's not the act of surrendering ourselves, but of surrendering our self-judgements *to* our true selves. We get hooked on a thing, and we have to surrender our attachment to that thing in order to make a gain. (../surrender)

This is another 'Banana Split': Surrender as a Consciousness is a totally different thing to surrender as a behaviour. You might well come out fighting. And a person surrendered to Consciousness and their True Self packs more of a 'punch' in life than someone who's in their head. This Binary Table is a representation of whether notions of 'Surrender' to the True Self are interpreted correctly, with Love Consciousness, or misinterpreted with Fear Consciousness:

Love Consciousness	**Fear Consciousness**
We understand it to be surrendering our self-judgements *to* our True Self	We trick ourselves into seeing it as giving up, as failing, as passive, as a negative surrendering *of* our True Self In so doing we remain locked in our False Self and deny ourselves our True Self

Now we have a great insight into the nature of The Binary, of Love Consciousness and Fear Consciousness, let's have a look at how we actually turn Fear Consciousness into Love Consciousness. And we'll also actually do some releasing, some clearings – yes, right here in the book.

www.KissingConsciousness.com/binary

Chapter Four

The Kissing Consciousness Tool

Change

In this chapter we'll address the part of Kissing Consciousness that deals with achieving change, but before we do that let's understand what dynamic change really is.

Time-Triggered Change, Event-Triggered Change and Conscious Change

Imagine you're building a website and you're designing an animation effect. Let's say a smiley face on your website is going to change colour from yellow to red. You have a decision to make as to what will trigger the animation effect:

1. **Time:** Either immediately as the browser loads the page, or after five seconds
2. **Event:** When the user clicks a button, mouses-over an area, or moves the scrollbar, etc.

There's no other possibility for what can trigger the effect … unless the web browser itself wakes up to a will of its own!

This is an important analogy for us to understand the nature of change and what causes or creates real change for human beings in terms of personal development, achievement, self-help and healing. A point in time can trigger a change in Consciousness, which in turn triggers a change in behaviour, and make it *seem* like a proactive, Conscious dynamic of change is happening there and then. However, the reality could well be that our psychology, much like our web page animation, was programmed to cause something to happen at a certain time.

As an example, let's say a person reaches a certain age and changes something. It may look like the dynamic cause of the change is happening in the moment: "Oh look, they're changing! Thank goodness." But they may have *always* had a self-image that when they were at that certain point in life (say 18, 21, 30 or 40 years old) they would become more confident, embark on a journey, settle down, whatever. Nothing actually changed in terms of their 'Permissions', their Flow and Stuckness levels. The change is part of their *already chosen, already programmed* life expressing itself, which may well have been an Unconscious assumption.

Another example: You turn 21 and inherit some money, which you use to start a business. This means you no longer have to interact with a difficult boss you can't handle because you have self-judgements. In this instance, you weren't the trigger for the outward changes. The passing of time which triggered the inheritance was a Time-triggered Change. The inheritance which allowed you to start a business and quit your job was an Event-triggered Change – the 'event' was the inheritance. So you as an individual haven't actually proactively changed anything. You've just rolled with the external events, and the self-judgement which causes the inability to interact with difficult bosses remains.

What I'm interested in defining for our understanding is **Conscious Change**, because this is the specific 'magic' of transmutation: The moment a Fear Consciousness (a self-judgement) is transmuted into Love Consciousness (self-acceptance), breaking the 'programming'. This is REAL change, in proactive power terms. This is an individual really taking on board their power to release the false blocks. All the rest is merely the domino effect.

> "Until you make the Unconscious Conscious, it will
> direct your life and you will call it fate." – Carl Jung

Are we aware what personal development activities are actually causing real change for us, rather than being a mere garnish for the processes of time-triggered and event-triggered change? After the 'pump up' of the seminar, is the sense of confidence that it gave us still there? Or did it fade along with the adrenalin of the event? Would we have found a way to achieve the thing under our own steam, anyway? These seem to me to be potentially useful questions to gain Awareness around. (../change)

What Self-Judgements Are

For a person whose soul's nature is to live authentically and joyfully awake, journeying from Ego-free childhood, through conditioned, Ego-based adulthood, to finally arrive at wise, authentic, free adulthood is like running on nice grass, then through a quagmire or barren wasteland, and then out the other side to nice, new grass again. It's fine to say the grass isn't greener on the other side, but when conditioned self-judgements cause you to pursue a career that you hate, or a relationship that isn't what you really want – likely leading you to compensate with food, drugs or other indulgences which result in a body you don't feel comfortable in – and then you release that self-judgement-based lifestyle, the grass of your genuine choices may well be greener. In fact, the former state of affairs, self-judgement denying Choice, isn't green at all. It's the stale, dusty brown of dead grass. Releasing self-judgements offers a return to the You that you recognise.

'Broad' and 'Narrow' Definitions of Self-Judgement

The Kissing Consciousness definition of what a self-judgement is doesn't just include the obvious, semi-conscious self-judging conversations which may be going on in someone's head and 'self-talk', but also the Unconscious blocks we have to our true selves and their full, natural, unfettered expression. In a wider sense, these are better thought of as *self-constrictions*. This is the Shadow, or our 'Shadow Baggage', that inhibits our full personality and character.

Self-judgements are either semi-conscious or Unconscious. Self-judgements are never fully Conscious, because if we were fully Conscious of what was motivating our thoughts and actions, they would be a Choice, and so couldn't be a self-judgement. There always has to be at least some Unconscious or semi-conscious element which is causing us to not be our True Self. Sometimes our only Awareness or clue that we have a self-judgement influencing us is a sense of its consequences or the false limitations we feel are imposed upon us, and the Unhappiness we feel as a result.

Self-Judgements Are Misnomers

Although we call them *self*-judgements, technically, the one thing they are NOT is *self-*, or *ours*. Self-judgements are actually other people's judgements which are imposed upon us (remember 'The Wake Up Test' from the previous chapter?). There would never, ever be any reason for a person to go out of their way to judge themselves. So there's never, ever been anything even slightly or remotely 'negative' that is You. (../misnomer)

The Grid of Six Self-Judgements

I suspect most people would think of self-judgement as being a single thing which resides in someone's mind and relates to how they see themselves. We're going to expand that perception now, along two dimensions.

Other-Judgement and World-Judgement are Self-Judgements

If we judge other people or the way the world is, it is always a reflection of the fact that we are judging ourselves. So all three of the following are expressions of self-judgement:

- Judgement of ourselves for the way we are
- Judgement of the way the world is
- Judgement of the way other people are

Judgement of the world basically translates as, "My world isn't the way it should be, because of this factor or event, etc., and I'm not okay with that arising in that way", which is a self-judgement, because *our relationship* with the world is a part of who we are, a part of our relationship with *ourselves*. So it is fundamental rejection of reality, and of self.

Similarly, judging that another person "Is not allowed to be the way they are" or "Should not be the way they are" is also a self-judgement, because again it is a fundamental rejection of the way the world happens to manifest.

And if another person is not allowed to be a certain way, that's just another way of saying that *we* are not allowed to be a certain way – even if we might not choose to be. (Remember Willingness?)

Any judgement that life shouldn't be the way it is, is a self-judgement. Without a self-judgement there is no inherent resistance to life being the way it is or to other people being the way they are. We might simply Respond to it, or them, as we see fit. Remember our principle of 'The Confusion of Self-Acceptance', though. Once we accept that things, ourselves and other people are the way they are, we can certainly also accept the fact that we may dislike or wish to change any of these such situations. We can call people out, or challenge their integrity, or identify crimes committed, etc. You don't have to like everybody to unconditionally love (accept) everything that arises about everybody and everything.

Self-Judgements Also Reside in The Body

Science has long-since demonstrated that all Shadow Baggage, all self-judgements, also reside in the physical body, specifically in the nervous system. Self-judgements are not just things of the mind. Any self-judgement also has its manifestation in our nervous system, in our muscles, in our bones, in our cells.

Knowing this is handy. It explains why so many people have thus far had disappointing results in letting go of self-judgements: They have thought of the process solely as an exercise of the mind. Shifting a belief system doesn't necessarily undo the constriction in the nervous system, though, and so doesn't fully turn a 'No' Permission into a 'Yes' Permission. We kind of have an intellectual sense that we *'should'* be allowed a 'Yes' Permission, but it doesn't really exist.

A judgement of other people, or a judgement of the way the world is, is a judgement of ourselves in disguise, and this also resides in our physical body. So in a sense we have a grid of six 'boxes' or 'squares' (what I call 'The Grid of Six') in which self-judgements exist: Three different surface appearances (self, world and other people), multiplied by two different locations (mind and body):

1. Judgement of ourselves, located in our mind
2. Judgement of the world, located in our mind
3. Judgement of other people, located in our mind

4. Judgement of ourselves, located in our body
5. Judgement of the world, located in our body
6. Judgement of other people, located in our body

(../six)

Anatomy of The Creation of a Self-Judgement

Let's look at an example of how a self-judgement may be created, how it exists in the body, and how it might have the superficial appearance of a judgement of other people, or of the world.

Imagine a child sharing his or her dreams with their parents or grandparents, including what they want to do when they grow up. In the middle of a series of well-received statements, the child makes one comment which isn't at all well-received. Maybe the adult is triggered by what the child has said, or has a judgement around that issue – and they let it be known, forcefully chastising the child for that view. The child, shocked, learns that it is not safe for them to be a person who has that desire or opinion, and so it is repressed – buried in the Unconscious part of the mind. From that moment on the child, without realising it, has to pretend to not have that desire, and thus the False Self is created. The child now (Unconsciously) holds a self-judgement about that desire. Confidence becomes lack of Confidence because it's not safe for the child to confide in themselves as to their true desire, and all other qualities in the Love Consciousness column *around this issue* also become Fear Consciousness qualities. This is all about survival and safety: It's safer to become false than to be defiantly true and risk an even stronger attack. As the true opinion is denied, a false opinion inevitably takes its place. Furthermore, at the moment of repression the nervous system of the child's body also has a reaction, and the self-judgement that is created gets stored in the flesh, so to speak, in the nervous system of the child. The child will even carry themselves differently, albeit imperceptibly to the untrained eye.

Now imagine, later on in life, that the child sees another person pursuing a career that the child was not allowed to. By now, the child has developed a story around the desire – to protect their own feelings – and judges the other person against that story. And so we see how a self-judgement gets disguised as a judgement of someone else. In fact, the second person need not even be pursuing the same career as the child wanted to; any person who is free to pursue their chosen career might trigger the child-now-adult – because *they* were not allowed to. Similarly, not being allowed to live in their Choice, they may learn to fundamentally reject the way the world is, because their False Self, shut down Awareness state of being cannot possibly Respond authentically to the way the world is.

And this is where Kissing Consciousness clearings come in. If the danger has passed, the repressed feelings can be felt and the True Self part can be reclaimed. Success is the other side of the avoidance of that feeling; as they say, "Feel it to reveal it."

> "Feeling a feeling is the price we pay for the information and energy which gives us greater self-allowance." – James Blacker

In both major and minor ways, to greater or lesser degrees, everyone in society is collecting these self-judgements around all aspects of life – particularly during childhood, when the impressionable mind is in early development and the chances of telling a judgemental adult where to go are slim to non-existent. Even a defiant child still holds the self-judgement, because they are in Reaction, not Response, not in their Choice and free will, which is why they still suffer and feel lousy. It's no wonder people smoke, drink, do drugs and eat too much, have mental health issues or become homeless. (../causes)

What You Can and Can't Let Go Of

You can let go of anything that is a lie, that isn't true. All self-judgements are lies, and so they can all be let go of. What you can let go of is:

- Anything that's a lie
- This includes a lie that *relates* to a truth

This therefore includes anything that isn't actually your real Choice, or makes you feel heavy or not quite right.

You Can't Let Go of a Truth (or a True Emotion)

What you can't let go of is:

- A truth
- This includes an authentic feeling or emotion

As noted above, though, you can let go of a lie that *relates* to a truth. This means you can let go of your *attachment* to a true emotion, or your *resistance* to one, and thus change the way you experience the emotion. You can't let go of love, because it's not a lie; you can only let go of attachment to love or resistance to it, which is fear, or the illusion of love.

You can also let go of a False Emotion that only exists because you're 'in your head'. When you become Conscious to a self-judgement, the False Emotion that it was generating immediately drops and falls away. Some emotion may remain, but without the Neediness and avoidance quality it had before it's completely different. (../what)

Facilitators and Facilitation

A person who listens to another person and invites them to let go of any self-judgements which become evident is known as a Facilitator. The practice is known as 'facilitation', or 'facilitating someone'. Later in this book you'll hear about the official Kissing Consciousness Facilitator's Programme. We'll also cover being an unofficial Facilitator, so that if you wish to you can help your friends and family, and maybe others, too.

When we choose to let go of things off our own bat, this is known as facilitating ourselves. It's not actually necessary to have another person facilitate us. Letting go of self-judgements (also known as 'releasing', 'doing a release', or 'clearing') is a natural capacity that's simply been forgotten and is now making a timely comeback! Receiving assistance from another person certainly can add an extra dimension, however, and it's understandable that some people may feel that they cannot let things go on their own.

Ultimately, Kissing Consciousness is about empowering you to realise that you have everything you need to facilitate yourself in any given moment. And please recognise that if you get help from another, and clear a 'No' Permission as a result, it was still your empowered, original 'Yes' Permission that allowed you to ask for (Receive) that help in the first place.

Whether to Use a Tool or Not?

Whether to Use a Tool or Respect Being

Before considering the question of how to let things go, we first need to consider whether it's appropriate to attempt to let something go in a given moment, situation or context.

A toothbrush isn't the right tool to mow your lawn with. A lawnmower *is* the right tool, but mowing your lawn right now might not be the right thing to do, if, say, the lawn was only mown yesterday, or your spouse is holding a garden party on it. You wouldn't want to spray your guests with grass cuttings! Similarly, seeking to use tools to let things go without Awareness of whether that's appropriate in the present context can lead to equally incongruous and ridiculous moments. (../use)

The purpose of doing clearings is so that you have more Being to enjoy, *not* to *interrupt* Being. If you are in a state of Love Consciousness, then there's not necessarily a need to let anything go, and the only reason you might do so is if you want to do 'Proactive Processing' (see Further Insights on Letting Go below). The first principle of Kissing Consciousness is to be aware of when you are in Love Consciousness or Fear Consciousness, so you know whether to use a Consciousness Tool, or to respect your authentic Being and Flow in that moment. The last thing you want to do is interrupt your own Flow because you've gotten into the conclusion – the judgement – that every moment requires a clearing tool.

Feeling the need to interrupt a moment of Being (in which there is no need to let go of any self-judgements) by suggesting there's a self-judgement that needs clearing, indicates that we judged that moment as wrong and were not able, not allowed, to Receive it. Judging a moment of Being as wrong has to be motivated by a self-judgement – Fear Consciousness – so we can ask ourselves, "What am I not Willing to Receive?", and then do a clearing to let that go, as we'll be discussing below.

In any moment where you feel that a clearing is required by someone, but it wasn't required by them, then a clearing is still available, just not for what (and maybe whom!) you thought it was! You can clear whatever it was that made you judge a Love Consciousness moment (of yours, or of another's) as if it were a Fear Consciousness moment. Again, what are you not Willing to

Receive? This is quite a common occurrence. People might say something that sounds negative or unwanted or whatever, but actually they're okay with it. This is where grace comes in.

Neediness in Facilitators

One of the most common causes of inappropriate facilitation of other people is Facilitators unwittingly trying to prove their value as a Facilitator. Their Unconscious self-judgement shuts down their Awareness of what is *really* motivating them to attempt to facilitate another person. It is not so much offering or giving someone a service of facilitation as trying to foist it upon them.

Relating as Facing vs Relating as Avoiding

aka: Conscious Relating vs Unconscious Relating

Quite often, exercises and facilitation will involve a person relating their experiences of the past, or their struggles in the present. Remembering The Illusion of Identical Experiences, there are two qualities of Consciousness from which a person may relate their experiences or their story or feelings: One Conscious and one Unconscious … one effective and one disempowered … one acknowledging (facing) the real, underlying, authentic feelings, and one avoiding them.

Love Consciousness	Fear Consciousness
Relating our feelings and/or our story	Relating our feelings and/or our story
Relating as Facing, from our True Self	Relating as Avoiding, from our False Self

A Conscious Facilitator who's on the ball will be in their own Awareness when people are Relating as Avoiding, and choose not to take their False Self at face value (see Chapter Seven for more on this). An Unconscious Facilitator might sit there for hours trying to reason with someone's False Self, and making no progress for the obvious reason that they won't, and can't, because the person isn't being real with themselves, let alone anyone else. Even well-known Conscious Relationship practitioners have been known to relate in such a way as to avoid what they are really feeling, convincing themselves they are Relating as Facing. And usually their audiences can't tell the difference, instead applauding them for their 'vulnerability' when they've actually been in '(Trying to) Control' mode. When you get used to the quality of Love Consciousness, though, you will likely be able to tell the difference very easily.

On rare occasions, people's relating from Fear Consciousness, whilst still Unconsciously motivated, becomes almost Consciously intentionally insincere relating. They might be intentionally deflecting from the real point because they don't want to acknowledge it, perhaps even with dishonest motives. It's not the job of a Kissing Consciousness Facilitator to listen to someone who wants to relate from conclusion and Fear Consciousness – other than to point out that they're doing so and invite them to let it go. Beyond that we have to respect our own time and Choice. You can't force people to choose something, and by the same token you don't have to spend your own time playing a game that you can see is an illusion, a diversionary tactic to avoid the real, underlying truth and feeling. There's no need to entertain Fear Consciousness. We can decline with compassion.

When people *are* Relating as Facing, however, and feeling into the reality, as they will be most of the time, they're *already in* the process of honouring what's true for them. This is Conscious Relating. They may also recognise what lies and falsehoods they can see beyond and let go of. Merely feeling an emotion for the first time releases aspects of Fear Consciousness and self-judgement, so this is valuable work and time well spent. We don't want to interrupt that process by pushing them to do more facilitation – at least not for the moment. We want to allow them to become at one with themselves, with what they're feeling and honouring. Facing one's emotions and feelings is Receiving.

Relating from Conclusion Rather Than Possibility

"We don't live in the past. We don't live in the future." – David Heard

Having let in, acknowledged and honoured our feelings about the past, what is *not* Conscious is if we start to use that past as a reason for why we can't do things now, or keep repeating it as some kind of mantra that keeps us locked in an Unconscious, self-limiting relationship to that story. Whilst the past may be the backdrop, what's relevant to current possibilities is what's true *in the present.*

In this context, true Awareness is about "What is stopping you *now*?" That question then generates different insights and true Awareness. So "I can't do this because in the past xyz happened" might become "I don't feel I can do this because I feel too scared, or too old, or I don't feel ready to (which is fine), or my body has cravings, or …" Okay. At least now we're talking about the immediate issue and can see whether it's possible to do anything about it.

Love Consciousness	Fear Consciousness
Living from a sense of what's possible now	Living in the past

Love-Generating Touch vs Process-Breaking Touch

If a person is feeling into the truth of something in their body, then someone else touching their body, even when it's intended to comfort and help, can have the opposite effect of denying them that process and the valuable, felt, experienced information it brings with it.

There is an art to sensing when, on the one hand, someone's emotional state is too much for them and so physical comfort adds a useful resource benefit to them (Love-Generating Touch), and when, on the other hand, people are able to handle and process their emotions and our attempt to physically comfort them interrupts that process for them (Process-Breaking

Touch). (And of course that includes whether or not we're someone they'd want to be touched by anyway, and other basic principles of consent – see The Boundaries Exercise below.) The merest touch of the body of a person who is feeling into their truth can temporarily repress and chase away that truth for them – because they are now feeling and focused on your touch instead of Receiving their own feelings! If they are experienced at honouring their feelings and appreciate the value of doing so, they likely won't thank you for interrupting that. Fortunately, Awareness is the key to the art of sensing what is required, and if you aren't trusting your Awareness you can always ask them! Offering consoling or supportive touch is yet another example of The Illusion of Identical Experiences. This Specific Binary Table shows whether we were effectively tuned into the other person, and (often) the sincerity of our own motives. Maybe it was ourselves we secretly wanted to comfort, or gain attention or affirmation for. (../touch)

Love Consciousness	Fear Consciousness
Love-Generating Touch	Process-Breaking Touch

You're Allowed to Make Mistakes

Your Awareness will always inform you as to whether it's appropriate to facilitate someone, either yourself or another person. If you're in your Awareness you'll get the decision as to whether to facilitate right, and if you're not in your Awareness you'll get the decision wrong. It's as simple as that. The thing to note is that it's okay to make a mistake in this way. If you aren't allowed to make mistakes we'll do a clearing on this shortly. Here's a Specific Binary relating to using tools:

Love Consciousness	Fear Consciousness
You'll make a Conscious decision as to whether to facilitate yourself or someone else	You'll make an Unconscious decision as to whether to facilitate yourself or someone else

How Do You Let Something Go?

"How do you let something go? You notice if it's at odds with your truth." – James Blacker

How do you let go of a self-judgement? You become aware of it. You become aware that it's a lie, that it's not your truth.

And remember that self-judgements also reside in the body's nervous system … so you become aware that it's a lie, that it's not true for you, whilst simultaneously being aware of your Choice to let it go, and being aware of your Choice to allow your body permission to let it go also.

So you can see that all of that was done with Awareness. No forced actions or even forced thought-based actions were involved.

Adding Awareness to a self-judgement is like shining light on a Shadow. That's why when we do Kissing Consciousness facilitation seminars, all we are doing all day long is bringing Awareness to that which isn't true, simply by bringing a focus of attention to it, and using questions to invite the release of the blocks. It's as simple as bringing Awareness to the self-judgement, and to your Choice, and an automatic process does the rest.

In the briefest moment that we *observe* a self-judgement-based thought, rather than *identifying* with it, we release its hold over us. In a moment in which Life presents you with a self-judgement:

<u>**Love Consciousness**</u>	<u>**Fear Consciousness**</u>
You identify with the person who is *aware of* the self-judgement	You identify with the self-judgement
"I am aware of that self-judgement-based thought"	"I am that self-judgement-based thought"

Consider how easy it is to pick up a piece of paper from the floor next to you, compared to picking up a piece of paper that you're standing on. You can't simultaneously identify with a self-judgement and release it (pick up a piece of paper you're standing on). Releasing happens in the moment that you realise that the self-judgement was never your true identity.

In addition to merely talking about our self-constrictions, approaches such as The Sedona Method, founded by the late Lester Levenson, and Access Consciousness, founded by Gary Douglas, use question-based tools to prompt a new choice of freedom. I believe this proactive question-based approach is a more effective way of addressing our perceived limitations, and suspect that in future the whole personal development industry will work this way.

Gary Douglas also noted that in order to let something go, it's more effective to get a sense of the energy of that thing to arise first, so you can better tune into whatever it is you're letting go. In alignment with that insight, Douglas arranged the wording used in Access Consciousness' question-based tools so that the focus of the perceived limitation is mentioned before the invitation to release or change it. Kissing Consciousness also adopts this approach of arranging the wording of the question to let the energy arise first, ready to be released.

The Kissing Consciousness Tool

Kissing Consciousness uses a two-part clearing tool to release self-judgements. Each part is a question – and invitation – and the second question is dependent upon the answer to the first question being 'Yes'. Here is the tool:

Would you like to let that go?

And (if so):

Would you like to ask your body if it would like to let that go?

The 'Body Question' is not always necessary, however, we usually start with the default position that we *do* use it, particularly for people who are new to releasing. If I am facilitating you and I invite you to let go of something, and I can see that you have let go of it fully, not just as an intellectual awareness, but that you have embodied the release, then I quite possibly won't ask you the second question. The release it invites may have already happened spontaneously as part of the first question.

There are some people who, when you invite them to let something go, automatically seem to understand that this is something which involves the body. If you were facilitating them, and you heard them give a deep breathing out sigh, and saw their shoulders lower and their eyes half-close, it might be a bit incongruent to ask them if they'd like to ask their body to let it go. Possibly you just saw it happen right in front of your eyes! But often, and particularly early on, people aren't always aware that letting something go is a full mind and body activity, so it's always well to follow up one with the other.

More importantly, the Body Question may release a different block *physically* that the first question doesn't. I have seen many people who have had a shift – even a physical shift – from my asking them if they'd like to let something go, and then, a minute later, a totally different shift from asking their body if it would like to let something go around that very same thing. The body may have its own, very different idea of what it would like to let go of physically from its nervous system than you do and may be aware of other self-constrictions that you aren't. So if in any doubt at all, you might like to use both. It's the default way. Of course, Awareness is always the guide: If my Awareness says "Ask", or "Don't ask", then I listen to that and follow that. You can apply the same principle to using the tool for yourself.

Are You a 'Natural' or a Learner?

People fall into two groups: Those who know they are able to release instinctively, and those who "Don't know how." (The latter group are also able to release instinctively; they just don't know it, aren't Receiving it.) Some people, when I ask them, "Would you like to let that go?", say, "Ah yeah, thanks, phew, uuungh!", and I can see them visibly release those tensions from their body, usually with a sigh or deep sound. They understand that the question is an invitation to let something go, and that it can be released from the body. Other people, when I ask them, "Would you like to let that go?", get into conversation. They say, "I'd like to! (… but)", or they say, "Yes", and I can see they're still in their head. They haven't realised that the question itself is an invitation to a Conscious Choice, and for something physical in the nervous system to happen. Releasing isn't a conversation, it's an *invitation* to make a decision.

> "When I ask people if they would like to 'let that go' I'm not making chit-chat!" – James Blacker

The invitation to let something go holds within it a question about your own intention. That *'intentionality'*, your free will, your Choice, is the necessary element, once there is Awareness of the self-judgement. So the first task in making The Kissing Consciousness Tool available to you as a tool for change is to find out whether you're currently a 'Natural' or a Learner, and if necessary, to help you to have an actual experience of doing a Conscious and physical release. Once you 'get it', then you're equipped for life.

Going Straight to The Body Question

As you get used to releasing, when you recognise that you want to release something, you may wish to do as I do, and go straight to the Body Question, asking the body – as also representing the Subconscious Mind – if it will let something go. So I often ask myself:

Would I let that go?

I am asking that directly of my Subconscious Bodymind. This also implies the freedom to clarify or let go of anything in my Consciousness that I may be Unconscious to. If I'm feeling a relationship with my Subconscious Mind, my Inner Guide, I might even talk to it as a 'you' instead of 'I':

Would you let that go?

This translates as:

Would you (my body, which I also consider to be my Subconscious Mind) let that go?

If in a given moment I'm identifying myself (thinking of myself) as my whole self, thus appreciating the Subconscious Bodymind as part of 'me', I might use "I." It really doesn't matter; it's all about how it feels for you in each moment. Personally, I do both. So you might notice that you're nervous or Self-Conscious in a particular situation, and just say to yourself:

Would I let that go?

... with a Willingness to let any tensions drop away from your thoughts and physical body. The brain is a part of the physical body, too, so the Body Question also allows for the Subconscious to release things in and from the brain.

Our use of these questions often evolves very quickly to the point that we don't feel it necessary to ask the question of ourselves out loud, but are aware of the question in our head. Kissing Consciousness calls this Silent Releasing.

You Don't Do Consciousness! You Let it Do You!

There is no need for the forcing of 'doing' anything. There is no "How do I do that?" It does itself once fuelled by Awareness. Awareness does it. In fact, the whole process is one of Awareness:

1. Awareness that you're operating under self-judgement
2. Awareness that it's your deeper truth and Choice to allow yourself to let it go (then your Consciousness may automatically shift)
3. Awareness that you choose to allow your body to let go of whatever it is happy to let go of (then the body automatically does as it sees fit)
4. ... all leading to Awareness of the shifts (probably) happening as a result of these Awarenesses

All of that happens in a split-second, a single moment. Two or three moments at the most. You can observe the whole process, once you realise what it is that you're observing. The trick is in allowing that Awareness process to do its thing.

The Elusive Emotion

'The Elusive Emotion' is *the* block which is undone when a self-judgement is released. When we are operating under the influence of self-judgement, there is some feeling that we are not feeling into, that we're avoiding, dissociated from. Kissing Consciousness calls this 'The Elusive Emotion'. If you're avoiding The Elusive Emotion you're unwittingly fighting against your own Conscience.

In the moment when Awareness replaces a self-judgement, this feeling is felt into. It may not always be deep or even particularly noticeable, depending upon both the person's Permissions around emotional strength, and the significance *to that person* of the topic being released. In fact, in some instances some people may not even notice it at all, but it is always there, because it is a shift, and that inevitably involves the body and the mind somehow. In such instances, it could even be thought of as 'The Elusive Awareness'. (../elusive)

> **Principle:** If you haven't realised that you can let go of something, you haven't fully felt into it authentically.

The Kissing Consciousness concept of The Elusive Emotion works in tandem with the core clearings of Emotional Infinity, which is covered later in this chapter. The clearings for Emotional Infinity clear the way for us to have no fear of feeling or facing The Elusive Emotion. This in turn allows us to operate in line with The Paradox of Love Consciousness. If someone is stuck, the first question is always:

> **What's The Elusive Emotion that you're avoiding feeling, that you're not letting in?**

... and, of course, followed up with:

> **Would you like to let (your resistance to feeling) that go?**

> **Would you like to ask your body if it would like to let that go?**

The Elusive Emotion question alone usually leads people to feel into the feeling, as the moment it's asked they realise what they've been shutting out. Even in these instances, though, the Body Question can still add additional value.

When I'm incongruent due to avoiding emotions, yet I notice the fact of my incongruence and being at odds with myself, I usually say to my Subconscious: "Okay, what do you want me to feel, or acknowledge?" So here is a second version, a variation of The Elusive Emotion Tool, that we can direct to our own Subconscious Bodymind:

Okay, what do you want me to feel that I'm avoiding?

And because feelings can have a mental as well as physical quality, we might also feel it necessary to ask:

What truth do you want me to face, or acknowledge?

Active Letting Go and Passive Letting Go

If you really don't want to feel into the feeling you're avoiding feeling, you can at least still do a clearing by asking yourself to let something go, and see what changes may happen organically over the coming days and weeks just from that request. Kissing Consciousness calls this 'Passive Clearing', or 'Passive Releasing', or 'Passive Letting Go', and it can work just as well.

Grief

Feeling into The Elusive Emotion may well be followed by crying or an emotional release of built up resistance. It's perfectly natural to experience some form of *grief* when we release something – to cry, or be sad, or angry, or whatever. To acknowledge a self-judgement is to acknowledge the period of time that we've been operating without being allowed to be ourselves in that respect.

If you have a self-judgement that prevents you from facing the fact that a relationship is over, or that a job opportunity or relationship that you had your heart set on is not going to go your way after all, then releasing the blocks to acknowledging this is also going to return a potential element of grief. But there may also be an element of excitement, as the blocks no longer hold power over you and you regain your inner strength and freedom.

Fear as Excitement in Disguise

What if the fear that you have as a resistance to something is actually excitement in disguise? The notion that fear may be excitement that's simply been interpreted differently is a common one, perhaps originated by the late British management journalist, Robert Heller, when he said, "Fear is excitement without breath." Something that's true about you is experienced as follows:

Love Consciousness	Fear Consciousness
Excitement	Fear

In releasing Fear Consciousness we gain a piece of ourselves back. It's natural that this may be accompanied by a sense of excitement. We can use this as a question tool by asking:

What if your fear is excitement in disguise?

And we might further enhance it by following it up with The Kissing Consciousness Tool:

Would you like to let go of anything that doesn't allow you to experience it as excitement?

And would you like to ask your body if it would like to let that go?

Merely Intellectualised Letting Go vs Embodied Letting Go

aka: Intellectualised (or Theoretical) Permissions vs Embodied Permissions, Intellectualised Freedom vs Embodied Freedom

This section identifies the difference between intellectualised freedom from a self-judgement and actual, embodied, *real* freedom from that self-judgement.

Intellectualised Letting Go is the Awareness that a self-judgement belief is false. If you clear something in this way you no longer believe the lie that you shouldn't be allowed something, are incapable of it, or that it's not your true identity. You're ready to be aware of it as *theoretically* being something that *should* and *can* be allowed for you. But you're not ready to *be* it. Or better said, your body and your full, deep self isn't ready for you to be it. Embodied Letting Go, however, is exactly that: The embodiment of the Permission to choose, do or be something – total freedom around that issue, to the point that it doesn't even distract the mind. So there are essentially two different self-judgements which can be released. If we only Intellectually Let Go of a blockage, our Permissions look like this:

Allowed to intellectually recognise an ability	Yes	
Allowed to embody (Receive) that ability		No

A person who intellectually becomes aware of the lie of a self-judgement breathes slightly easier as a result and will have a certain shift in their nervous system, so there is still some form of release from the physical body. But it will not be to the greater degree they might experience if they did Embodied Letting Go. Crucially, it will only allow them to cognitively *understand* their capacity for freedom around whatever issue it is, not *live* it. So Intellectualised Letting Go isn't really letting go. It's not actually shifting the thing.

This is why people often say, "Oh, I thought I'd cleared that belief (or wound, self-judgement, baggage or material)!" In this scenario, your Consciousness is quite likely continually re-raising the issue in your mind in an attempt to invite you to let it go from your body and nervous system, and even your physical brain's wiring, in addition to just clearing it from your mental beliefs and conclusions. As a society, we don't know to ask the body to let go of a self-judgement. We don't even know to think about it. We barely have any Awareness of our natural ability to release at all, but what little Awareness there is mostly relates to mentally letting go of things. We really need to establish the notion of asking and allowing the body to release self-judgements until it's as familiar to our culture as the alphabet.

> "Bottom line is that the study of human psychology has been far too cognitive and doesn't understand the bodymind. Similarly, all the work on consciousness tends to see only that which we are aware of and think about, which is the top 5% (or however many). The brain is evolutionarily recent." – Jon Freeman

Cognitive understanding is optional, and if it comes at all, it typically comes *after* the release of a self-judgement. This is in contrast to the notion that cognitive understanding needs to happen *before* a self-judgement is released, in order to make it possible. If you are aware that something is your genuine Choice, and you have a nervous system that can handle the idea of you allowing yourself to Receive it, why on earth would you need to cognitively, intellectually understand it? More to the point, why would you *insist* on doing so before you were Willing to Receive the benefit? Needing to understand something in order to allow yourself to have it is a self-judgement. The curiosity as to how it works might be optional, and reasonable, but to deny oneself because something is not cognitively understood is a self-judgement. Jon Freeman, the author of 'The Science of Possibility', explains: "I don't think that you need to know why any of the techniques work. It does sometimes help to know what is underneath what you clear, because it may take you to something of value. But it doesn't matter that much because whatever else needs to come up will do so sooner or later." As he also often remarks, "The brain is the most important organ in the body, according to the brain", akin to the old Emo Philips joke, "I used to think that the brain was the most wonderful organ in my body. Then I realized who was telling me this."

Anywhere you've bought into the lie of having to cognitively understand your wounds and false limitations in order to benefit from releasing them, would you like to let that go?

And would you like to ask your body if it would like to let that go?

A 'Non-Nervous' Nervous System

A Non-Nervous Nervous System is your fulfilled potential for everything. Quite apart from its obvious benefits, having a non-nervous nervous system is what *allows* Success, making it both possible, and automatic. As we've seen, the alternative to a nervous system that lets you be you is Frustration, which is the opposite of Success. Everybody, pretty much, is aware that they'd *like* a million dollars, or that they'd *like* to be slimmer, or that they'd *like* a great intimate relationship, or even that they'd *like* to get up on stage, but the real key is not whether they are capable of *wanting* it, (anyone can always want something), or even whether they can get their head round the idea (which is indeed necessary), but most crucially, whether they can get their *body* around the idea. This is not (yet) often taught in personal development and self-help, but it is indeed the way of Success.

- If you ask Life for a million dollars, you require a millionaire's nervous system in order to be able to Receive it
- If you wish to be slim, you require a nervous system that allows you to flow naturally with your hunger, thirst and desire for physical activity
- If you wish to have a true love relationship you require the nervous system of a person who is able to Receive one

The only reason the body took on the self-constrictions of its (your) nervous system in the first place was to keep you safe. As an organic system with no Ego it has no interest in doing anything other than maximising its Life Force – your Life Force – just as a flower or a tree does. So when the body is invited to let something go, it's generally going to be more than willing to let go of that shut down effect in its cells and muscles, its bones and tissue, unless there's a bloody good reason not to. If there is a reason, it's generally safety – emotional, psychological or physical.

The brain, unlike the mind, is a physical thing, and so when the body releases self-judgement from its nervous system, this includes changing the wiring in the brain which had previously associated the 'No' Permission with the subject matter, making it into a 'Yes' Permission. Jon Freeman observes: "Not just in the brain. Neuro-endocrine chemistry, release of held muscle tensions, shifts in the acupuncture meridians (which is how EFT [Emotional Freedom Technique] works) and probably a lot more. I don't think that we have got beyond 1 or 2% of the potential understanding in these areas."

'The Quickening'

As kids we watched the 'Quickening' process that Connor MacLeod went through in the film 'Highlander' when he becomes immortal, body shaking as electric energy is unleashed in it. As an adult, I'm struck by how very similar to that movie scene it is when I do clearings, asking to let go of stuff in my Consciousness, or putting Awareness into my body that has been Unconscious for decades; this is exactly the kind of feeling I experience, as electricity pulses and my body realigns itself. The experience may be somewhat different from person to person. One way or another, we're talking about the trapped nervous system unleashing itself. It really is a remarkable phenomenon. I can't think of any other name for it. 'Transmutation', I suppose it is. You can see a video of me demonstrating the mind-body relationship and the energy in it at the link below.

www.KissingConsciousness.com/bodymind

You Can Release a Notion, or Even Just an Energy or Feeling

This leads us to yet another great, empowering freedom. You don't have to have an intellectual understanding of what it is you want to let go of, you can just 'say' to yourself, "That!"

What if you didn't have to intellectually understand anything in order to heal it, let it go? Or didn't even have to name something in order to release it? What if it's just an energy, a sense, which you can choose to let go of?

You can just get an intuitive sense or feeling of the energy in your mind, or in your Awareness, in your body even, and know it as "That!", and simply release *that*! You can word The Kissing Consciousness Tool accordingly, for example:

I'd like to let go of *'that'*, please!

Body, would you like to let *'that'* go?

Proactive Presencing: Stepping into The Real You

'Stepping into' in this context merely means 'allowing Awareness of'. This process is a proactive 'step' (Choice) into the space of a 'No' Permission. You say to yourself (in your Awareness, although out loud will do), that you're choosing to be Confident around something which is currently a 'No' Permission. At a Consciousness level, you (metaphorically) step into the space of the 'No' Permission. As you do that, all of the internal representations – thoughts, feelings, etc., – of that 'No' Permission will naturally arise in your Conscious Mind and body.

And then what you do is 'hold Presence' to that – you allow it all to arise, without resisting any of it. In essence, you're taking a stand in defiance of the 'No' Permission by refusing to React to it from Unconscious Fear Consciousness – and note that this refusal to React Unconsciously also includes needy desperation to succeed in the process. And as you *observe* it all, without identifying with it, you become aware that you'd like to let it go, and that you give your body permission to let it go, too. This is simply asking the two questions of The Kissing Consciousness Tool at the Awareness level. And you become aware that your Choice is to step into the real You, the "Yes' Permission You', so to speak.

And if it passes, all those internal representations and bodily feelings drop away and you automatically step into the image and embodiment of yourself honouring what's true for you, and you stay in that feeling, until you have no resistance to feeling it. By staying in this process you are reclaiming the energy of the new you, which is also actually the real you that never got a chance to show up before. What I'm describing here is what I described in the previous chapter as 'Nature's NLP': You let something go, and whatever internal representations of the mind, bodily feelings, vision, impulses, instincts, imagination or sense of power is required for you to achieve or do something, arise naturally and automatically as a result of the newly cleared Consciousness and nervous system. You don't need to think about or concern yourself with how to do 'Nature's NLP'. You just let go of the 'No' Permissions and what remains takes care of itself. That's the beauty of it. That's the natural, unfettered way of your True Self.

Once Proactive Presencing is successfully completed, the individual gets what I call 'The Divine Desire Power Rush' (see below).

A Mere Flick of the Consciousness

It may seem like there's a lot of detail here, and that the process of letting go of a self-judgement takes time or is tricky – it doesn't and it's not. Letting go actually takes the moment of Awareness, so is barely even measured in time. The feeling and honouring of emotions that arise may take a little while longer, but with practice even they can arise and pass at the speed of non-thought.

I promised earlier that we'd do a clearing on making mistakes:

Anywhere you've picked up self-judgements that you're not allowed to make mistakes, would you like to let that go?

And would you like to ask your body if it would like to let that go?

I describe releasing as a 'flick of the Consciousness', the Awareness equivalent of a flick of the wrist. I'd like to give you an experience of that now. Become aware of your thoughts. As you do that you may recognise that you're free of them, and so can choose in spite of them. Your body doesn't need to move (though it may react) and you don't need to think anything (though you may become aware of new thoughts in that moment). You just become aware to yourself in that moment. We're talking about something that happens in less than half a second. As you do that, freedom of Choice comes flooding back in. Now, can you 'flick your Awareness' several times within three or four seconds? (../flick)

"Has it Gone?"

After The Kissing Consciousness Tool is used to release a self-judgement, we might ask the question, "Has it gone?" to see if the letting go has worked, or more likely if we sense that it hasn't – e.g. a person's face still looking stressed and doubtful, lacking in Confidence.

There are two main reasons why letting go doesn't happen:

1. **Avoidance:** The person trying to do the release is in a state of Fear Consciousness, unknowingly avoiding feeling The Elusive Emotion, and therefore in the wrong state of Consciousness to release anything.

2. **Safety:** The person's Subconscious Mind doesn't consider it safe to release the fear.

The following two Kissing Consciousness processes address each of these respectively, and we'll look at each of these in turn:

1. Unlocking The Moment
2. The "Has it Gone?" Process

The moment always needs to be 'unlocked' for a clearing to work, however, to save time we usually assume that the moment is unlocked, and only circle back to use the Unlocking The Moment process if it is needed. If a clearing question doesn't work, Unlocking The Moment is always the process to try first.

If the moment is 'unlocked', or then becomes 'unlocked' through the process, and the clearing still doesn't work, or there's some kind of obvious block, then we move on to the second process, the "Has it Gone?" Process. This doesn't always provide a 'Yes'. Sometimes the deeper self has its reasons for not being ready to let something go.

There's also a third possibility as to why something may not have cleared, and that is that it's not really that person's real Choice. Ask for help to stop smoking when you don't really want to stop, and no Facilitator can help you with that. It's impossible to facilitate someone against their Choice. In this instance we might then just let go of whatever self-judgements caused us to think we *'should'*.

Unlocking The Moment

aka: Unlocking The Consciousness, Unlocking The Desire

"It all starts with Unlocking The Moment." – James Blacker

What a verb is to a noun, Unlocking The Moment is to The Paradox of Love Consciousness. Unlocking The Moment puts The Paradox of Love Consciousness *into action.* The Paradox of Love Consciousness is the insight or teaching, and Unlocking The Moment is the tool for letting go that goes with it.

Again, because of The *Primacy* of Consciousness, we're looking for that action to be a Consciousness Act of Awareness, not a thought-based behaviour or physical activity-based action. To refresh our memories, The Paradox of Love Consciousness states: "The moment you stop fearfully needing to jump across to the Love Consciousness path, it automatically moves itself underneath your feet."

Love Consciousness	Fear Consciousness
Not minding whether you're in a state of Love Consciousness or Fear Consciousness	Having attachment to being in a state of Love Consciousness and resistance to being in a state of Fear Consciousness

How to Unlock The Moment

"We were all born with an unconditional relationship to life. We then learned a conditional relationship to life through self-judgement." – James Blacker

Unlocking a moment is achieved by moving from the first of the following states, to the second:

1. It's *not* okay to not get some thing or some outcome ("I'm not okay with this!")
2. It *is* okay to not get some thing or some outcome ("I'm okay with this.")

In this context, "not okay" means fundamentally resistant to the very arising of reality. To resist reality itself is to reject ourselves. Let's just confirm how a Binary of Unlocking The Moment looks:

Love Consciousness	Fear Consciousness
Unlocked Moment, Unlocked Desire, Unlocked Consciousness; your Consciousness is Unlocked	Locked Moment, Locked Desire, Locked Consciousness; your Consciousness is Locked in Fear Consciousness

Love Consciousness	Fear Consciousness
Conscious (of current motives)	Unconscious (of current motives)

To Unlock The Moment we must release the state of Fear Consciousness *with regard to the thing we wish to achieve or have*, and thus become in a state of Love Consciousness about it. You may remember this quote from the last chapter, regarding being in your power:

"Being in self-acceptance the gates of your power are open. Being in self-judgement the gates of your power are closed." – James Blacker

This applies to releasing anything. Being in your power to release self-judgements is merely a subset of being in your power generally. You can only let something go while you're in a state of Love Consciousness.

Let's say you want a new job, or for your ex to get back with you, or to be fitter and get out of breath less. To be locked around that desire is for it not to be okay that you don't get it, to have a self-judgement – of yourself, of life – if you had to be without it. The resistance and shut down Awareness inherent in that self-judgement prevents you from being in an effective state to release a self-judgement. It's like trying to drive a car with the handbrake on.

"No effective processing happens on 'Planet *Should*'." – James Blacker

When we release the 'handbrake', i.e. the resistance to 'not getting', we can Receive ourselves and our power fully. If it's not okay not to have something, then you inevitably *have* to try and achieve it from your Fear Consciousness, from your state of being at odds with yourself. That is neither empowered nor effective. When it is okay not to have something, you can seek to achieve it via your self-love, in tune with your Inner Guidance, in the state of being at one with yourself: In your power.

Unlocking The Moment still uses the same Kissing Consciousness Tool for releasing attachment, just applied to a different self-judgement: Not the self-judgement that says you aren't allowed something, but the self-judgement that says you aren't Willing to accept yourself if you don't get it. This is, again, Unconsciously avoiding The Elusive Emotion. As all Fear Consciousness is False Self and self-judgement, the Unwillingness to face an emotion is also caused by a self-judgement, and so can be released, too. We use The Kissing Consciousness Tool to unlock a moment as follows:

> **Anywhere you're not allowing yourself to be okay with not getting this outcome, would you like to let that go?**

And if so:

> **Would you like to ask your body if it would like to let go of anything that's not allowing you to be okay with not getting this outcome?**

And whilst there may be a grief response (such as crying) to that release, that is an empowered response – you've got your Consciousness back. This is not mentally telling ourselves that we don't *care* about the desire or outcome, but genuinely not *minding* because we have released the Charge around it. There is no emotion or feeling we are avoiding.

The X-Factor in Understanding Letting Go

Before we go on, let's look at a neat way of remembering and understanding the two key factors of letting go, by using an 'X' or criss-cross on the Binary Table below. Imagine drawing a diagonal line between the two positive statements, and another between the two negative statements: (../x)

<u>Love Consciousness</u>	<u>Fear Consciousness</u>
Nothing in this column (state) can be released	Everything in this column (state) can be released
You can release anything whilst in this column (state), i.e. with Love Consciousness	You cannot release anything whilst in this column (state), i.e. with Fear Consciousness

'Infinitize The Opposite'

"If it's not okay for you to not get something, then your relationship to life is skewed, and like a prison." – James Blacker

If, upon realising that we are attached to a certain outcome (and resistant to its *opposite*), we then use The Kissing Consciousness Tool to release that attachment and resistance, then the moment may well unlock naturally and effortlessly as a result. (And if it does, we have also *automatically* 'Infinitized The Opposite', probably without noticing).

If it doesn't release automatically, however, then there is a more 'manual' process we can go to as a backup, called **'Infinitizing The Opposite'**. To do this, we *'infinitize'* the notion of the opposite of the aim or desire. By 'infinitize' I mean 'make it into infinity' (in our imagination and Consciousness).

In this process, we imagine never having the thing we desire or wish to happen. We imagine how it would be and feel to stay in the experience of not having it *forever*, and we allow ourselves to be present to (we 'hold Presence to') that feeling and Consciousness until we no longer have any Charge around it, until we no longer have any resistance to not having it. *Or* ... if the issue relates to something we want *not* to happen, or something that we want to *end*, we hold Presence to the idea that it will never end, until we have no resistance to that notion. Either scenario is likely to bring up many feelings and resistance, and this is where The Elusive Emotion comes in again. Whenever we are in a 'Locked Moment' there is inevitably something we're avoiding feeling or being, and facing that Elusive Emotion behind the avoidance is the key.

Because we've been brought up with the lie that we can only handle half of our emotions – the 'good' ones – there will be a lot of these scenarios for people to release, all of which can be easily dispelled with Awareness, once they realise their (and everyone's) underlying emotionally competent nature.

Let's take that example of wanting to get back with an ex-partner. To 'Infinitize The Opposite', you imagine what it would be and feel like if you *never* got back with them, until both your Consciousness and your body can be totally okay with that. Only then can you 'live in the moment' about it. This is naturally going to involve feeling into some feelings which had previously shut down and been buried. All of the feelings and emotions which relate to that desire will poke their heads up for attention, acknowledgement and honouring. But this is the whole point. We *want* that Charge to arise –

so we can process it to clear it. By feeling those feelings, you get your power back, as those feelings had been controlling you throughout the time you were Unconsciously or semi-consciously resisting feeling them … and usually also causing you to give your power to that ex-partner! (../infinitize)

The Divine Desire Power Rush

aka: Freedom for Dynamic Activity

People may initially think that Unlocking The Moment means giving up on what they desire, or that it will distract them from their focus. Not so. Actually, the freedom created is like opening your metaphorical kite to the wind, as the true Desire that you have for that thing, if it was ever real and true – *or for whatever is true for you in its place* – comes rushing into and through you from that place of infinite power in you: Love Consciousness. Before this, you were trying to drive it from your Fear Consciousness. Upon Unlocking The Moment, the internal feedback message, "You aren't allowed this!", is naturally replaced by the sense that you are being guided to achieve it if at all possible. And if it – or whatever is true for you in its place – is possible, you feel you are about to be driven into the heart of your desired goal, almost against your will, like a hurricane drives a blade of grass into a tree.

The Divine Desire Power Rush is the name I've given to the phenomenon of the arising energetic quality that you get when you let go of a self-judgement. It is your basic nature being unleashed in support of your true desires. This is the same thing that I believe Sri Sri Ravi Shankar was talking about when he said that "Turbulence always seeks peace, yet peace seeks dynamic activity." We can 'translate' that into Kissing Consciousness speak as "Fear Consciousness always seeks Love Consciousness, yet Love Consciousness seeks dynamic activity." If we interpret this into The Binary, we may consider 'turbulence' to be the experience of self-judgement, and peace as self-acceptance.

Love Consciousness	Fear Consciousness
Peace	Turbulence

Love Consciousness	Fear Consciousness
… Seeks dynamic activity	… Is seeking peace

In any moment of Fear Consciousness we are, of course, seeking to achieve the state of Love Consciousness – we are attempting to heal and ease our pain and be (become) at peace. Yet if and when we return to a state of Love Consciousness, what flows from that state is dynamic activity. It can be dynamic stillness or movement, silence or sound, but always the quality is dynamic.

Unlocking The Moment is the key that gifts you the inner peace – and thus the dynamism – to pursue a genuine Desire *effectively*. The truth of the Desire is what drives itself and you forward, the same way gravity drives a stream downhill or a released object to the ground. The quality of its own truth is what makes it the new destiny that's 'zeroed in on', because it always was Nature's intention, and now there's no human mind (or compromised nervous system) getting in the way of that, you get a rush! (../rush)

Principle: You can allow the energy of truths, of Being, to achieve what's true for you.

Just because you've released all attachments to achieving something doesn't mean it's possible. Nothing we do here makes the impossible possible, we're merely maximising our *allowance* of what *is* possible. People are never really bothered by what's genuinely impossible for them, anyway. It's the false blocks to what *is* possible that Frustrate and sadden us.

Principle: Consciousness doesn't offer a future guarantee that you'll get anything.

Faking Unlocked Consciousness: 'The Futile Paradox Hack'

Sometimes people observe that they don't get The Divine Desire Power Rush that they would hope for. They haven't really Unlocked The Moment, but have merely paid lip service to it in their head, perhaps trying (in vain) to trick their own Conscience and Consciousness so that they can have the thing they want from a place of attachment, without really giving up the attachment to it. (Or as Alan Watts might say, after people realise they need to stop 'Trying to Control', "You try 'not trying' – trying to get it that way!")

You haven't created a genuine freedom of Consciousness around the thing, and so your (lack of) power is still coming from your 'Trying to Control' Ego mind and Fear Consciousness. I call this 'The Futile Paradox Hack', because you're trying to 'hack' – cheat – The Paradox of Love Consciousness by pretending that you're not attached to something (trying to 'not try'). It's a common phenomenon and futile because Fear Consciousness is Fear Consciousness, no matter what we pretend. If you realise you've done this, then you need to release the attachment and face The Elusive Emotion. Then you have a real feeling to feel. (../hack)

The Paradox of Unlocking The Moment

aka: The Paradox of Letting Go, The Paradox of Freedom to Fail, The Paradox of Surrender

Half-Unlocking The Moment

People are very often encouraged to allow it to be okay however they are, however they show up in the world, and to not judge themselves for not being or not having or not doing certain things. All well and good.

In many of these instances, though, the very things they're encouraged to not judge themselves for not being or not having will be things that it's their truth to be, or their true desire to have, such as Confidence, or connection, or prosperity, or a healthy, fit body, or anything else. Nobody's personality is lack of Confidence, for example. And this presents a hidden trap, a paradox as to what truly, *fully* being okay with 'not having' or 'not being' something is.

The mathematical or logical operator ≠ means 'does not equal' or 'not equal to'. Here's the paradoxical truth:

Not okay to have ≠ Okay not to have

For ultimately:

Okay not to have = Okay to have

Making it 'okay not to have something', or 'okay not to be something', is crucial and has value. But if it's 'not okay to have something', can it *truly* be 'okay *not* to have something'? No, not really, because there will still be Charge around the matter; our 'okay not to have' cannot be coming from freedom. If you aren't really free to Receive something then you aren't entirely free to be in self-acceptance and genuine Choice around being okay with *not* Receiving it. In dating and courtship, for example, if you can't hear a 'No' when you invite someone out (i.e. fear of rejection), then you can't really, truly Receive a 'Yes', either. And vice versa. To be okay not to have something and to be okay *to* have something are two sides of the same coin. You can't put one side of a coin in your pocket without also putting the other side in your pocket.

If a moment is locked, there are two self-judgements to release, rather than one:

1. Unlock the Moment: Let go of the self-judgement that you're not okay without something
2. Unlock the Non-Permission: Let go of the self-judgement that you're not allowed something

'Permissions' for being only half-way through the process of Unlocking The Moment look something like this:

Intellectually Conscious of the notion that you can allow yourself to stop judging yourself for not having or being something – which will include a *somewhat* embodied freedom	Yes
Allowed to stop judging yourself at either a Consciousness level, or an embodied level	No
Allowed to have or be the thing	No

Assuming that you're not allowed some desired outcome, which we'll call 'x', then:

Principle: Your relationship to x *isn't* that you're okay not having it, your relationship to x is that you *need* to *not* have it – because you're not allowed *to* have it.

Without this 'Yes' Permission for actually being allowed to have or be the thing (x) to make the 'okayness' whole and complete, people's feelings will always be tinged with a little Unconscious Unhappiness and they'll be Self-Conscious. The *cognitive* mind may be *half*-unlocked, but the individual is inevitably still going to feel a certain quality of self-judgement which will still reside in the body and nervous system. There will always be some nagging, Unconscious elements remaining, driven to wake you up to the not-yet-unlocked true part of you.

In many Conscious communities there are a lot of people telling themselves that they're in self-acceptance around certain notions, whilst semi-consciously knowing or feeling that they're retaining the heaviness of self-judgement and lack of self-given Permission. They are still judging themselves for not having or being something. I call this **'Half-Unlocking The Moment'** or 'Half-Unlocking The Consciousness'. Typically it's only going to be an Intellectualised Letting Go, rather than an Embodied Letting Go. (Note that even a merely intellectual Awareness of a notion of self-allowance has a certain representation in the nervous system that's better than being without it entirely, as acknowledged above in the wording, 'which will include a *somewhat* embodied freedom'.)

Ultimately, we get to a point of realisation that if something is both possible and our Choice, then to be *totally okay* with not having it means getting it! … or at least allowing ourselves to Receive it, as and when the opportunity arises. Or if it relates to *Being* something, then you are able to honour it as your Being.

Of course, it is both unhelpful and unkind to judge people for only Half-Unlocking The Moment. But it can also be kind and helpful to help them realise that they still hold the essence of the self-judgement – and how they might release it.

The Divine Pull to Proactive Presencing

aka: The Divine Pull of Self-Acceptance

There is a phenomenon that arises naturally – or at least in theory ought to arise naturally – when we feel into being totally okay with not having something, with not being something, and truly allow that. It is the same principle as The Divine Desire Power Rush, but a step earlier in the process.

Instead of a 'Divine Rush' to achieve or be something, there's a 'Divine Rush' to Receive the 'Yes' Permission relating to that thing.

Automatic Proactive Presencing

Whilst in theory we Unlock The Moment first, and then unlock the *specific* Permission, The Paradox of Unlocking The Moment shows us that in reality they kind of have to happen simultaneously. When you say to your Consciousness, "I'm totally okay with not having something", and mean it, then the impulse to step into the Being of having it will automatically arise in you. The 'Unconscious but true part of you' is driven to wake you up. It has been 'activated' – disturbed – by your request to be totally okay to be without something! So it may be that the self-judgement that we are not allowed something clears naturally as a consequence of Infinitizing The Opposite.

But if it doesn't, we have a final clearing to do to allow ourselves to step into the possibility of Receiving the thing we desire: **Proactive Presencing** (as explained above) to 'Infinitize The 'Yes' Permission', to be infinitely okay with Receiving the desire in question.

You can ask a couple of introductory questions of yourself or others to focus into the resistance that you or they may have about this. The exact wording isn't crucial:

> **How would it be to Receive the thing you wish to achieve?**
>
> **How would it *feel* to Receive the thing you wish to achieve?**

And then perhaps follow up with The Kissing Consciousness Tool:

> **Would you like to let go of anything that wouldn't allow you to feel okay and be okay at the prospect of Receiving the thing you wish to achieve?**
>
> **And would you like to ask your body if it would like to let go of anything that wouldn't allow you to feel okay and be okay at the prospect of Receiving the thing you wish to achieve?**

In the Automatic Proactive Presencing scenario, these questions get automatically 'asked' (in non-verbal form, possibly without thinking about it) – by The Divine Pull to Proactive Presencing.

A Moment or Two Explained in Several Pages

The **'Unlocking The Moment'** process is only *truly* completed when it is followed up with the **'Stepping Into The Real You'** process. They work very well as a pair, because you're 'dragging' the Consciousness both this way and that. You're saying to the Consciousness that it can be whatever it wants. You're giving yourself *genuine* freedom.

Unlocking The Moment isn't just a tool for letting go of Neediness to have something, it's also for unlocking the 'Yes' Permission for having or allowing that thing.

> "If you open yourself up to the force of evolution, it will carry you wherever you want to go." – Dr Deepak Chopra

And again, although this has taken pages to detail, these processes can happen in mere seconds or split seconds. (../unlocking)

The "Has it Gone?" Process

If I'm looking at a person I'm facilitating, and after inviting either them or their body to let go of a self-judgement I can see in their face, demeanour and body language that they still don't feel any happier or lighter, I ask them this follow-up question, to which I pretty much already know the answer:

Has it gone?

If they are really on the ball they might say to me, "That hasn't gone, James, shall we ask again?" But usually people have a bit of fear of failing to let something go, so it's up to me (or whoever is facilitating them – it may even be you!) to notice from their body language, facial expressions and such like if they haven't shifted the thing, ultimately trusting Awareness on that. This is quite easy most of the time, because when people do let things go there's a visible relaxation, even a subtle 'celebration', which is notably conspicuous by its absence when it doesn't happen. (../gone)

The Power of Acknowledging a 'No'

This is one of the most powerful aspects of the process, because without it people might not become Conscious of the fact that it hasn't worked. Acknowledging when something doesn't shift or release 'scores the points' of Awareness, self-love and Confidence that aren't otherwise gained if Fear Consciousness causes us to pretend to ourselves that it has released. If you ask something to let go and it doesn't, but you acknowledge the fact, you have still made a gain. It's still taking you to where your True Self wants to go.

Love Consciousness	Fear Consciousness
Appreciating that a 'No' is just as welcome news as a 'Yes' – and just as powerful	Interpreting this as not what's wanted, and inferior to a Yes, and being afraid to face it
You see this as it is: As useful feedback	There's the temptation to pretend to yourself that it did release, or judge it as a failure

If, upon asking the question for a second time, it still hasn't released, that has at least established that the deeper self has a reason why it is unready to release. A slightly different question may now serve us.

Safety and Survival

If you as your Conscious Mind wish to let something go, and have Unlocked The Moment, and the thing still hasn't gone, then the resistance is in the deeper Subconscious Mind and the body, and is almost certainly related to safety and survival. Good questions at this point might be to ask the body:

- If it has a good reason for not being ready to let go of the judgement?

- If it can tell us anything about that, or if it would like to?

My next question to the body is usually:

- What do you need the person to know or be aware of before you are willing to release the self-judgement?

As long as one is respectful of the body's answer, there's no inherent reason why we shouldn't follow up a "No" answer with a further "Why not?" question. However, if our Awareness says, "Leave it for now", we want to go with that.

Energy in the Body

Another questioning approach I often take at this point is to ask where in the body people can feel things – where the judgements are remaining, physically. They may say "Arm", or "Chest", or whatever, and after we've invited the body to let that go, they may then say, "Now it's in my stomach", or "It's moved to my shoulder", or that it's now gone completely. This is all normal, all good clearings happening, and it may help to loosen up the dialogue and line of communication with the body, the Subconscious Bodymind. It's a game of asking and responding to the feedback. You'll get the hang of it by doing it. It's just talking to a friend, after all. But believe that your body, as your Subconscious Mind, is on your side. Your Inner Guide is NOT interested in telling you things like: "I'm not going to let you for the sake of being nasty, because I'm not on your side." It only has one agenda, to keep you safe and as well as possible. It really comes down to: "Is it safe for you to achieve a Success and Happiness?"

This might seem like a silly question, but if you have someone close by who would resent your Happiness and Success to the point that they might hurt you, physically or otherwise, then it becomes hugely relevant. Indeed, this is how self-judgements are created in the first place – because it's not safe for us to show some aspects of our expression or free will. The first thing I would consider is the safety of the domestic living environment. Who there might be judgemental, and even dangerously so? If it's impossible or impractical for a person to move out they may have to live by adopting someone else's personality just to survive in the home. They may have to adopt a false sense of self in order to survive, to pretend to be someone they are not. And that may well be done Unconsciously. Our Subconscious Mind helps us with this in order to protect us, to keep us alive. After the home, I would consider the working (or school) environment, and then perhaps after that the social environment.

A Closed Eyes Process

In one-to-one sessions particularly, I might invite someone to close their eyes for a few moments, and then ask the body, the Subconscious Bodymind, some questions to invite it to confide in the individual, in the Conscious Mind. It's 'horses for courses', but some people might find it easier to tune in to and establish a relationship with their Inner Guide with their eyes closed. And, of course, you can do this for yourself: Close your eyes and invite a positive relationship with your Subconscious Mind, any time you want to. (../eyes)

Emotional Infinity

aka: Emotional Innocence

"You have an innocence about you,
but not in a naive way." – Claire Floyd

"We've all been brought up with the lie
that emotions are scary." – James Blacker

Would you like to have total freedom from fear of your emotions? Would you like to have the total Confidence of walking the world without worry as to what emotions or feelings might arise? It's actually a simple and natural state of being. The first thing is to illuminate the false cultural assumption that emotional freedom, emotional authenticity, is a tricky quality:

Love Consciousness	**Fear Consciousness**
Emotional freedom is no big deal, and is actually a natural quality which we all had as children	Emotions are scary things and emotional freedom is an unnatural and rare quality for people to have

Once you have that Awareness, you always have the ability to crack open 'The Elusive Emotion'.

"Emotional Infinity: We have learned how to be bad at naturally honouring our emotions." – James Blacker

How to Face any Emotion with Confidence

Are emotions and feelings the same thing? There's a suggestion that emotions are associated with the body, while feelings are related more with the mind, however, we're not going to use that distinction. There's a much 'cleaner' way we can differentiate between the two things which are happening with regard to what we might call emotions or feelings:

1. Events of the mind
2. Events of the body

And we can be *aware* of both events of our mind and events of our body. Whether we call them feelings or emotions doesn't matter. There are only two reasons why you wouldn't be able to face any emotion:

1. You can't get your head around it
2. You can't get your body around it

Actually, there's only one reason – self-judgement – but that one reason breaks down into these two factors, and that's the invaluable insight here. This means that there are only two forms of freedom you need to allow yourself in order to have emotional freedom and total Confidence:

1. Allowing your mind to do what it wants (when any thoughts or feelings arise)
2. Allowing your body to do what it wants (when any emotions arise)

Once you have freedom of mind and body, you have Emotional Infinity, Emotional Freedom, Emotional Invincibility, Emotional Innocence, Emotional Purity, Emotional Imperturbability, Emotional Authenticity, whatever you want to call it. Personally, I like the word 'imperturbability', meaning that no emotion or thought can bother your sense of self (literal translation: 'unable to be bothered'). It's also Emotional 'Infinity' in the sense that you have a full emotional freedom range that allows you to have the full breadth of your Consciousness, and thus no need to separate yourself from it. This is what gives the basis of total Confidence. It's Emotional 'Innocence' in the sense that you have no knowledge of any self-judgements which could cause you to adulterate your straightforward and natural experiencing of emotions and feelings.

None of this means that emotions don't hurt. Grief is grief. It means they don't create conflict within us. It also means we don't cause ourselves additional pain or distress because of our resistance and avoidance of them.

"Are our emotions complicated? Or is it just our beliefs and self-judgements that make us think that our emotions are complicated?" – James Blacker

Let's remind ourselves of The Paradox of Love Consciousness, and of Sub-Paradoxes, so that we don't go off in an Unconscious, fearful pursuit of Emotional Infinity (The Paradox of Emotional Infinity):

Love Consciousness	**Fear Consciousness**
Not bothered whether we have Emotional Infinity or not	Attached to having Emotional Infinity, afraid not to have it

Our two tasks of getting our head around an emotion or feeling, and getting our body around it also, are solved with wisdom and body wisdom:

1. You can't get your head around it (an absence of wisdom)
2. You can't get your body around it (an absence of body wisdom)

Events of The Mind: Allowing Your Thoughts and Mind to Be Free

Any resistance you have to letting your mind do what it wants is a self-judgement. If we have self-judgements then we have resistance to what our thoughts might be, or what information about our lives might come into our Awareness, as these inform our sense of identity. A person who has no self-judgements has no attachment to any given identity for themselves, because they are Willing and more than happy for that identity to be self-defining by whatever is true of them. Flexibility of identity thus becomes a cornerstone of Emotional Freedom and emotional flexibility.

"Only in the Western World have we developed this bizarre idea that hearing voices and having strange ideas has no meaning at all." – Dr John Read

Events of The Body: Allowing Your Body to Be Free

There are various ways that self-judgements – both individually and culturally held – turn the mind into the tyrant of the body. Part of effectively processing and handling an emotion is to allow the body whatever it requires in order to accommodate that … but how on earth is that going to be possible if there are all these rules and judgements about how the body is *and isn't* allowed to be and express itself? We can't be socially afraid of the human body. If you're afraid of the human body you're going to inhibit the ways in which it is allowed to Surrender into its own emotions, and that shuts down your Awareness, your Confidence and Success.

"I allow nature to have its way with my body." – Peter Ragnar

If you allow wisdom, reality, truth and love to have its way with your identity (and therefore your thoughts, and contents of mind), and then allow Nature to have its way with your body, you have all the ingredients for total Emotional Freedom.

> **Anywhere you've got self-judgements that would deny you either of those two freedoms, would you like to let that go?**
>
> **And would you like to ask your body if it would like to let that go?**

Crying

If you cry from False Self, with inauthentic or Unconscious (needy) motives, that may be frustrating and unfulfilling for you. But if you cry because you are now letting in emotions and feelings that had previously been shut out, you are *reclaiming your Life Force energy*, reclaiming more of yourself and your truth. Crying is natural – for both sexes! – and the *freedom to cry* is a necessary element in good psychological and physiological health.

> **Anywhere you've bought into the lie that you're not allowed to cry, would you like to let that go?**
>
> **And would you like to ask your body if it would like to let that go?**
>
> **And anywhere you've got self-judgements to the effect that you're not allowed to cry in public, or in front of others, would you like to let that go?**
>
> **And would you like to ask your body if it would like to let that go?**
>
> **Anywhere you've bought into the lie that it's weak to cry, or unnatural to cry, would you like to let that go?**
>
> **And would you like to ask your body if it would like to let that go?**

And one for safety:

> **Anything that has shut down your Awareness that it's dangerous or against your best interests to cry in front of certain people, or in certain situations, would you like to let that go?**
>
> **And would you like to ask your body if it would like to let that go?**

Goodness, I could do a load more clearings on crying … but we're going to run out of book space if I do dozens of clearings on each area!

Screaming or Shouting

I'm watching a trailer of the CRAZYWIZE documentary film. In the video a man is screaming into a pillow. So where's the problem? To me there's no problem. If he feels the need to scream into a pillow, fine, no problem. I don't need to make it a problem. Or comment. Or judge.

There's no problem unless you make a problem, but conventional, judgemental society often does just that. The feeling isn't going to go anywhere by being judged and denied! We all have various feelings at one time or another which wish for a certain expression, so when we all buy into the idea that expressions of feelings are not allowed, we also lose out somewhere down the line. Decades of outdated and fear-based approaches to psychiatry that were judgemental of many of the ways in which a human physical body needs to express itself have created a society in which most adults have lost that capacity for Emotional Infinity that they all had as children, because they are too worried about how they might be perceived or judged.

Being Sick

Freedom to be physically sick is just another strand to Emotional Freedom, another way in which the body is allowed (or not) to handle feelings the way it needs to. If you're Unwilling to feel an emotion or truth which might risk making you sick, then you won't get the 'Yes' Permission to whatever it is that's true for you that you're not allowed to honour. You might jokingly say "Fine!", but what if that 'No' Permission relates to allowing yourself true love, or a career that allows you both health and fulfilment?

Anywhere you have resistance to being sick which is causing you to avoid feeling your feelings, which in turn is shutting out the Awareness that is crucial to allowing yourself the Success you desire, would you like to let that go?

And would you like to ask your body if it would like to let that go?

Love Consciousness	Fear Consciousness
No resistance to being sick	Resistance to being sick

This principle applies to whatever the body needs to do to accommodate an emotion; cry, scream, shout, go for a run, collapse to the ground – all are fine, until we resist them.

You can feel an emotion from a place of Love Consciousness, and you can feel an emotion from Fear Consciousness. Possibly a few emotional moments can be a mixture of both. And if you're generally resistant to feeling emotions then the experience may take longer, maybe much longer, because you are not fully or not really feeling into them and they may continue to arise in order to be felt. Conversely, fully feeling emotions and feelings may mean that they pass very quickly.

All Emotions Are Neutral, Never 'Negative' or 'Positive'

At a Consciousness level, an emotion or feeling is what it is. Even grief, considered by some to be 'negative', holds underneath it the love that we had for whomever or whatever was lost – a feeling to be felt, part of life's truth, however painful.

People who are upset or down in the dumps, or who's body is feeling low on energy, have said to me "Sorry I'm not feeling very positive!", or "Sorry I'm not being very positive right now." And I say to them, "What do you mean, positive? You are being positive – you're honouring your feelings!" Or you're listening to your body and honouring that. There's no 'positive or negative' about emotions. They simply are.

I have also read an article about "Why it's good to embrace negative feelings." It made a good point about seeking to embrace all emotions and feelings, but there's no such thing as a negative feeling or emotion! To label them as such is what keeps people trapped in attachment and resistance – attached to 50% of all emotions and resistant to the other half.

50% of Life

Thinking of some emotions as negative leads us to reject half of all of our life. If we avoid feeling those 'negative' feelings we are shutting out half of what's true for us, because we simply aren't allowing ourselves the information. Emotions and feelings don't exist for no reason. They have inside each of them a kernel of truth, even if it's just about how we relate to emotions. Emotions without the Fear Consciousness of self-judgement are just packets of valuable information about what's true for you. By allowing them you 'Get The Information'.

Love Consciousness	Fear Consciousness
Feelings are welcomed, including the feeling that you don't want to welcome a feeling	Feelings are unwelcome, resisted and ignored
You get the information about what's true for you	You don't get the information

We reject the experiences we judge as worthy of being rejected, and this starts with emotions. But the fact that we resist 50% of all of our emotions, and therefore 50% of all the information about what's true for us, means that we *never* have a moment where we're *fully, totally at one with ourselves.* And so in a sense 50% of life actually gets us 0% of life ... because we never get to a point that everything is honoured. We never allow the full picture of who we really are. So in that context *everything* is 'chosen', at least in part, from a False Self basis, and we never get to the full Consciousness of being allowed to choose what we truly desire.

Once we have reclaimed an authentic relationship to feelings and emotions we can allow in all of life, and this is exactly what this section on Emotional Innocence provides a way to achieving.

What if someone tried to take your grief away from you? Underneath that grief is love and truth – the precious knowing of your treasuring of that person, or some other way of life. What if someone tried to take fear away from you? Underneath that fear is love and truth – a gift of how and who you really are. What if someone tried to take discomfort away from you? Underneath that discomfort is love and truth – a gift, a new habit, an opening to your strength. Without discomfort you wouldn't even know what comfort was. What if someone tried to take anger away from you? Underneath that anger is your truth, and your love, a reflection of what you stand for and care about, what you value the cherishing or protection of, and the energy to defend it.

Principle: Love and truth is underneath all authentic feelings and emotions.

Emotion Isn't The Problem, Resistance Is

When you have Emotional Innocence, you still feel your feelings, but you feel them without resistance. It's the resistance that makes them uncomfortable. Before resistance, they are merely a physical feeling or a thought, to be felt or allowed to pass through.

Facing emotions may make you cry, but what does that matter? It's only crying! But shutting out emotions makes you unhappy, stressed, constricted. You can actually be happy once you release the resistance to facing your emotions.

When people are feeling into their emotions and crying or similar, I sometimes involuntarily smile – particularly if I know that they themselves are aware that they are okay with it all because it's only emotions and feelings – because I appreciate the gain that they are making by doing so, that it is good for them. They are Receiving themselves, where once they had shut themselves out, and I'm pleased for them.

Emotional Purity and False Emotions

As we know from the previous chapter, Fear Consciousness creates additional, false aspects to emotions. Thoughts of self-judgement may interpret things more scarily and more uncomfortably than they need to be interpreted, which in turn may create an additional – and *false* – extra experience in the body. That feeling in the body may in turn lead to further triggering of the self-judgement fears, and so the whole thing goes around and round like a merry-go-round, a vicious cycle, picking up more and more problems.

Let's say a person declines your invitation to a romantic engagement! That's disappointing. But that disappointment might only need last a nanosecond. However, let's say that you have a self-judgement about what that means about you, and another about how that threatens your sense of your dream for life ... all of a sudden there are a whole load more uncomfortable feelings added to what was initially there to be felt. But those additional feelings are *false* feelings because the self-judgements which created them are false. By releasing those self-judgements, declining their additional effect on that feeling experience, we can leave ourselves with just what was naturally felt. This is what I mean by stripping an emotion or feeling down to its purest form (Emotional Purity). It is the difference between an Ego-based experience of emotions and an authentic experience of our emotions. If you don't Unconsciously assign meaning to feelings via self-judgements then you experience them in their true form, their pure form. Emotional Authenticity acknowledges the choice to release self-judgements, so that the experience which remains is only what's authentic and felt, not that which is additional false drama.

Anywhere you've made emotions and feelings more dramatic than they need to be, would you like to let that go?

And anything that wouldn't allow you to strip the experience of them right down to their bare-bones truths, would you like to let that go?

And would you like to ask your body if it would like to let go of all of that?

Love Consciousness	**Fear Consciousness**
You get the information of the feeling or emotion in pure form	You don't get all the information, you get a false or at least partially distorted experience

"I'm not sure what I should be feeling!"

This is a major area of self-judgements in emotional life. If you're thinking about how you *'should'* be feeling, then you're not feeling the reality! In this moment you're *intellectualising* the notion of feeling and judging yourself, rather than feeling anything. There is no 'should' to how you should be feeling. You either feel something or you don't.

"I'm not very good with my emotions."

You are. You've just been conditioned to have to pretend that you aren't, so your capacity has gotten buried a bit. Your relationship to emotions has been adulterated, as most of ours have.

'Spiritual Bypassing'

Coined by psychotherapist and Buddhist teacher, John Welwood, the phrase 'Spiritual Bypassing' refers to a tendency to hijack spiritual notions and ideas to avoid feeling or facing unresolved emotional issues and the wounds caused by self-judgements. An example might be someone who considered themselves "Too spiritual to get angry."

You Kinda Get to Choose Your Feelings!

In a sense you get to choose your feelings, because anywhere that your feelings are influenced by self-judgement, you can realise that, *release that*, and thus allow the false aspect of the experience to dissolve.

There isn't a 'solution' to authentic emotions, because you can't let go of a truth. Authentic emotions are there to be felt. There *is* a solution to:

1. One's resistance to feeling them
2. Self-judgements which add false aspects to them (False Emotions)

Emotional Flexibility, Emotional Infinity

"You can go from painful crying to hearty laughing to sad again, to melancholy in an instant!" – James Blacker

Emotional Purity inevitably gives us emotional flexibility. The quote from Claire Floyd, "You have an innocence about you, but not in a naive way", was a compliment to me which gave me more insight to my own emotional wisdom. I realised I was able to move through extremes of emotions in moments without any of them sticking or requiring either Egoic analysis or resistance.

"Shifting quickly through emotions is often seen as the gift of the master … Yet we all have this inner ability when we are ready." – Kristy Foley

The weather can change in an instant – particularly in Scotland – from sun to sleet to dry to rain to snow – and that's exactly how a humans emotions are designed to naturally flow. People have (temporarily) lost the emotional authenticity they were born with. You are not your emotions, you are like the sky, through which the weather passes without attachment or resistance, without judgement or praise. As the weather is to the sky, emotions and feelings pass through you, both unbidden and unblocked.

None of these emotions need to stick to you. Whilst I've been at pains here to explain that we might not want to avoid feeling or facing any feeling or emotion, once they are felt, or rather as long as they are not avoided, we really naturally exist at a Consciousness that doesn't get particularly identified with them. (../flexibility)

'Channelling Energy or Anger'

You may have been told to "Channel your energy", or "Channel your anger", or heard it suggested to others, either in real life or in the movies.

There are two ways in which we can approach our emotions and feelings: We can either Respond to them, or React to them. These show up as *three* different things we can do with regard to them, because there are *two* different ways in which we might React (Unconsciously) to emotions as a result of not knowing how to handle them: Either suppress and deny them, or lash out uncontrollably, physically and/or in the way we speak (to ourselves or others).

1. Repress (React)
2. Uncontrollably lash out (React)
3. Hold Presence; feel and integrate them into Conscious Choice (Respond)

The third of these, holding Presence, is the way of channelling the energy, your Life Force. This is Emotional Infinity, allowing the mind and body to be as they are. This also means allowing the process to take as long as it takes, however long one may have to hold Presence to it for, without giving in to the temptation to either repress or lash out. Holding Presence will transform into making Conscious choices, if it's not already.

Love Consciousness	**Fear Consciousness**
Holding Presence; allowing feelings to arise (Response)	Lashing Out (Reaction), Repressing (Reaction)

Emotions are filtered through either self-acceptance or self-judgement. In those moments when they are filtered through self-acceptance, nothing is a problem, because we naturally take the Choice we wish to take. We know the appropriate Response or path, and have no self-induced blocks preventing that. We're not at odds with ourselves as to how to either feel or express that emotion.

When emotions are filtered through Fear Consciousness, however, it can be good to release whatever is stopping us from feeling the emotion authentically. By releasing the self-judgement and feeling the emotion authentically, we allow whatever action or Response we take from there to be coming from genuine Conscious Choice.

As part of listening to our bodies as to what we might want to do, we can get a sense of how uncomfortable (and unhealthy) it is to repress our feelings. We can also observe and become aware of how unfulfilling it feels to lash out uncontrollably, out of alignment with our truth. This may help us realise that we'd really rather decline doing so and choose something else, as it's a self-destructive path and leads to False Emotions and Frustration.

I invite you to imagine surrendering the control of your arms and legs in your body. Either sitting or standing, it doesn't matter which (but not whilst driving!) Now, whilst staying in that state of 'limp limbs', imagine that a feeling of great rage and anger is arising in you, in your body, so you can feel it in your stomach and coursing through your veins. And imagine this while not allowing yourself to 'push the feeling back down' (repress) to avoid feeling it; allow yourself to feel all of it fully. Notice that even with the feeling inside of you, without your own volition, your free will, your *Choice* to move your arms or legs, there's no way that *the feeling itself* could actually carry out a physical manoeuvre or action. It certainly couldn't throw a tea cup or hit somebody. It couldn't burn a letter or even shout at someone. It couldn't send a destructive text. For all that, you yourself would have to give the permission to your hands and arms, legs or voice to do so. Anger cannot punch; choice does. This exercise shows that we may regain freedom from our uncomfortable feelings.

You may have to allow your body to breathe in a deeper or fuller way than it might have previously, and there may be an experience of the body seeming to 'expand' as it takes on and integrates all of your truth, but that's all okay, just flow with it, let it do its thing. This is your whole self-system adjusting to accommodate that extra bit of your Life Force and sense of self. You're becoming more fully true to yourself, so there's the feeling of the process of Receiving that in, of reacquainting with your energy. This is what we do to 'integrate' or feel any feeling or emotion, whether it be anger, fear, pessimism, joy, sadness, or anything else.

From there, once that feeling, that anger or whatever, has been integrated and you trust yourself around it, if you feel it appropriate to do so you can indeed choose – *choose* – to throw a cup, or shout at someone. Awareness is non-self-judgement, so Awareness isn't going into conclusion that we definitely won't want to express ourselves in any particular way, or that we *'shouldn't'*. We may well feel it right to do so. But this is the key: It is no longer 'the emotion' or 'the anger' doing anything (not that it ever really was), it is *you* choosing to do it. This is what makes any action healthy – if it is coming from a Conscious place.

Anywhere you've shut down your Awareness to your natural ability to neither repress a feeling nor be uncontrollably driven by it, but

just be with it for as long as it wishes to be with you, would you like to let that go?

And would you like to ask your body if it would like to let that go?

So emotions and choices are different things:

Love Consciousness	Fear Consciousness
Your choices are not dictated by emotions	You're allowing your choices to be hijacked by your emotions

"Anger experienced as Love Consciousness is Love Consciousness." – James Blacker

This is why such suggestions as "Anger is not empowerment", implying that anger *cannot* be Conscious or empowered, are misleading at best.

There's nothing inherently wrong or Unconscious with venting your spleen. In some instances it might even be desirable to do so. It just depends where it comes from, and most of the time I suspect it's not coming from a Conscious place. Again, though, Consciousness is primary – a physical action or behavioural level act is *in and of itself* neither inherently Conscious nor Unconscious.

Anywhere you haven't allowed yourself to be aware of the difference between emotions and Choice, would you like to let that go?

And would you like to ask your body if it would like to let that go?

Emotional Infinity and The Elusive Emotion

If you don't have Emotional Infinity then you have self-judgements around your relationship to emotions and feelings. You don't have to clear all of your self-judgements in order to have Emotional Infinity, just your self-judgements around what emotions are, what your relationship to them is, and to an extent, how you might be allowed to express your emotions, particularly in the body, but also in the mind.

Now we have the tools to allow ourselves our own natural comfortability with emotions and feelings, and can have a relationship with The Elusive Emotion of knowing that emotions are nothing to be afraid of. Given that the only resistance that's left is the immediate, paper-thin wall of Unconscious resistance that is always there when we are in Fear Consciousness, we can know that that resistance itself is the only issue. And knowing that resistance alone has no substance, we can snap it like a Consciousness twig with our Awareness and intent. (../infinity)

'Physioactive and Supersonic'

aka: Supersonic and Physioactive

I'm delighted to introduce this Kissing Consciousness concept to you. As someone who has spent decades doing Shadow Work, often finding it depressingly slow or demoralizingly unsuccessful, it's exciting to see the possibilities for all of us to release self-judgements at a rapid rate of knots.

'Physioactive' means affecting the body. 'Supersonic' means greater than the speed of sound, and in this context we are using it metaphorically. Actually, I think of it in terms of the speed and frequency with which the computer game character, Sonic the Hedgehog, collects all those gold rings and scores points. If you haven't seen it, no worries. I imagine at the very least you will have seen a single example of a computer game screen (everyone's seen Space Invaders, right?) where the player's score is in the hundreds of thousands or millions, and increases by tens, hundreds, thousands in every moment? Please remember that image.

Consider the time it might take to intellectually analyse all of our self-judgements. It could take an hour (or a year!) to unravel a single one. To do a thousand? To unravel a hundred might take a lifetime! What if we didn't need to intellectually analyse it?

'Physioactive and Supersonic' asks the question: What is actually necessary for releasing self-judgements, our blocks to true Success? Two things:

1. The person's Conscious will, intent and Choice; and
2. The releasing of the associated blocks from the person's physical body's nervous system and brain wiring.

So we'll now continue where we left off in our work on letting go of self-judgements, and see how that practice can quickly evolve into the capacity to be 'Physioactive and Supersonic' in the way we do it.

A Subtle Intentional Notion

Let's look at three evolutions in our practice of letting go:

Evolution 1: When we ask the Kissing Consciousness Tool questions "Would you like to let that go?" and "Would you like to ask your body if it would like to let that go?" out loud there is always, included, a subtle notion of intention which makes the thing happen. That's the element of your free will that sets the aim. When we evolve to asking clearings of ourselves in our head, this subtle intentional notion is of course still there. After a few weeks or even just days, most people will naturally evolve the practice to asking clearing questions in their head (or muttered under their breath). As long as the 'subtle intention' is there it still has effect.

Evolution 2: So we shall likely evolve to asking the letting go questions in our head, and can even evolve our practice of releasing self-judgements further, to the point that we barely even need to say the questions in our head because we are *already* aware of the will and the intention that we wish to let go of self-judgements at every opportunity.

Given that it's impossible to let go of a truth, I take an approach that, by default, I always want to say "Yes" to any invitation to let go of a self-judgement. Even better if we don't hear the letting go question that's being asked, since it will certainly have totally bypassed our Conscious Mind and there's no False Ego getting in the way.

Evolution 3: Once you realise what self-judgement feels like in the body, you can do your letting go as bodily notions and subtle movements and energies, rather than as mental activity, which can allow you to shift them in much greater numbers, maybe thousands of times greater. This makes the process of releasing limitations (self-judgement) 'supersonically' quick.

Principle: You can let go of self-judgements as quickly and as many as your nervous system can cope with or is happy with.

> "Flick of the wrist? Letting go is a flick
> of the Consciousness!" – James Blacker

If you went down a regular gym to do regular physical exercise, you wouldn't want to overdo it to the point that it caused your body problems. Nor would you want to do so little that you became sluggish and uncomfortable. Working in tandem with your Awareness, your body can regulate the practice of letting go of self-judgements in the same way, by giving you feedback. If you want to choose it, you can have an ongoing 'arrangement' – an understanding – with your deeper self, whereby your body is clearing self-judgements from your Consciousness, mind and body in a spectacularly efficient way. You can ask your Subconscious Bodymind to clear self-judgements from its nervous system at every opportunity it feels appropriate, increasing your health as it goes. And it can prompt a thought into your Awareness each time, so you can choose whether you want it to. It's a flick of the Consciousness, and the permission for the body to do what it needs to, to 'do its thing', to release the conditioning of self-judgement from the flesh.

So if you want to be as rich as you possibly can be, you don't have to force behaviours against yourself. Stand or sit where you are, ask your body to let go of all of the self-judgements which would prevent that, and allow it to do whatever it needs to or wishes to, to shake, shudder, rattle and release those self-judgements out of your nervous system, and out of your Consciousness. And thank goodness we have our insights for Emotional Innocence, in case the body wants to cry, etc.

Anywhere you've shut down your Awareness to how quickly and how easily you can release wounds and self-judgements from your entire system, would you like to let that go?

Please remember, you don't have to intellectualise anything, or know 'how'.

And would you like to ask your body if it would like to let that go?

The Body in Kissing Consciousness and Dialogue with The Body

"As you become Conscious, you're moving from a way of living whereby the mind is the primary intelligence, to one in which the body and your Awareness, in tandem, is the primary intelligence, and the mind is its servant." – James Blacker

My body and I talk to each other all the time. Having a physical body, there's so much information being provided all the time if you choose to listen for it. Kissing Consciousness sees the body as the home of the Subconscious Mind, also called the Subconscious Bodymind. My body often confirms what I believe my Subconscious, my Inner Guide, is saying, via feelings in the body and words or insights coming into my brain. The body has access to all of the information available to you at any level. Your Conscious Mind doesn't have all the information of your Subconscious Mind, or of your Unconscious, so your body is more informed than 'you' are, if you mistakenly think of 'you' as just your Conscious Mind. This is why people who have shut down their bodily intuition struggle.

The body represents both the nervous system AND the Subconscious Mind. Have you ever tried asking someone out on a date when both your nervous system and your Unconscious self-judgement programmes are working against you? Or asking for a business sale or job vacancy? The body is the ultimate permission giver, and so Kissing Consciousness is a somatic approach to Success and Happiness.

The Brain Rewiring

The brain and the mind can be considered different things in that the mind is non-physical, but the brain is physical: You can touch it, even cut it open if you're a Neurosurgeon! Therefore, the brain is part of the physical body, and as part of the body's activity of letting go of a self-judgement from its nervous system and letting in new possibilities, the brain is also unlocked. Perhaps the brain chemistry changes, meaning in turn that the mind also changes, as new visions of seeing yourself achieve something related to being true to yourself replace the previous internal mental representations of self-sabotage.

Whilst that chain of events relates to the release of a single self-judgement, the collective, cumulative effect may soon be a total change in brain chemistry, resulting in a brain and nervous system that are incompatible with self-judgement. This affects the mind as well, which is why all this activity is not just *'physioactive'* – affecting the body – but technically *'psycho-physioactive'* – if there is such a word – affecting both the body and the mind, back and forth, all for the good.

Just as ice cannot survive in a volcano, when you realise and reclaim your true nature, self-judgement will have no way to exist in your Bodymind. For those who feel there are too many emotional or psychological 'wounds' to heal, this way may offer an antidote.

'The Consciousness Gym'

'The Consciousness Gym' is a process which can either be done formally and proactively in bulk, or informally as a response to allowing the body to release self-judgements in individual moments as required. It can help with all manner of things such as such as relationships, weight management, releasing cravings and career. (../gym)

First let's look at 'Body Unscrunching', a key component of both formal and informal uses of the process.

When Unconscious self-judgement is generated, the body and its nervous system also constricts. We might have clenched hands more often than we'd choose, curled toes as we've learned to be tight, anxious or even afraid – possibly for good reason in the moment of trauma! Our back might be hunched, shoulders lowered, tummy tightly held in, breathing shallow. As we notice all these things, though, the tendency is often to physically straighten them ourselves, to unclench them ourselves, to push our toes open, whatever. You might, through Awareness training, notice that you're holding your hands tightly, and so you take the action to straighten them, perhaps stretching your fingers out. As much as I can understand the motivation to do this, I'd like to suggest that it doesn't actually create permanent change, *and* that there is a better way which does.

Anywhere you've shut down your Awareness to the possibility that manually and intentionally forcibly straightening your conditioned bodily constrictions doesn't necessarily create lasting change, would you like to let that go?

And would you like to ask your body if it would like to let that go?

Here's how I do it. If I notice my hand clenched, perhaps with nervous conditioning affecting my hand, wrist, forearm, I don't personally straighten my hands or fingers, I observe it all. You can hold Presence to any part of your body, or all of it, any time you want to. Continuing to observe, I then give my body permission to straighten it if *it* wishes to. Invariably it does. Why would a body want to stay in a constricted, unhealthy, uncomfortable, unnatural state? What happens then is that the body *unwinds itself.* On the surface this might look like the exact same thing has happened as if I had done it manually – the clenched fist releases, the fingers straighten, etc. But it's not. The body *itself* is doing it. It's a totally different dynamic. More importantly, it's a totally different level of influence and *deconditioning*; this is the releasing of self-judgement *in action*. Again, it's a subtle difference, but crucial. If the body hasn't been allowed to unstraighten, then me forcibly making my hand/fingers do so won't last any longer as a solution than until the moment I stop forcing it! On the next occasion I will likely notice that the situation has reverted entirely to its previous conditioned state: Clenched and guarded, a 'No' Permission manifested in physical form.

Again, can you see how this is all based on declining forced behavioural action?

Love Consciousness	Fear Consciousness
Flow behaviour; the body unwinds its own nervous system constrictions effectively by itself, with your permission	Forced behaviour; you make your body be a certain way but it reverts back the moment you stop making it do that
A release and Permission change is achieved	No Permission change is achieved

All this is merely the *basic* activity of letting something go. You can try this for yourself now. Hold your hand out and give your body permission to release any physical constriction in it. You may then see it unwind. And you can try this with any body part. The conditioned constriction can, and probably has, affected it all, from the chest to the leg muscles, toes, eyes, forehead, shoulders, bottom, belly, hips, liver and kidneys, groin and even genitals. Often particularly genitals. One of the biggest sources of judgement that humanity has seen has been around sex, so the genitals may be holding any degree of trauma.

But let's look at an example like toes, or shoulders. How are either of those for you right now? If either are constricted, what happens if you place your attention on those parts of the body, surrender the will in your body, and allow your body to uncrinkle the knots and tensions for itself?

Even these changes aren't necessarily immediately totally permanent. You may find it takes a few goes to fully unwind something. It takes as long as it takes. But each little step is a permanent mini-change in its own right, and is moving what can be shifted in that moment. With these mini-changes there's a gain across the board of Permissions, nervous system, Consciousness, and internal representations.

If you meet me I might not appear totally 'unscrunched', but everything is relative. As a young man I was so constricted I had to sit my A-level exams in a room all by myself, away from the other students. I had panic attacks which meant that some of the most basic tasks were scary. Public speaking was definitely a no-go area. By 2013, I was giving an interview on the radio with 80,000 people listening in – a major shift for someone who was uncomfortable merely leaving the house. And thanks to these insights I'm now able to take this process into 'hyperspace'. (../unscrunching)

We can look at breathing similarly, too. It often happens at workshops, Conscious dance groups, retreats or similar that the whole group will be involved in an activity, most of them nervous and in their heads and focusing hard on what they're doing, and the instruction will come in from the host on the side-lines: "Breathe!" Again I'd like to suggest that there is a better way than this.

Firstly, "Breathe!" is imperative grammar, telling people what to do, and as such it doesn't really support them in being Self-Referral. Secondly, breathing is an involuntary action. It doesn't work to force it. You can't force your breathing from your mind for very long before it inevitably reverts back to its conditioned base level, because, by nature's design, breathing is a function that the body regulates, not one which the Conscious Mind regulates or even can regulate to any great or long-lasting effect. Forcing it is essentially 'Unconscious Breathing'. Crucially, by telling people to "Breathe!", unless they happen to be Conscious to all this, we're denying them the opportunity to have their body straighten out their breathing for them! We're *overriding* the possibility for Body Unscrunching.

So as an alternative approach, I might *invite*, not instruct, your *attention* to this matter and say, "Would you like to notice how your breathing is?" Notice how that wording is much less likely to engage an Unconscious Reaction in you. Then you might simply notice, *observe*, how your breathing is. You're not being triggered into behavioural level action, but are invited to Respond at the Consciousness level. If you choose to do so, you can then allow your body to do as it wishes with regard to changing your breathing. And then if, as suspected, you are holding your breath because you're nervous or concentrating too hard, *it* can release that to allow a fuller breathing to return – and this can also contribute to the more permanent establishment of more relaxed breathing, because the change is happening on a nervous system level, not merely the behavioural level. Subtlety. Everything here is about subtle differences and subtle intentions.

Breathing is a key thing to let crinkle out, and is considered by many to be the gateway to Consciousness, between the mind and the body.

The Consciousness Gym: Formal Sessions

Now we can address the notion of formally deciding to spend an hour, or just a few minutes, "down The Consciousness Gym."

As a formal process or exercise, you might decide to spend fifteen minutes of a morning, afternoon or evening putting your attention and your Awareness into your body, without assumption, control or judgement, giving it permission to clear and release whatever self-judgements as are stored in your body as it sees fit. As you do that, the body itself might decide that it will lead your Awareness to a particular part of the body. Or it might not. You might also get intellectual insights into some of it, but it doesn't matter at all if you don't, as that's not the aim. You don't need to cognitively understand any of it.

If you wish – and this is probably how I most formally envision it – you can lie flat on the floor in a star shape, so that all of the floor is taking your weight. Even then, as Alan Watts observes, you might find that your muscles are still holding themselves up, even though there's nothing between you and the ground. That might even be a good place to start, to ask those tensions to let go and allow the ground to take your weight. You have the intention set, physically you are supported, and your muscles and all of your body can release a raft of constrictions for you. By law of averages, we can all guess that there might be all kinds of judgementalism locked in our system, and this way may allow vast swathes of it to disappear overnight.

After you've done this, you might get a mental sense of how much more empowered you are, how much less you have disempowering belief systems dominating you. Who knows if that energetic shift you felt wasn't a 'No' Permission to true love leaving your body? Or a 'No' Permission to a dream holiday on a tropical island? Sometimes self-judgements can leave without us knowing what they were.

Equally, you can do this in five minutes while waiting for a bus. If you are standing up, your body is smart enough to only release things that can be released while retaining your ability to stand up. Sitting in a chair waiting for an appointment is another fine opportunity. People think they can't make money while waiting for an appointment – but if you clear a 'No' Permission around earning six figures, isn't that the same thing? Any spare moment can be used to unlock you further.

You can also do a session of The Consciousness Gym with a specific target in mind. For example, as you start you can say to your body "Please release anything that's getting in the way of me having a better relationship with my kids", or "Please clear anything that is a block to my prosperity."

A person witnessing all this might understandably mistake it for a fit. There is a video of one demonstration I gave at a live seminar that shows the body reacting "quite violently", as one observer put it. This is where non-judgement, Awareness and Knowing come in: The last thing we want to do is to perceive the basic – and natural – process of releasing things as undesirable, and so not do it, judge it and impede both it and our health. This is *re-embodiment*, because we were totally embodied at one stage in our lives, and this process returns us to that. You have almost certainly inadvertently let Unconsciousness into your body. We all have … to hugely varying different degrees possibly, but everyone is subject to this. This is inviting Consciousness back into your body. (../supersonic)

Asking Life for More: Infinite Possibilities

[Where will you find me in ten years' time?] "Stepping into the field of infinite possibilities." – Dr. Deepak Chopra

What's *really* possible for you? We can all live from freedom and a sense of possibility in any and every moment. Inviting in Awareness can open up your world and invite all manner of wonderful things in.

Inviting in Greater Awareness

Inviting in Awareness is a different expression of the same basic principle that we've already been using. Since self-judgement shuts down Awareness, while we might ask to let go of self-judgement, we might similarly ask for increased Awareness around something, a specific issue or desire perhaps, and invite Awareness to come in. Questions are great ways to invite in Awareness.

Asking for Things

We can ask ourselves and Life for anything. Your own Awareness and Inner Guidance is pivotal. You might ask for someone wonderful to come into your life. You might ask for more social opportunities, or a richer variety of life. You might ask for greater physical energy and vibrancy. And to have all of these things be asked for from the right place (Love Consciousness), you would do so unconditionally, so not attached to the outcome, or 'how' it might arise. I knew someone who had a list of 150 things they were asking Life for, all manner of things relating to a variety of aspects of life, and they told me how they were intending to increase that to 1,000.

Whether to ask for things ought to be informed by our Awareness. We don't want to get into the conclusion that we should always be asking, or that it necessarily suits all of us the same way. Feeling that we should always be asking for more may be a personal development-caused (or general society-caused) false dissatisfaction.

Love Consciousness	Fear Consciousness
Asking for things as a natural by-product of one's Awareness and Choice	Feeling that you *'should'* always be asking for more, the energy of craven desire

Tools Are Effective When They Emanate from Your Being

We come back to The Illusion of Identical Experiences: There's a difference between asking for something in the Love Consciousness state as compared to doing so in the Fear Consciousness state. They are not identical experiences, and so will not yield identical results.

Love Consciousness	Fear Consciousness
Asking for things, inviting in Awareness	Asking for things, inviting in Awareness

And as we also know from studying Consciousness-Behaviour Splits, and the example of prayer, there's a difference between asking as a physical behaviour, and doing so as a Consciousness. Just because a person asks a question out loud in words, or even in their head, doesn't mean they're asking a question in terms of their heart, their intention and their Consciousness. (../asking)

The Desire Feedback Principle

'Negative' Thoughts are Invited in by Us!

The reason you have supposedly negative thoughts come into your head? You're ambitious. And I mean that in a good way. You wish to respect your True Self, or at the very least a Subconscious part of you does. You desire things, and essentially you've asked yourself for things (whether Consciously or Unconsciously). You've asked for things to be a certain way. Maybe you've asked for You to be a certain way. Okay, fine. So far, so good.

In order to help you deliver on that desire, your Inner Guide, your Subconscious Mind, needs to make you aware that you have conditioned self-judgements running around your Unconscious Mind which are blocking you from Receiving You, so that you can release them – because you can't Receive what you have a self-judgement and Non-Permission around. The releasing is necessary to allow the 'No' Permission to become a 'Yes' Permission, and your Subconscious knows this. The only problem is that you, or certainly often, people, judge these thoughts as they arise as 'negative'. If you allow them to arise without judging them, you can then see that they are also, simultaneously, an invitation for you to let them go. As I'm typing this I just asked my body if it would like to confirm this on behalf of my Subconscious Mind, and it just gave me a "Yep" back, by sending a subtle pulse of energy through my body.

These pieces of information only become negative critical voices because you judge them for arising, and judge yourself for them arising. Prior to that they are just neutral bits of information arising on the surface of your Conscious Mind.

Once you get out of that habit of judging (neutral) information as 'negative thoughts', you can simply have what I'd call a "normal" relationship with your thoughts – i.e. knowing that they are there for your benefit and your service. The alternative is a conflict-based relationship with your thoughts whereby you mistakenly think they are there to beat you up.

You will release the perception that your thoughts are in conflict with you to the degree that you release your self-judgements around your relationship with them. I still have the odd moment of perception of my thoughts as conflicting with me, until I wake up to them. And then I see what I am being invited to let go of, what strength or truth I am being invited to reclaim. Interpretation is the key, and that is of course dependent upon our Consciousness state.

Love Consciousness	Fear Consciousness
Observing thoughts as neutral bits of information	Interpreting bits of information as 'negative' thoughts

The Self-Disgust Principle

As thoughts arise in our Awareness as a result of becoming Conscious, they may shock, scare, disgust or horrify us: "How can such terrible things be in my mind?" There may be a temptation to avoid even doing clearings and letting go of such thoughts if they cause us embarrassment or shame when we acknowledge them. However, if you don't judge these things you can realise what this means: The very fact that such thoughts do disgust us, horrify us or make us feel ashamed is itself proof that they aren't truly ours! So The Self-Disgust Principle is curiously reassuring. (../disgust)

The Inner Critic is The Inner Servant Misinterpreted

The Inner Critic doesn't exist – and we shall realise this if we interpret 'neutral information' as exactly that: neutral. It's our Unconscious habits and conditioned self-judgements that cause us to interpret neutral information as critical, self-criticising, or unfriendly, self-denying, self-sabotaging or even hostile. This is understandable, but a trap we can empower ourselves to avoid. So whilst The Inner Critic doesn't exist, we might say that the 'Self-Criticising *Interpreter*' does, whenever we are in a state of self-judgement:

1. An event happens, either at the behavioural level or at the Consciousness level (for example, someone declines our offer for something, or we have the thought that we desire to achieve something).
2. This triggers a thought about what this means for us. The information that we hold a self-judgement around that matter becomes relevant, and so it arises in our Conscious Mind.
3. Without realising it, we *interpret* that thought, that information, *through self-judgement, as a criticism.*

It's just a habit of how we interpret our thoughts, but for most people, probably a pretty ingrained one. This Binary Table shows how we respond to a piece of information *about* the self-judgements we currently hold: (../critic)

Love Consciousness	**Fear Consciousness**
Accepting inner Awareness of self-judgements as they arise, and thus being able to Receive their information, and even let them go if we wish	Interpreting the Awareness of self-judgements as self-criticism, and thus remaining blind to the possibility of releasing them

If we approach this from Love Consciousness, we can realise that the *otherwise neutral information* is an invitation to let go of a self-judgement – and thus change what happens in Step 3 above. All we have to do is release the habit of interpreting our inner information as a self-criticism and cultivate the habit of Receiving instead, to Receive the gifts that come with letting go of the self-judgement. And so we see that the so called 'Inner Critic' is actually trying to give to us all the time, by offering us a choice. Information itself is always neutral. It has no 'side', or prejudice. (../feedback)

Love Consciousness	Fear Consciousness
Seeing the so-called 'Inner Critic' as an invitation to let go of a self-judgement you no longer need	Seeing the so-called 'Inner Critic' *as* The Inner Critic

Presence

Presence is *the* key, the quality that allows change and healing to happen. We can hold Presence to anything. This is also often called 'holding space', particularly if we do it to facilitate other people.

Some people are already able to hold Presence to themselves, giving themselves a space of non-judgement; others have yet to realise that they can do that, and so believe themselves to be dependent upon external groups or others to provide the base of safety that allows them to touch their Awareness into some things. One-to-ones or group events may make things easier or quicker, or provide prompts we may have taken longer to get to by ourselves, but ultimately it is incorrect to say they are the source of our power. Just as with Emotional Infinity, holding Presence for ourselves is a natural capacity, and a basic prerequisite for a full and fulfilled life, yet the weight of self-judgement may have convinced many people that it is some lofty ability that only a few can have. If that's you, would you like to let that go? (../presence)

Love Consciousness	Fear Consciousness
Being able to hold Presence to any emotion is just a basic ability, no big deal	Being able to hold Presence to any emotion is a rare ability only a few people can have

Holding Space vs Filling Space

If we want to hold space, either for ourselves or for others, we can't fill that space. Sometimes, people will attempt to 'hold space' for others but fail to provide a Conscious atmosphere of non-judgement, instead imposing their own opinion, judgements, conclusions or will on the conversation. That's not holding space, that's filling space. If you're filling space with your judgements, beliefs, conclusions, etc., you can't help yourself or anyone else achieve change. This is a 'Universal' Binary (applies to every moment of life):

Love Consciousness	Fear Consciousness
Holding Space	Filling Space

This is why a good Facilitator can ignite healing and influence positive change with their mere Presence alone. That itself is the invitation, offered in a safe, judgement-free space, like a magnet to that which is ready to adhere to and match with it. It's a kind of paradox as to where the power is in Consciousness Facilitation: An effective Facilitator effortlessly finds themselves aligning with people who are ripe and ready to choose for themselves, like a desert thirsting for water. (../filling)

Responding vs Reacting

Whether on our own, or interacting with other people, we either Respond from self-acceptance or we React out of self-judgement. Presence ensures that we Respond rather than React, even to our Fear Consciousness.

You can't Respond from 'should', only React. And Respond doesn't necessarily mean 'slow', nor does React always mean 'quick'. Nor does taking responsibility, in the sense of having a creative response to the situation, necessarily mean we're acknowledging that we 'caused' something or that it is our 'fault' (although it might). I didn't personally cause the broken world economic model, yet I choose to Respond to it, rather than React to it. "Taking responsibility" is just another way of saying "having Choice" in how we Respond to that moment, whether we caused it or not.

Music, Your Body and Your Consciousness

Sometimes my Knowing, my Inner Guide wants me to go back in time by listening to music from my past, for example to do Shadow Work, releasing self-judgements. The music (or a book, picture, place, person, anything) can trigger a memory, which can remind us of a truth, personality or capacity of ours, which, with that Awareness, we can reclaim. Sometimes my Knowing wants me not to do that at all, to have the music off, so I can live from a moment in a different way.

Listening to music can be a Conscious Choice, and a contribution to one's energy, but like anything at the behavioural level, it can do us a disservice if its motivation is Unconscious, such as when we use music to drown out the sounds and rhythms of our own body, or our capacity to be comfortable in our own skin during moments of silence. This could well be avoidance: Unconscious self-judgement and resistance to feeling into your own body. David Heard, in our audio on 'Strength for Life', related that people at his gym would ask him if he minded if they changed the music? His reply: "I don't even hear the music. I'm so intent on what is happening in my body. There are things going on, and we can make a difference [if we listen] ..." I wonder if a whole gym full of people would have the courage to work out in silence, to really hear what is going on for them.

Going Cold Turkey on Not Living in the Moment

This is a phrase I've coined to help people understand the process of returning to the way of being of living in the moment. In our culture, we are habituated to, even addicted to, many things which all shut down our Awareness and our Being. Central to all of them is an avoidance of how we feel and what we are really experiencing in the present moment.

For many people, the habit of thinking in terms of the future, avoiding feeling the 'now', has gotten so strong that the choice to start living in the moment brings up all kinds of feelings, thoughts and resistances which frankly can take quite some Receiving. In this instance, people unwittingly want to 'Escape the Moment'. It is totally understandable that living in the moment may be a big deal. In my case at least, avoiding the present moment in favour of living in the future and living conceptually 'in my head', rather than experiencing reality directly, had gotten so ingrained over three decades that it has very much been a case of 'going cold turkey' on that state of avoidance, in exactly the same way as a drug addict would experience withdrawal symptoms, albeit with potentially less fatal outcomes. It is one thing to eat, drink, smoke, watch something, concern ourselves with something, think about something we're doing 'next' out of Choice, but quite another to do it when we'd rather not but are habituated into avoiding the present moment. The opportunity here is not just for a single moment of becoming present, but returning to an entire way of life of Presence.

Let's not beat ourselves up for how difficult it might be simply to be present with ourselves in the moment. It sounds on the face of it a silly thing to suggest is a difficulty, but it's really not. And let's make sure we don't get judgemental with ourselves or others for choosing to escape the moment. You are allowed to escape the moment. We have to create that freedom of non-self-judgement first, so that any attempts to release our resistance can have a chance of working. Here's a Binary Table for our own response to noticing we are seeking to escape the moment:

Love Consciousness	**Fear Consciousness**
Consciously choosing to escape the moment is a perfectly fine thing to do	We judge ourselves for escaping the moment or avoiding any feeling, and this makes it worse

The 'cold turkey' of avoiding living in the moment is largely played out in terms of not being present to our bodies. We have our tools for that: The Kissing Consciousness Tool and 'The Consciousness Gym'. It also plays out in our emotions. Again, we have our tools to become comfortable Receiving The Elusive Emotion, so we're equipped to approach the challenge of not avoiding the present moment.

I was sent into office work: A physical animal, as we all are, forced to sit still doing menial tasks in a constricted and immobile body position for eight hours every day in tight-fitting shoes and a jacket and silk noose (tie). Others have to work in factories, similarly forcing their body against what it can handle. Fuck me, who wouldn't want to escape the moment in those circumstances?! In that sense, it can be thought of as an intelligent thing to do.

A survival mechanism, maybe. Hence we see the Friday night phenomenon of half a nation's workforce wanting to get 'out of its head' just in order to 'survive' the week.

Although possible, it might take some wisdom and clearing of self-judgements to Receive the creativity available to us in every moment of a job stacking shelves. But as we begin to use The Kissing Consciousness Tool to improve our quality of life, to regain more Choice and to live with more self-love and natural joy, we might well want to start living in the moment again – and after decades away, that can take some getting used to. (../cold)

Meditation

We've talked briefly about meditation as a Consciousness-Behaviour Split. In its broadest sense, though, meditation is an ever-present state of Presence, rather than just being something that occurs in the fifteen minutes or hour of what we might call 'formal meditation' (eyes closed, legs crossed).

Clarifying 'Grey' Consciousness

aka: Facilitating/Purifying Grey Consciousness, Purifying Desire, The Mastery of Desire

As we saw in the last chapter, lots of 'black and white' Consciousness mixed up together can give 'The Illusion of Grey Consciousness'. The process for dealing with that is kind of like the 'zooming in' function on Google maps: You start seeing one big shape – a lump of grey, we might say – but once you zoom in you can see all the detail of it in black and white.

We can use the process around any issue, but for now, let's say you have one big mess of a bunch of feelings around a relationship issue. Until they are untangled they may seem to only present two extreme opposing options for how to approach the situation: Leave now or stay forever. As you sit with the feelings, however, you can allow each individual aspect to be felt objectively, without judgement, in your Awareness and particularly in your body, and this allows you to see where your boundaries and truths are, where your 'bottom line' is, so to speak.

So a string of moments of Awareness may arise as follows, as a conversation with oneself: "What this person said makes me feel like I want to end the relationship with them. Yet I feel heavy about shutting them out completely. Is it true that I want to shut them out completely right now? No, that doesn't feel true. Okay, but I feel like I don't want to compromise and be with someone who doesn't share my views. Does that feel true? Yes, that feels true. So how can that be? Okay, I see, it may be possible to talk to them about it, to see if they understand and might choose to align with that? Yes, that feels true. Okay, and if they don't is it true for the moment that I don't want to stay in that relationship? Yes. Okay, so if they don't agree I will leave, decision made. Is that my truth? But I feel a little uncomfortable about that, so why is that? Okay, I see, it's because I'm deciding in advance how I will feel and thus what I might decide, is that correct? Yes. Okay, so what if I agree with myself I won't make any decisions in advance of the moment? Yes, that feels true. Okay, so I'm not going to leave right now, but I am going to speak to them about it, and if they don't align with that then the way I feel right now I am currently inclined to leave, so I'll bear that in mind as an Awareness, but I won't make any decisions just yet, as further information may arise which may inform my choices in that moment, is that right? Yes. Right, okay great, so now I understand exactly how I wish to approach the situation, based on honouring all the things around it that are true for me." *That* is a person who is now fully equipped to honour themselves, without causing themselves any unnecessary pain, and a tremendous Confidence goes with that. Obviously, because it *is* self-confiding fully.

Another example could be around doing some work: "I'm having resistance to working, so is it true that I don't want to work? No. Okay, so if it's true that I do want to work, and yet I'm experiencing resistance to working, is it true that the way I'm approaching the work is influenced by self-judgement? Yes. Okay, so I do want to work, but not in this way, correct? Yes. Okay, so what's wrong with the way I'm approaching the work? I'm approaching it from the mindset of wanting to get it done, rather than enjoying it in the moment. Okay, so I need to allow myself to enjoy it in the moment? Yes. And not be attached to the outcome? Yes."

Your body can feel through each individual aspect of your Awareness as you consider all of the various ins and outs of any situation, and let you know which individual bits are true for you, and which are not. The key is that rather than Reacting to a feeling, you hold Presence to it, and so can Receive its message for you. (../clarifying)

Further Insights on Letting Go

Proactive Processing

It's handy that a friend of mine commented once that he was surprised when I said I was going to "Pop off and do a couple of hours of processing", because he hadn't realised that processing could be done proactively. This gave me the insight that other people might also have not realised this possibility. Processing can actually be proactive in two different senses:

1. You don't need a Facilitator or event host to do processing.
2. An issue doesn't need to have arisen. You don't even need to have any knowledge of an issue in order to process it.

The difference between those personal development approaches which use what we might call 'Consciousness Tools' (questions/invitations to invite people to let things go) and those which don't, is perhaps most easily observed during the lunch breaks and tea breaks of their workshops and events ... when people are standing around in the corridor chatting. In those groups which use Consciousness Tools, even during a break, a workshop participant mentioning an issue they have might be met by an invitation to let that go by a fellow participant – or perhaps they would just say the same to themselves. In groups which don't use Consciousness Tools, however, such an observation is often met with the suggestion: "Maybe the event host can help you with that when we resume the next session." The sense there is that nothing can be done without an event host to lead, and that participants are powerless until then. It's the old saying about "Give a person a fish and you feed them for a day, teach them how to fish and you feed them for a lifetime." Do we really want a planet of powerless participants? I say let's go 'tooled up', if you'll pardon the expression, and invite people to empower their own clearings, healing and releasing – and then let hosts and others *add* to that, to enhance it, maybe, but not be depended upon. (../proactive)

What I really mean by 'Proactive Processing' is expressed in the second point above, what we might call 'Mining for Gold'. You might have no sense whatsoever of any self-judgements you have around money, or your body, or love, or sex, or other people, but once you get a sense of how life works in terms of these energies, how so much of society is based on repression and judgement, you might just decide to clear loads of stuff 'on the off-chance that it is there', which it probably is. So just for 'fun' I might choose to clear "Any self-judgements I've picked up about money", "Any self-judgements I've Unconsciously taken on board as a result of the way sex is a taboo in our society", etc. I might even just clear a 'heavy' energy: "Would I let go of any heaviness I'm holding onto in my body around self-expression?" … or more generally, "Any heaviness I'm holding onto." We can clear anything, whether we know it exists or not. As always, your Awareness informs you whether or not it's ideal for you to do Proactive Processing in any given moment.

Inverted Avoidance

Let's say you're avoiding facing a feeling, because it's scary, because it's uncomfortable, because you sense it will hurt. But then later you face it, and you realise that that makes you feel more in control of managing the pain of the feeling. Perhaps it's less uncomfortable to feel in control of facing it than to have the sense that you don't know when you might have to feel something. And so there then develops the tendency to proactively pursue the activity of facing feelings and letting go – but Unconsciously motivated by Fear Consciousness. It becomes something we feel we can 'control'! But that desire to control is caused by *avoiding* feeling something (ironically, another **Elusive Emotion**). We have inadvertently gotten *attached to* 'facing our fears' because it feels 'safe'. This is an attempt at Proactive Processing, but motivated from Fear Consciousness.

Kissing Consciousness calls this 'Inverted Avoidance'. We can get caught in its trap by ourselves, and it also happens when event hosts get too keen to encourage audience members to face their fears. When we try and force our feelings to be felt, that is when they (our *real* feelings) elude us and run away. You can't force that feeling to be felt, you can only notice when your *'facing'* becomes *'attachment to facing'* (avoiding). Again, this is about the difference between a Consciousness Act and an Unconscious Behavioural Act. Letting go is a Consciousness Act. (../inverted)

Love Consciousness	Fear Consciousness
Proactive Processing	Inverted Avoidance

Dance and Exercise: Changing State vs Permanent Change

Dancing is a very popular activity in the Conscious community, and often praised as being therapeutic. So let's consider the difference between therapeutic benefit and actually releasing a self-judgement.

Dancing (in itself) is a behavioural level act, not an Act of Consciousness. You can't dance away a self-judgement. You can only choose away a self-judgement – however subtle that quality of 'Choice' may be as it occurs in your Conscious Awareness. You may be able to *temporarily* dance away the *effects* of self-judgement. And actually, why not?! Dancing may also provide a context that feels safer, or more appropriate to lending itself to letting stuff go. It may also be a way your body uses to realign and express itself *after* you release a self-judgement, or as it releases. But releasing a self-judgement – even if it happens *during* dancing – requires at least a hint of Conscious Choice.

If driven by an Unconscious motive, dancing could potentially be a repression of a feeling or Consciousness, an avoidance of it (The Illusion of Identical Experiences). I've seen the sadness in people's eyes when they've been told they can dance a feeling away; without realising it, they intuitively sense that they won't have changed anything permanently by just dancing and hoping their issues will go away. They won't have addressed the real wound in any empowered way that actually changes it, and would still be left with the heaviness of those self-judgements, and the feelings and self-denials they generate. Without asking a self-judgement to leave, or without becoming Conscious to a lie, and only dancing away the *effects*, the self-judgement will still be there in your Bodymind and your Consciousness the next day. It actually still exists *while* you dance, even though it may not be at the forefront of your experience in that moment. The same goes for exercise, such as running. You can exercise away the *effects*, and the stress in the body that may have built up as a result of self-judgement, but that doesn't change the *underlying conditioning in the Bodymind.*

If we recognise all this then we can see the opportunity that a Conscious (non-judgemental) dance floor can provide as a *complement* to intentional proactive releasing – by using it as an optional space to cater for the expression of The Divine Desire Power Rush as it occurs when we choose to hold Presence to our Fear Consciousness, either prior to dancing, or during dancing. Any shift our body's nervous system may wish to make can be accommodated!

When we let a self-judgement go, we get a Divine Desire Power Rush; if we resist this and block it, we're effectively blocking our full Willingness to release the self-judgement, and so it doesn't (fully) happen. If we are Willing, though, when Divine Desire Power Rush comes we essentially 'dance' into our new nervous system's Bodymind (the 'us' that we are now that we are free of the self-constriction of the self-judgement). This becomes the dance of life – the dance of the newly reclaimed You. The final moment of truly letting go of a self-judgement is found in being allowed to express our new, truer selves after that true part of us has been reclaimed. (../dance)

Self-Judgement is a Double-Entry Bookkeeping System

We looked earlier at how a self-judgement is created, and we can now look at how that self-judgement manifests afterwards. Accounting is a double-entry system, which means that for every credit a banker makes into an account, they have to make a debit (or debits) from one or more other accounts which add up to the same amount. I worked in a bank once, and I know that the computer won't let you process a transaction until the debit and the credit equal each other. The same is kind of true of self-judgements as well: For every self-judgement that stops you doing something you want to do, there's a 'Reaction' activity you do that you don't really want to do. This is the principle that "For every action there is an equal and opposite reaction" (Newton's Third Law). If you knock a brick out of a wall there is *both* a hole in the wall, *and* a brick on the floor. When the True Self is disallowed, the False Self is created.

In any moment of Fear Consciousness, you're not doing or not focussing on something you want to be doing or focussing on. You want to go to the museum, but your peer group tell you it's for nerds, so you don't go.

And what are you doing that you don't want to be doing, but are doing because you aren't allowed to do what you *do* want to do? That is your 'Displacement Activity'. You want to go to the museum, but you don't go, so what do you do *instead*? You go and watch The Simpsons! Or the news! Or you eat, or watch TV. So you might get into the habit of doing something you didn't even choose! You aren't allowed to be an artist, so you get a job as an insurance broker: The job as an insurance broker is your Displacement Activity. You are ridiculed for thinking you could start your own business, so you go and smoke a cigarette instead: The cigarette is the Displacement Activity.

So wherever you're not doing something you want to be doing, and doing a clearing on that, you might also look to what you are doing as a Displacement Activity that you don't want to be doing, and do a clearing on that also. And where you're doing things you *don't* want to be doing, you might ask yourself what it is that you would rather be doing instead, if you had no self-judgements. (../further)

> **Anywhere you've shut down your Awareness to the fact that you do things in Reaction to not being allowed to do other things, would you like to let that go?**
>
> **And would you like to ask your body if it would like to let that go?**

Habits

"Habits are, by definition, Unconscious." – John Christian

Would you like to take a smart and effective approach to habits? Habits are by their very nature Unconscious: They are behaviours driven by Unconscious motivators (self-judgements). If in any moment a habit were Conscious, that would be a Choice, not a habit.

Therefore, given that the nature of a habit is that it is Unconscious, the way to end habitual behaviour is by:

- Bringing Conscious Awareness to it

Yet the way in which people have traditionally attempted to deal with habits is by:

- Forced behaviour

… which only stretches the elastic band until you let go of it.

Willpower: Free Will vs Power Over

"The key to unravelling habits isn't behaviour, it's Presence." – James Blacker

As we have seen in Chapter Three, in 'The Elastic Band Principle', forcing behaviour never lasts, and is counter-productive. Forcing behaviour is driven by self-judgement, and is an Unconscious act, and so actually makes the whole situation of trying to deal with habits worse, because we are trying to solve Unconscious behaviour with more Unconscious behaviour! That's like trying to fight a fire by throwing petrol on it.

Whether 'willpower' is healthy depends on what you mean by willpower: The free will which comes from being at one with yourself and the genuine Choice which that provides, or the 'Power Over' yourself which leaves you at odds with yourself. Usually, by 'willpower', people mean forcing against themselves, so I tend not to like the word.

The Bad Habit of Admonishing Yourself for Bad Habits

aka: The Bad Habit of Bad Habits

"Most people are trying to fix their habits from their self-judgement, rather than from self-love. That's never going to sustain results." – James Blacker

Wherever there is a judged bad habit there is also the habit of admonishing oneself for it. They tend to go hand-in-hand. This means, for example, that you develop the habit of smoking, watching TV or eating unhealthily, *and* you develop the habit of judging yourself for doing so – struggling against yourself – in order to remedy that. It's like struggling as a strategy to get out of a fisherman's net. It's never gonna work that way. So it's a double-whammy: Struggling to force the behaviour of a good habit, and struggling in self-judgement for not doing so.

Dissipate The Charge

We want to take the Charge out of habit and addiction. Our whole approach is based on moving out of the Fear Consciousness column and into the Love Consciousness column around the matter in question. You might like to ask yourself this: What are you choosing in that moment of admonishing yourself for continuing those bad habits? Are you choosing to release the Charge around those habits? Or are you choosing to make it worse by creating more Charge? You see? By criticising yourself after making a 'mistake' or bad choice or regret, you just make it more likely that you'll do the same thing again next time – and *less* likely that you'll realign your nervous system and Consciousness to your truth and Choice. Nothing is processed or released when you go into self-judgement around a behaviour. By Responding Consciously it can be.

> **Anywhere you've shut down your Awareness to the possibility that your self-judgements cause you to admonish yourself for bad habits – and that this actually makes the situation worse, would you like to let that go and let in all that new Awareness?**
>
> **And would you like to ask your body if it would like to let that go?**

If I were to beat myself up over a habit, it would set a pattern of: Make a mistake, beat myself up, make a mistake, beat myself up about it, make a mistake, beat myself up. I don't want to set that pattern, I want to erase it, so I allow myself Awareness of the mistake, and hold Awareness (in my mind, but particularly also in my body and nervous system reaction) to the temptation to beat myself up about the mistake. You see, it's all being healed by Conscious Awareness, and by not judging ourselves – particularly in our nervous system reaction – we create new physiological responses, brain patterns, thought habits and neural associations. (../admonishing)

The Habit of Forced Good Habits

> "Even the way society tries to deal with habits is a bad habit." – James Blacker

People try to address unwanted habits by forcing the opposite behaviour, which just creates a second, 'Equal Opposite' habit. That doesn't achieve an absence of the unwanted habit. It simply results in a second habit being created alongside the first, so there are two bad (unwanted) habits instead of none. What they want to be doing is becoming Conscious to their habit-based behaviour in the moment, and then transmuting it, then letting whatever behaviour or actions are desired to flow from there. (../forcing)

> **Anywhere you've shut down your Awareness to the Reactive, 'secondary' or 'Equal Opposite' habits you've gotten into as a result of trying to stop the first habits, would you like to let that go?**
>
> **And would you like to ask your body if it would like to let that go?**

The Three Habits of Bad Habits

So there are typically three habits of bad habits:

1. Do something out of habit when you'd really rather not (The Unwanted Habit)
2. Criticise yourself for doing so – also out of habit (The Habit of Admonishing Yourself)
3. And then try and force the opposite behaviour – also out of habit (The Habit of Forced Good Habits)

They're all Unconscious. That's a whole trilogy of Unconscious behaviour driving us away from the Conscious quality which is the antidote to habit that we're looking for. What we actually want to achieve is 'Conscious Habits' – because there's no such thing as a Conscious Habit, it becomes a contradiction in terms – and at that point it instantly becomes Choice.

The Gain of Realising Something is Already a Choice

A Conscious 'habit' is a Choice. If we are carrying out some kind of act or behaviour Unconsciously, and then we 'get Conscious' to our motivations for doing so, we might actually keep on doing the thing as a Choice. It might turn out to be merely that we had a judgement about what we should or shouldn't be doing. On the face of it, this could be considered by some as being 'no gain', but there is a gain because you've moved from a place of doing something in the state of Fear Consciousness, to doing something in the state of Love Consciousness – and as we've seen, there are a hundred different ways to appreciate the quality of life that comes with that state.

"If you're going to sin bloody well enjoy it!" – Bridget Foster

And when we let ourselves 'sin' without judging ourselves for it, this also opens up the space for us to realise, if true, that we no longer really want to be doing the thing. There is no 'sin', as we have seen in Chapter Three. There's only Frustration around not acknowledging your true desires.

Being Honest with Yourself About If and Why You're Choosing Something

If you're Conscious, how can you be discontent with yourself about the behaviour you're choosing? You're choosing it! It's like asking for chips and then being upset because someone brings you chips! It's only when you have self-judgements operating on you that you get the sense that (1) choosing, and (2) not being content with your actions and choices, go hand-in-hand. And the reason for this of course is that you weren't aware that when conditioned judgementalism is operating upon you, operating upon what you *'should'* do, that isn't really Choice.

Love Consciousness	Fear Consciousness
Choice-based behaviour and thinking	Habit
Content with the behaviour you're choosing	Discontent with the behaviour you're doing
Conscious behaviours	Unconscious behaviours

Symptoms Getting Visible

If your habits are getting worse, or let's say more annoying to you in your perception of them, it might not be that they're getting worse in the sense that you're moving further away from resolving them. It might just be that you're getting more Conscious to them, and that that in turn is helping you to release them. But let's not make that a conclusion. You can ask yourself for your own Awareness around them on that question.

Get Your Body Around It

> "Dissolving habits is about letting an energy back into your body. That can be unfamiliar at first." – James Blacker

Anywhere you've shut down your Awareness to the role that trusting your body has to play in getting rid of unwanted habits, and allowing it to Receive the real you back in, would you like to let that go?

And would you like to ask your body if it would like to let that go?

The Bicycle Keeps Freewheeling After The Pedalling Stops

If you stop pedalling a bicycle, never to pedal it again, have you taken the action which will inevitably cause the end of the bicycle's movement? Yes, you have. Once you stop pedalling though, does the bicycle stop moving immediately? No, because it still has a certain momentum. It continues freewheeling until it runs out of momentum. This is the 'Freewheeling Habits Principle'.

The same is true after you stop putting your forced behaviour Consciousness into a habit or behaviour or approach to something. There may be a period after which the habit continues, however, if we are aware of what is really happening, and we don't judge the fact that a habitual action has reoccurred, we can allow the 'bicycle wheels' of the habit to come to a halt in their own time. The body will likely have a lot of wisdom of its own as to how it wants to do things.

If we don't have Awareness of this phenomenon (if it is what is happening), then we 'bite' in on our self-judgements and feel the need to try and force or push more behaviour. By having Awareness of when we've stopped putting our 'False Self momentum' into a habit we no longer want, we can avoid sabotaging or slowing down our desired outcome out of a sense of fear or frustration that it isn't working or going through its process effectively. You might want to let the body's nervous system – and your Consciousness – iron itself out.

> **Principle:** Just because the 'wheels' of your habit are still going around, doesn't mean you're still pedalling them! Awareness will tell you whether or not this is the case.

Are There 'Good' and 'Bad' Habits?

What there really are, instead of other people's opinions of what are your 'good' or 'bad' habits, are either 'wanted' or 'unwanted' habits – according to the you who is free of self-judgement. It's never a 'bad' habit because of the judgementalism of another person; who are we to say what another person should be choosing?! It comes down to how happy, or not, a person is with their behaviour, including their thought-based behaviour. So whether or not an action is a habit has nothing to do with the action or behaviour, but the Consciousness in which it's done: (Conscious) Love Consciousness or (Unconscious) Fear Consciousness.

As all habits are Unconscious behaviour, there is always an opportunity cost when we act out of habit: i.e. what Choice from our truth are we missing out on? A notion of 'good' or 'bad' could be said to come in with regard to the significance of the consequences (and note also that this would also be *as perceived by the individual*). If we exercise every day by running a mile and one day we shut down our Awareness and Inner Guidance to the inspiration to modify the routine with a sprint finish that our body is asking for, or a walk in the middle which may respond better to our body's immediate feedback, that is a habit-caused missed opportunity. If we harshly chastise ourselves for making a mistake at work, or for drinking alcohol or eating sugary foods that we don't really want, that is a habit-caused missed opportunity. There is always a missed opportunity with an Unconscious habitual moment, as it's a quality of being unaware to what we really want to be doing out of everything that's possible. Saving money through Unconscious habit is perhaps a less damaging habit than spending all one's money on gambling, but it is a habit, nonetheless. (../habits)

Intuitive Loving Touch (ILT)

Intuitive Loving Touch is a process I first trialled while hosting a seminar for women in London in 2015, called 200 Women Changing at The Speed of Love.

The very basic and natural phenomenon of touch has huge health and psychological benefits, and so I've chosen to develop a way that it can be harnessed on a daily basis by everyday people without any barriers to it such as a requirement for specific training. (We don't train to breathe or drink water, so why should touch require training?!) By formalising it as a 'thing' it can give people the vehicle, the notion and the prompt to even think to take advantage of the very natural and obvious possibilities which the combination of touch and loving intention offers. It's free and the benefits are many.

The basic intention of loving intent – the intention to bring the quality of loving wish, caring wish, for someone – sets the direction of the activity, sets a cause in motion, and the freedom to flow with the quality of intuition ensures that possibilities aren't shut down by unnecessary rules, and that the good which may be done by harnessing Love Consciousness isn't in any way cancelled out by the Fear Consciousness of being in conclusion. Freedom to follow intuition avoids going against the body and the True Self. Of course, any judgement which denies intuition is Fear Consciousness, and so removing this completely retains everything done as pure of motive, and so purely beneficial.

When we trialled this in 2015 the amazing thing, which convinced me it was something to be taken further, was that all the recipients of the process said afterwards that they felt as if the person giving the service to them was a professional of some sort of similar practice, and had done so before. All of the givers, which was all of them, as they all had a turn at each role, confirmed, with one exception, that they weren't healing professionals at all, and that this was the first time they'd done anything like this. This is the power of the intention of love, particularly when it is not diluted or compromised by any "shoulds" overriding intuition. A safe, unconditional (non-judgemental) environment is also pretty much essential.

Establishing Boundaries

As one person, 'the receiver', lies down, ideally on a massage table, the other person, 'the giver', starts by asking whether it's okay if they touch the receiver as part of the process. As a default, they also state that this will not be on or around the genitals, bottom, or, in the case of women, the breasts. At this point the receiver can also state if there are any other areas of their body where they'd wish to not be touched. Choice is paramount in these exercises, and this includes being free to choose not to pair with a particular person if you'd rather not. The giver may also check that the receiver is warm enough and comfortable enough with blankets, pillows, etc.

Energetic Touch Only

If the receiver would rather not be touched at all, they don't have to be, and can also see if the giver is willing to provide non-contact loving intention, either hovering hands above the body, or even just sitting there, alongside and still. You may be surprised what can be positively affected solely by the intention, attention and presence of one person to another.

The giver then gives Intuitive Loving Touch, usually for an agreed amount of time, maybe five minutes, maybe fifteen, by allowing their own intuition to guide the placing of their hands on the receiver's body. They should also do so without any intention or expectation of what the receiver *'should'* heal, or what should happen for them. The giver has no business seeking to control or manipulate the receiver's will or pre-assume the outcome. At the end of the process the giver and receiver may swap roles, so that the giver gets to receive.

Intuitive Loving Touch is typically conducted in pairs. Two is the minimum number of people required, however, the ladies attending the seminar in 2015 did it in groups of three, and this can easily be done if the numbers at an event require it, in a round robin style, with each person sitting out once as an 'observer'. As a two-person process, it is ideal for arranging ILT 'swaps' with friends or family on a regular basis, or as required.

Talking

It's 'intuitive', so talking is an option if you feel to do so. When we first pioneered the process it was done in silence, (Silent ILT), so that may work well as a basic, or 'default' approach. However, I myself usually choose to talk, particularly if I sense that may be more effective – perhaps if I get an intuition that something is a good question to ask, for example to invite a clearing. I may also ask the receiver's permission to ask questions directly of their body, or relate with them about what they're feeling, or what's going on for them, to see if they themselves might like to ask things of their body. Frankly, I would become at odds with myself if I didn't honour and follow my own Awareness to use The Kissing Consciousness Tool to (offer to) facilitate the receiver, if that was my instinct. If a skilled Facilitator gets an intuition that talking may help, they are unlikely to want to let a self-judgement convince them to bury that intuition. It will likely keep occurring in their thoughts until it is honoured, in any case. The Kissing Consciousness Tool is a separate thing to the ILT process, but the flexibility of the ILT process totally allows for the option to use The Kissing Consciousness Tool as part of it.

The receiver, too, has the option to talk if they wish. They may wish to ask a question, or request the giver focus and/or place their hand(s) on a particular area of the body, or even focus on a particular subject or issue. It's all about the giver and the receiver working together to gain Awareness of what is in the best interests of the receiver.

Intimate Areas: 'The Kid Left at The School Gates'

With regard to boundaries, I said that as a default, the giver would state that touch will not be on or around the genitals, bottom, or, in the case of women, the breasts. That said, such areas of the body often get neglected exactly because they are erogenous and subject to sexual stimulation. However, genitals etc., are not *just* sexual organs *instead of* being regular parts of the body, but *as well as*, and we must remember to honour them as such. Otherwise, those parts of the body kind of get the unhealthy energy of being the 'kid who gets left behind at the school gates', neglected and forgotten about, when all the other kids have been picked up. Emotion of trauma is stored in the body, in the nervous system, and this is often even more so the case for such areas of the body. (Think about the extreme effect of society's judgements around sex, and cultural expectations of the body around sex, not to mention the extent of abuse of it). In that sense, silly as it may sound, these parts of the body can be said to have feelings, even a personality, and they certainly have sensitivity to the way they are treated and respected, or not. We'll cover the mind-body relationship more in Chapter Six on Body and Health.

There is currently some fantastic and invaluable work being done by many women's groups providing 'Yoni healing', (Yoni being a Sanskrit word for the vagina), to heal the trauma that may be stored there. For men, too, healing the Lingam (Sanskrit for the penis) is equally potentially relevant. There is also a suggestion that even *Unconscious* beliefs around homosexuality may cause many men, gay or straight, to shut down their Awareness of, and sensitivity to, their bottom as a part of the body, potentially leading to 'dis-ease'. All parts of the body need to be listened to, not ignored. Ignored body messages become symptoms. At a basic level, every part of the body has its own function, as well as being part of the whole of the body, so it's incredibly important not to dishonour parts of it for mental or cultural (self-judgement) reasons. There is no place for coyness around such issues when health, happiness and even life are at stake. None of this is covered in ILT, but society desperately needs to be aware of it. (../yoni) (../lingam)

Anywhere you've got self-judgements preventing you from addressing such potentially embarrassing conversations effectively and maturely, would you like to let that go?

And would you like to ask your body if it would like to let that go?

It's as Much About The Giver as The Receiver

Both the receiver and the giver can benefit from the process, and the giver is equally in their Choice. The giver's boundaries must be fully respected, just as the receiver's are. They too have the choice if they'd rather not work with someone, and they also have the choice to pause, or rest, or stop, as they feel they wish to do so. If a person has been leaning over someone in the same position for a few minutes, and starts to find it straining their back, or whatever, what is the point of them carrying on – to gift to one person at the expense of taking away the honouring of the body from another? All of these caveats are perfectly in line with the whole of the Kissing Consciousness philosophy of Awareness, Choice and Love Consciousness. You can watch a video of ILT in action at:

www.KissingConsciousness.com/ILT

The Boundaries Exercise

I am particularly passionate about this exercise and what it can do for people. It might just change your world. Society deeply needs a fuller respect of boundaries – both other people's and one's own – and yet our conventional education and society doesn't train us in this. If we can make this exercise commonplace the way Starbucks or meditation or yoga is, it may revolutionize the way people treat each other and themselves, and transform our world.

The aim of The Boundaries Exercise is to learn about your own boundaries and those of others. It allows you to practice stating your boundaries and respecting those of others. Finally, it's a great aid to connection and intimacy. It's a very dynamic and powerful tool as a learning experience. I first participated in the exercise when it was hosted by Jan Day and have since led it myself many times. I find it one of the easiest things a workshop leader can host, as it's simple to set up and orchestrate, and yet the material and experience it produces is almost always rich. And the good news is that I have spoken to Jan about its origins and there is no copyright issue about us using the exercise. In fact, anyone can host or participate in the exercise, which is good news if it is to become a household 'name' (exercise) used to underpin a healthy society.

There tends to be a wealth of insight to be gained from repeating this exercise many times, with the same or different people, perhaps across many different occasions. It's like a fruit that can be squeezed of all its juices until you are totally able to respect your own boundaries, and all other people's. You may soon start to notice just how prolific boundaries dynamics are in society.

How it Works

Two people participate in the exercise as a pair, however, space permitting, you can have any number of pairs participate in the exercise at the same time – two rows of people in pairs facing each other. Typically, it is done with one male and one female, or more specifically, with the gender or genders you are attracted to. It is primarily a tool for understanding and honouring boundaries in relationships, so it is most effective with the gender you're attracted to, however, there is still potentially much to be learned and gained from the exercise when that's not the case.

The two participants stand facing each other, a few yards apart, and take turns at two roles: The 'signaller' and the 'responder'. The 'signaller' has two body positions to use as signals to the second person, the 'responder', to let the responder know in each moment whether they are – or aren't – welcome to walk towards the signaller. Both hands down at the sides, palms facing forwards, arms straight, means "You're welcome to move towards me." Both hands in front of the chest, palms facing forwards, elbows bent, means "You're not welcome to walk towards me – please don't come any closer."

Over the course of the two or three minutes of the exercise, the position of the signaller's hands may move back and forth between the two positions at will, from not welcome to welcome to not welcome to welcome, etc., as they see fit. If the hands are down by the sides to indicate that the responder is welcome to walk towards the signaller, the responder *may* do so, but they don't have to. As with the Intuitive Loving Touch process above, both participants are *always* entirely operating with choice. If, whilst the responder is walking toward the signaller, the signaller moves their hands back to the "You're not welcome to walk towards me" position, the responder must stop moving forwards immediately. The responder is not required to move backwards in this instance, although they may choose to do so. Both parties always have the option to move backwards at any time if they so wish, which is why it is always a good idea if both start at least a yard away from the wall. However, it is not particularly the aim of the exercise that the signaller moves backwards, as they are in control of the degree to which the responder is *allowed* to move forward. Theirs is essentially a standing still role. In return, the responder is in control of the degree to which they choose to move forward *based on what the signaller invites*. After the first exercise the participants swap roles, and the responder has a go at being the signaller, and the signaller gets to be the responder. If, for whatever reason, the responder does not respond to the signaller's boundaries I would terminate the exercise immediately, though I have never seen that happen. And, of course, any participant may stop the exercise at any point if they wish to. It's all a matter of choice.

Sharing a Debrief

Optionally, the two participants may sit down together after the exercise for a minute or two to share their experiences with each other: How you felt, what it brought up for you, etc. There is a wealth of insight available in these exercises, not least because there is often the phenomenon that the responder takes it personally when the signaller puts their hands up, yet this isn't necessarily the case if and when one hears from the signaller during a debrief. You can also share what you enjoyed.

Additionally, particularly in the context of a Kissing Consciousness environment, you might conceivably share what self-judgements – blocks, attachments, energies and feelings of resistance, etc., – you may have chosen to let go of *during* the exercise, or that you'd like to clear after the fact as a result of the exercise. For many people, it is a challenging enough exercise in itself, particularly the first time, so don't worry if you weren't able to let anything go during the exercise, or even able to think about doing so. I totally understand. That said, I would be failing you if I didn't point out that that option is always there ...

The Boundaries Exercise + Consciousness Tools

In 2015 and 2016, I co-hosted two workshops with the Access Consciousness Facilitator, Fiona Cutts, called 'Love, Sex and Consciousness Tools', a Tantra style workshop. We both saw that there was an opportunity to combine the power of such Conscious Relationship exercises as The Boundaries Exercise with the power of question-based Consciousness Tools for releasing blocks. I believe we were the first people ever to combine these two.

The Boundaries Exercise is particularly powerful in the context of an approach that uses Consciousness Tools. Not only can the use of Consciousness Tools during a post-exercise debrief support the proactive clearing of any self-judgement limitations – nerves, doubts, anxieties and other blocks (all of which are 'No' Permissions, of course) – Consciousness Tools can even be used *during the exercise itself*. Let's say you wanted to walk toward someone, or tell them to stop, but found you couldn't. Given what we have seen about the subtle, silent and instant nature of letting go, particularly with the 'Physioactive and Supersonic' insights, letting go during The Boundary Exercise itself is certainly possible, and could allow you to return to a 'Yes' Permission and relate the way you'd like to right there and then! In life, relating with others won't always be an exercise, there won't always be an opportunity for a debrief, so what value the option and the ability to be able to let go of a self-judgement in the moment? That might be in the moment of passion with a partner, a conversation on a first date, or anything else.

Given that recent reports suggest some young women are going out at night with the belief that young men have the right to touch them without permission, the situation could not be more urgent. At all other levels of interpersonal relationship, too, there is much positive change to gain from fully establishing the principle of honouring boundaries and choice. Everything that's good about how society works starts with respect of boundaries. We'll cover this a lot more in Chapter Seven on Relationships and in Volume II.

You can watch a demonstration video of The Boundaries Exercise at:

www.KissingConsciousness.com/boundariesX

The "We" Space Tool

"… the mysterious and miraculous "We" space in which we come into mutual resonance with one another." – Ken Wilber, A Miracle Called "We"

The Kissing Consciousness Tool relates to the individual's mind and body. It would be tricky to use a similar question tool to unlock collective social challenges, because it would have to be worded something like "Would you like to ask your *society* if it would like to let that go?", and that isn't entirely practical.

That said, we *can* actually use The Kissing Consciousness Tool in this way collectively in group situations, and that may achieve the 'mutual resonance' which the quote above rightly identifies as key. In fact, given the title of Volume II of this book, 'Co-creating a World Beyond System Failure', we can start with that most direct clearing for collective wellbeing:

Anywhere you've got self-constrictions that wouldn't allow you to Receive a world beyond system failure, would you like to let that go?

And would you like to ask your body if it would like to let that go?

That sentiment is neutral enough not to get into judgements of what the 'right' worldview 'should' be. I imagine "We" Space Tools are going to be an important part of humanity's salvation. The energy and Consciousness *between us* has a crucial role to play in determining our cultural, social and global systems, which are the priority in humanity tackling its four or five main challenges. As such, the personal development world and Conscious communities are likely to be some of the main places where Collective Consciousness Tools evolve, and where 'mutual resonance' may take its lead. I have asked my Subconscious Mind for any more "We" Space Tools it can come up with, in addition to using the basic Kissing Consciousness Tool collectively, and I'll see if anything comes of that.

And just a cautionary note: The last thing the world would want, or needs, is if somebody were to join in with a "We" Space Tool against their true Choice as a result of peer pressure. If we're judging people for not joining in, then that's not helping either. The last thing we require is people doing things from 'should' rather than from Choice. As an expression of self-judgement, that would just add to the collective Fear Consciousness in the world, rather than adding Love Consciousness. Being in allowance of any who didn't wish to participate would *also* aid the evolution of Consciousness. (../we)

www.KissingConsciousness.com/tool

Chapter Five

Happiness and Your Inner World

Reclaiming You

"Everywhere you haven't been allowed
to love you is a lie." – James Blacker

The three main areas we think of in terms of happiness and quality of life tend to be relationships, money and our physical health/body. However, there's a fourth and more direct area which encompasses all of these: Our inner world, the broader picture of our thoughts, feelings and emotions.

Happiness, as we've already seen, is primarily about the state of self-acceptance (or the absence of self-judgement) that we're calling Love Consciousness, which also has as its consequence the qualities of Confidence, Success, Being, Receiving and many more.

Whether or not we do something amazingly grand is not what makes us happy. What makes us happy is whether we do what we want to do, rather than deny who we really are. Where self-judgements become significantly numerous – where people aren't allowed to 'Receive' themselves to significant degrees – we can develop such things as general unhappiness, anxiety and depression.

Psychology is Not Personality – And We've Lost Both

Our culture often mistakes psychology for personality. Once we understand that our psychology is not our personality, then we can reclaim all of our personality – *and* reclaim our true, positive psychology as part of that – because we no longer believe the lie that we're going against our true personality if we change our *psychology* for a more positive one. Quite the opposite: We realise that this is about showing that personality in its true light.

Nobody's true personality is negative thinking, although that may temporarily be their False Self's psychology. Nobody's true personality is a loser – though that may temporarily be their False Self's psychology. Nobody's true personality is that they are unlovable, but this may temporarily be their False Self's psychology, their current belief. Nobody's true personality is to lack Confidence, to hate themselves, or to not know their own mind or wishes. You might think of your personality as a light, and your psychology as the dimmer switch for that light. The dimmer switch determines how brightly the light shines or how dimmed it is, not the light itself. So shall we see what we find if we turn the light on fully to show the whole of the real personality?

Shyness provides a great example of how a person's psychology is not their personality. There's a difference between having a quiet, private personality and being shy. Shyness isn't a personality trait; it's the fear of self-expression. There's a caveat to go with this, but yes, shyness is a fear. It's the constriction of Choice, the denial of Choice. Shyness is the wish to express oneself somehow which has gotten repressed by one or more self-judgements.

> **Are there any shyness-causing self-judgements that you'd like to let go of? Would you like to let go of those now?**
>
> **And would you like to ask your body if it would like to let that go?**

It's always going to come down to your own Awareness as to whether you're not speaking, not socialising, or whatever it is, due to shyness or because you don't wish to. Shyness isn't an original personality trait. (../shyness)

'Reclaims' and Your True Personality

Our true personalities have been buried and denied to us by the conditioning of self-judgements, by the False Self. We want to reclaim both our true personalities and our true (non-negative) psychology, i.e. non-judgemental Consciousness to what arises.

In the last two chapters we learned about 'The Binary' of Love Consciousness and Fear Consciousness, and how to let go of self-judgements using The Kissing Consciousness Tool and other processes. Now in this and upcoming chapters we can start to use The Tool to 'Reclaim' our true personality back from underneath those self-judgements, a process which is also called 'Shadow Work' and is like unwrapping your Shadow 'presents'. Kissing Consciousness calls these 'Reclaims'. As emotional as it may be to release some self-judgements, we're always gaining a part of us back, and if that doesn't get you hugely excited you probably haven't understood it. Both in quality and quantity, these Reclaims may gift you many hundreds or thousands of times more joy and happiness than those presents you get at Christmas or on other occasions. Intuitively, but Unconsciously, these Reclaims are what many of us vainly hope to find in our birthday gifts, even though we know deep down that this is not how they can arrive … because such things cannot be given to us by other people.

In this chapter, we will cover Reclaims of happiness and inner experience in a number of areas, all of which are ultimately about Reclaiming self-love. (../reclaims)

Reclaiming Reclaims

The first thing we might start with is Reclaiming the ability to Reclaim things itself:

Anywhere you've shut out your Awareness to your natural ability to Reclaim your true personality, would you like to let that go?

And would you like to ask your body if it would like to let that go?

Anywhere you've got self-judgements which wouldn't allow you to see opportunities to Reclaim your True Self, would you like to let that go?

And would you like to ask your body if it would like to let that go?

Anything that wouldn't allow you to use The Kissing Consciousness Tool to its fullest possible effect, would you like to let that go?

And would you like to ask your body if it would like to let that go?

Happiness

The Elusive Emotion isn't always sadness. Half the time it is joy, happiness or elation that we aren't allowed to feel. If we've grown up in environments where Happiness was frowned upon, or our natural joy was met with judgement or abuse because it triggered those around us, the very arising of even the mere *possibility* of Happiness or happy, joyful feelings may trigger us before we're able to properly let it in. Even though we want it, we instinctively know we're not 'allowed' it. Our *nervous system* is conditioned to not allow it, so when those possibilities of happy feelings trigger us, we sabotage them and can't allow them in.

Anything that wouldn't allow you to be happy, would you like to let that go?

And would you like to ask your body if it would like to let that go?

Anything that wouldn't allow you to feel happy feelings and emotions, would you like to let that go?

And would you like to ask your body if it would like to let that go?

Adopting The Approach of Resting as Happiness Consciousness

There's a theory about a certain level of happiness that is based on nothing – not based on *any* condition *whatsoever* – yet we know that both unhappy feelings and Fear Consciousness Unhappiness exist within our human experience, so that's neither quite right nor helpful. With our Binary Structure, though, we can see that the quality in question occurs when the state of Love Consciousness allows us to honour simple Being. This is not based upon any *other* quality or any specific outcome or gain, but on the allowance/acceptance of Love Consciousness (which we can also understand as the *absence* of Fear Consciousness).

"When happiness has a cause, unhappiness will follow.
When there is no apparent cause, then one's true nature
has been allowed to surface. A counterfeit happiness that

> depends on people, things or conditions will always leave one wanting. Seeing beyond those is seeing the source, one that has no beginning or end." – Peter Ragnar

If you base your happiness on an upcoming party, then when the party is over that happiness disappears. Base it on some food and when that food is eaten the happiness disappears, too. You could base happiness on the security that you think money brings, and that happiness may disappear even while you still have the money, if you fear its loss!

If, however, you get back in touch with that quality of Happiness *as a Consciousness* that is prior to – not dependent upon – circumstances ("people, things or conditions"), then the varied and rich array of emotions, joys and experiences which life offers can arise without rocking your boat, without being held onto too tightly, and can be enjoyed as part of life's glorious and colourful tapestry.

Anywhere you have self-judgements that wouldn't allow you to choose the inherent value in simple Being, would you like to let that go?

And would you like to ask your body if it would like to let that go?

Anything that wouldn't allow you to recognise or inherently Know this quality of Happiness as simple Being, would you like to let that go?

And would you like to ask your body if it would like to let that go?

Contentment and Self-Contentment

'Happiness as Contentment' – and self-contentment – is simply another perspective on the quality of Love Consciousness. The commercial world distracts, even dehumanises us from this because it wants to sell us 'things', and therefore seeks to manipulate us into a state of *artificial* discontent. (We'll address the systemic causes of discontent in Volume II.) Incidentally, I would suggest that the more self-judgements a person has, the more likely they are to initially resist the notion that Contentment can provide them with any Happiness, because they are quite a way away from seeing – experiencing – that it would actually feel good or be fulfilling to them. Of course, in the case of our 'No' Permissions, discontent is actually appropriate, and is the thing that wakes us up to the opportunity to release a self-judgement. (../contentment)

Love Consciousness	**Fear Consciousness**
Contentment	Discontent

Letting Love Consciousness Lead to Happy Emotions

Your emotions and feelings are at least partially determined by your Consciousness, which means that if you prioritise and achieve Happiness as Love Consciousness, by and large this will lead to the *feelings and emotions* of happiness, of being happy and joyful. It will lead to the optimum, maximum possible joy.

Love Consciousness	**Fear Consciousness**
Happy emotions, wherever possible, are allowed	Wherever possible, happy emotions are not allowed

The Two Aspects of Happiness Consciousness

Happiness as a Consciousness is derived from:

- Happiness as simple Being
- which means an absence of 'No' Permissions to being yourself

So we can clear the one major self-judgement that doesn't allow us to enjoy and appreciate the inherent value of all moments and adopt the approach of resting as simple Being. Even so, unaddressed 'No' Permissions *will* pull us out of Happiness and pull us out of our Being as and when they are triggered.

So as part of our Surrender to our Being, to keep the wheels turning smoothly we may wish to practice 'catching' (noticing) our 'No' Permissions so that we can hold Presence to them and Reclaim them as they arise.

Consciousness Itself Calls Us to Fulfil Our Success

We can then see that Conscious Living is not about just passively accepting things, putting up with our unsatisfying self-denials, or going without our heart's desire or fulfilling our potential. The very moment Consciousness accepts going without, it seeks to allow Receiving. True acceptance includes accepting our ability to Reclaim our buried truths, so Happiness inevitably includes Shadow Work, where appropriate. And since we've all been brought up in a dysfunctional and traumatised world, Shadow Work is going to be required for pretty much everybody.

The Paradox of Happiness

"... so a key here is to not *mind* whether
we are happy." – James Blacker

The Paradox of Happiness is a subset of The Paradox of Love Consciousness: By Needily needing to be happy, we actually push Happiness further away. Happiness and not being okay unless we get Happiness are polar opposite energies. The notion of the 'pursuit' of happiness that we've all grown up with is better replaced by the *Receiving* of Happiness.

From 'A' Happiness Moment to 'The' (Happiness) Moment

"If we take eternity to mean not infinite temporal
duration but timelessness, then eternal life belongs to
those who live in the present." – Ludwig Wittgenstein

We can see Happiness not as lots of little moments of Happiness that arise one after the other in time, but as one single eternal moment that has no beginning or end because it is an ever-present Consciousness. In this sense, Happiness is not just *a* moment, but *the* moment. Again, we understood this as children. And yet again, whether adult or child, 'No' Permissions will always drag us out of this 'one moment of our natural state of Being, of Happiness'. This is why I prioritise the removal of negatives (of all kinds) from my life, rather than the acquiring of 'positive' 'things'.

The Paradox of Living in the Moment is another subset of The Paradox of Love Consciousness, so we don't want to judge ourselves if we don't make the Happiness moment last forever without any interruptions. That's just counter-productive. We can't achieve the state of living in the moment by trying to control or force our living in the moment. All these things arrive unbidden, when we stop trying to control them.

It's partially true that there is only one moment. We just happen to experience it from lots of different perspectives that we call 'time' and circumstance. There is certainly only one Consciousness, one quality of Awareness and 'witnessing'.

"The only thing that's happy is The Witness,
because it's already free." – Ken Wilber

Success in Achieving Goals and Happiness are The Same Thing

It's a misunderstanding to think that a Conscious – and remember that's a True Self – approach to achieving goals and a Conscious approach to Happiness are two separate things, and could therefore possibly be in conflict with each other. I invite you to see these two as a single drive, as the same expression of Love Consciousness: Self-acceptance, self-honouring.

Under a Conscious Living approach we have Happiness Consciousness (Love Consciousness) as the 'goal', and we let optimum happy and joyful emotions follow from there. This is exactly the same as the achieving of goals approach: We have Success Consciousness (Love Consciousness) as the 'goal' and let optimum achievement of goals and aims follow from there. Thus we can address Happiness and Success as one single 'aim', as it were, rather than mistakenly seeing them as different priorities competing for our attention.

There is inherent value in life, and in any moment of life. In fact, the very nature of pure, unadulterated Being is enough to make us laugh hysterically, or smile like a Cheshire Cat, or just soak in the feeling of being alive.

For this reason, many wise people seek to remove and eliminate negatives in their lives before they pursue the 'trappings of success', if at all. They prioritise the removal of anything that compromises their experience of Being, or that inhibits their Life Force, compromises their nervous system or causes physical discomfort. This often starts with addressing any issue which inhibits the body – and there are plenty of those to tackle. It may also include distancing oneself from controlling people who don't allow us to be ourselves or negative people who seek to suck the joy out of us. And, of course, 'No' Permissions. Even then, 'getting things' often merges with and is driven by the wish to eliminate negatives, e.g. achieving a spacious, peaceful home surrounded by nature, with kind people around to hug and interact with eliminates the negatives of cramped living conditions, turbulence and noise, being distant from nature and isolated from human contact.

On a collective level, any unfair broken economic system that forces us to work twice as long and hard for the same or even lower quality of life is also a negative to be removed. This is particularly so if it is also destroying our soil and food quality, devastating our environment, imposing dehumanising surveillance and manipulative commercial messages on us, and more … and I've written an entire second volume of this book to address such things. Whilst you, like me, are dependent upon our collective effort to address most of this, there are also plenty of things you can do for yourself to allow you to be in your Being as much as possible.

Our Lifestyle: Our Relationship to Emotions

We can actually change our emotions, at least in part, by changing our relationship to them such that we're no longer avoiding them.

Emotions and feelings don't have free will. They don't need to inhibit our Choice or behaviour. There's a group of people who recognise this and who integrate their feelings as they arise, and then transcend them. This means that the emotions and feelings provide both experience and feedback, but they are subservient, 'weightless' background elements that don't need to clog down the individual going about their life. I call this the Integrate and Transcend Approach.

Another group of people don't transcend or integrate their emotions, but instead identify with them and get stuck in them, meaning they allow them to dominate. Some people take yet another approach of 'transcending' their emotions and feelings without feeling and integrating them, which means they are not actually transcending them at all but avoiding them. There is indeed a 'higher vibe' of Consciousness beyond emotions and feelings, but avoidance ain't it. These are both Fear Consciousness relationships to emotions. Emotions need neither be avoided nor allowed to be dominant.

Anything that wouldn't allow you to have a free and light (Integrate and Transcend) relationship to emotions and feelings, would you like to let that go?

And would you like to ask your body if it would like to let that go?

Reclaiming Emotional Authenticity: Being Grounded

Being 'grounded' means being in touch with what we are truly feeling, and what's true for us in the moment. It's neither avoidance of feelings, nor the adulteration of them through judgements about what and how they should or shouldn't be, which is also a form of avoiding feelings. There are no wrong feelings (although there can be False feelings). If we have the view that there are no wrong feelings, then how we behave and express ourselves can come from Love Consciousness, allowing everything to be authentic, effective, and psychologically and physically healthy. Let's take a look at a few different examples of how we can be grounded in response to our emotions.

Anger: You can be grounded and be angry at the same time.

Some people would like us to believe that anger is always Unconscious. It's not. Anger isn't so much a problem for the body as *judged* anger is, because judged anger is resisted anger, which means repressed anger, and repression causes a block of energy, a block of your flow, and potentially ill health. Unhindered, uninhibited anger, if related to Consciously, arises and then passes as appropriate. It can also provide fuel and authenticity to emphatic or aggressive expression – quite handy if you or someone you care about are being attacked.

> **Anywhere you've got self-judgements about how you should and shouldn't be with regard to anger, that have made you judge your authentic anger for being what it is, would you like to let that go?**
>
> **And would you like to ask your body if it would like to let that go?**

Fear: You can be grounded and be afraid at the same time.

> **Anywhere you've made yourself wrong for having fear, would you like to let that go?**
>
> **And would you like to ask your body if it would like to let that go?**

Sadness: You can be grounded and be sad at the same time.

An Unconscious person might say "Cheer up!", but a Conscious person wouldn't. Instead, they would be delighted that you were feeling into what is authentically true for you. People don't realise that sadness can be self-contentment because they never give it a chance. They judge it – every time – before they give themselves a chance to experience it in pure Consciousness, and so they always conclude that sadness is something to be feared and avoided. That prohibits the true discovery, that underneath all emotions is love and peace and truth.

Grief: You can be grounded and grieve at the same time. Grief can be both Conscious and Unconscious.

You can be cheerful or joyful yet not be grounded. And we can also Reclaim elation and joy. Again, The Elusive Emotion isn't always sadness. (../grounded)

Inner Strength

What if inner strength isn't something you wish for, but something you already have that simply requires acknowledging because your self-judgements have buried it in a way that made you not allowed to acknowledge it? Everyone has the inner strength to be everything they want to be. The problem is that where we have self-judgements, we won't be allowing ourselves to acknowledge that inner strength or use it to achieve our goals and enjoy life's moments.

Love Consciousness	**Fear Consciousness**
You allow yourself to acknowledge any inner strength you have	You don't allow yourself to acknowledge all of the inner strength you have

... and in Love Consciousness, you allow yourself to achieve and Receive those things you choose which require that inner strength. In Fear Consciousness, you don't.

> **Anywhere you've got self-judgements that aren't allowing you to acknowledge the inner strength you have, would you like to let that go?**
>
> **And would you like to ask your body if it would like to let that go?**

Total Strength of Psychology

There are weaker, average and stronger psychologies, but there's a definition of a psychology that goes beyond the comparative of 'stronger' to 'total': 100%, indomitable. You can Reclaim that attribute by being Willing to see reality the way it is in every moment. This is actually natural, indeed we have it as young children before it is knocked out of us.

This is achieved by having no self-judgements around who you have to be, or *how* you have to be, such that who you are is totally flexible, and can – and does, of course – define itself. Your Willingness to have your identity defined *by its own true nature* is this total strength of psychology.

When you have no attachment to any sense of a finite, fixed definition of yourself, and therefore have no need for things or the future to be a certain way, there is no need to 'skew' your perceptions of reality to accommodate needy hope, self-delusion or fear of your emotions.

Anywhere you've got self-judgements which prevent you from allowing yourself to be as you are and align with your true nature, would you like to let that go?

And would you like to ask your body if it would like to let that go?

How powerful – empowered – would you be if there was no truth you weren't Willing to face?

Similarly, wishful thinking is a *learned, conditioned*, false psychology trait – the effect of self-judgement. Nobody's true personality is wishful thinking. Not in adulthood. Wishful thinking arises out of unprocessed emotional pain and fear. Would you like to word your own clearing to allow you to release any self-judgements which cause you to engage in wishful thinking?

Complacency

Complacency isn't the same thing as choosing to not do something or choosing to rest. Just as shyness is the fear of self-expression, complacency is the fear of Success. So nobody's true personality is complacency. Therefore, complacency is another opportunity for a Reclaim. (../strength)

Personality and Character Reclaims

Personal Interests and Passions

Our accumulated self-judgements may have caused us to deny our interests in anything and everything from arts like dancing, singing, acting and playing musical instruments to passions for adventurous activities, travel, cookery, sport or stamp collecting. Maybe you were told that because you were academic you had no capacity for practical things, and you would secretly like to take apart the engine of a car and put it back together again. Or perhaps you have an honoured practical side and a denied academic side!

Maybe you were ridiculed for playing nerdy games, and so pretended to yourself that you didn't like them or had 'grown out of them' (whatever the fuck that's supposed to mean – wait for death, I think!). With so many potential clearings, rather than word them all individually, I'll word them in groups, giving just a couple of examples, and you're welcome to pick the ones you want to clear.

Anywhere self-judgements have caused you to deny your interest in dancing, singing, music, art, acting or poetry, or anything else, would you like to let that go?

And would you like to ask your body if it would like to let that go?

And please bear in mind that there's no downside to running that clearing, or any clearing! – it can't make you like the arts against your will!

I have already shared that it took me until age 39 to Reclaim dancing. At the time of writing I'm starting to wonder if I have an acting interest, too. But how are these things for you? What is there waiting to be Reclaimed?

Anywhere you've got self-judgements that deny or inhibit your interest in adventurous activities, travel, a hobby, sports, 'nerdy' pursuits, or anything else, would you like to let that go?

And would you like to ask your body if it would like to let that go?

None of this – not a single Reclaim or clearing – ever requires forced activity. It's all about what may happen to flow automatically and with ease after we've cleared the block. You don't have to *'do'* anything. You don't have to get the courage to do any of these things. If you clear them, and they are true for you, you can simply allow whatever flows from that.

Personality Reclaims

In telling jokes or anecdotes it's not so much the content that makes something compelling or not – a 'hit' or a 'miss' – as whether we 'own' it. Two different people can tell the same joke, but if one does so almost apologetically because they aren't allowed to be seen, or be in the spotlight, or be charming or compelling, it's that 'No' Permission that's going to make the difference.

People say they're "No good at telling jokes" or "Can never remember them." I think this is the False Self. Why did the chicken cross the Möbius strip? To get to the same side! That's fourteen words, certainly not beyond the basic memory capacities of an adult. But if we factor in our self-judgements, it changes the picture entirely.

Charisma is a subject that people have a lot of Charge around. I agree that some false or manipulative versions of charisma can be repulsive. But any person's Being, which emanates from Love Consciousness, is naturally charismatic. Nature has its own charm, and thus so does the human personality when it's not separated from itself. Again, I'll 'group' the clearing to save space:

> **Anywhere self-judgement has denied you your pure charisma, or your natural capacity for making conversation, communicating, interacting, telling stories, anecdotes or jokes, and 'owning' all of that, would you like to let that go?**
>
> **And would you like to ask your body if it would like to let that go?**

There's a difference between being childlike and being childish, but unless we appreciate that, we may allow Unconscious self-judgements to cause us to deny our childlike qualities as adults. Do we become 'grown up grown-ups' (who grow with time), or 'adulterated adults' (who have their true, joyful natures *adulterated* by judgements of how an adult *'should'* be)? (../personality)

> **Anywhere you've taken on self-judgements that have prevented you from appreciating the difference between being childish and being childlike, thus denying you your childlike nature, would you like to let that go?**
>
> **And would you like to ask your body if it would like to let that go?**

Characteristics

Any characteristic, from shrewdness to thrift, wit, presence, calmness, independence, and millions more can be lost to self-judgement – and also then Reclaimed. Perhaps you have self-judgements preventing you from acknowledging that you are good in a crisis? Or perhaps you always have to be the "strong" one and would like to feel free to fall apart once in a while! A healthy freedom from self-judgement would be having the option to acknowledge one's strengths, but not *having* to.

Anywhere you've got self-judgements that have buried your natural shrewdness, thrift, wit, presence, calmness, independence, or anything else you might like to Reclaim, would you like to let that go?

And would you like to ask your body if it would like to let that go?

You can literally choose any other characteristic or character trait that you'd like to ask for and Reclaim. You can also ask for things which you don't even think you are – that's often the point of having characteristics and strengths repressed. You might not have everything you ask for lying in wait for you, but there is no downside in asking. It's like the more balls you throw at the coconut shy, the more coconuts you hit. And it's free!

Projected Character and Characteristics: The Other-Admiration Principle

aka: Projection

One of the ways in which our buried character traits, characteristics and repressed personality aspects show up is by our Projection of them onto other people. Because we are not allowed to acknowledge our own capacity for these qualities in ourselves – but they are nevertheless true underneath the surface – we notice and admire them (or possibly dislike them!) in others. The very fact that you can appreciate the quality in others shows that you yourself have the capacity for it, however, in your case it hasn't been allowed to be honoured. This experience may also 'press our buttons' if it causes pain that they are allowed to own the quality, but we are not. We might call this 'The Other-Admiration Principle', which is a part of the principle of Projection.

This is the same principle as The Self-Disgust Principle, working in reverse. Instead of realising that an 'ugly' quality in our own thoughts and identity isn't really ours by the very fact that it repulses us (The Self-Disgust Principle), we realise that the beautiful qualities which we admire and appreciate in other people are ours also, by virtue of the fact that we are engaged by and appreciative of those qualities.

Maybe, for example, you would like to be one of those people who "Never miss a trick." If so, then you *are* one of those people who never misses a trick and have merely projected the quality onto others. The very fact that you can appreciate the quality in others shows that it resides in you.

Anywhere you've got self-judgements that prevent you from acknowledging yourself as one of those people who "Never miss a trick", would you like to let that go?

And would you like to ask your body if it would like to let that go?

One group of people we might frequently project our qualities onto are celebrities, not least because they are often in front of us. We might admire the gravitas of Morgan Freeman, the courage of Anne Frank, Freddie Mercury's stage presence, the drive of Oprah Winfrey or Michael Jordan's humility. "So are you saying I can Reclaim the gravitas of Morgan Freeman, Anne Frank's courage, Freddie Mercury's stage presence, Oprah Winfrey's drive *and* Michael Jordan's humility?" Yes, that's exactly what I'm saying. And you might see these qualities differently to me – you can Reclaim what you see and like.

You might have to release a heck of a lot of self-judgements to have the Presence to stand in front of 100,000 people in Wembley stadium without wavering into 'self-apologetic Consciousness', but ultimately it's just standing upright. The dance moves that Michael Jackson showed at the 1993 Superbowl carry his own personal signature. But the ability to hold one's nerve enough to remain still and silent for a minute, as he did, is ultimately just a matter of self-allowance, because other than self-allowance there's no actual specific skill required.

It doesn't even need to be people! I've managed to project one of my qualities onto the space invaders of the computer games of the late 1970s and 1980s. I noticed in them a non-Egoic persistence that I admired, and then realised I wished to Reclaim. We all had space invader persistence as children. At least at first. (Until we learned from adults how to quit on our truth … or deplete our energy by being talked into having determination to pursue that which was not our heart's desire). As kids, we didn't start to build a 'base' out of chairs and blankets and then give up 'cos the side or top fell down. We rebuilt it a slightly different way. (../projection)

Anywhere you have self-judgements that prevent you from owning the egoless persistence of a space invader, would you like to let that go?

And would you like to ask your body if it would like to let that go?

Reclaiming Indefinable Intangibles

We can even Reclaim those indefinable, invisible notions, feelings and nuances which touch our soul. Any time we even have the slightest feeling that there's something wonderful about life that we can't quite grasp or comprehend or get a sense of, we can still ask to let go of the non-allowance of that, and also ask for it to come into our lives.

Anything that wouldn't allow that amazing ... whatever it is, back in, would you like to let that go?

And would you like to ask your body if it would like to let that go?

There may even be a 'something' that is so intangible you can't define it, or you aren't even really sure what it means or is. That doesn't matter. If it has a certain energy or vibe, resonates in some way for you, or has a certain feeling for you, you can ask for it back. (../intangibles)

Peace of Mind

Would you like to Reclaim your peace of mind? It's not about having a certain personality, or having to achieve a certain outcome in life; it's just about releasing the self-judgements which don't allow peace of mind – and so it is everyone's birth right. In the Love Consciousness state you have peace of mind: You are at peace with yourself. Even so, for some people that may be very unfamiliar. It may take some getting used to, and allowing in on a more permanent basis.

Love Consciousness	Fear Consciousness
Peace of Mind	Troubled Mind; at odds with yourself

Conditional Peace of Mind and Unconditional Peace of Mind

There are two types of peace of mind. The first is what I think of as 'Beach' peace of mind, which is dependent upon circumstances being the way each individual personally requires them to be in order to feel at peace, for example "If I was at the beach …", or "At home with my feet up and no noise." This is conditional peace of mind. The second type is 'anywhere' peace of mind, which is brought about by a totally trusting relationship with self, not dependent upon the current life circumstances. This is unconditional peace of mind. Both types have value and can contribute to our quality of life. Conditional peace of mind is rather fragile, however, as circumstances can – and do – change, and so we might also ask for unconditional peace of mind, where we simply realise that we are fundamentally and inherently okay.

Anywhere your self-judgements have denied you unconditional peace of mind, would you like to let that go?

And would you like to ask your body if it would like to let that go?

Conscious Stillness

We can consider a 'Consciousness-Behaviour Split' with regard to stillness. What's the difference between stillness at a behavioural level and stillness as a Consciousness? We can even consider the difference between stillness at the thought-based behavioural level and stillness as a Consciousness. People tend to value the body and thoughts being still, but if your Consciousness is still – not needing to judge anything that arises – then both your mind and behavioural activity can be as messy as they want.

When your Consciousness is still your mind can be as turbulent and chaotic as it wants without you losing your peace of mind – because stillness is unconditional and total when you have it at the level of Consciousness. This is also particularly useful if you want to get the most you can out of attending a personal healing seminar such as a Kissing Consciousness event. Someone who is Willing for their mind and body to be as unstill as they want to be can open up to achieve a level of healing that is not accessible for the person who is overly concerned about how peaceful and still they appear to others. The first person has a still Consciousness and an unstill mind and behaviour/body (which is still Love Consciousness); the second person might have a still mind and behaviour, but their Consciousness is well and truly lodged in the Fear Consciousness column and anything but still. You can't have stillness Consciousness while you're attached to either your mind or your body being still. You are not your thoughts; you are not your body. So you can *observe* either, and not be bothered what they do.

"Peace of mind isn't about not having thoughts.
It's about not judging one's thoughts, or the mere
fact that they have arisen." – James Blacker

This is not about not having turbulent thoughts arising; it's about not judging them. If you think about it, if your peace of mind were dependent upon not having turbulent thoughts arising you'd be attached to that notion. That wouldn't be freedom, and couldn't possibly deliver unconditional peace of mind because there would be the fear of loss – fear that a turbulent thought may arise and destroy the peace.

Ultimate freedom can never be based on anything, because anything that's based on something being the case is always subject to fear of loss: It's always conditional. That which has no fear of loss is free.

Anywhere you've got self-judgements that have caused you to judge either your mind, your thoughts, your body or your behaviour for not being still, would you like to let that go?

And would you like to ask your body if it would like to let that go?

Uncertainty as Freedom: Are You Okay Not Knowing?

Being okay with uncertainty and not knowing is a basic part of unconditional peace of mind. Naturally, that goes hand-in-hand with being okay *with* knowing. Resistance to either indicates avoidance of an Elusive Emotion.

> **Anywhere you've got self-judgements which have compromised your natural ability to be okay with the uncertainty of either knowing or not knowing, would you like to let that go?**
>
> **And would you like to ask your body if it would like to let that go?**
>
> **And anywhere you've got self-judgements which have hidden your natural creative excitement in the face of uncertainty and not knowing, the very nature of the quality of vulnerability of the Love Consciousness state, would you like to let that go?**
>
> **And would you like to ask your body if it would like to let that go?**

Freedom from Compliments

Believe it or not, compliments can make us a prisoner of them, and so can also interrupt our peace of mind. To receive a compliment is fine, but the moment we take that further in our minds and attach or cling to the good feeling of the compliment (which we will likely do if we have low self-esteem) we imprison ourselves. We might hear someone say something about us – that we're funny, always speak our mind, or are kind to others – then, the moment we attach to any feel-good feeling around that notion we Unconsciously feel the need to match up to that in future, to keep the sense of the compliment alive. This means we Unconsciously feel we have to behave a certain way, rather than let our natural personality generate its own behaviour. This in turn shuts down our Awareness, and that shut down Awareness and state of 'being in our head' stops our peace of mind.

> **Anywhere you've shut down your Awareness to the fact that compliments that we hold on to become a prison for us, would you like to let that go?**
>
> **And would you like to ask your body if it would like to let that go?**

Comparison with others and gossip are different views of the same prison trap. Most Western TV soaps are driven by gossip and judgement. I even switched the mainstream radio stations off when it became obvious that they too were fuelling their shows on a diet of gossip and judgement. This is psychologically unhealthy for society. What are you feeding your mind with?

How to Stop Your Mind Racing

"Can somebody please turn off
this 'tape recording' in my head?!"

It's a very common complaint. People would like the 'drip, drip' of their minds to leave them alone.

Conscious Response to a Racing Mind

The brain isn't designed to stop, or to not have thoughts. Even when you sleep it's working. The only way the brain stops is when it gets insufficient oxygen … when you're dead. It's therefore important to realise that the problem is not the thoughts themselves, but *resistance* to the thoughts – the Unwillingness to have them. It's the *resistance* to the thoughts that gives them that quality of seeming to pester us and beat us up like Chinese water torture. And remember, resistance is a quality of self-judgement, which means it can be released. Change the quality of your relationship to your thoughts and you change your experience of your thoughts. That doesn't mean they'll cease without you Receiving the message about your truth that they're trying to give you.

> **Anywhere you've got self-judgements that your mind 'should' stop, would you like to let that go?**
>
> **And would you like to ask your body if it would like to let that go?**

So the solution to stopping the mind 'racing' is simple: Stop avoiding The Elusive Emotion. Let go of your resistance to feeling The Elusive Emotion, feel it, and you become at one with yourself. And when you do that, the quality of the dialogue inside your head automatically changes.

We can also think of this as 'The Paradox of Peace of Mind', that by Needily craving peace of mind we don't have it, and by Surrendering that Neediness we do have it. (../racing)

The "Don't Think!" Bind

When you're 'in your head', and you don't want to be, how do you think about not thinking? You have some self-judgement thought beating you up, so how do you think your way out of not thinking about that? That's the "Don't Think!" Bind.

You might try to think about not being in your head, but that cannot possibly work. You might try it the other way and try to 'not try' to think about the issue: "Ooh, look at me, I'm not even trying to *not* be in my head", but that's the same bind in different clothes: The 'Futile Paradox Hack' (see Chapter Four).

> "How can I decide not to decide? How can you focus on not thinking? You stop trying. You stop 'not trying' … trying to get it that way! You see, there is no way out of that bind." – Alan Watts

But ultimately there is a way out of that bind: To stop fighting it. Acknowledging the futility of the bind itself is what's useful. The only option left to you is Surrender. Surrender to The Elusive Emotion. Surrender to your True Self. You do this by becoming Conscious, by becoming aware of what you're doing, and releasing your own resistance to the situation. And once you do that, things happen for themselves.

For personal reasons, I think of trying to quieten the mind with other thoughts as 'The Shoulder Buster'. Once, when I was trying too hard to appear calm and relaxed – as a result of a 'No' Permission which was causing me to sabotage attempts at connection with other people – I was given advice along the lines of 'try to think calm thoughts around not doing that', and 'try not to do that'. But that can never work, because it's either forced behaviour, or forced thought-based behaviour. As part of 'trying to show I wasn't trying too hard' I got into a bind and unwittingly tried all manner of False Self and ill-fated ways to be, ending in an attempt to be cool by diving into the snow on the ground. The result was that I injured my shoulder. This a vivid example of what happens when Fear Consciousness drives forced thought-based behaviour, which in turn drives forced behaviour. The effective solution I needed at that time was to be invited to let go of my resistance to *not* coming across as calm and relaxed, as this would have returned me to myself, and in so doing would have been the very quality of Being I was seeking: Love Consciousness.

Of course this would have brought in The Elusive Emotion question: "What feeling are you shutting out that relates to the resisted prospect of not coming across as cool and relaxed? Would you be Willing to let that feeling in?" You now have feelings to feel, but you are no longer in your head. You're in a natural state of Being, at the point of no longer having any resistance. (../bind)

You're Perfect!

"We are perfect. That was the best bit."
– A Participant of my Wisdom Course, 2013

You're perfect. In actual fact, you transcend the very notion of being either perfect or not perfect. There's no basis for *any* definition of what could conceivably make a human being 'perfect' or 'not perfect'. The only thing that could even make it seem that way is the phenomenon of self-judgement. So rather than being either perfect or not perfect, what you are is free: Free from any sense of – and any reality of – imperfection … and perfectly wonderful just as you are.

"There's nothing wrong with you at all." – Alan Watts

So this is a part of happiness, to realise that the very notion of whether people are 'perfect' or not is utter nonsense. There's nothing you have to measure up to. Anyone who tells you otherwise is abusing you. We'll come to what I call 'Control and Abuse Consciousness' later.

"The first thing is to allow ourselves to accept that we can even *be* perfect." – Dr Deepak Chopra

Wow, there's a lot of Charge around this notion: "I'd better not say I'm perfect or people will think I'm big-headed or lack humility!" So we hold on to the self-judgement that we have to find a way to consider ourselves imperfect, at least in some way. But this is false humility on the part of the entirety of society. Not to mention that it compromises our immune system. It's no big deal to consider oneself either perfect or immune to the very notion of perfection, as these are just the realisation that self-judgement is an illusion. For society to be healthy we need to start acknowledging that. (../perfect)

Anywhere you're not allowed to consider yourself as anything other than less than perfect, would you like to let that go?

And would you like to ask your body if it would like to let that go?

The Potential Blindspot of 'Perfectly Imperfect'

A phrase that has arisen as people have attempted to avoid taking on the judgement that they are not where or how they 'should' be, is to describe themselves or others as 'perfectly imperfect'.

The danger with the notion 'perfectly imperfect' is that, except in a very rare few cases, it's an example of The Illusion of Grey Consciousness. There's a good intention in there that we don't want to judge ourselves for being where we are, but it's still mixed in with the Unconscious self-judgement that we *do* judge ourselves for being where we are, as evidenced by the very fact that we have felt the need to *qualify* the description of ourselves as 'perfect'. We could have described ourselves as 'perfect', (or even, preferably, not felt the need to define ourselves at all), but we chose instead to qualify that to 'perfectly imperfect' … which still buys into the idea that there *is* a notion of where or how we 'should' be. A difference between what we are and what we *'should' be* is a self-judgement.

Of course, we may still have real wounds we want to heal, but there's no need to think of ourselves as imperfect until we do, and that is neither an effective nor a compassionate basis for releasing them anyway. Yet sadly people still Unconsciously and unwittingly buy into the lie that they are imperfect, and that in any way whatsoever it's even possible for them to be not good enough.

Everything exists in a state of grace. On top of that are human perceptions clouding the issue. (../imperfect)

Self-Esteem and Self-Worth

The trouble with the notion of 'loving ourselves' is that love isn't the problem; it's the conditioned self-judgement that is all over the top of it that's the problem. Releasing that self-judgement will allow the self-love to shine through. The self-love has always been there; it just got buried. The self-love is just acknowledging your truth and Choice.

People get caught up on whether they 'deserve' something. Consciousness has no interest in that because it's a judgement. You don't need to 'deserve' something but the sense that you *don't* deserve it will get in the way of you achieving it.

> **Anywhere you've shut out your Awareness to the notion of deserving things being based on self-judgement and unreality, would you like to let that go?**
>
> **And would you like to ask your body if it would like to let that go?**

"Ideally, my self-esteem is based on nothing." – James Blacker

Self-esteem is how we feel about ourselves. Unsurprisingly, this is based on the sum of our self-acceptance and self-judgements, as clearly we're going to feel good about ourselves where we're allowing ourselves to be us and allowing our Choice, and won't feel good about ourselves where we (think we) are not even allowed our own free will. Self-esteem follows, responds to, is determined by our Permissions, so I wouldn't worry about trying to achieve self-esteem directly, I would instead release the self-judgements that block your Choice, and let the self-esteem follow on from that and take care of itself as a consequence. And again here's a sub-paradox, The Paradox of Self-Esteem: By letting go of the need to have it, we have it.

Love Consciousness	Fear Consciousness
Self-Esteem	Lack of Self-Esteem

So self-esteem is, on the one hand, conditional upon our Permissions, yet if we choose to have no resistance to being in a state of lacking self-esteem, the very fear of not having it loses all power over us and ceases to have any relevance. Our lack of resistance automatically returns us to a state of Love Consciousness – which we now also know is self-esteem. In this way we have Unconditional Self-Esteem. (../esteem)

As we've seen above, we're all of us immune to the very notion of imperfection, so the same principle also applies to our inherent worth. If we take self-worth as read for all human beings as default, then we as a society may avoid the unhealthy temptation to try to prop up our *authentic* and *inherent* self-worth with false notions of feeling superior to others, which actually just cause us further problems because it is merely papering over the cracks. Whether we *have* worth and whether we *feel* we have worth are different things, of course, so again as we release our self-judgements we'll start to see the real picture.

> "To think that there is anything in the entire Universe that is more worthy than you is to lack self-esteem." – James Blacker

Crickets in the Spanish countryside don't feel lacking in worth in any way, nor do wolves in Canada, so why should people? In our society we have phrases such as 'First Lady', which of course also suggests that the president is the 'First Man'. What's the implication? That the rest of us are 'second best'? Same with The Royal Family: We sing "God save the Queen", and "Long to reign over us", and of course, HM stands for "Her Majesty." But what does that imply for the rest of us? She's majestic, but you're not and I'm not? And she 'reigns over us'! So we're 'underneath'. Are we even free?! And then we sing that God will save the Queen/King. God will save the Queen/King … but not us? Why don't we sing "God save all of us"? All of these messages have the same theme: We're inferior, we're second-best, we're underneath, we're different to them, we're not good enough. What kind of Unconscious message do you think a person is sending themselves by singing for God to save someone else, but not them themselves? What do you think that does to a nation's mental health? Regardless of whether you're a monarchist or a republican, religious or atheist, The Unconscious is called that for a reason, and I would suggest that virtually all of us have picked up Unconscious inferiority messages from birth which need to be released if we're to be healthy, both mentally and physically.

Anywhere you've shut down your Awareness to the fact that our world is full of subtle messages about our inherent inferiority, both intentional and accidental, would you like to let that go?

And would you like to ask your body if it would like to let that go?

Consciousness is capable of seeing the reality behind the judgement that humans engage in: That all of us are born equal. A simple understanding of Alfred Adler's notion that a 'superiority complex' is merely a False Self attempt to hide a sense of inferiority and lack of self-esteem, a lack of self-love, completes the picture. Many of those 'at the top' require our compassion for their 'superiority' (Unconscious sense of inferiority) self-judgements every bit as much as those whose sense of inferiority isn't camouflaged by superiority. At Kissing Consciousness we don't take the False Self at face value (see Chapter Seven). There is a saying, "A truly secure person is never unkind under any circumstances."

Anywhere you've shut down your Awareness to the fact that all of us are equal, and that people who believe otherwise are actually using that to cover up their own insecurities and compensate for their own sense of denial and lack of self-love, would you like to let that go?

And would you like to ask your body if it would like to let that go?

Nature knows that all human beings are born equal, so why don't we? There is nothing we need feel inferior to.

Where Lack of Self-Respect is Appropriate

Where people have self-judgements, and thus a False Self, they lack self-respect to that degree. But there's one way that's quite appropriate: Why would you have respect for something that isn't you?! So in a way we can be proud of our lack of self-respect, where we are rejecting a False Self that's been imposed upon us. That's a healthy starting point from which to let go of the False Self. (../worth)

Mental Health

Word on the street is that one in four of the population (25% of us) has had mental health issues. My own sense is that it's between three in four (75%) or almost four in four (99% of us), so the good news might be that we're all in it together. In fact, checking the official statistic, "1 in 4 people in the UK will experience a mental health problem *each year*", which tallies more with my instinct. Given that most countries' citizens see more trauma than the UK's, we could say we have a traumatised world system that makes mental health issues likely and predictable. Very rarely do I meet people whom I can sense are totally together. In fact, at a recent business event I attended, no one else in a roomful of 20 people said they considered themselves to have wellbeing – and this was a group of social leaders and entrepreneurs, headteachers and other professionals with very long, distinguished careers in various fields. So we're all sensibly invited by nature to unite as one big unofficial team to 'hold space' for us all, for each other. We're all understandably finding this 21st century terrain a bit of a challenge. (../mind)

Guilt and Shame

> "Holding guilt and shame are seriously
> bad for our health." – Angèle Beaudoin

In order for your Conscience to work effectively, it's important to retain some sense of the possibility that both guilt and shame can be genuine and may guide us to identify where we've done things that go against our authentic sense of right and wrong, which we can address. That said, for the most part, guilt and shame are likely to be false, created by self-judgements being imposed upon us, and here we are invited to let those go.

Anywhere self-judgement is compromising the genuine, natural, healthy sense of right and wrong that you had before our dysfunctional society dumped its ills and opinions on you, would you like to let that go?

And would you like to ask your body if it would like to let that go?

You aren't less than a saint because you eat chocolate or like sex. You aren't less than a saint at all. You're allowed to be free of toxic guilt and toxic shame. You don't have to apologise to anyone about what you are and what you're not. (../guilt) (../shame)

Anywhere you've bought into the lie that you are inferior to a saint because you like things that make you feel good, such as food or sex, or for any other reason, would you like to let that go?

And would you like to ask your body if it would like to let that go?

Worry and Anxiety

"Worry is impossible without self-judgement being present." – James Blacker

Whereas guilt and shame can be either real or false, worry is always a False Self interpretation of your inner information because it has no upside, no positive benefits. It just drains our energy.

There are two causes of worry:

1. A self-judgement that you're not allowed to be something, so you worry that things may turn out that way.
2. A self-judgement that is stopping you from doing something you know you wish to do about a situation. Maybe you are not acknowledging your genuine fight or flight messages, for yourself or someone else, or maybe there is an opportunity for positive gain that you are not taking.

Either way, your worry is an invitation to let something go. That's its purpose, to get you back communicating with yourself Consciously. You can't force your behaviour, or even force your thinking to not worry, but by letting go of the self-judgements the worry removes itself because there is no longer anything generating it.

To Consciously dissolve worry requires us to acknowledge the true message of our inner information. It may be that we can only replace our Unconscious worry with Conscious deep grief and pain.

Anywhere you've got self-judgements which may cause you to engage in the unproductive activity of worry, would you like to let that go?

And would you like to ask your body if it would like to let that go?

Sometimes people will say "I'm worried such and such will happen if . . .", and oftentimes it's not that they're worried that it *might* happen, but that they *know* that it *will* happen! In this case, what self-judgement is preventing us from facing the fact? Would you like to let that go? (../worry)

Similarly, by letting go of our self-judgements about all the various outcomes which may or may not occur, clearing them from both the resistance aspect of our mind, *and* our body's nervous system, we can lessen anxiety's hold on us until it disappears. The question here is what state of being would best serve us, and so would we like to let go of anything (worry or anxiety) that wouldn't allow us to have that most useful and self-supportive state? In actual fact, every self-judgement we've released so far, and every one we ever will, is decreasing our worry and anxiety.

If anxiety is slight, we might think of it as being closely associated with worry, almost the same thing. Where anxiety is more dominant and a bigger issue, however, it tends to be associated with the conversation around things like depression and mental health, PTSD and so on. (../anxiety)

Depression

"When a flower doesn't bloom, you fix the environment in which it grows, not the flower." – Alexander den Heijer

"How dare a footballer have depression? If he has that kind of money he's got no reason to be depressed." It doesn't work that way. As we've seen, Consciousness is primary and it's not about what you have.

Blimey, who wouldn't be depressed. After being brought up by a society that's based on self-judgement, one arrives at adulthood to find that the tax money we pay disappears down some black hole into a world economy that doesn't even adhere to the basic principles of accountancy. Even if humanity is starting to envision an age where love can come shining through, the place it has come from has been anything but that, and it is still very much a work in progress.

I see depression as primarily being about the environment in which human beings are expected to live, and the things we are required to tolerate. In that sense, depression is actually appropriate – a natural way for a human psyche to respond to inhumane life conditions. It's a survival response.

All Fear Consciousness is repression, and that isn't much different to depression. Without saying that releasing self-judgement is going to cure all depression – which would be irresponsible – I would still suggest it's a pretty good place to start and see where it takes us.

The First Step: Release Judgements Around Having Depression

Depression is said to be a 'secondary' emotion: You aren't allowed to be angry, so you get depressed, or you aren't allowed to be passionate, so you get depressed. You aren't allowed to speak your mind, so you get depressed. You aren't allowed, or aren't able, to stand up against injustice, so you get depressed. So if instead of making the depression 'wrong', we honour it, and in so doing honour ourselves, we can see what curious service it provides.

> **If you have depression, if you've judged yourself for having depression, would you like to let that go? There's no reason you have to judge yourself for having depression.**
>
> **And would you like to ask your body if it would like to let that go?**

If the Elusive Emotion release on that clearing is big, of course please take as much time as you want before continuing reading.

The Second Step: Release Judgements That Cause Depression

Depression isn't to be judged any more than an upset stomach is. What we want to do is clear the self-judgements that have contributed to or caused depression. What are we not allowed to be that is causing us to be depressed? Is there a part of you that hasn't yet been allowed to be loved? … and honoured? Quite possibly there are many parts.

Wherever self-judgements have caused or contributed to depression, either entirely or in part, would you like to let those go?

And would you like to ask your body if it would like to let those go?

Johann Hari made an observation that mirrors my own long-standing thoughts on this matter: "We all know that every human being has basic physical needs: for food, for water, for shelter, for clean air. It turns out that, in the same way, all humans have certain basic psychological needs.

- We need to feel we belong.
- We need to feel valued.
- We need to feel we're good at something.
- We need to feel we have a secure future."

He continues: "And there is growing evidence that our culture isn't meeting those psychological needs for many – perhaps most – people. I kept learning that, in very different ways, we have become disconnected from things we really need, and this deep disconnection is driving this epidemic of depression and anxiety all around us."

We are all affected by the actions of those around us, and we'll talk more about society later. For now we can ask ourselves what can we do *as individuals* for ourselves, to maximise our mental wellbeing and create a nurturing, relaxed, supportive way of life for ourselves as best we can? We are too short on space in this book to offer as many clearings as I'd like to, but there are any number of clearings you might like to ask yourself.

Wherever you have self-judgements blocking your Awareness to the ways in which you might improve your overall environment in any way, would you like to let that go?

And would you like to ask your body if it would like to let that go?

Wherever self-judgements have blocked your potential in any way, would you like to let that go?

And would you like to ask your body if it would like to let that go?

A Collective Third Step: A Revolution of Society

Society simply isn't designed to prevent depression and disorder; rather, it's designed to manufacture it on an industrial scale. Up until now, society has been built on Ego and the False Self. This has gotten worse at the exact same time as vast swathes of collective human Consciousness have started to recognise our psychological needs.

"Is there a lesson? Let us please take depression very seriously, in ourselves and in others. If in ourselves, let us speak our pain openly, let us not be limited by childhood conditioning into hiding our anguish, into being shamed into silence. And if in others, let us find the patience and compassion to hear that pain, to invite it to exist without judgement, without easy answers, without blame. Let us share. And let us understand that the prevention of mental illness begins in the crib, in how we hold and attend to our children." – Dr Gabor Maté

Anywhere you have self-judgement that wouldn't allow you to speak your pain openly, or ask for help, would you like to let that go?

And would you like to ask your body if it would like to let that go?

Depression and medication are addressed a little in Volume Two. We'll also take a further perspective on depression and anxiety in the last chapter of Volume Two on Wisdom. (../depression)

Lifestyle Reclaims

"Love is the only lifestyle that isn't a dead end." – James Blacker

We can Reclaim all unfulfilled aspects of our desires for lifestyle, covering such things as Ease, which we addressed in Chapter Three, more free time, freedom from social approval, even being cool or smooth (it doesn't have to be a dirty word!). We can ask our Subconscious for more life in our life. We can ask for less drudgery, in fact we can ask for zero drudgery. We have infinite opportunity for the Ease we can ask for in our lives. Maybe you'd like to Reclaim your capacity for a lifestyle without procrastination … or to stop judging yourself for procrastinating and just enjoy it. What Awareness might you have underneath the self-judgements of procrastination? And we can certainly ask for any of our own individuality back that we may have mislaid along the way. Maybe you have a party animal side you've never been allowed to honour.

Anywhere you have self-judgements preventing Ease from being your experience of life, would you like to let that go?

And would you like to ask your body if it would like to let that go?

Would you like to make more use of your time? How can you earn £50 waiting for a bus for a minute? Maybe you can't directly (or maybe you can!) but you can certainly do a clearing from an infinite array of choices, which may lead to all manner of desirable outcomes once those false blocks are removed. I might write a letter: "Dear personal Consciousness, what can you do for me? Whatever you've got that's good for me, just keep it coming …!"

Anywhere you have self-judgements about not being allowed to ask Life for more, or about what you're not allowed to ask for, would you like to let that go?

And would you like to ask your body if it would like to let that go?

Maybe you'd like to remove any blockages that wouldn't allow you to notice ways that you can start to increase the amount of rest and personal space time you manage to get for yourself, maybe noticing what trustworthy people might be able and more than willing to help with your workload.

'Owning It'

You might like to do a clearing to allow yourself to 'own' your own style and personality. In fact, every clearing you'll ever do is about you re-'owning' something.

"If you're going against your truth, then no
amount of fashion or stylish clothes are going
to give you a good look." – James Blacker

Discovering The Joy of Other People's Opinions and Lives

As you become complete within yourself, the need to impress others or influence others disappears, and you may find that your own words, if they are habituated ways of speaking which were generated by Fear Consciousness, become boring to you. You may realise you are bored of the sound of your own Ego, your own explaining, your own defensiveness, your own approval seeking, Neediness and desperation to gain a rapport. This leaves the space for many things, one of which can be Receiving the views and interesting pictures and stories of life which others share as something that interests you and enriches your life. (../lifestyle)

And in the next two chapters and continuing into Volume II we'll cover Reclaims around the following three areas as they relate to happiness and quality of life:

- Physical Body and Health
- Relationships
- Money, Society and Prosperity

www.KissingConsciousness.com/happiness

Chapter Six

Body and Health

Trusting The Underlying You

"The countryside is empty and the hospitals are full. There's a big clue in there!" – James Blacker

With such things as Success and Happiness, we've taken the approach that we simply require an absence of negatives, and that in those circumstances the positives take care of themselves. We trust the underlying truth. With health we take pretty much the same approach – that our inherent Life Force takes care of itself, congenital conditions aside, and we're simply required to avoid negatives, or remove the negative influences upon our Life Force and our health.

Unfortunately, we now have to keep our Awareness open to the possibility that some of these negative influences come from the very medical professions, free market products and governmental health messages that we have been brought up to trust to look after us. Most people are aware these days that lobbyists and corporate interests influence what information is shared with the public, and corporate interest is susceptible to putting its own financial interest ahead of transparency of research and the interests of the people. In short, if a walk in nature is better for you than a pill, it takes a person (or company, government, economic system) of integrity to tell you that, rather than sell you the pill. The world is currently selling us the pill.

The human Life Force has never yet really been allowed to shine at its fullest in mainstream society. Only in the cases of a few isolated individuals can we start to see even a glimpse of what's possible for us as human beings. (../trusting)

A Recent History of Human Health

To understand what's going on with human health, we might consider the difference between the following two types of disease:

- Infectious Disease
- Degenerative Disease

A hundred years ago and more, people mostly died of Infectious Diseases such as Tuberculosis, Influenza (the flu) and Pneumonia. A combination of improved sanitation, hygiene and the good work of those who have found cures and advanced medical science means that Infectious Diseases are no longer the major cause of death in the developed world. Today, the more common causes of death and suffering are Cancer, Heart Disease and Stroke, Osteoporosis, and forty or fifty other Degenerative Diseases.

Whilst such things as fortune and accidents of birth do play a part, the essence of Degenerative Disease means that there is definitely a role to play for the individual. I was first taught the important distinction between Infectious Diseases and Degenerative Diseases by Dr Myon Wentz, Founder of Sanoviv Medical Institute. In the same lecture, he disclosed statistics stating that the primary contributing factor to Cancer is diet: What we eat and drink. The second contributor is smoking. These are things we have some control over as individuals. As the saying goes, we are digging our graves with our teeth. Society cannot expect all of the responsibility for tackling Degenerative Disease to lie with the doctors the way it did with Infectious Disease. It's simply not the same kind of scenario. (../recent)

Body Wisdom

Listening to The Body

I was very fortunate to be taught to listen to my body by David Heard in 2002. Heard was the founder of The National Rehabilitation Centre for The Paralysed, for which I worked, as well as its sister charity, Sportability. His testimonials for his work with elite athletes include those from the then

England Cricket Captain, Andrew Strauss. In 2002, when I interviewed David to record an audio product on 'Strength for Life' and ageing, he had just completed a challenge to cycle a thousand kilometres around Vietnam, at the age of 62, in temperatures of 90 degrees and in 90 percent humidity.

Whether with elite athletes, for people at his rehabilitation centre, or everyday people in all walks of life, Heard told me how he always worked with people with a view to getting them to listen to their body. This is about paying attention to what's going on in your body: What are the signals being given to us, what information is being provided? I asked if this was like a mechanic listening to a car engine and getting a feel for it. He agreed, adding, "You're reading the runes of your own body."

As we've seen previously, we can create a Universal Binary for listening to the body. Although we aren't going to spend every moment focussing into our body, if we're in Awareness we are at least open to its information, such that, if the body wanted to, it could let us know something it wished for us to do to help it, for example change our posture, drink fluids, or even stop thinking so hard, if that is causing us brain strain.

By listening to our body we can tell when we want to eat or drink, and when we don't, and even *what*. We can tell if and when we want to move, and even *how*. And all of this goes for every single moment. If we get the desire to walk, and so walk, but then get the desire to either speed up to a run, or slow down or stop, we can respond to that. We can respond to that, *if* we notice, and if we allow ourselves to (i.e. if we're Conscious). The more we develop the art of listening to the body, the more information we can receive and respond to, and the more we can allow our Life Force to be free to maximise itself and give us optimal health.

Listening to the body is a *fundamental principle* of Awareness and Conscious Living. Our body is with us in every moment, as is our mind, and as Heard observed, "You don't divorce the two." Body and mind are inextricably linked.

Symptoms

Listening to the body is the cornerstone of health because when we ignore our bodies we get symptoms of discomfort and disease. It goes something like this: You do something and your body gives you signals to say it doesn't like that thing, or that it makes it uncomfortable, and if you've never thought to listen to your body you might not actually notice these signals at first, as they are very subtle. As you continue the behaviour, the signals become more noticeable, and let's say you carry on doing the thing which caused them. The body then has to 'shout' even louder to get your attention, and the feedback from the feelings in the body is more clearly uncomfortable. What if you still ignore those signals? Well then the body has to 'shout' even louder still, and if the symptoms still aren't listened to then soon they may become a full-blown illness or disease.

What traditionally happens then? We go to the doctor and take pills for the symptoms as if they were the cause. Why? Partly because we haven't been taught to master our emotions, haven't been taught to let go of self-judgements, haven't been taught to listen to the body: All attributes of Conscious Living. And partly, again, because the health system is not currently separated from the profit system. But we all know that if we have rats because of a build-up of rubbish bags in the street, the solution is to get rid of the rubbish, not the rats. This is part of what's known as 'The Feedback Principle'. Life is always giving us feedback.

"He who eats until he is ill must fast
until he is well." – Arab Proverb

Aside from Infectious Diseases, congenital conditions and the like, symptoms and ill health are generally the consequences of continually ignoring the body.

Sensitivity

Sensitivity is merely the intelligence to honour your Life Force. A person who rejects their capacity for sensitivity is gradually depleting themselves.

With an interest in doing so, over time you ought to be able to sense – and read (interpret) – the slightest impulse in your body. It's saying, "Pay attention to me." You don't necessarily have to translate it into words, you can keep it as an intuitive feeling or energy communication, but you'll know what it's 'saying' on some level. At the most basic level, it will be saying, "This is good and your truth", or "This is bad and not your truth", usually followed with "Do this!" or "Don't do this!" (../listening)

The Needs of the Mind vs The Needs of the Body

You may well find, if you start the practice of listening to your body, that *even though you are able to hear your body, and wish to honour it*, you aren't necessarily always responding to it in the way that you'd like to. This leads to an insight, also taught by Don Miguel Ruiz, that there is a difference between the needs of the mind and the needs of the body. It's crucial for our health that we learn to notice this difference.

> "The needs of the mind are not the needs of the body. If the need for food is in the mind, if the need for sex is in the mind, you cannot satisfy the need." – Don Miguel Ruiz

If the need for food is in the mind, there's no way you can satisfy that need with food. Similarly, if the need for sex is in the mind, there's no way you can satisfy that need with sex. The same goes for drink, and even exercise, and any other confusion of mental needs and bodily needs. If you think about it, it becomes obvious. So we have to sort our needs into two 'piles': These are the needs of the mind, and these are the needs of the body. An upside of this is realising that we can achieve effective weight management without having to deny ourselves anything we like, and without having to force our body to do any exercise it doesn't want to. (../needs)

Principle: Nobody's body overeats. Only your mind can overeat.

The 1-2-3 of Health

After realising that listening to the body was not enough, that we also needed to calm the mind enough to allow ourselves to actually honour the requests of the body, (and six years after being taught to listen to the body), I created the teaching concept 'The 1-2-3 of Health', and confirmed the theory with David Heard as accurately reflecting reality. In fact, if you want to see a 'retro' video of mine, there's only one: A somewhat nervous three-minute video explaining The 1-2-3 of Health was the first teaching video I ever recorded. It was done on an actual camera (no video phones) and took sixty-three takes. (../123)

The 1-2-3 of Health is the basic breakdown of what determines good health and how to achieve it, congenital conditions and Infectious Disease aside, and is as follows:

1. Listen to the body
2. Appreciate the difference between the needs of the mind and the needs of the body
3. Free the body from the tyranny of the mind so that we always honour the body, whatever that takes

Of course, it's no good merely identifying the difference between the needs of the mind and the needs of the body if we then go and do the thing even though we know the body doesn't want it. As Don Miguel Ruiz observes, we have to free the body from the tyrant that is the mind. The body might say "I don't want another piece of chocolate cake", and the mind might reply "Yes, you do!" We are required to do whatever it takes to actually tame and integrate the mind sufficiently such that we honour the body in all moments. And so, like everything else, this comes back to Awareness and, if necessary, letting go of the self-judgements – both in our Consciousness and particularly in our nervous system – that otherwise keep us locked in an abusive relationship with our own body.

Honouring the body 'half the time' is better than nothing, but it's not gonna get you optimal health because, by definition, you're also *dishonouring* the body half the time, and as we've said that can bring symptoms of discomfort and disease. Why would you want a moment in which you were dishonouring your body? Answer: Your True Self wouldn't, only your False Self would.

Listening to The Body and Your Practical Agendas

You may think, "Well, I can't honour the body all the time, I'm going to have to get *some* things done." As we've already seen, however, the body, being one with your Subconscious Mind, is well aware of this, and integrates itself with you wherever that course of action is in your best interests. If you have to 'bust a gut' to arrive at a new situation which is better for you, whether for an hour or for a year, the body will understand. And it will support you – *unless* it has a better idea that you're not listening to – remember, the body has access to all the Consciousness that you do, and of what's true for you, *and more.* This is why your body is your key intelligence and key implement of Success, and why listening to your body will not only maximise your health, but also your prosperity, and not listening to it will cost you prosperity.

Centauric Consciousness

What's the easiest jigsaw puzzle in the world? Two pieces, right? One jigsaw piece isn't a jigsaw puzzle, just a picture or an object. So a two-piece jigsaw puzzle is as easy as it gets!

What if those two pieces of puzzle were your mind and your body? What if the key to health is effectively integrating these two? Integrating mind and body is like doing a two-piece jigsaw puzzle for optimal health. On the face of it, integrating mind and body sounds easy. The difficulty comes because most people only 'see' one of the pieces of the jigsaw puzzle: The body. This is because they think they *are* the mind. That's like trying to do a two-piece jigsaw puzzle with one of the pieces hidden behind your back, except in this case, the second piece, the mind, is 'hidden' behind the eyes. So they can never complete the puzzle. They can never integrate mind and body. The way to do so is to stop identifying with the mind, and instead see it as an object. See its thoughts, feelings, emotions and beliefs as objects.

Figure 6.1: Seeing mind and body as objects to be integrated

In personal development, specifically Developmental Psychology, the stage of personal development at which a person is able to integrate the mind and the body is known as the 'Centauric' stage of development. Ken Wilber, Hubert Benoit, Erik Erikson and others use the centaur to symbolise the integration of the Bodymind. The centaur is a mythological being with a horse's body and a humans chest, arms and head; as a metaphor for a human, this represents integration of the (animalistic) body and the mind. The 'lived-in' experience of the physical body of a person who's achieved the Centauric stage of Consciousness differs considerably from that of someone who hasn't. And we're not just talking about things like slimness here – which might not even be the case. The whole feel and way of being is different. There is a freedom from the mind which can be felt in the body, and thus also in the daily experience of life.

"Hence, centaur – mind and body are both
experiences of an integrated self." – Ken Wilber

I need to be frank with you here that this is *not* 'no big deal'. We can't just click our fingers and leap to a Centauric stage of Consciousness in the same way that we can let go of a self-judgement. It's a fairly lofty stage of Being. Statistically, only about 30% of people have reached the stage *before* the Centauric. Perhaps 2% to 5% of the population are at the Centauric stage as of 2018. However, every moment of Presence and every usage of The Kissing Consciousness Tool supports the capacity to experience the mind and its contents as objects, and also Reclaim embodiment. So even if we aren't at the Centauric stage, we are doing everything we can to liberate the body from the effects of our own self-judgement. And that starts with The Paradox of Love Consciousness: Letting go of resistance to the judgement that "We're not there yet." That tool itself is aligned with the Centauric, and so is kind on the body. (../centaur)

We'll explore further perspectives regarding this topic in Volume II. For now let's look at some examples of the ways in which the mind dictates to the body, both for us as individuals, and collectively. Why do we allow the mind to tyrannise the body?

Illuminating The Tyrant That is The Mind

"I let nature have its way with my body." – Peter Ragnar

What a great quote! At the walking group I attend, some people observe those who stretch their legs before starting, and comment that "I feel I'd like to stretch, but I'd feel embarrassed", or "I feel the need to stretch, but it looks a bit pretentious." Bang! Just like that, self-judgement has compromised the health of billions of people; I'd say everyone in society, to some degree. There are many such cultural views that affect us all collectively. Another is the saying, "A gentleman may walk but never run." What absolute nonsense. Ladies and gentlemen, this is no intelligent way to run a society. We all do it, but can we stop now please? Can we stop the stupidity of self-judgement at the expense of our health and happiness? Isn't it time to be smart enough and wise enough to honour the body … and to recognise that as the way of health? (../tyrant)

Anywhere you have self-judgements that wouldn't allow you to honour your body, would you like to let that go?

And would you like to ask your body if it would like to let that go?

Liberating Your Optimised Immune System

"Your immune system is eavesdropping on
your internal dialogues." – Dr Deepak Chopra

Our immune system has been described as a circulating nervous system. The nervous system is compromised by self-judgement; so is the immune system. It's just as well that we understand The Paradox of Love Consciousness then, isn't it, otherwise the first thing people might do is panic about getting into the state of Love Consciousness to support their immune system. By not minding whether you're in a state of Love Consciousness or not, you *are* supporting your immune system. The effect of our Consciousness on our immune system is:

Love Consciousness	Fear Consciousness
Optimised immune system	Compromised immune system

None of this information makes anything worse for you, or for any of us. Bringing Awareness to it simply makes it possible that we can make things better. The way to a healed nervous system is asking your body to let self-judgement go, each bit. Personally, I have it running permanently, with the established instruction from me to my body: Let go of whatever you can, when you can. And in return, I always aim to listen and oblige it when I get requests back.

Your Life Force

We've talked about 'The Consciousness Gym' and Reclaiming an embodied body, and how this unlocks the full power of your Life Force. The Life Force is merely the growth of life that happens in us automatically, the same way a plant doesn't have to force anything in order to grow, as all the 'instructions' and drives are already inherently there. All that is required is to remove negatives from the environment, as expressed earlier in the quote about the flower (in the Chapter Four section on depression). The reason our Life Force might seem like a mystical thing is how little of it is understood or acknowledged by our societies up until now. Having repressed, denied and ignored our Life Force to such an extreme extent, it stands to reason that we might be surprised to realise we're sitting on a seemingly 'magical' amount of energy and wellbeing. (../immune)

Eat Unconsciously, 'Bowel Unconsciously'

If you eat things that your body doesn't ask for, or if you eat things in *quantities* that your body doesn't ask for, or even at *times* that your body doesn't ask for them, you'll likely experience interruption or discomfort when the body has to process it later on. Cause and effect, the Unconscious behaviour leads to an unwelcome experience. (This is not to say there aren't also other health issues which affect the bowels.) (../bowels)

Drink Unconsciously, 'Bladder Unconsciously'

By the same token, this may also apply to what you drink, how much and when. Unconscious drinking also leads to unwelcome experiences. (../bladder)

Farting, Sweating, Consciousness and Embarrassment

Let's say a person has self-judgements which prevent them from being calm or comfortable in their own skin. In different periods in my past I've asked ladies out with varying effects on my physiology. On one occasion I started sweating profusely almost the moment I began talking. Years later the capacity was there to carry out the same task with no particular effect on my physiology. So what was the difference? It's the Permissions that we have, whether we're allowed to ask for something, whether we perhaps feel shame at doing so, and related matters. The embarrassment of sweating in those circumstances was not due to the physical act, but rather, a symptom of Fear Consciousness. In the state of Fear Consciousness there is an embarrassment or false shame about doing something, which affects the physiology. By holding Presence to the things that cause us embarrassment we can release their hold over us and thus prevent their effects.

Similarly, when we are uncomfortable in our own skin, we perhaps don't honour our body so much, and often around food. When eating, we might not be calm, we might eat in a turbulent rush, and so swallow more air, particularly if we see food as our only source of pleasure, excitement or happiness in life, and also particularly if we have Charge around food. Self-judgement is Stress, and stressful eating affects the body differently. We might also chew our food less, and as a result of all that we might fart more. We might be embarrassed to fart because Subconsciously we know it reflects the fact that we're not comfortable in our own skin, which might in turn reflect a Subconscious (and definitely untrue) message we may have received that we're unlovable. It may also be linked to the moment our nervous system was initially compromised by unkindness or abuse, and that experience may also have caused us toxic (false) shame. Of course, there's no real shame in it. (../body)

Empowered Health

To help understand your relationship and humanity's relationship to health, I've defined the influences of health into the following groups:

1. **Independent Health:** Health you can allow for yourself.
2. **Interdependent Health:** Health which is achieved through co-operation with your fellow humans.
3. **Dependent Health:** Health which you depend on others for, such as scientists, researchers and doctors.
4. **Impossible Health:** Health which cannot be achieved by oneself or by anyone else.

The suggestion I offer is that people start with what they can do for themselves first – Independent Health – and only move on to Dependent Health if that alone isn't enough. In other words, what health and wellbeing can we achieve through our own self-honouring, without having to visit the doctor or the hospital?

Independent Health includes listening to the body, and so not degenerating one's body through Unconscious choices like overeating, ignoring the body's desire to move, and the body's natural ability to heal itself, wherever and to the extent that that exists. It also includes avoiding negative people, gossip and turbulent situations which cause sensory overload. Letting go of self-judgements promotes mental health, bodily nervous system health and immune system health. It also contributes to Interdependent Health.

Interdependent Health includes such things as a peaceful cultural environment in which we're not triggering each other's fight or flight responses all day long, and promotion of a healthier physical environment by not creating pollution, retaining and rewilding natural spaces, regaining soil quality for food and air quality for breathing, and preventing projects which expose us to harmful influences, such as 5G. It also includes the protection of people from harassment and other crime, as well as the removal of negative influences on our psychology, such as manipulative advertising, Orwellian authoritarianism and abuse of our privacy and private data. This is addressed in Volume II.

Dependent Health includes cures to Infectious Diseases, and more recently – in part – cures to Degenerative Diseases like Cancer and Heart Disease. We will not, however, find all the cures for things like Cancer unless we recognise the roles that both Independent Health and Interdependent Health play in Degenerative Disease. Here's a little critique of, and addition to my work:

> "For category 3 you don't appear to cover the issue of cures to genetic conditions, where the initial cure is dependent but subsequent health is not." – Jon Freeman

Independent Health, Interdependent Health and Dependent Health are *all* currently devastatingly compromised by the existing system failure of the global economic model. In Volume II I'll also touch on such things as vaccines, hugging, food quality, health care and Cancer.

Impossible Health

I'm not sure I like the idea of anything being in this category, and certainly should qualify it against absolutistic and authoritative diagnoses like telling people they'll "Definitely be dead in six months", or "Will never regain movement in that body part."

Jon Freeman added his own contribution to this debate: "There are too many stories of people achieving supposedly impossible things in the health arena such that I would not have a category 4 [Impossible Health]. Those who have read 'Science of Possibility' as referred to by James will know of my witnessed example of the reversal of HIV/AIDS in a man who had already been administered the last rites."

At The National Rehabilitation Centre for the Paralysed, people with Spinal Cord Injury who twenty-five years previously had been told by the best SCI units in the country that they wouldn't walk again, did indeed walk again, twenty-five years later. Whether we consider this category of 'Impossible Health' empty, or aren't ready to do that, I'd suggest we approach the notion of the impossible with extreme caution, and certainly with Conscious Awareness. (../empowered)

The Wisdom Diet

"I think The Wisdom Diet material and the concept is really interesting. I think it turns conventional dieting on its head, and I think it's absolutely needed in our culture and our society." – A Participant of my Wisdom Course, 2013

James Blacker: "If I only ate what my body wanted, and not what my mind wanted, I'd be ..."

David Heard: "... you'd be svelte."

In 2008, I wrote 'The Wisdom Diet', an eBook for weight management. As I explained in an interview about it, "It's a psychological approach; it's an interior approach. People take an exterior approach to dieting, so they'll try and force themselves round the block, or they'll deny themselves a bit of chocolate cake, but that really is an expression of the interior [in Kissing Consciousness terms, the behavioural level is an *expression* of our Consciousness], so what I'm doing is turning the five basic principles of dieting on their head, in terms of the thought process and the psychology that goes with it. The five main things that are wrong with dieting are that:

- There's denial
- There's forced exercise
- You can fail them; there's no guarantee of results
- It takes time
- And you can quit them

So there's a psychological way to turn all of that on its head to make it work for you."

"What if conventional dieting has been hammering away at the wrong 'rock'?" – James Blacker

1. Allowing Yourself Food and Drink (Conscious Eating)

As we've seen with The Elastic Band Principle, forced behaviour invariably snaps back and ultimately fails when the Unconsciously motivated force runs out. Forced behaviour is not enjoyable during the attempt, either, as that is life lived in a state of Fear Consciousness. Perhaps the most classic example of this principle can be seen with dieting and weight management.

Any good economist will tell you that decreased supply generally causes a spike in demand. We see this when the news reports a fuel shortage, and cars are soon lined up and down the road outside the garage. When I used to wake up thinking about a chocolate bar, but then denied myself this, it created a false sense of demand (and a False Self sense of demand!) as it caused me to think about it every moment throughout the day. Had I just allowed myself to have the thing straight away, the sense of demand would have been realistic.

I've said before that Love Consciousness is direct and *real* experience of reality while Fear Consciousness is conceptualised experience of reality. There are two totally different experiences of eating a chocolate bar, or anything else: From conclusion – "I shouldn't eat this, but I've intellectually decided that it's delicious" – compared to eating it from Awareness, which provides genuine experience and insights, and might well show us that we actually find the experience unenjoyable. Perhaps we can feel the thing blocking our arteries as we eat it, or maybe we realise we simply don't enjoy the thing. Maybe we realise it is making us feel nervous, or shaky. This is like the scene in TV's Minder, where Arthur Daley was hypnotised into thinking he no longer liked cigars, and he couldn't find one he liked. But we're not being hypnotised when we practice Conscious Eating. It's the opposite: We're releasing the hypnotism of conceptualised experience. We're waking up to reality.

The Conscious Eating approach is a more mature and responsible approach because it trusts the individual to be honest with themselves. If we were launching an ocean liner, we wouldn't want to just drop it into the water from a great height. We'd want to lower it in gently so that the water could take its weight without damaging it, until it could float on its own without the need for supportive ropes. In the same way, we don't want to be reckless with the notion of just letting ourselves eat what we want when we want. To be sensible it must be done *in response to* an increase in Awareness. And continuing the nautical theme, some of those big ships require 12 miles to turn around in, to change direction, so we may wish to appreciate that our body, too, may require us to be equally patient if we choose to change it, and us, from being control-based to being freedom-based. What does your Awareness say?

The Two Ways People 'Eat Their Emotions'

Hand-in-hand with the failure to listen to the body when making eating and drinking decisions comes the habit of emotional avoidance – comfort eating and the like. In this sense, people can be said to be 'eating their emotions', because they would rather eat something they don't really want to eat than face and feel into their emotions and physical feelings. This is the biggest contributor not just in terms of the obesity crisis, but of Degenerative Diseases generally, and as such it offers the greatest opportunities for potential gains from increased Awareness and the Emotional Infinity insights to help us Receive The Elusive Emotion. This is why Emotional Freedom is the core of Kissing Consciousness.

The main driver of comfort eating (and other related drugs) is denied desires and dreams. So we might clear our self-judgements around what projects we're not allowed to try, what pursuits we've been ridiculed for, what relationships we're not allowed to have, and perhaps most of all, what physical and sexual nature we have that we've been taught to repress, that we're not allowed to honour, or show.

> **What are you not allowed to do such that because you're not allowed to do it you eat instead? Would you like to let that go?**
>
> **And anywhere you have self-judgements that you're not allowed to do nothing, but you're allowed to eat and so you eat because you aren't allowed to be in your Being when that would mean doing nothing, would you like to let that go?**
>
> **And would you like to ask your body if it would like to let all that go?**

People also 'eat their emotions' based on certain qualities that foods and drinks have. If we consume a lot of sugar-based foods, toxic foods, or alcoholic drinks, we can expect the emotions and feelings that come with that. You might reasonably decline a sweet on the basis that you don't want the emotional drop that would follow.

Nurturing Food and Junk Food

The Kissing Consciousness definition of junk food is anything that your mind wants, rather than what your body wants in full Awareness. If the body wants something it has a good reason, and so of course the Kissing

Consciousness definition of *nurturing* food, or food that's good for you, is food that your body asks for, says "Yes" to, in full Awareness.

Love Consciousness	**Fear Consciousness**
Nurturing food or drink	Junk food or drink

If you just follow the rules of what the nutrition textbooks say, you'll be totally excluding the requests and feedback of the body. Does that really sound like a recipe for health? An example is the person who's been pushing water down their throat all morning, complaining of feeling bloated, but forcing themselves to drink yet another glass, because "The book says you have to drink 8-10 glasses a day." That's really self-abuse. I'm watching this and thinking to myself, "Doesn't the body get a say in all this?"

Conscious Nutrition

None of this means that nutrition doesn't have a place. And all things being equal, as the population becomes more aware they are most likely going to consume less of what we conventionally understand by the term 'junk food'. As with the mind, though, if there are no self-judgements then nutritional insights are the servant, not the master. Just because you know something to be 'unhealthy' by conventional definitions doesn't mean your body Awareness can't be genuinely asking for it. There might be a million and one good reasons why it is. And by the way, are we to believe that the body itself hasn't learned anything about nutrition?! The Subconscious Bodymind? I would guess your Subconscious Bodymind almost certainly has a stupendously vast wealth of nutritional insight.

Conscious Cravings

In the same way that we can fully feel into emotions like anger, grief and sadness without judging them, and find that there is love and truth underneath them, we can also fully feel into a physical craving, i.e. feel it without judging it, listen to the body *with originality* and get a totally different set of information than if we judge it. We find what the body really wants, and thus likely also what *we* really want. Underneath what we *think* the body is *craving* for is likely to be what the body is really *yearning* for. And it will tell us if we listen to it. It might be water, it might be deep breathing, it might be physical activity. It could even be the thing we crave itself: The body will know better than our Conscious Mind how it best wishes to decline and release the craving.

Anywhere you've confused cravings with what you genuinely desire, would you like to let that go?

And would you like to ask your body if it would like to let that go?

And anywhere you've judged your body's genuine request for an item that you crave, would you like to let that go?

And would you like to ask your body if it would like to let that go?

You see, we want to get you out of judgement and conclusions in *both* directions, not just assume one way will always be the 'right' way, as that shuts down Awareness.

2. No Forced Exercise (Conscious Movement)

In the same way that most people have a false (and False Self) relationship to what they're eating because they're in their heads, they also have a false relationship to exercise. By holding the judgement that we *have* to exercise, and *should* exercise, but that it's something we hate to do, we fail to ever have the experience of freedom around moving our bodies which may give us the realisation that there are times when it's more enjoyable to do so than not to. Incidentally, education is similar: We're all forced to learn from age dot, so very few of us notice that education can actually be enjoyable. Same goes for work! Anyway, back to movement … and let's bear in mind that formal exercise is simply a subset, a *part* of overall movement.

'No Pain, No Gain' is a No-No

"Pain is the body's signal that something is wrong, so 'no pain, no gain' was always going to be a dodgy premise." – David Heard

As David Heard also pointed out, "No pain, no gain is a no-no." Exercise is a part of movement, and movement is designed by nature to be enjoyable, so I often consider that if people are not smiling during it, or are feeling worse after it, they are probably doing something from 'should' (from their mind) rather than from truth (from their body). Some people reject this notion, saying they "love the pain." Well that's not actually pain they're talking about. It's crucial to understand the distinction between the enjoyable sweet spot of stretching oneself, and actual bodily pain or damage.

Anywhere you've bought into the self-judgement that you have to feel pain in order to be healthy, fit or slim, would you like to let that go?

And would you like to ask your body if it would like to let that go?

Anywhere you've got self-judgements that have denied you joy of movement, would you like to let that go?

And would you like to ask your body if it would like to let that go?

Sluggishness vs Laziness

For Conscious Movement, we don't force exercise or movement. We also don't *deny ourselves* exercise or movement, don't let Unconscious self-judgements deny us our true relationship with movement and the true joy of movement.

Laziness is a judgement. There's no such thing as laziness. It doesn't exist. Either it's sensible rest (all good trainers know to respect the rest period) ... or it's something that someone else wants us to do but that we don't want to do, which is probably sensible to resist their controlling nature ... or it's something we *do* want to do but we have a 'No' Permission around it and Unconscious self-judgements clouding the issue of our passion and our feelings. The 'solution' to so-called laziness isn't to work, but to stop judging yourself.

Sluggishness isn't a judgement, however. It's the reality of how you feel when self-judgements stop you from being as dynamic as you would like and are able to be, through your own genuine Choice. But rather than take my word for it – which I wouldn't want anyway – you can ask yourself for your own Awareness as to how enjoyable it is to feel sluggish, mentally as well as physically? This is yet another way in which Awareness leverages The Wisdom Diet to make authentic movement *automatic*, not forced.

> **What Awareness do you have underneath the judgement of yourself or others as ever having been lazy? Would you like to let that judgement go?**
>
> **And would you like to ask your body if it would like to let that go?**
>
> **Anywhere you've got self-judgements that mean you have to experience sluggishness against your will, would you like to let that go?**
>
> **And would you like to ask your body if it would like to let that go?**

Resistance and Perceived Exertion

An important principle of Conscious Exercise is that it doesn't matter what weights or speeds other people are achieving, or even what you *should* be achieving; what counts is how you *perceive* your own level of exertion. Resistance is another useful concept to appreciate here. If you're walking or running and flat terrain becomes uphill, that's an increase in resistance. Paddling upstream gives more resistance than paddling downstream. You have the opportunity to assess whether the level of resistance in any given moment is too much *for you* or too little *for you*. And this will likely change from day to day, even moment to moment. This is why I encourage everyone to try spinning (indoor cycling on a static bike) at least once. The degree of control that one has over the resistance whilst spinning, adjusting the resistance moment to moment as it gets too hard or too easy, is a great way to learn about tuning into and mastering your own relationship with physical resistance so that physical movement is enjoyable and energises us to want to do it again. It's a great way to get into your own zone, to find that sweet spot between not hard enough and too hard. You don't have to listen to the guy at the front telling you to go quicker. You're there to serve you, not him or her.

"Better that you do something that you enjoy, and will do it regularly, than you have some weird idea that you *should* be doing this, and actually you won't. It's not about punishment." – David Heard

Conscious Personal Fitness Trainer Client

... Which brings us to Conscious interactions with personal trainers and the like. It's important that this is a two-way street. If a personal trainer tells you to do something and your Love Consciousness says it's alright, then fine. But if your Love Consciousness says "No" to it, and doing what the trainer says would take you into Fear Consciousness, then if it were me I would simply tell them "No." I would supportively explain what my Awareness around it was. If they don't accommodate your information in that moment, any time they push you to force against yourself, they're just going to 'elastic band' you (remember The Elastic Band Principle). You don't want the Ego (or even simple innocent ignorance) of your trainer dictating against your body's genuine realities. A good trainer will understand this.

> **Anywhere you have self-judgements preventing you from saying "No" to people, would you like to let that go?**
>
> **And would you like to ask your body if it would like to let that go?**

The body does have *genuine* limitations. When I heard Peter Ragnar say, "Don't let your mind fail you", I was relieved to hear him add, "It's okay to let your body fail you." An immature trainer who doesn't understand that the body can have limitations, either in terms of fitness or health, can be a dangerous, destructive and counterproductive influence.

Living in the Moment, Conscious Goals and Being True to Yourself

The three remaining things that are 'upside-down' about conventional dieting are: (1) you can fail them (there's no guarantee of results), (2) it takes time and (3) you can quit them. The way to make this work for you is to have a goal that is based on being true to yourself in each and every moment – and to have any desire or wish you have to be slim or a different weight be *subservient* and secondary to that. And, of course, to have no attachment to any outcome. Attachment to a future outcome is Fear Consciousness; 'Conscious Goals' have no sense of attachment to them. This in turn means that we are free and able to operate effectively and enjoy life in the moment, including listening to the body.

So instead of, "I won't eat this pizza because I want to lose weight", we might ask, "Does my body actually want this pizza?" If not, it's not a *denial* to decline it, but a choice. Instead of, "I'll go for a walk because I want to lose weight", we might ask, "Does my body actually want to go for a walk?"

We can move away from being enslaved to the concept of goals with a 'reward' date set several months into the future, sacrificing huge chunks of one's life in the hope of results, and instead replace them with goals that have their reward date right now, in the moment. In every moment.

Thinking that we will be waiting for ages to get results can be a very uninspiring, disempowering and demotivating thing – particularly when there is no guarantee of results! So we need to turn this on its head. When you are doing things for the wrong reasons, e.g. denying yourself something, or forcing physical activity, an hour or even a split second can be a struggle, let alone three months, six months or a year. So you can always be asking, "What's the true thing for you to do *now*?", according to the principles above such as listening to the body and declining the tyranny of the mind.

So we commit to doing what is right and what will make us truly happy in the moment. When you start to do this effectively, the future will take care of itself. And not only will the future take care of itself, the future *must* take care of itself, for you can only ever live in the now moment, and that is the only place you will ever find any positivity or power.

The beauty of The Wisdom Diet is that it is impossible to give up on because it is impossible for us to give up striving to be true to ourselves, which is the cornerstone of the approach. The Wisdom Diet isn't a diet. It's the natural consequence of Conscious Living. The alternative is to approach weight loss by going against yourself. (../diet)

Sleep and (Circadian) Body Rhythm

When the longevity pioneer, Peter Ragnar, was asked about the factors that help him achieve great results, the first word out of his mouth was "Sleep." At the same time as I interviewed David Heard on 'Strength for Life', I also conducted three interviews with the UK's top sleep expert, Dr Neil Stanley, then Director of the HPRU, The Human Psychopharmacology Research Unit, and later Chairman of The British Sleep Society. The highlights were that we don't all need eight hours sleep; anything between three and eleven hours can be considered normal. ... Whatever the spread of our sleeping hours, we are designed to be asleep between the hours of 2am and 4am. And you need the amount of sleep that will, quite simply, allow you to feel awake during the day. (../sleep)

The Stupidity of 'Alarm' Clocks, Changing The Clocks and The 24 Hour Society

It's not just about sleep, it's also about rhythm. You may have heard the term 'Circadian Rhythm', which refers to our biological processes, and in this regard we might appreciate the fact that we evolved on a 24-hour planet. It's all very well for the clocks to be put back or forward an hour, but can your body's rhythm be moved around quite so easily? Dr Stanley informed me that if a person wishes to shift their sleep-wake cycle, for example if we're regularly waking at eight and we wish to regularly wake at seven, it takes at least a week to comfortably shift it by an hour. Yet we are expected to do this overnight when the clocks change twice a year.

How many of us can truly say we've gotten into a rhythm with our bodies? Very few. It's no wonder that society's health is struggling if every time the body has a chance to get into its natural rhythm, it is knocked off kilter again every six months. The European Parliament has finally seen sense and taken steps to end clock changing in 2021. It only took them 20 years to catch up with my rather basic and straightforward Awareness. The UK Conservative government, disappointingly, has indicated it will keep changing the clocks, assuming a Brexit happens. (../clocks)

Biological Torture

Scientists at Oxford University carried out a study showing that starting work before 10am is biological torture because it disrupts the body's Circadian Rhythm and natural timers, which regulate our various functions. Researchers found that obstructing the Circadian Rhythm can have effects that resemble being tortured.

Dr Paul Kelley observes: "This is a huge society issue. Staff should start at 10am. You don't get back to [the 9am] starting point until [age] 55. Staff are usually sleep-deprived. We've got a sleep-deprived society. It is hugely damaging on the body's systems because you are affecting physical, emotional and performance systems in the body. Your liver and your heart have different patterns and you're asking them to shift two or three hours. This is an international issue. Everybody is suffering and they don't have to. We cannot change our 24-hour rhythms. You cannot learn to get up at a certain time. This applies in the bigger picture to prisons and hospitals. They wake up people and give people food they don't want." (../torture)

> "Society teaches people to live on a weekly rhythm.
> Whereas our basic nature is screaming at us to
> live on a daily rhythm." – James Blacker

Our bodies evolved on a 24 hour a day planet, yet our social constructs impose a *weekly rhythm*, not a daily one, whereby we have different sleep-wake cycles at the weekend than we do during the week. This is the cause of the 'Monday morning feeling', because we have interrupted our Circadian Rhythm. As part of honouring our Circadian Rhythms, we might also consider the unhealthy nature of our 24-hour society. Unsurprisingly, depression and divorce rates among shift workers are higher than for the rest of the population. Dr Stanley also pointed out to me that whilst drink drivers are four times more likely to have an accident, sleep-deprived drivers are forty times more likely to have an accident. That's quite alarming, which brings me to my next suggestion. Even the name of the device, an 'alarm' clock, is a most ridiculous reflection of society. If you'll pardon the pun, it shows how asleep we are (in a Consciousness sense) as a society, how 'in our heads' and dissociated from our bodies and our Awareness, that we mess around with our Circadian Rhythms, and think nothing of starting every day with an 'alarm'. We're supposed to be an intelligent race! Words have psychological power; they have their own interpretations in our Bodymind. What does your own body say? (../alarm) (../rhythm)

> **Anything that wouldn't allow you to honour your body's desire for sleep and rhythm, would you like to let that go?**
>
> **And would you like to ask your body if it would like to let that go?**

And if you get insomnia, does it help the situation any if you judge the fact that you have insomnia?

> **Anywhere you've judged the experience of insomnia, or judged yourself for having it, would you like to let that go?**
>
> **And would you like to ask your body if it would like to let that go?**

Detoxifying Various 'System Failure' Toxins

In Volume II we address the underlying dynamics of the health and life destroying consequences of our destructive global economic system. Here are a couple of early examples of symptoms of it, both its products and its messages.

Toxin Free Toiletries

In my life, the move from conventional, toxic products to natural ones that are kinder on the body is picking up speed. Aluminium-containing deodorants have been replaced in my cabinet by PitRok, a natural deodorant. The same principle applies to toothpastes and shampoos: Conventional products are awash with toxins. Our water contains toxins and the steam from our showers gives off toxins from the metals in it. Even our clothing is toxic. (../toiletries)

Body Love and Body Shaming

Male or female, we could all use less body shaming. If I had a pound for every time I'd judged my body! Judgements because we're blonde – or because we're not blonde; we're too tall – or we're not tall enough.

> **Everywhere you've judged yourself for the way your body has happened to be in any given moment, would you like to let that go?**
>
> **And anywhere you've made yourself wrong for ever wanting to change your body in any way, would you like to let that go?**
>
> **And would you like to ask your body if it would like to let all of that go?**
>
> **Anywhere you've got self-judgements that stop you appreciating your natural beauty, would you like to let that go?**
>
> **And would you like to ask your body if it would like to let that go?**

Men are judged for the way their bodies look and given all kinds of negative messages simply to sell them products they don't need, or worse, are bad for them. In the case of women and girls, however, that judgement and negative messaging goes into extreme overdrive …

Female Hygiene and Big Business

> "Ever notice how there's a Female Hygiene Aisle in every pharmacy, but there's never a Male Hygiene Aisle!" – Liz Plank

Women are starting to observe how certain types of products are being sold to women that would never be sold to men because retailers wouldn't get away with it in our current culture, and realising that much of it is a con. I agree. Sadly, much of the commercial world has become sick. As we'll learn in Volume II, global industries cannot be effectively regulated at present. Dr Natasha Chinn explains: "The vagina is self-cleaning. It does not need douching, or intimate sprays. Women do it, and then they end up getting a bacterial infection because *now* they've shifted their pH balance, and *now* there's overgrowth of bacteria that normally live there, and *now* they need a doctor when they didn't before." As Plank points out, these products are causing the problems that women think they are fixing. (../hygiene)

> "It's like, instead of being labelled as "Oh, make everything fresh!", it should be "Use me and you'll need antibiotics!" – Dr Natasha Chinn

"Hair removal, excessive hair removal; there is no reason for the vagina to be bald. The hair is there as a protective agent. It can protect you from getting yeast infections. It's your first barrier of defence from getting sexually transmitted infections as well. And when you shave it you can get shaving bumps, and that actually can make you more susceptible to get infections." – Dr Natasha Chinn

Ageing

> "When my mind stopped racing, my body stopped aging! How can it be more simple than that?" – Peter Ragnar

That's quite a statement from the author of *'How Long Do You Choose To Live?'* That said, Ragnar's unique exploits and results, which are touched on in Volume II, suggest a wealth of insights.

Longevity is a personal interest of mine. As a young child I had the feeling I would have a very long life. That sense has since expanded further. My favourite curiosity of Peter's longevity "Work in progress", as he calls it, is his observation that mammals have a life expectancy of between 10 and 20 times the age at maturation. This would put the *natural* human life expectancy at anywhere between 100 and 320 years or higher.

> "Science knows of no disease caused by the simple passing of time." – Dr Myron Wentz

Science has never actually proved the existence of time, either, though Jon Freeman points out that that would be impossible to prove or disprove. There are many angles from which conventional society hasn't yet considered ageing.

Freeman himself appeared on 'Wogan' in the 90s to talk about ageing from the perspective of the nature of reality. In the 1960s it wasn't even widely understood that smoking was bad for us. So who yet has lived beyond 'three score years and ten' in a world that got even the basics of life promotion right? Answer: Nobody. So we just don't know 'how high is up' in terms of what our Life Force is capable of.

"Anything that isn't Love Consciousness
is violent on the self." – James Blacker

The approach of living in the state of Love Consciousness is the primary approach to optimal ageing. More precisely, it reduces *false* ageing to zero, so you Receive all of what's possible for you. More specifically still, it reduces false aging to zero *within the sphere of* ***Independent Health***. In Volume II, I talk about the concept of 'Rat Park' and define 'The Prosperity of Unity'. These are the bases of optimised **Interdependent Health**: Optimal health in the optimal social-global environment, supported by an appropriate global economic system.

In Volume II, we'll also address Alzheimer's and Dementia. (../alzheimers)

In 2002, while recording *'Strength for Life'*, I asked David Heard what truth, if any, there is to the notion that "you should take things easy at your time of life", or being advised to stop going down the gym, or exercise with less weight, or to exercise less strenuously? His reply: "Given that there are no medical conditions that pre-empt that, then it is total rubbish. There is no reason why, and I do stress, given that there are no medical reasons, i.e. heart condition and lung condition, etc., that have been diagnosed, there is no reason why, *as a matter of course*, one should:

a. Exercise less
b. Exercise less intensely

... and this comes back to what we said right at the top of the conversation about listening to your body, knowing what you can do."

David also shared some compelling accounts of people who were demonstrating the point: "There are a number of interesting studies by The Keiser Institute for Aging in America. It's very well worth following this through. What Keiser Institute have done is taken people in their late 60s, 70s and even 80s, and put them through intensive resistance training (what we would normally call weight training). And the gains in strength are absolutely phenomenal. We're talking of the order of 40% strength gains over a period. Phenomenal, absolutely phenomenal."

> "It's not about being Peter Pan and turning back the clock. It's about removing the artificial barriers." – David Heard

Heard continues, "At The National Rehabilitation Centre for the Paralysed we ran a pilot programme, not with paralysed people but with elderly people. They were not immobilised because they had paralysis, or had had a stroke, or had any health or medical condition that made them immobile, but they were immobilised because it was easier to manage them. They were in homes, I'm talking about care homes for the elderly, and they were plonked in front of a television every day, because actually that was what was easier to do.

"I had read some research on this, and so we carried out our own study. We took these elderly people from the home, and we put them through an exercise programme, not very vigorous, but twice a week, over a period of six weeks. In other words, they had twelve sessions. And the kind of exercises they were doing was walking ten metres in the parallel bars, or going from sit to stand. Sometimes they had to be assisted. Obviously, we prescribed the exercise programme to suit the condition that they were in.

"In *every case*, they made, and remember just twelve sessions – they made tremendous gains. To the extent that one of those people was able to go unaided from sit to stand, from a wheelchair, and walk 20 metres. She had not done that for five years.

"Now that is an absolutely extreme example of how society conditions people, and conditions them negatively. Because it was considered acceptable for her, and you know, in a patronising way, "Well, it's easier for you, dear!", "We'll put you in the chair, and wheel you about, because it's a bit of a strain, isn't it?" And so it's self-fulfilling. It's totally lowering quality of life because all of her options were closing down. It's a self-fulfilling prophecy that will happen if people impose it upon you." (../ageing)

www.KissingConsciousness.com/health

Chapter Seven

Relationships

A Walk Around The Four Quadrants

There's an exercise I've run a couple of times at seminars. It's not mine; it's from the Integral community. To run this exercise you ask people to walk round a space in the room randomly, without focussing on the other people, but with just enough care not to bump into them, either. You might first ask them to focus their attention into their body. After a while you ask them to focus their attention inwards, into their own mind and thoughts. Then you ask them to focus on the room itself and the environment: The walls, ceiling, floor, chairs, etc. And then, finally, you ask them to notice the other people walking round the room, to make eye contact. If you've done this before, you know in advance how they will react to that last one: They all start smiling and get quietly giggly at acknowledging other human beings. Giggles aside, what they have just experienced is a direct appreciation of how life itself manifests. These four are defined in Ken Wilber's 'AQAL' model as 'The Four Quadrants':

> "... the four profound dimensions or perspectives
> that hold your universe together." – Ken Wilber

Draw a huge plus ('+') sign on a piece of paper, and you have four quadrants, four spaces to label. The top two quadrants are the individual, the bottom two are the collective. The right-hand two are the physical, the left-hand two are the intangible (non-physical). Everywhere we go we are followed around by these four quadrants: (1) the individual's inner 'world' of thoughts, feelings, ideas, (2) the (physical) body – including the brain, (3) culture – the collective intangible realm of shared meaning making and relationship, and

(4) the physical environment and social systems. In every moment of our lives, these four have always been present, and always will, even when you're asleep. It's also handy to realise that meaning can only be found in the left-hand quadrants. There's no meaning in your elbow, a kiss or a lump of rock, other than what you choose to give them.

It's necessary now to introduce The Four Quadrants, because while people normally have no question that other people exist, the inquiry into spirituality, wisdom and enlightenment that seeks to go beyond the separate Ego quite rightly brings up the question of 'Oneness', which has led to confusion when approaching relationships. Conscious Relationship has to navigate the world of relationships at the very same time as many people are starting their journey into the understanding of 'Oneness'. Having a relationship with someone who believes you're merely a construct of their mind, with therefore no free will of your own, might not be your idea of fun. More to the point, it's not relationship because the other person is not *relating* to you; it's confused narcissism. A person doesn't *relate* anything if they think they are the only thing that's 'real', and that the other three quadrants (including you!) are merely the consequence of their own individual interior thoughts.

So far this book has addressed you as an individual. We now start to also include the areas in which you interact with other people. In Volume II, we will expand our view further to look at how you are affected by society and the rest of the world, and vice versa. For now, on to relationships, including intimate or romantic relationships, friendships, parenting and family relationships, social activity and even business interactions.

Connections Pre-Exist in Nature

"Relationships are easy; it's self-judgements that make them difficult." – James Blacker

The one consistent, simple thread running throughout this book is the removal of self-judgement from that which is already in its natural state. This applies equally to relationships, because our connections with other people also pre-exist perfectly. Self-judgements influence relationships in the following two ways:

1. You don't allow yourself to do what you want to do
2. You do what you *don't* want to do

And as we said when we explored self-judgement as a 'Double-Entry Bookkeeping System', these two often go around as a pair: You aren't allowed to have a glorious relationship with someone who's right for you, so you have a frustrating relationship with someone who's not. You don't speak your truth with someone, so you instead go for a drink or a snack or a smoke you don't want. If you release your self-judgements so that you no longer do what you don't want to do, and you *do* do what you do want to do, you will find *your own relationship to relationships* to be totally self-fulfilling.

Anywhere you haven't been allowed to pursue and Receive your true desires and connections with people, would you like to let that go?

And would you like to ask your body if it would like to let that go?

The Theory of Pre-Existing Relationship

The natural state of our connections and relationships to other people exists *prior* to our self-judgement of those connections, and how they should be, and of ourselves and of other people. In the very same moment that our opportunity for an authentic interaction with another person arises, so too does our Consciousness, which decides whether to allow it without interruption or deny it in some way.

Of course, if we have 'No' Permissions around certain relationships, or even around certain individual aspects of them, (maybe we're allowed relationships, but we're not allowed someone who compliments us in public), then we can't *Receive* those relationships, or those aspects of relationship. This triggers us when such opportunities arise and sends us into the False Self state.

Let's say you are the colour blue and I am the colour yellow. The connection between us could be said to be 'green', as that's what you get when you mix blue and yellow together. Even before either of us has to do anything, nature has already created a 'green' connection for us by our very existence. So we don't even have to do anything to be that connection! How hard is that? You be blue, I'll be yellow, and together we'll be green. But if you have self-judgement that you're not allowed to have and Receive a 'green' connection, then you have to pretend to be something you're not. You have to pretend to be something other than the 'blue' person you are when a 'yellow' person comes along.

Every day, as we come into contact with people, from getting married to buying a newspaper from someone, we have pre-existing truths about whether we are going to like someone, or won't like them, or wish to interact with them, or not, and a million other details. Other than in the case of abusive people, those who push beyond our boundaries, none of this is a problem if we're honouring what's true for us.

The Illusion of Relationship Frustration Due to Another

There's an Unconscious trap of self-delusion, whereby we might say that we are not enjoying the situation of a connection because the other person is not Receiving the connection, so we can't have it either (because it requires both people, it takes two to tango, so "I'm ready, I'm true, but they're not playing their part!"). But whilst it may be true that someone is not able to Receive a connection with us due to their self-constriction, it would not trigger us, nor inhibit our own capacities to Receive connection with others as the opportunity arises, unless it reflected a self-judgement we ourselves hold.

If a person is not ready or able to Receive a connection, then the opportunity for that connection with that person *in that way, at that time* doesn't actually exist, and 'now' is the only time we can be sure of how something exists or is true. It's up to us to be okay with that. So if we feel Stress, the connection is not quite what we're telling ourselves it is – in that moment, at least. If we can't be okay with things being – or not being – a certain way, that is our self-judgement, our Fear Consciousness. To want a connection that the other person can't give, or can't give yet, is to want unreality, to want an illusion. So the other person is never 'the problem' when it comes to us fulfilling our potential to Receive the natural connections that are readily available to us. If we are 'clean', then we interact with others appropriately according to wherever they happen to be. This is a challenging notion (which can also be exciting if we Respond to it Consciously) because it requires us to take full responsibility for all our choices and actions, for all our Consciousness.

The Confusion between Happiness as Self-Acceptance and Happy Emotions

It is because people haven't made the distinction between (1) Happiness (or Unhappiness) *as a Consciousness*, and (2) happy emotions vs sad emotions, that we get confused about whether other people have control over our Happiness when in relationship of any kind with us. Another person cannot take you out of your self-acceptance, and thus cannot deny you your Happiness *as a Consciousness* – as Contentment. Only your own self-judgement can do that. But you sure as heck can feel human sadness when someone who loves you withholds that love, for whatever reason (usually their own Fear Consciousness). Or when someone who likes you withholds friendship, or even mere interaction. Or when they aren't strong enough to be honest with us or do better than be unkind. Even with strangers: It's heavier when people separate from integrity. We can feel it when people withhold truth from us. However, we can still be in self-acceptance at the same time, realising that there is a certain unhappy or sad feeling or emotion that doesn't necessarily mean we're not 'in our power', or that we've 'given our power away' to the other person. It's the subtle distinction between healthy human feelings and not being Needy. And actually, fully feeling the feeling will usually prevent the Neediness.

1. You can hold Presence to any sad or unhappy emotions that arise
2. Without giving your power for Happiness *as a Consciousness* away to other people

A Match Made in Heaven

"Let love speak up itself." – The Beautiful South

Every time a connection arises – and we allow it to be what it is – then we have what can be called a 'Match Made in Heaven', whether it be in love, sex, business, friendship, sport, or any other sphere of creativity, or even a temporary exchange where you chat with someone you meet on the path. You may even have heard people talk of such things as having 'commercial chemistry' in business. What any of these 'Matches Made in Heaven' are may have no bearing on what we might judge that a connection *'should'* be. As always, the "What does xyz [insert an aspect of Consciousness e.g.

Confidence, Success] look like?" question has no specific answer, other than that it reflects the qualities of harmony, Flow and self-acceptance.

Unconditional Love in Relationships

The expression of Unconditional Love for someone else is only, and can only ever be, the reflection of Unconditional Love for oneself. It simply means allowing them to be who they are – not controlling them but being Willing to take responsibility for our own choices as to how we Respond to them. It has nothing to do with having to pretend we like everything they do, or with doing what they tell us to, or staying with them, or not. Of course, if we *need* them or the relationship to be a certain thing, that compromises our capacity to be unconditional with them.

A misunderstanding that can make people resistant to trust the empowered Unconditional Love approach is that it is interpreted as meaning passive acceptance and us not speaking our mind or not doing anything about unwanted circumstances. Absolutely we can speak our mind, we can let people know how we feel, let people know what our 'bottom line' is – what we are and aren't prepared to tolerate. We can make requests and we can even give ultimatums, which are simply inviting others to make choices based on our boundaries. If we take responsibility for all of that, we won't feel the need to *control* other people, because we are happy with how we are taking control of (taking responsibility for) our *Response* to them, and the situation, and perhaps also taking responsibility for our actions and consequences. Unconditional Love isn't about being a doormat.

The Primacy of Self-Intimacy

> "Freedom and Sincerity are inextricably linked. You can only have sincerity where there is freedom, and only where there is sincerity is there true authentic fulfilment: Happiness. This is the key to life." – James Blacker

Due to The Primacy of Your Consciousness, the intimacy that you have with yourself is the primary basis for any intimacy you could have with anyone else. Connection with oneself determines whether one shows up in interaction with others from a place of Love Consciousness or from Fear Consciousness. And as we've seen, this determines such things as sincerity and authenticity. Let's remind ourselves of the basics:

Love Consciousness	**Fear Consciousness**
Authentic Connection with Others is Possible	Authentic Connection with Others is Impossible
Speaking Your Truth (including Silence)	Not Speaking Your Truth (including Silence)
The *Option* of Sincerity with Others	The *Certainty* of Unintentional Insincerity with Others

Realising that Presence to ourselves is something that we can enjoy is the starting point and the key to connecting with others. In each moment, intimacy with ourselves can be sought *whether we then interact with others or not.*

I'd like to introduce you to another term, **'The Healing Power of Self-Intimacy'**. By holding Presence to ourselves we can heal our wounds. This brings us to a profound insight: We can generate the experience of intimacy *for ourselves*, merely by being present to what we truly feel, by 'holding space' for ourselves. This is great for our joy and pleasure, just as it can be good for our efforts to dissolve unwanted habits and addictions. But bear in mind, if you are in self-intimacy, and your life's flow and truth move you to interacting with another and you don't allow yourself to Receive that, your self-intimacy will drop again in those moments. The other person doesn't give you self-intimacy; you allow (or don't allow) yourself to Receive it whilst interacting with them.

Self-intimacy allows us to be sincere in our interactions with others. The word 'sincere' comes from the Latin 'sincerus', meaning 'clean, pure'. Clean and pure are two great words for getting the essence of Conscious Living. If our Consciousness is 'clean' our motive will be pure. Purity of motive is Happiness. Impure motive is Neediness, which we'll come to shortly. (../self-intimacy)

#DTTFSAFV

#DTTFSAFV is a Kissing Consciousness Tool which stands for 'Don't take the False Self at face value'. If your Awareness is that other people aren't coming from their Awareness and Choice – which may be quite easy to tell if their energy is incongruent, heavy or has an unrelaxing effect upon you – then you don't have to take their False Self at face value. This is a crucial Awareness. (../DTTFSAFV)

Love Consciousness	Fear Consciousness
We don't take other people's False Self at face value	We take other people's False Self at face value, and so we are inadvertently interacting with an illusion, a falsehood

Critiquing The Behaviour vs Criticising The Person

There's a common understanding, particularly in parenting, that if people do bad things that we 'criticise the behaviour, not the person'. And 'critiquing' is an improvement on 'criticising', as the latter may imply judgement, and so also put *us* in an 'offside' position. Consider the difference between:

- "That was a thoughtless thing to do!" and
- "You're a thoughtless person!"

The first of those statements correctly addresses the issue. The second incorrectly attributes a single behaviour to a whole personality, and worse, potentially conditions the person to believe they are a thoughtless person (and that is an example of the *creation* of Shadow Baggage).

As we now understand that people's behaviour is a consequence of their Consciousness, we can see that an effective approach is to recognise people's False Self Fear Consciousness, rather than to only see the behaviour without seeing its cause. Hating a person rather than hating their behaviour which is driven by their Fear Consciousness causes a lot of heartache which we can avoid by not confusing the person themselves with their behaviour. If we all understood this and didn't buy into each other's False Selves, we could heal society almost overnight. It can help us with our relationships, too: What happens when a person has a false sense of their motives for committing to a relationship with us, or a business venture?! It would be good to be aware of their state of Consciousness, wouldn't it? (../connections)

Harmonious Relationships

Not Making Yourself Their Enemy

When you want for someone something different to what they want for themselves, you inadvertently make yourself their enemy. This is not an act of love, but an Unconsciously motivated attempt at control. Most people tend to do this, even though not doing so is the key to harmonious relationships. So what causes us to do this in the first place? As always, it's some form of Unconscious, conditioned self-judgement.

Tuning into The Other Person

In any form of interaction, tuning into the other person – rather than just focussing on what we want to get – is an invaluable habit. If we're in any way interested in interacting with integrity with the other person, we're seeing the exchange as a two-person team activity. This may involve the natural skills of noticing and paying attention to people's body language, demeanour, speech, energy, etc. As well as knowing we are in Love Consciousness, we can consider whether what we're inviting the other person to participate in is putting them in Love Consciousness or Fear Consciousness. This can apply to everything from big choices to all the little intricate details and moments of interaction. (../harmony)

Neediness (and When Using People and Needing People is Called Loving People)

Needs are just that. We all have needs: For oxygen, water, sleep, human touch, etc. Neediness is a different thing.

Neediness is when a person has the inner resources to provide or resolve something for themselves, and their deepest truth is that they have the *desire* to do so, but they aren't aware of those two truths because they also have conditioned self-judgements which stop them from recognising both their ability and their desire to solve the thing self-sufficiently. (If they didn't have a self-judgement operating on them and limiting them, yet they weren't able to meet the need for themselves at all, it would simply be a straightforward need.) The result of people's Neediness, of their inability to recognise that they can resolve the thing for themselves, is that it drives them to attempt to gain the thing from another person or other people, leading to their company being unattractive to others. And the greatest cause of Neediness is not recognising that we can handle our own emotions and feelings (Emotional Infinity) if other people do or don't choose certain things, often leading to the feeling of needing to control those people. Here's how to understand Neediness:

Love Consciousness	Fear Consciousness
Allowed to recognise one's own strength or ability to either meet the need, or cope without it	Not allowed to recognise one's own strength or ability to meet the need, or cope without it
(Not Needy)	(Needy)

The way to help someone out of Neediness is not to judge them or to try to get them to force their behaviour to be different, but to invite them to let go of the self-judgement, which would empower them if it clears. (../neediness)

Anywhere you haven't allowed yourself to recognise the full extent of your ability to meet your own needs, emotionally, physically, financially or otherwise, would you like to let that go?

And would you like to ask your body if it would like to let that go?

Having Harmonious Relationships

Releasing the self-judgements that cause Neediness is the key to being able to align with the relationship wisdom truth which Lester Levenson so eloquently explained when he said:

"Want for the other person what they want for themselves."

This Love Consciousness stops you making yourself the other person's enemy, in any way – assuming you choose not to. And when you allow yourself this, you can have harmonious relationships which you will be able to enjoy and be yourself with, because you are not bending under the strain of needing to manipulate your own actions in order to try to get anything from the other person by manipulating them.

"If you change the way you think it will change the way you act. When you change the way you act it will change the way people treat you. When you change the way other people treat you, you're free." – Dr Paul Solomon

This principle applies to attempts to get people to do what we want in romantic relationships, family relationships, friendships, business relations such as office politics or attempts to make sales against a person's will, interactions at social clubs, or any other sphere of human interaction. It can also include an Unconscious Consciousness Facilitator (if that isn't a contradiction in terms) needily trying to get a client or audience member to let something go in order to prove what a competent Facilitator they are, or needily trying to get someone to attend an event or online call. Many life coaches, healers, doctors, school teachers, soccer parents etc., over the years have invested their own Neediness in their client's or their student's results, or in their own attendance figures.

There's No Such Thing as a Needy Person

Bear in mind, again, as it's the False Self, that there's no such thing as a needy person. There's only needy *behaviour*, caused by Fear Consciousness. There are only non-needy (empowered) people who have been *conditioned*, through self-judgement, to *behave* in a needy manner in some instances. If you think you are a needy person, look and you will find self-judgements. There is no Neediness without self-judgement. We explored some creative extensions of Love Consciousness in The Anatomy of a Moment in Chapter Three, and here are some more to follow that up:

> There is no Neediness without self-judgement.
> There is no lack of Confidence without self-judgement.
> There is no worry without self-judgement.
> There is no unwelcome emotion without self-judgement.
> There is no Stress without self-judgement.

And we could look at this another way …

> There is no Neediness without a block to self-confiding.
> There is no lack of Confidence without a block to self-confiding.
> There is no worry without a block to self-confiding.
> Etc.

We could keep this up all day!

> If you think you are a needy person, look and you will find self-judgements.
> If you think you are a shy person, look and you will find self-judgements.
> If you think you are a person who's not confident by nature, look and you will find self-judgements.
> If you think you are a negative person, look and you will find self-judgements.
> If you think you are afraid of emotions, look and you will find self-judgements.
> There's no such thing as a needy person, only a person who's been conditioned to that Consciousness.
> There's no such thing as a negative person, only a person who's been conditioned to that Consciousness.

There's no such thing as a shy person, only a person who's been conditioned to that Consciousness.
There's no such thing as a naturally non-confident person, only a person who's been conditioned to that Consciousness.
Etc.

And all of these apply to *all* of the Fear Consciousness elements of The Binary.

Communication

Communication creates (or maintains) a *communion*: You and the other person *become at one* as a result of authentic communication.

Neediness Communicates with The Energy of Fear Consciousness

When a person attempts to satisfy their Neediness by trying to 'get' from the other person, they are communicating from Fear Consciousness, which also of course has the *energy* of Fear Consciousness, and which therefore *communicates* the energy of Fear Consciousness … which has never been a persuasive communicator! (Except to other Fear Consciousnesses, to other people's Neediness.) When we communicate from Fear Consciousness we offer other people (our) Fear Consciousness to interact with, which is why Conscious people decline it. It's like walking up to people and asking them if they'd like something crappy. The energy that Fear Consciousness communicates always repels good and the energy that Love Consciousness communicates always attracts good. This can be great news, because by releasing self-judgements we may become more and more appealing to other people. Specifically, what's happening is that you are releasing the *blocks* to your natural appeal that already exists. This is adults learning – remembering – to connect with each other naturally and effortlessly the way small children do. (../communication)

Love Consciousness	Fear Consciousness
Communicating with the energy of Love Consciousness	Communicating with the energy of Fear Consciousness
Communicates	Miscommunicates, and inadvertently communicates the False Self

The Relief of Conscious Communication

Communication is only effective, real and authentic if it emanates from Love Consciousness. It is the effect of Love Consciousness and happens automatically *as a consequence of* the Love Consciousness state. It can be a relief to realise that we don't have to worry about how we communicate. Authentic communication is natural. You can just let go of the negatives, the self-judgements about how you *'should'* communicate, and the underlying you always knows how to be you.

"It makes no sense to learn contrived ways of communicating." – Colin Turner

Body language is a part of this, so we don't need to worry about that, either.

We've also seen that charisma – the genuine, healthy kind – is a natural product of Love Consciousness. In each moment of Love Consciousness, a person who is in their Being is naturally charismatic and automatically and effortlessly authentically communicating that Being.

Love Consciousness	Fear Consciousness
Natural Charisma	Buried Natural Charisma

You Can't Abdicate from Consciousness

"You cannot not communicate" – Colin Turner

We cannot abdicate from either Consciousness or communication. Even abstaining from a vote or remaining silent communicates something. Behaviour communicates and absence of a behaviour communicates. We create and communicate from our Fear Consciousness as well as from Love Consciousness, it's just that *what* we create and communicate from Fear Consciousness will not be what we want. It creates a mess, so we might want to put a stop to that habit.

No Fear Consciousness = Infallible Communication

Happiness Projection

"The less self-judgements you have, the less you see the illusion of your happiness depending on other people." – James Blacker

Love Never Hurts

Love is a battlefield, apparently. Is friendship a battlefield? I only have friends with whom it's not! So why would love need to be a battlefield? What is the difference? Well … if we Unconsciously think other people control our Happiness, we have to (try to) control their actions to make sure those actions are the ones we want them to take in order to secure our Happiness. It's a completely bizarre notion. And yet it is the basis of the majority of human love relationships, and many family relationships and friendships until now: This person is responsible for my Happiness.

'Love is a Battlefield' is a great song, but a lousy piece of advice for Conscious Living. Like a lot of these songs, the music and singing are great, but the message is conditioning society to stupidity, lack of self-respect and Fear Consciousness. "Ahh, I can't go on without you!", claim any number of modern songs. Love isn't a battlefield. Love is Heavenly. It's everything else you do that isn't love that makes relationships a battlefield.

Anywhere you have self-judgements causing you to experience possessiveness or sexual jealousy, would you like to let that go?

And would you like to ask your body if it would like to let that go?

Being The Focus of Other People's Happiness Projection

We can see how 'Happiness Projection' happens in both directions: You projecting your Happiness onto other people, and them projecting their Happiness onto you. If a person enjoys you as a result of their own sense of allowance, then they won't make you responsible for the Happiness that interacting with you may bring them. If they don't see it that way, and they instead see things in such a way that they believe you are the *source* of that interaction, they're going to (mistakenly) make you the source of their Happiness, and therefore also the source of their power. So you may sense their fear of loss being directed around you. What are other people's approaches to you? Bear in mind, this Binary Table is representing *their* state of Consciousness, not yours:

Love Consciousness	Fear Consciousness
You are free to be yourself with them	They may need you to be a certain thing, so you may feel 'imprisoned' and may wish to 'escape'

The Paradox of Self-Sufficient Joy from Relationships

So how do we square being the source of our own power with the fact that relationships and interactions with other people clearly give us joy, pleasure and happiness? If other people can't make you happy, how come we get joy from them? You get joy through *allowing* yourself to *Receive* the potential connection-in-waiting that already exists. I call this 'The Paradox of Self-Sufficient Happiness and Joy from Relationships'.

Love Consciousness	**Fear Consciousness**
Receiving happiness and happy experiences which involve interacting with others	The mistaken belief that other people are the source of the good that comes from interactions, whereas really it's our lack of Permission(s) which causes the pain of not Receiving those interactions

Facilitating Beyond Happiness Projection

"I can't give you that which you demand of me." – Dr. Wayne Dyer

The main reason for suffering in relationships is the failure to correctly answer the question: "Who is responsible for your Happiness?" You can't be your own person while you still see the illusion that your dream partner, or anyone else, is the source of anything of 'You' or your experience. And so Facilitating the release of people's Happiness Projection is *the* core aspect of the Kissing Consciousness approach to relationships. Once we facilitate letting go of this illusory self-judgement fear, everything else happens in freedom, and you experience harmony as your way of relating and Receiving. Of course, the people you relate with aren't necessarily experiencing the same harmony. They will have their own Consciousness status. As we facilitate Happiness Projection, we're also facilitating our Permissions to Receive relationship and other interactions as a consequence. (../HP)

Anywhere you've bought into the self-judgement that you have to make other people the source of your Happiness, would you like to let that go?

And would you like to ask your body if it would like to let that go?

Fear of Rejection

There's no such thing as Fear of Rejection. There is only Fear of Self-Rejection. Another person cannot reject you; they can only decline you. It is you, who then, by your Consciousness, interpret that by either rejecting yourself if you have self-judgements or accepting yourself if you do not. This table shows how a 'No', i.e. a declining of your invitation, is received by you:

Love Consciousness	Fear Consciousness
The 'No' is simply accepted for what it is, a 'No'	The 'No' is interpreted as a rejection of who you are

Let's say you ask someone if they'd like a cup of tea, and they say, "No." Then you ask them if they'd go out on a date with you, and they say, "No", and a reaction to that comes up in you, maybe feelings in your stomach, thoughts in your head. Actually, in themselves these thoughts and feelings aren't a problem. But you may interpret the experience as a rejection of you. What was the difference between the two Noes you received? Nothing; they were identical.

To further see that it is impossible for others to reject us, consider the ridiculous idea of a person going out of their way to 'reject' a person who had no self-judgements about such things. They might walk up to that person and say, "Hey, I'm rejecting you!" The self-accepting person might reply, puzzled, "Err, okay. Fine."

If you have no Fear of Rejection, you can ask a thousand questions, and even if you only get 10% response, you've got 100 Yeses! What could you do with 100 Yeses? So what self-judgements would you like to let go of to allow all of your Awareness around the illusion of Fear of Rejection? Note, however, that fear of being unkindly or even violently declined is of course real, and quite rightly, we want to allow our Awareness to guide us to avoid that wherever possible.

Anywhere you've bought into the lie that other people can reject us, would you like to let that go?

And would you like to ask your body if it would like to let that go?

Fear of Rejection is Fear of Acceptance and Fear of Self-Acceptance

As we talked about in the Binary of Receiving vs (Trying to) Control, when we think we have Fear of Rejection there's always a part of us that has Fear of Acceptance (fear of someone actually saying 'Yes' to us), because we lack self-acceptance; we aren't allowed to Receive. When we accept ourselves, we don't want 'Yeses at all costs', we want clarity and the truth. So what's the relationship between Fear of Rejection and Happiness Projection? They are totally linked, part of the same dynamic, because one is the off-shoot of the other:

- "This is what I want from this person..." (Happiness Projection)
- "And this is what I fear if I don't get it." (Fear of Rejection)

When I ask someone something, whether it's in relationships, social or business, I'm not looking for a 'Yes' rather than a 'No', I'm looking for a clean answer, rather than a confused, Unconscious one. I wanna know what the truth is, what's grounded, what's sustainable. I want to hear from their Love Consciousness, their Being. Only being interested in that keeps me in *my* Being. This is the position of Love Consciousness. An Unconscious 'Yes' will waste your time. (../rejection)

Love Consciousness	Fear Consciousness
Valuing a clear, Conscious answer above a confused Unconscious answer	Valuing a 'Yes' above a 'No' (and secretly afraid of a 'Yes')

Being Triggered and Triggering Others

aka: Having our Buttons Pressed

If you aren't familiar with the term, being 'Triggered' or 'having our buttons pressed' means anything that causes resistance and an uncomfortable reaction in us. Often, it is other people who trigger us, and of course vice versa.

Responsibility Dumping and Inappropriate Apologising

The first thing to note about pressing other people's buttons or triggering them is that unless it's done intentionally, it is never your fault or responsibility. Equally, if someone triggers us or presses our buttons, it is never the fault or responsibility of that person. We cannot blame someone for merely being who they are. A person could be triggered by a certain mannerism, hair colour, style of clothing, a scent, a certain word or phrase, an opinion, or a million others things which may remind them of an uncomfortable experience in the past, or, in some way, make an Unconscious self-judgement that they may have immediately relevant to the current moment. We can't, for example, blame an old man just because his white hair triggers us into a bad memory of someone else who had white hair. A trigger brings a self-judgement to the surface of our experience. For example, the self-judgement that one is too big for a swimming costume lies dormant until the beach season comes around. These triggers happen all the time, every day, in all walks of life. Kissing Consciousness defines the following set of trigger aspects to help in navigating the dynamics around triggers.

Trigger Apologising

In the past, I had people come up to me and tell me I made them uncomfortable – because I jumped around too energetically, for example. In my ignorance, I made myself wrong for that; I told myself I was wrong, often apologising, and certainly constricting my natural self-expression as a result. But this is not Conscious; I should not have to apologise for this. So I call this Trigger Apologising. (../TA)

> **Anywhere you've made yourself small or lesser in order to be acceptable to other people, would you like to let that go?**
>
> **And would you like to ask your body if it would like to let that go?**

Trigger Communicating

It's fine for a person to tell another person that something they do triggers them (Trigger Communicating), as long as they are only informing them. As part of that, they may even also let the other person know that they can't, or don't wish to interact with them because of it.

If we do choose to Trigger Communicate, it might sound something like this: "Hi, just to let you know that when you do/say that thing it triggers me, it makes me feel [insert as appropriate: e.g. uncomfortable/scared/unloved]. Of course, it's my responsibility, I just thought I'd make you aware that it was having this effect on me." Or use (your own) words to that effect, depending on what exactly you want to say. (../TC)

Requesting Trigger Stopping

The triggered person may even ask – without any expectation or sense of a right to demand – if the other person is willing to modify their behaviour. They have that Choice to ask that, if they wish, and, of course, the other person has their Choice as to how they wish to respond to the request. If they're a reasonable person they will likely at least bear it in mind, if not simply decide it's no downside to them to simply not do the thing – but they're not obliged to! That's the point. Asking someone if they will modify their behaviour could either be a Conscious or an Unconscious act (if driven by our Neediness). (../RTS)

Trigger Dumping

Going beyond communicating or making a request, to blaming the other person for triggering us or expecting them to change their behaviour, is what I call 'Trigger Dumping'. It is not respectful and does not take responsibility, and so is not Conscious. If you are tempted to do this to another person, the answer, as always, is to release any self-judgements.

> **Anywhere your self-judgements have caused you to attempt to make other people responsible for your Reactions to innocent events, would you like to let that go?**
>
> **And would you like to ask your body if it would like to let that go?**

In fact, after I explained the definition of the term, my friend realised it had happened with a friend of hers earlier that day, remarking: "She totally just Trigger Dumped on me!"

Trigger Dumping is also an example of 'Control and Abuse Consciousness', as explained below, since it occurs when somebody who is Unwilling to take responsibility for their own Reactions seeks to force someone else to do (or stop doing) something innocent. (../TD)

Declining Trigger Dumping

This is what we do when people try to dump blame or criticism for their triggers onto us, and we're not having any of that. The phrase "not my circus, not my monkeys" comes to mind; we don't need to get involved in other people's Shadow Baggage. The act of declining itself could also be either Conscious or Unconscious. An Unconscious Reaction might be as rude as "Get lost!", whereas a more respectful, helpful response might be to point out what is happening, and who is responsible for the person's *Reaction* to the trigger. If you become a Kissing Consciousness Facilitator, a test of your sharpness if someone tries to Trigger Dump on you might be whether you then invite them to have you facilitate them around it when you decline the blame for triggering them. That might sound like this: **Trigger Dumping**: "Hey, you did this, and it made me feel uncomfortable!" **Declining Trigger Dumping**: (politely) "What are you telling me for?! Do you need my help in letting go of whatever self-judgements caused you to React Unconsciously?" (../DTD)

Trigger Owning

The good news about a trigger bringing a self-judgement to the surface of experience is that if we are indeed aware, we can catch it (observe it), and process it. By acknowledging our responsibility for our own Unconscious Reaction to the innocent event that triggered us, we are 'Trigger Owning'. (../TO)

Trigger Releasing

Now we're talking! If we choose to we can let go of the energy of the self-judgement that caused the Reaction in us, which is 'Trigger Releasing', of course. The sad side of being triggered is when people don't realise what's going on and put up with the restrictive effects: They 'suffer in silence', which we might call 'Trigger Suffering'. As we know, there's no need for someone to keep hold of a self-constriction that triggers them. (../TR)

Here's the rundown of the various dynamics of how people handle triggers, and whether they are a Conscious *Response*, or an Unconscious *Reaction* …

Trigger Owning	Conscious	Taking responsibility for what triggers you
Trigger Dumping	Unconscious	Blaming others for what triggers you
Trigger Apologising	Unconscious	Allowing others to blame you for what triggers them
Declining Trigger Dumping	Conscious	Not allowing others to blame you for what triggers them
Trigger Communicating	Optional, Conscious or Unconscious	Respectfully letting someone know that what they do triggers us
Requesting Trigger Stopping	Optional, Conscious or Unconscious	Asking someone if they would consider stopping doing something that triggers us
Trigger Releasing	Optional, Conscious	Letting go of the self-judgement that causes an innocent event to trigger us

Table 7.1: Kissing Consciousness Trigger Dynamics

Third Party Trigger Dumping

What on earth would Third Party Trigger Dumping look like? Well, if a mother was frustrated that her husband was very late back, and she wanted to involve the kids in the drama, she might say to them, "Where's your father got to?!" A person in this situation who wanted to take responsibility is more likely to word it, "Where's *my husband* got to?!" But it's *your* father, you see, so *you're* to blame! You're now involved in the saga, even though you did nothing. *That's* Third Party Trigger Dumping.

Maybe a guy gets ribbed by one of his mates about his girlfriend and it presses his buttons; it makes him feel embarrassed, so he goes home and criticises his girlfriend. That's Third Party Trigger Dumping. (../TPTD)

Being Triggered and Being Abused at the Same Time

Just because you're being triggered doesn't mean you're not also being abused or mistreated. Your boss might speak to you rudely, unkindly or unacceptably aggressively, which isn't a trigger but an abuse, but the event might also trigger you because you have a conditioned Unconscious self-judgement that you're not allowed to speak up and state your right not to be mistreated. However, the lack of ability to state your case doesn't negate or justify the abuse. Nor does it make you responsible for it.

Intentional Triggering

"Intentional Triggering is abuse." – James Blacker

Intentionally triggering someone is usually also Control and Abuse Consciousness (see below). A possible example of when it might not be is if a therapist has gained a client's consent to bring a challenging emotion to the forefront of their Conscious Mind. In the absence of consent, though, it's a selfish, abusive act to cause someone to have a reaction against their will, even with the claim that it was done in their best interests, to help the person get out of their judged limitations in whatever way. It's False Conscience. (../IT)

www.KissingConsciousness.com/triggers

Boundaries and Barriers

"Boundaries are not barriers. They are not limitations. They are *Choice,* in self-respect form. All boundaries are a 'Yes' to you, and all are positive." – James Blacker

A Boundary is a person's truth about the extent to which you or they are – and *aren't* – happy to be spoken to, or for, touched by others, interacted with, misled, stared at or anything else that affects them in a way they don't have personal control over, but which relates to their individual right to be both left in peace and treated fairly.

The Two-Sided Wall

A Barrier is a self-judgement which is not allowing you to Receive a connection with another person as much as you would like, or in a way that you would like. Maybe you would like to tell someone you admire them, but you have been chastised for trying to connect with others in the past. So an Unconscious self-judgement exists that prevents connection – that is a *Barrier* to connection. A Barrier's original purpose was to keep us safe. As that need ceases to be relevant, however, if the Barrier remains it continues to prevent us from connecting with other people … and the same wall that keeps others outside also keeps us alone inside. As you release any self-judgements you may have around connecting, you remove your Barriers to connection. We may have no Awareness at all that a lot of our Barriers exist. One way to find out might be to ask for ever-deeper levels of connection and freedom, and see what arises. (../barriers)

Essentially, the 'ideal' one might choose is "Connecting without Barriers and with Boundaries." The Boundaries Exercise from Chapter Three is available for you: To view the demo video to get an idea of it, and to practice for yourself if you wish. You may even take part in the exercise at a Kissing Consciousness event, or similar. Here's a clearing, and like many clearings on big subjects, you may feel the need to ask this a few times as new layers of You are revealed.

Anywhere you have Barriers to connection, would you like to let that go?

And would you like to ask your body if it would like to let that go?

We also have Boundaries *collectively*, as citizens, relating to our right to be treated fairly, not be misled, conned or in any way stolen from, legally or illegally. Volume II looks at how we can all assert our Boundaries in Response to living within a global economic system which is no longer fit for purpose, and which causes virtually all other Boundary disrespect social issues.

Boundaries and Consent

No means no. Silence also means no. Not answering means no. If you or they are not sure, this also means no, as it isn't a 'Yes'. If something isn't a 'Yes' then it's a 'No'. A 'Yes' becomes 'No' if it is replaced by a 'No' or a 'Not sure'. (../consent)

Anywhere you've bought into the self-judgement that you aren't allowed to state your Boundaries, or that you aren't allowed to have them respected, would you like to let that go?

And would you like to ask your body if it would like to let that go?

Even though you may have a Barrier around something, that Barrier is still also a Boundary to be honoured and respected. People don't have the right to say, "It's a Barrier, so you must go beyond it!" (usually associated with "… and connect with me!") in order to get their way. It's up to you. In theory, you shouldn't even have to make a decision on it, as silence means no. All of this doesn't just apply to sex, it applies to *everything*.

Tantra's Three 'Yeses' of Consent

Whilst conventional society accepts just a verbal 'Yes' as legal consent, the following approach is the actual natural truth of consent … and everyone's true Conscience intuitively knows it.

In Tantra, there is actually an approach of requiring *three* 'Yeses' of consent prior to having sex, and all three must be present. These three are:

1. A 'Verbal Yes'
2. A 'Body Language Yes'
3. And a 'Genital Yes'

A 'Genital Yes' may also be called a 'Yoni Yes', or a 'Lingam Yes', as these are terms used for the female and male sex organs respectively. Even with verbal consent, incongruent body language is still taken as a 'No', and so that is considered not to be consent. Can you see how this approach is not about justifying *getting*, but genuine respect: We only want something if it is also the other person's true wish? If someone says yes to you, but you can see that they are not at one with themselves about it, that is a 'No'. And even with both a 'Verbal Yes' and a 'Body Language Yes', there may still be a 'Genital No', which also means no consent, because the body itself doesn't want to play ball. Whilst at the time of writing, the law may consider a 'Verbal Yes' to be sufficient, what we might call 'Conscious Consent' essentially does not. It requires all three, as it directly relates to a person's Conscience, and their Knowing. People generally know when they are in that *'getting'* energy.

Everyday Boundaries

A couple of my friends shared the view that if a work colleague wanted to give them a hug at Christmas they had to accept that; it would be rude to not allow it. It's not rude. It's not consent. You have a right not to be hugged or touched by anyone you don't want to be hugged or touched by. We can do a clearing about how you might decline a hug or ask someone not to do something in a calm and sensitive manner, but even if you don't manage that calm state you still have the right to say "No." The lack of Conscience is actually on the other person's part, if they don't respect that, and they can do a clearing on what causes them to be so needy or controlling.

Our Body Gives Us Boundaries

Incidentally, we talked about listening to our bodies, about Receiving its information about what it wants to eat, how it wants to move, or not, etc. When we go against such requests we are not respecting our own body's Boundaries. Fortunately, the body has no capacity for refusing us forgiveness. Our bodily experience will feel different according to whether or not we are honouring our consent in the regular sense (Embodiment vs Disembodied).

Natural Boundaries vs Legal or Cultural Boundaries

The test of **Natural Boundaries** is kindness, consideration and respect. Just because something is legal or considered common practice, doesn't mean it respects a person's Boundaries. As I write, the BBC has just blogged a story about a minor celebrity's life choices and provided a public comments section, in which, not surprisingly, she is being attacked by many commenters. This is currently legal, and may even be considered perfectly acceptable practice, but it's not something a respectful, self-respecting person would do. In a Conscious society, there would be much more appreciation of that individual's life than to make her 'open season' as a target for everyone to vent their spleen. This comes back to the principle: "A truly secure person is never unkind under any circumstances."

www.KissingConsciousness.com/boundaries

What happens when consent is not respected, or people just choose to push others anyway? Well, this is the horribleness, messiness and tragedy of the world …

Control and Abuse (Un)Consciousness

You are your own authority. Yet Control and Abuse Consciousness says, "I exercise authority over you."

When people:

1. Have an innate understanding of the importance of respecting other people's Boundaries, choices and right to personal peace and freedom
2. And yet they choose to go beyond those Boundaries anyway,

… this is typically because their wounds have caused them to shut out the voice of their True Conscience, their truth. They know in their Conscience that the behaviour isn't right, and isn't their truth, but they aren't able to allow that voice of Conscience in sufficiently to correct their own False Self. Kissing Consciousness calls this 'Control and Abuse Consciousness', which is in part a misnomer, because unless people were born unkind, sociopathic or evil – and I don't think I've ever met someone who was – it is ultimately their *Unconscious* wounds which are driving their controlling and abusive behaviour, while they tell themselves they are operating from Conscious Choice. Below the surface, such people generally feel wretched.

At less extreme levels, right down to very subtle means of control, we see people seeking to control and abuse others in relationship (see 'Imperative Grammar' below).

Virtually everyone has that basic understanding of what we might think of as "Do no harm." This is often known as our 'basic moral intuition': Don't attack or kill people, don't steal from them, don't lie, mislead or misrepresent things in order to steal from them, or gain indirectly by that. Many of our politicians and billionaires are currently guilty of several of these! This is about remaining aligned with that true joy of spirit, natural Happiness, rather than succumbing to the separation of Ego.

When people engage in Control and Abuse Consciousness, their self-judgements prevent them from accessing their strength to do any better. Their behaviour may also be a crime. Primarily, I think of it as being about people who can't let the love in. Yet. And that may be a psychopathology, which can maybe change and be healed. Remembering the difference between Power and Power Over, whilst abusing others is a force or 'Power-Over', it's essentially a weakness and a lack of Power. Control and Abuse Consciousness is really a disease of the heart.

"Being in self-acceptance the gates of your
power are open. Being in self-judgement the
gates of your power are closed." – James Blacker

Love Consciousness	**Fear Consciousness**
In Your Power	Not In Your Power

You don't have to hate the person; you can realise that the malevolent influence you dislike is the Fear Consciousness that is driving their behaviour. But not everyone can be safely treated with innocent compassion. Some people are so distanced from their true Consciences, their truth is so buried, and their basic moral intuition so lost in the sands of time, that they are simply dangerous.

'Evil' as Unconsciousness

What we think of as 'evil' is perhaps merely an extreme form of the False Self, brought about by trauma and self-constriction that takes people so far away from their true nature that they are lost to themselves, to that beautiful self. Of course, not everyone who experiences unkindness and trauma takes that out on others in a way that resembles 'evil'. (../abuse)

Imperative Grammar

Imperative Grammar is the language of telling people what to do: "Shut up!", "Stop crying!", "Don't interrupt!", "Do this, do that!" For the most part it is controlling and therefore also abusive. It's encouraging people to be External Referral (Fear Consciousness) rather than being Self-Referral (Love Consciousness). They don't want you to do what you want to do; they want you to do what *they* want you to do.

I say "for the most part" because being controlling is about more than the language and the grammar itself; it's about when using Imperative Grammar is the *energy* of Control and Abuse Consciousness, because a genuine friend could jokingly tell you to "Shut up!" and not be trying to control you. That said, a seemingly innocent joke *could be* controlling or psychologically abusive. Is the energy playful or does it make you feel heavy and your true joy repressed?

Saying "Let's" is also often a very subtle form of control, as it translates as "This is what we're *all* going to do." It speaks *for* other people, rather than letting them speak for their own truth. This is often to control debate: "Let's focus on the...", or "Let's not get distracted by ... [a truth?]" Similarly, defensive politicians and sports coaches will say "Look..." (or "Listen...") when interviewed. Even if they mean no malice, they still unwittingly betray a Fear Consciousness resistance to people taking other points of view. (../lets)

"Get over it!" is Usually Control and Abuse Consciousness

"Get over it!" is an abusive statement. It's controlling. It's invalidating. It's dismissive of something that's true because it's inconvenient to the Fear Consciousness state of the person saying it to face the truth of the reality for the other person – usually because of what it reflects for themselves.

"Man Up!" is Control and Abuse Consciousness

Being External Referral isn't going to result in any kind of authentic personality, but Control and Abuse Consciousness is not interested in that. There's a great spoken word performance by Guante, in which he states his ten responses to the imperative "Man up!" If it's still available, you can watch it at the link below. Here's his second response: "If you want to question my masculinity, like a schoolyard circle of curses, like a sword fight with lightsabre erections, save your breath, because, contrary to what you believe, not every problem can be solved by 'growing a pair'. You cannot arm-wrestle your way out of chemical depression, the CEO of the company that just laid you off does not care how much you bench [press]! And I promise, there is no light beer in the universe full-bodied enough to make you love yourself." Generally speaking, "Man up" is Control and Abuse Consciousness.

www.KissingConsciousness.com/up

The 'Character-building' Lie and Insult

When people live in such a way that they often allow themselves to indulge in Control and Abuse Consciousness, they'll frequently also lean on the lie that abuse or bullying is 'character-building'. That's like someone stealing your wallet, and then telling you they should get away with it because it does you good, and that you should be grateful. But actually it can be like someone stealing years of your life, because it can take time to undo all that stuff.

Sad as it is to say, Control and Abuse Consciousness does also happen in personal development training and therapy.

Energy-Checking People

Instead of fact-checking people, we may be better off if we energy-check people! Is it peaceful or turbulent? Is it the energy of Love Consciousness or the energy of Fear Consciousness wrapped up in unkindness, deception or even hate? Is their *motive* a truth or a lie? Is their motive benign or malignant? Is it coming from their heart, or their negativity?

> **Anywhere you've shut down your Awareness to your ability to assess people by their energies, would you like to let that go?**
>
> **And would you like to ask your body if it would like to let that go?**

This is where Integrity relates to energy, because you can tune into the energy of another person, and, of course, yourself. You can tune into the intention of another person – at a level of truth *prior to* their vocal words or even physical body language, actions or behaviours. You can do this via your natural ability to Receive that energy Awareness. This is the same natural ability that animals displayed prior to the 2004 tsunami in Indonesia, knowing that the storm was coming before they could visibly see it. In this way, we can trust our Knowing with friends, lovers, employers, media, politicians, strangers. We can tune into the energy of the person or the establishment it is coming out of: Is it benevolent or is it malevolent? Does it feel true, or does it feel shadowy or heavy? Does it make you feel relaxed or tense? Being in the company of someone who cares about your wellbeing should make you feel relaxed. (../checking)

Natural Integrity

If we take the subjectivity out of the term 'integrity', and instead look at the origin of the word's stem, we find that its meaning is 'whole': To be whole, or to make whole. An integer is a whole number. 'Integral' Philosophy is about seeing the *whole* picture. To *'integrate'* is to combine things to form a whole. So integrity can be thought of as operating in a way that respects the whole, such that all other elements of the whole can function like clockwork. But we might then ask, "What 'whole' are we talking about?" There are two ways we can consider this.

The first is that 'integrity' relates to the person in question, to each individual. The powerful question is not whether you compromise *my* sense of ethics, but whether you compromise *your own*. And this is largely what makes something Control and Abuse Consciousness, where people know deep down that what they are doing goes against their best self and doesn't really align with their truth.

"Integrity is the ultimate sign of self-belief." – James Blacker

Worldcentric Integrity and Win-Win-Win Behaviour

Looking at things a slightly different way, there are three or four main 'levels' of a potential answer to the question, "What 'whole' is your integrity oriented around?" You may remember in The Power of Love chapter that we defined three Levels of Care and Compassion. We can add a fourth to this:

Stage 4: **Kosmocentric:** Care for all sentient beings: anyone or anything that can feel

Stage 3: **Worldcentric:** Care for all human beings

Stage 2: **Ethnocentric:** Care for oneself, one's friends, family, tribe, culture or country

Stage 1: **Egocentric:** Care only for oneself

There's a theory that 'Win-Win' deals, arrangements or behaviours are inevitably good and ethical: This deal is good for me and you. But there is also a 'them': Other people, and potentially the planet itself. This means that a 'Win-Win' deal or way of behaviour or attitude actually has up to *three* elements, i.e. it can be a 'Win-Win-Win' or a 'Win-Win-Lose' situation. The way the economic-political Neoliberal elite have done deals has mostly been 'Win-Win-Lose', dumping on their own citizens, as well as those of other countries. Bearing that third element in mind, we might argue that 'Ethnocentric Integrity' isn't really what we mean by 'having integrity'. So I would suggest that the 'integrity' we most need in today's world requires us to operate in such a way that the wider world is also looked out for, what I'd call 'Worldcentric Integrity'.

For an Egocentric person, to have integrity to look after 'the whole' means only looking after themselves. This is relatively easy to achieve – we all care about ourselves – but on its own it isn't much use to society, in fact it creates most of the problems. The term 'Egocentric Integrity' is an obvious oxymoron. And don't expect a relationship with an Egocentric person. There's no such thing as a relationship with a person who only cares about themselves; there's only the *illusion* of relationship. (../integrity)

So far in this chapter we have addressed principles that apply universally, across *all* dynamics and types of relationships and interactions with others. Now we shall look at specific areas and types of relationship.

Your Three 'Fingerprints' of Love, Sex and Relationships

Until we choose to put them together, love, sex and relationships are three entirely different and separate things. You can have sex without love. You can have sex without relationship. You can have sex with love but without relationship. You can have sex with relationship but without love. And you can have sex with relationship *and* love. All these are valid choices. You can have love without sex. You can have love without relationship. You can have love with relationship but without sex. You can have relationship without love, and you can have relationship without sex. All of these are valid and possible choices. If any of these combinations trigger you, then you likely have a lack of freedom of Choice regarding them and may wish to clear any self-judgements you have around that.

Not only are these three things different, the way you do love, the way you do sex, and the way you do relationship, will be entirely unique to you. To that end, I devised this concept of your three 'fingerprints': Your fingerprint of love, your fingerprint of sex, and your fingerprint of relationship, so that you might choose to have Awareness and freedom around all of these three. (../fingerprints)

Anywhere you have anything other than total freedom around the issues of love, sex and relationships, would you like to let that go?

And would you like to ask your body if it would like to let that go?

Romantic Relationships

"Our purpose in the relationship is to nurture the other person." – Dr Deepak Chopra

Actually, our purpose in the relationship can be whatever we want it to be, including to nurture ourselves as well as the other person. Chopra's words sound like a pretty healthy basic attitude and approach, though. If you're choosing that then you're choosing nurturing relationship.

The creator of the TV Show 'Will and Grace' called it that because in order to have a happy relationship you have to have the will to choose it and the grace to Receive it.

Conscious Relationship

In conventional assessments of judgement-based success in life, there's a general, unspoken sense that if we scored each other out of ten for the main areas of life, we might score people high financially if they have a lot of money and low if they don't, and high at physical body if they're in shape, and low if they're not. When it comes to the relationships category, the general misconception is that whilst someone is in a relationship they are 'scored' between one out of ten and ten out of ten (a minimum of one because they at least *have* a relationship), but a single person always scores zero at relationship – because they have no relationship, so they're 'scoring' zero at relationship. This is totally incorrect and unhelpful. It's actually part of a collective Unconscious misunderstanding of relationships. Just to give a couple of quick examples, a person who is being discerning and not just saying yes to the first offer of relationship that comes along that they don't really want is demonstrating Conscious Relationship, and their life will have a certain fulfilling quality of life because of that. A single person might be capable of engaging in Conscious Relationship to a high degree, even 100%, whereas a person in relationship might be operating totally from self-judgement. Consciousness doesn't consider being in a relationship as either more or less valuable than being single. It's a value judgement to believe that life in a relationship is inherently better than a single life. From the perspective of The Binary, it's not whether you're in a relationship, it's whether your *approach* to relationship is *true to self*, or not. There are also scales of maturity and responsibility in relationship. Whether we are single or not bears no relation to how far up this scale we are capable of relating from.

Part of Conscious Relationship is seeing things as they are, not how you want them to be. There's a difference between objectively observing the dynamics of a new connection to see if it's a good match, and subjectively interpreting everything so that it looks as if it is. The same goes with assessing the state of an existing relationship – and at each given point.

Love Consciousness	**Fear Consciousness**
Objectively Assessing a New Connection or Existing Relationship	Subjectively Interpreting a New Connection or Existing Relationship

The Myth of 'Failed Relationships'

Unconscious society might consider it a "failure" for a relationship to end, but that's merely a judgement. The Kissing Consciousness definition of a 'failed' relationship is not one that ends, but one that either continues against someone's true Choice, or is not allowed to start when it is both parties' Choice. The world is taught to congratulate people for being in a relationship, and pity them when they are not. A healthy alternative to this is to congratulate people when their relationship status authentically reflects their truth and support them when it does not.

Conscious Dating

People talk about having nerves – butterflies – on a date in the same way they might talk about something unwelcome. If they really understood the positive quality and nature of them, though, and what the experience was prior to their learned habit of *judging* their nerves, they'd relate to them in a very different, perhaps completely opposite way, as something welcome and delightful, rather more like they're having an energetic orgasm, or chocolate cake, or someone's just given them a million pounds. It's delicious. It's the excitement of vulnerability. But before we get a chance to taste that we've already judged it, and so we don't inhabit it, and so we don't honour it as our Being. We experience it as a concept in our head rather than a dance in our skin and body.

Of course, if the body's signals are alarm bells of a dangerous or disrespectful person, that is a different thing to Receive Awareness about.

"I Can't Fall in Love with Your False Self!"

If you have nerves and you relate that openly and honestly to the person you're dating, at least that's authentic and you're communicating from Love Consciousness. And maybe your nerves are really excitement in disguise.

Are you trying to date or court someone from your Being, or from your self-judgement? Doing so from your self-judgement is the False Self. Whilst Conscious people might have every compassion for you, and every non-judgement that you do that, the False Self is *not* something that someone even has the *chance* to connect with. People can't authentically fall in love with your Fear Consciousness because it's a False Self, and so it's not real. For the other person it's like being invited to shake hands with a ghost. Not to worry, though! Whenever we want to return to our True Self and provide the other person with an authentic version of us they can interact with, we can do our usual thing and release our self-judgements. We can remember The Paradox of Love Consciousness: By having no resistance to being triggered into our False Self we begin the return to being our True Self.

Everywhere where you've tried to court and date people from your self-judgement, would you like to let that go?

And would you like to ask your body if it would like to let that go?

Fear of Being Single

As tough as it sounds, you have to be Willing to be alone forever in order to choose relationship for Love Consciousness reasons! If you're not, then you've chosen relationship in order to try and avoid a fear, rather than to choose for love, from freedom. A 'choice' of relationship that's driven by Unwillingness to be single is not Choice, but Fear Consciousness.

Anywhere you have a fear of being single, would you like to let that go?

And would you like to ask your body if it would like to let that go?

Anywhere you have a fear of being in a relationship, would you like to let that go?

And would you like to ask your body if it would like to let that go?

All these principles that apply to dating continue to apply as we proceed in relationships. If you're presenting a False Self, that denies the possibility of authentic connection. If you've got fear of being single, you're likely going to be interpreting things subjectively, rather than objectively, bending over backwards or walking on eggshells just to keep the relationship going, and perhaps not realising the degree to which you're not speaking your truth. A person with no fear of being single is much more likely to respond to crap relationship with "Fuck that shit, I'm outta here!", and so more likely to only accept good ones.

Anywhere you have self-judgements that you have to accept a love-starved or sex-starved, intimacy-starved or respect-starved marriage or relationship, would you like to let that go?

And would you like to ask your body if it would like to let that go?

'Dinner for Two' is Really 'Dinner for Four'

By the time the voice of our self-judgements have had their say, dinner for two is really 'dinner for four'. The more of them we have, the more our talking to the person in front of us is interrupted by the chatter of our internal dialogues, and the same is also true for the other person. This doesn't necessarily stop when dating becomes a full-fledged relationship, either. It stops when there are no self-judgements left that are getting triggered. (../dating)

Commitment

"Commitment to another is merely an offshoot of commitment to ourselves." – James Blacker

Commitment is also relevant to business and all other kinds of relationships. We can only effectively commit to others if that arises naturally out of, and as a result of, our Love Consciousness commitment to ourselves. Otherwise, false commitment is being forced by our Fear Consciousness, and even if we sustain it, it will be a strain on our Life Force. It's no wonder so many people have issues with commitment to others, when the important principle of commitment to ourselves is so little understood.

Promises and 'Nevers'

What's the relationship between living in the moment and making someone a promise, which, by its very definition, implies something you will do in the future? When a future moment arrives, you can either do what you said according to the promise, or you can do what your Awareness says. These two may be the same thing, but if they're not, fulfilling the promise means going against your Awareness. This is not Conscious Living. It's not Love Consciousness, either. It's fear and attachment. To "want for the other person what they want for themselves" means wanting it to include us only if it is in their best interests. As Jan Day says, "Would you want to have dinner with someone who didn't want to be there?" This may even be Control Consciousness, too, if a friend holds too tightly to what was agreed. We make decisions in each moment. I might say, "Right now my intention is to do this", but in the future the moment will be new.

A 'Conscious Marriage' appreciates the potential catch 22 situation of either breaking a promise or dishonouring one's Choice and operating from Fear Consciousness. Many people are starting to write their own marriage vows so that they don't clash with their views of living from Choice and Awareness. Simply, if something isn't Choice it isn't Love Consciousness; we wouldn't really want someone to do something they didn't want to do just to make us feel loved. And a 'Never' is merely the equal opposite of a 'Forever' promise, so is potentially a Fear Consciousness resistance, too. The fact that most marriages, and other relationships fear these outcomes and *attach* to the promises is what causes the relationships to go stale, because the fear of loss inhibits each party's original self-expression. Addiction to the status quo becomes the prison. Those energies of the first flushes of love are difficult to Receive under such circumstances, because the key ingredient was creative originality of life, born in the fires of freedom from fear. (../commitment)

Attachment and fondness are different things, by the way. Nobody's saying be cold or aloof.

Intimacy

> "If you don't know yourself, how can you know the value of anything you're giving to anyone else? Answer: You can't." – David Heard

Due to The Primacy of Your Consciousness, intimacy with another person can only ever be the effect of your own Consciousness. Intimacy is neither guaranteed by certain physical acts, nor ruled out by them.

You cannot say, for example, that gazing into each other's eyes is definitely an act of intimacy, or that it's impossible for shouting at each other to be an act of intimacy. For that matter, you can't say that *avoiding* eye contact is definitely not intimacy. It may well be – avoiding eye contact, in a given moment, may well communicate the authenticity of how you feel in that moment.

Disagreement is *not* necessarily an opposite of intimacy. It's perfectly possible to have intimacy while disagreeing on something. Again, this is because intimacy is primarily a Consciousness!

So intimacy is any behavioural level expression that is authentic. In this way, you and a love partner (for example) can be intimate all day, every day. Intimacy as physical contact may or may not be a part of that.

Eye contact is the activity most frequently assumed to equate to intimacy. But if you are in a mindset of "eye contact = intimacy", you are in your head. The person in front of you is not interacting with you, but with a belief system! You are offering them your 'mask' (the notion that "eye contact = intimacy") to interact with. In short, you are hiding from connecting authentically and intimately with them behind the belief system.

Everyone associates 'slowly' with 'Conscious'; very few associate 'quickly' with 'Conscious'. The truth is that 'Conscious' is inherently neither. Someone might say, "Look into my eyes, nice and slow and Conscious." Well, which? If 'slow' and 'Conscious' happen to diverge which would you prefer?! (../intimacy)

Conscious Monogamy and Polyamory

A truly Conscious approach may require us to weed out the false limitations, illusions and judgements of the culture and context we grew up in. It does with regard to money and personal health, and with regard to relationships, also. If we're to choose monogamy, for example, and we have a resistance to polyamory or celibacy or any other choice, we might want to do clearings on that first, beforehand, so that we can then approach our pursuit of monogamy from a Conscious and therefore effective place, in order that it be fulfilling.

Most of us were brought up in a monogamous culture, and as part of that we grew up with Unconscious resistance to anything that doesn't fit that model. But if we were brought up in a polyamorous culture, we'd think that was normal, and we'd have resistance to anything that didn't fit *that* model, including monogamy. If you have a judgement around polygamy or polyamory you won't be free and able to choose them. But you won't be able to *choose* monogamy, either. You can only 'end up in it', by default. This is why so many people end up Unconsciously resenting their own lives – they weren't allowed to genuinely choose for themselves. So the first thing is, if you really want to do monogamy, and you want to do it effectively and have it be fulfilling, it must be a *Choice* of yours, and not a *Reaction* to society's fears. It can't be a Reaction to the fear of polyamory, and it can't be a Reaction to the fear of being single. People may say, "Ahh, you're promoting polyamory!" No, I'm promoting Choice. (../monogamy)

While we're on this subject, I'll offer a clearing, relating to guilt around having spiritual, soul-level connections with more than one person, what we might call 'Multiple Soul Loves', or simply natural love-based connections. We might have them; we might not have them; we might have them and not be *aware* that we have them.

Anywhere you've got guilt around having love-based connections with more than one person, would you like to let that go?

And would you like to ask your body if it would like to let that go?

A 'Marriage' Made in Heaven

"Nobody ever manufactured true love." – James Blacker

As we saw earlier, if you have a relationship that arises of its own accord, that isn't forced, then that is a relationship 'made in Heaven'.

In spiritual traditions, and as nature has it, and as it relates to our Consciousness, a 'marriage' is understood to be a 'marrying of energies'. Two people happen to find that not just their intellectual Ego's wishes, but their energies, their Beings, have come together in some way without Forced Behaviour. The 'marrying of energies' is a spontaneous occurrence that happens naturally. The legal contract document of a marriage is a different thing to an actual 'Energetic Marriage'. It's possible to have a conventional legal document marriage without a genuine marriage of energies, and it's possible to have an actual genuine marriage of energies without a legal contract marriage. It's sad that so many people get a legal marriage because they're kidding themselves that that alone will automatically give them the authentic joy of a genuine Energetic Marriage, as nature understands and governs it. So a 'Marriage Made in Heaven' is a real thing in nature. Of course, I'm loosely translating 'Heaven' to mean Love Consciousness. (../marriage)

I read a news article about a couple who engaged in a ceremonial activity to bind themselves spiritually. There's no such thing as a behaviour, ritual or ceremony, or even a mental behaviour or process, that can bind you spiritually or energetically to someone (... which doesn't mean you can't have a nice ceremony to celebrate Energetic Marriage *after* the fact!) Spiritual binding, as connection by a different name, pre-exists in nature. If it's real, the truth of saying, "Yes, I'll marry you", exists before the words come out of your mouth. You can say in your mind as many times as you want that someone is your true love, or your spirit – it won't make it true. The truth of that is deeper. You can *imbue* the behaviour with a Consciousness, *if that Consciousness is already there*, but you can't rely on a behaviour *in itself* to provide a certain Consciousness or natural reality.

And just because you have a love connection with someone, doesn't mean the behaviour you wish to engage in with them necessarily has to be marriage, or even living with them, or even sex, or anything else. Behaviours and choices are their own thing; they are totally a separate thing to whether you have a love energy with someone. Let's 'map' saying "I love you" in terms of The Illusion of Identical Experiences.

Love Consciousness	Fear Consciousness
Saying "I love you"	Saying "I love you"

Easy Come, Easy Go

"And it will not say goodbye, just like it didn't say hello." – The Beautiful South

To be Willing to play the game of authentic relationship without False Self is to accept that the same truth of nature which gives a true love connection can take it away just as instantly. And because it arrived without force, if it is to remain then it remains without force. Just as it cannot be contrived into authenticity, it cannot be contrived to remain in authenticity. Nor is it Conscious to try. One day a person may find themselves in love, another day they may wake up and find that the drive is no longer there. Or they feel it's time to take a different journey. It doesn't mean anything bad, it's just the way it is. There may also be grief, which may be healthy. But if we engage in Happiness Projection, then the fact of a relationship's energy being no longer true is seen as a problem.

Just as 'Energetic Marriage' is a separate thing to the paperwork of legal marriage, 'Energetic Divorce' is a different thing to legal divorce. (../divorce)

"Energetic 'Divorce' is itself inherently painless." – James Blacker

Even if the other person in a (legal) divorce is not interacting respectfully, there may well still be self-judgements that people can clear to make the process as easy as possible for themselves.

Anywhere you have self-judgements causing divorce to be more painful or difficult than it needs to be, would you like to let that go?

And would you like to ask your body if it would like to let that go?

The Honeymoon Period

In our culture, The Honeymoon Period is a couple of weeks holiday in the sun. In nature, and in wiser cultures, however, The Honeymoon Period is something different. It's a period of approximately six to nine months that allows people to see if they can sustain a relationship after the initial 'adrenalin' of passion and tendency to see each other through rose tinted spectacles wears off. They want to be sure that something other than that is what is driving the relationship forward. Some people call this 'The Test of Friendship'. The wiser cultures knew that if a couple lasted beyond The Honeymoon Period then they were probably able to sustain a marriage. So even a honeymoon has a natural reality in Consciousness! When I recorded John Christian's 'Relationships, Communication and Sexuality' audio with him, John identified a six-stage model of relationship. I'm going to suggest a two-stage version of that for you to consider:

- Stage One: The Honeymoon Period
- Stage Two: The Test of Friendship

Here's where our notion of Happiness Projection comes in. If we don't Happiness Project, then we can allow the dynamics of The Test of Friendship to explore themselves earlier, and more effectively, *alongside* whatever initial passion, sparks and fireworks may be happening. When people do project their happiness onto others, it can lead to a much more challenging and turbulent time when the (natural) Honeymoon Period comes to an end. In short, the more illusions you see, the more gaps in reality you have to process once the illusion is undone.

For those seeking a sustainable relationship, having an aim of establishing the success of the connection *beyond* the effect of The Honeymoon Period, 'aiming' more at assessing The Test of Friendship, is something I invite you to consider your own Awareness around. Incidentally, this Honeymoon Period also applies to non-romantic relationships, business relationships or new jobs, mobile phones, new lifestyle habits or anything else. (../honeymoon)

Conscious Choice of Relationship

Society has not yet become very aware of the existence of its Shadow Baggage. As a consequence, very few people are aware that they actually have a Shadow and a 'hidden self'. In my experience, it becomes obvious only when we start to do Shadow Work that there is much more to us and to our true personality than we realised. This means that a lot of people – in fact, I'd say most people – choose relationships without really knowing who they are, what suits them, or what they really want from relationship. This, of course, has various consequences, particularly if people sign legal contracts binding themselves together, and even more so if they have children. To be Conscious to this dynamic, you can become aware that you're operating from a sense of yourself that perhaps hasn't yet been entirely allowed to flourish and show itself. As a general trend, I would suggest that the more you know yourself, the better you're going to be able to choose a partner who is a good match for you.

Self-Acceptance Increase During Relationship

You might not want your partner to have to try (in vain) to make up for that which can only be restored by your own, whole sense of self. But people often choose relationships with that Unconscious intent. So revealing more of your True Self may also reveal that a current relationship was only ever a match for your False Self. If you have low self-respect and increase your self-respect and you're in a relationship, the person you're in a relationship with may very likely have the choice to either 'upgrade' with you, or, if they can't meet the standards of self-respect that you now insist on for yourself, they may find the relationship being ended.

Women Choosing Men

Here's an observation I've shared to help women: If you want a man who is genuinely committed, and real, you really have to look them in the eyes (not literally) and see them for what they are, beyond what you hope for, and not ignore the tell-tale little details. It takes a bit of 'seeing' to be able to tell when men say all the right things early on, but actually they are either incongruent, or just haven't explored themselves enough to really know what's motivating or driving them. In response to this, one woman said, "Speaking totally for myself this is right on the nose – 'beyond what you hope for, and not ignore the tell-tale little details.'"

Men Making Themselves Available to Women

And an observation that may help men attract women? I always had the best of intentions, but could certainly repel women with my Neediness and self-sabotage at a rapid rate of knots. Then I learned to be present to myself, to let go of the self-judgements, fall in love with my own energy, be comfortable in my own skin, and the kindness that I always was could then finally be offered to women in a way that they could Receive – presuming they themselves had 'Yes' Permissions around that. When you let go of your self-judgements you have no Neediness, and don't need to go chasing women because you can Receive yourself. When you can Receive yourself, you're also able to Receive your natural connections with women.

Men Making Themselves Safe for Women

To not want anything from a woman that she doesn't want to give to you is integrity. To do that without feeling you're unfulfilled or missing out is to know yourself so well, inside out, that you are clear with yourself on what you genuinely wish to offer, and to whom. You are not going to be interested in anyone who doesn't wish to choose that – hence, no need for manipulation, no desire to manipulate, and you can be the energy of 'safe', the energy of integrity, for a woman.

> "Women glow differently when they are
> treated right and loved properly."

It's anecdotal, but I've also clearly observed this. And of course, all of these insights and principles have value for all genders, and work both ways.

Men

The media tells us that it's difficult for men to know who they're supposed to be these days, and then some men buy into that story.

If you have no self-judgement it's easy to know how to be a man, because you are what you are. In fact, a man who has no self-judgements doesn't even feel the need to worry about *if* or *how* he's being a man; you're just a person who happens to be male. This all comes back to the same principle of things being naturally self-defining. 'What it means to be a man...', often with the words added, '... in the 21st century', presents difficulty and confusion for men simply because it is all about self-judgement. Even articles about it are destructive because they're motivated by money. Nobody's going to extract money from others with a two-word article that just says, "Be yourself."

- You're allowed to cry; in fact it's unhealthy to repress that
- You don't have to be any more macho than you really are; in fact, you don't have to be macho at all
- Gentleness and kindness is a strength
- Who are we kidding when we tell ourselves 'male role model culture' makes it difficult to know how to respect a woman's consent and boundaries in all matters?

"In Touch with Your Feminine Side"

The phrase itself almost sounds like a 'feminine side' is not you, or not something you're supposed to have. I would just say, "Are you in touch with your own emotions, your own kindness, heart, humanity, gentleness?" If you are, then – again – I'm sure anything you are meant to be will take care of itself.

Unconscious 'Macho'

This is about getting the approval of other men (or perhaps women) that one is "macho enough." It's yet more 'rules' to skew the underlying nature.

Love Consciousness	Fear Consciousness
Levels or qualities of 'Macho', if any, self-define	Where there's self-judgement around being 'Macho' these cause false, insincere attempts to demonstrate whatever that person perceives to be 'Macho'
This is Self-Respect	This is *not* Self-Respect
Healthy 'Macho'	Unhealthy, false 'Macho'

What Life's Like for Many Women? Male Empathy is Invited

Jackson Katz has a great exercise, in which he asks men, "What daily steps do you take to prevent being sexually assaulted?" Puzzled looks and awkward silences ensue. Katz reports that aside from the odd comment about staying out of prison, the response is essentially that men do nothing, and don't even think about it. Then he asks the women …

"As the men sit in stunned silence, the women recount safety precautions they take as part of their daily routine. Here are some of their answers: Hold my keys as a potential weapon. Look in the back seat of the car before getting in. Carry a cell phone. Don't go jogging at night. Lock all the windows when I sleep, even on hot summer nights. Be careful not to drink too much. Don't put my drink down and come back to it; make sure I see it being poured. Own a big dog. Carry Mace or pepper spray. Have an unlisted phone number. Have a man's voice on my answering machine. Park in well-lit areas. Don't use parking garages. Don't get on elevators with only one man, or with a group of men. Vary my route home from work. Watch what I wear. Don't use highway rest areas. Use a home alarm system. Don't wear headphones when jogging. Avoid forests or wooded areas, even in the daytime. Don't take a first-floor [ground floor] apartment. Go out in groups. Own a firearm. Meet men on first dates in public places. Make sure to have a car or cab fare. Don't make eye contact with men on the street. Make assertive eye contact with men on the street." – Jackson Katz

That's no way for society to cause women to live. And that's without even considering the hugely imbalanced economic punishment, legislative punishment and cultural repression of women that is explained in Volume II. The idea that men have it as bad as women – or worse – is a false, pathological political narrative peddled by demagogues and cowardly career politicians who are themselves psychologically broken and frankly need therapy.

www.KissingConsciousness.com/men

Women

As a woman, what might freedom in love, sex and relationships look like for you? If you have rules around such things, are they your rules acquired through Choice, or judgemental Barriers imposed upon you by society? Are you free to explore yourself as much as men do?

Anywhere you have self-judgements that you're not allowed to explore yourself, would you like to let that go?

And would you like to ask your body if it would like to let that go?

While men are mostly judged on whether they are 'macho', women are hugely judged on their appearance, of course. That often means a whole raft of opportunities for women to let go of doing things they don't want to do and similarly honour their True Self.

Anywhere you attend to your appearance out of self-judgement rather than out of Choice, would you like to let that go?

And would you like to ask your body if it would like to let that go?

And there are also many societal judgements of women's choices that are simply not applied to men.

Anywhere you've bought into society's judgements about your choices and what they may mean, would you like to let that go?

And would you like to ask your body if it would like to let that go?

www.KissingConsciousness.com/women

The Facilitating Conscious Relationship Caveat

Are you Willing to get Conscious to your relationship, even given the theoretical possibility that it might reveal that your Choice is to leave the relationship? Or that that's the other person's Choice, or both? The moment we start working on facilitation with more than one person, or involving more than one person, the possibility arises that people might want different things, so we may wish to mention **The Facilitating Conscious Relationship Caveat** to them. It's possible – indeed, it is the nature of Unconsciousness – that people might be Unconscious to what they really want. They might think they want something different to what they actually do. So people in relationships should know that bringing Awareness to their relationships could potentially bring them to an end.

"Most people don't have the courage for love
so they settle for connection." – Tony Robbins

The only thing I would tweak about that is that actually people *do* have the courage for love, but their self-judgements dissuade them from acknowledging it. If you have that self-judgement would you like to let it go?

Finally, here are some powerful questions from Jon Freeman: "What would happen if we took all the labels off the box? What would happen if we stopped believing in romanticised and chocolate box presentations? What would it be like if we rose in love and didn't fall in it? What would it be like if we stopped believing that there is one right way that fits all, and projecting our own views onto other people? What would it be like if we were all secure in our being and sexuality? What would it be like if we didn't externalise morality?"

Sex

Sex is our basic nature, our Life Force. For humanity to somehow manage to *fear* sex really takes some doing. That is a testament to the power of the human intellect, and the human race relying on belief systems at the expense of its Awareness and Knowing.

Growing up in a culture full of judgement about sex – and pleasure in general – destroyed the joy of the first few decades of my life, and I dare say that of many millions, probably billions of others, too. I don't think there is a person whose life hasn't been negatively impacted in some way by this world's repressive and fear-based relationship to sex and pleasure. Would you like to let that draining influence go?

Anywhere you have self-judgements that you *'shouldn't'* have a frank discussion about sex, or aren't allowed to, would you like to let that go?

And would you like to ask your body if it would like to let that go?

I'd like to suggest an intention for this subject that we address it with as much sensitivity and kindness as we can.

Anywhere you have self-judgements that wouldn't allow you to approach sex and your own sexuality and sexual energy with self-kindness and self-compassion, would you like to let that go?

And would you like to ask your body if it would like to let that go?

Sex is one of the most judged areas of life, shutting down possibilities in all directions. If we step out of judgement around sex, and step into reality and direct, real experience of it, what new and different realities might open up for us? What might be different for our bodies? And if your relationship to sex were to change, how might that change your relationship to food, or other things? Is it possible that the world's fear and judgement of sex is a primary cause of the obesity crisis?

Buried under the lies that create shame, guilt and judgement around sex is a blissful, natural world of Unselfconscious sex, sexual energy and relating to others from that sexual energy. We have an option here of seeking to release that buried reality.

And 'relating to others from that sexual energy' may have nothing to do with actually having sex, and often won't. It simply means relating to others in a way in which you are allowing yourself to 'own' all of your energy and Being, which includes your sexual energy and your Life Force, which are totally intertwined. It means acknowledging the sexual energy that you have, and that you are, without having to do anything about it.

Anywhere you have shut down your ability to communicate fully because you aren't allowed to communicate as the sexual being that you are, would you like to let that go?

And would you like to ask your body if it would like to let that go?

It's important to realise that for many people the negative effects of being brought up by a world that fears sex, judges sex, doesn't understand sex, punishes sex, and doesn't have a healthy relationship with it, may have been added to further still by the experience of trauma caused by abuse. That trauma may have been sexual, however, non-sexual trauma may also have the effect of inhibiting our sexual nature and expression. Many people are so traumatised by abusive experiences in life that the mere thought of any kind of sex is challenging. Anything traumatic or abusive is going to shut down the body to some degree, and our sense of allowance for joy, pleasure and happiness. But we may invite those areas where we have been shut down energetically and sexually, physically and emotionally, to open up again, if they and we wish to do so.

Boundaries

The first thing to address is understanding how to honour our own Boundaries and those of other people, so everything that follows has that crucial element nicely in place. The Boundaries Exercise (see Chapter Four) is a great way to go beyond any blocks to honouring yourself and can help provide a basis for understanding total self-respect in readiness for everything else that may follow in your sex life, and elsewhere.

Releasing Sexual, Emotional and Energetic Wounds

I'm sure you're familiar with the wake of a ship, the watery trail of disturbed water that flows out behind the ship as it moves through the water. The wake follows the boat, not the other way around. In the same way, as much as our past experiences may have been traumatic, if we're to be effective we are invited to Respond to the here and now. This enables us to honour any relevant emotions, rather than intellectualising them.

This means something like, instead of saying "I can't do this because this happened in the past", we say to ourselves, "I can't do this because … what *right now* is stopping me from doing this?" It is either going to be something physical, or something emotional/psychological, or both. For example, "I can't do this right now because … my body can't do it." Or, "I can't do it because I feel too emotionally hurt or in pain."

Intellectual freedom from self-judgement – having a *cognitive understanding* of our right to a happy and relaxed relationship to our own sexual energy and activity – can only go so far. At some point, the desire for full freedom requires the involvement of the body, and likely asking the body to release its blockages. Of course, asking our body to let things go is a good starting point. (../wounds)

Using Intuitive Loving Touch May Help

In Chapter Four on Tools we introduced the Kissing Consciousness process of Intuitive Loving Touch, or ILT for short. This process may help you, perhaps if you work on it with a safe and trustworthy lover, and I would encourage you not to underestimate the power of your own ability to provide touch-based healing for yourself. You might, for example, lie on your back and rest your hand on any part of your body, sexual organs or otherwise, that you feel you'd like to bring Awareness, love and honouring to. That may bring up emotions, but if you can hold Presence to yourself to allow yourself to be with what arises, to cry, for example, that may not need to be a big deal, and you'll get a gain in energy and wellbeing from any releasing.

Body De-armouring

Body De-armouring, or just De-armouring, is another popular process of releasing the trauma stored in our bodies.

"The pain body is spread throughout the whole physical body, and it contains all the pain, trauma that we accumulated since birth. So we're working with that, we're working to replace the pain body and replace it with love. Heal it. Bring it to light and hold it in our heart, hold it in our body until the energy dissipates, dissolves, relaxes and integrates. Sooner or later I feel every body needs to be freed from pain, and aches, and pent-up energy, and stiffness." – De'an Matuka

Exploring The Wonderful World of Conscious Sexuality

Delicious, ecstatic and emotionally and sensuously luxurious possibilities for sex and intimacy are available to us. These greater possibilities will almost certainly also yield greater outcomes for our health, Life Force and happiness. Let's explore some of the juiciness on offer.

'The Touch of God'

Unconscious self-judgement comes across in our touch, our voice, etc. If we have self-judgement around what we are doing, that turbulent energy is going to travel from our Consciousness, down our arm, into our fingers, and the other person is going to feel it in our touch, possibly Consciously and definitely Subconsciously. Given our understanding of The Paradox of Love Consciousness, the first thing we can do to *Respond* if this is the case is to allow it to be okay that it happens. As we release our need to be a certain way, and as we release the self-judgements we hold which come across in our touch, our state of Surrender allows our natural self to come through, in turn allowing our natural touch to come through, resulting in a quality of touch that comes straight from the Divine, what we might call 'The Touch of God' or 'The Touch of The Divine'. (../touch)

For men particularly, a practice you might like to consider is to be 'slow like honey' when touching or caressing. Simply run your touch along your lover's arm, for example. Now do it slower. Now slower still. Even more slowly than that. And slower still – such that you are not thinking about the next thing. Even if it's not your *Choice* to do slow during intimacy, having the *capacity* to have the option to do so may benefit the levels of self-control you have on what you *do* want to do. (../honey)

One thing women often say is they'd like men to be a bit less "A, B, C, D, E." They would like to feel a little less like sex is a conveyor belt with a fixed agenda of points to be run through in order. Conscious Sexuality is about allowing Awareness and Choice into what you do, so that it is fulfilling rather than obligation.

Tuning into The Other Person

With sex, just as with all other aspects of human interaction, tuning into the other person is invaluable. This allows sex to be a couple in tandem, in harmony, rather than two people solely focused on their own 'getting' and paying no attention to each other's flows, energies, speeds, wishes and signals. Again, practicing The Boundaries Exercise is great for developing this tuning in 'muscle'. Of course, tuning into the other person doesn't mean just doing what they want. In coercive relationships, those being controlled may do better to tune into their own wishes. (../tuning)

Energetic and Full Body Orgasms

Our ill-informed sexual world is slowly but surely being introduced to a veritable smorgasbord of sex insights, pioneered by practitioners of such things as Conscious Sexuality and Tantra. These include such things as Full Body Orgasms and even Energy Orgasms, which can be achieved without touch. (../orgasms)

Having Sex with All Three of Your Bodies

"In our schizophrenic sexual culture – whether sex is moralistically repressed as sin or hedonistically expressed as 'fucking' – sex tends to be reduced to a mere physical act: Tab A in Slot B, or some variation thereof. This, of course, is only the gross dimension of sex. But could you have sex – or really make love – consciously in all 3 bodies?"

That quote from the Integral Life Practice handbook by Wilber, Patten, Leonard and Morelli introduces an understanding that is destined to become more acknowledged by humanity, that we all each actually have three bodies: A gross physical body, a subtle (energetic) body, and a causal (very subtle) body. These correspond to your waking, dreaming and formless (or deep sleep) states of Consciousness.

> "Without you and your partner's conscious participation, [gross, physical level sex] would lead fairly quickly to male orgasm and the end of the encounter." – Integral Life Practice

"At the subtle level (which begins before the gross and continues beyond it), you and your partner could share a deep emotional exchange. ... By focusing your attention on the subtle dimension of sex, achieving orgasm might become less important, and the joyful play of energies up and down, in and out, and in every other direction, could become an amazing source of pleasure. Your heart centres could open and mutually resonate perhaps even merge into a singular vortex of profound and passionate loving. ... The play of energies and depth of emotion could themselves become free-flowing subtle orgasms.

"At the causal level, you could rest in perfectly still, unobstructed awareness – the silent, conscious, spaceless space that's holding your gross and subtle bodies, and hearts and minds, throughout the sexual act. And finally, in the nondual union of all your bodies, that still and silent witness consciousness might reveal itself as inseparable from boundless radiant love. And that all-pervading love might find itself making art out of the caress of two naked human beings. Pure emptiness could hold the dance of undulating flesh and the frolic of subtle electricity, and release them into an ecstatic luminescence that's utterly transcendent and yet tenderly intimate – even in the sweetness of your lover's lips." – Integral Life Practice

Reading the final chapter of Volume II will illuminate the terms 'causal', 'witness', 'emptiness' and 'nondual' a bit more for you. (../bodies)

Pornography and Erectile Function

> "You probably want to know why any porn-loving guy in his right mind would give it up? Two words: Erectile dysfunction. Internet porn is killing young men's sexual performance." – Gary Wilson

Whilst potential causes of erectile dysfunction are varied and mostly well-known, many people are not aware of the new and extreme threat that internet pornography is. Stating numbed pleasure response, how opposite it is to actual sex, and the fact that constant novelty at a click can cause addiction, TEDx presenter, Gary Wilson, shares that internet porn is assessed to be far more compelling and destructive than previous versions of pornography. According to Wilson, whilst it takes older men 2 months of abstention to recover from porn-induced erectile dysfunction, it takes younger guys 4 – 5 months to recover. The reason? Even though older guys had been using porn longer, they didn't start on today's internet porn, whereas today's young teens *start* on high-speed internet connections when their brains are most vulnerable to addiction. As Wilson explains, "Widespread, youthful erectile dysfunction has never been seen before." Oh, what are we doing to our children's wellbeing as a society? (../function)

"This movement, to unhook from porn, is growing rapidly. In fact, groups are springing up all across the web, and in Europe, too." – Gary Wilson

Conscious LGBT+

Any judgementalism of a person for choosing something for themselves that doesn't harm other people is a sign of insecurity, lack of self-esteem and fear on behalf of the person doing the judging. We've said before that a truly secure person is never unkind under any circumstances, and you might like to let go of anywhere you've shut your Awareness down to the notion that other people's judgementalism is a reflection of their issues, and not yours. There may have been a lot of unkindness around this, too, and so maybe some clearings on the body's trauma would serve. One thing I would invite people to check in with themselves around, though, is that they are making their choices *from Choice*, and not from self-judgement. A person who considers a gender change, for example, is no more immune to the phenomenon of Shadow Baggage and the False Self than anyone else. Whatever people want to do is fine, of course, but I'd hate to think somebody made a life-changing decision for something they didn't really want, as a result of self-judgements that had been imposed upon them which repressed their true personality. This principle works both ways, as there will also be people whose self-judgements prevent them from acknowledging their homosexuality to themselves, for example, or their genuine desire to change gender. And maybe a realistic Awareness is that it's not safe to acknowledge that in a given culture. (../LGBT)

www.KissingConsciousness.com/sex

Other Relationships

Friendships

"A friend is someone you can be yourself with."

We'll address friendships first, because we might like to choose that all other relationships also include the quality of friendship – particularly when it is understood by this saying above. Would you want a friend, parent or lover, employee, colleague or boss you weren't free to be yourself with? (../friends)

Conscious Parenting

"What usually has the strongest psychic effect on the child is the life which the parents have not lived." – Carl Jung

It's the most tragic thing, for a parent to want the best for their child, yet inadvertently come from an Unconscious place of wanting less than the best for their child because seeing the child be fully happy and what they are capable of Being, having and Receiving, triggers the parent's own Unconscious emotional pain. Parents may not realise that they are getting triggered by all the things they themselves weren't allowed to be, or do, or have. When we have our buttons pressed by our children's greater freedoms and opportunities, can we catch ourselves and not put our judgements onto them?

"If I think about it, I only have five more years, five summers, and I'm not the centre of their Universe." – Jason Momoa

Here are four principles which we've already covered, plus one we'll address in Volume II, that can aid Conscious Parenting hugely:

- Critiquing the behaviour, not criticising the child
- Encouraging the child to be Self-Referral, and not External Referral

- Tuning into the other person, i.e. the child
- Avoid Third Party Trigger Dumping
- Appreciating that the current education system is sub-optimal, even dangerous and destructive, and children will naturally sense this and wisely have valid concerns and resistances

Please consider these two alternatives:

> "Go to school."
> "I don't want to."
> "Go to school!"

> "Go to school."
> "I don't want to."
> "Why not?"
> Starts a conversation that leads to ... "I'm being bullied" or "The big kids are trying to push me into buying drugs."

Third Party Trigger Dumping: The child has green hair and earrings. The grandparents don't like it, or someone at the bowls club makes a snide comment, so the parent Reacts. Or the parent was so starved of love themselves as a child that they'll do anything to gain the approval of society or their own parents – so they criticise the child for a mere act of self-expression. "How it reflects on me!", they might comment. Why let the judgementalism of society get in the way of respecting yourself and loving your family unconditionally? I always think that if you meet the child halfway, don't judge them for things which are benign, and don't try to control their career choices, social preferences, etc., then they will more likely listen to you when you need them to about the important things such as keeping them safe. They will *want* to socialise with their friends and boy/girlfriends in your home, rather than avoiding it because they can't be themselves and going who knows where on the streets to find some personal space.

www.KissingConsciousness.com/parenting

Family Relations

A Conscious approach to family relationships is simple: What would you like to do or not do? No judgement need get in the way of that. (../family)

Jokes as Unconscious Alternatives to Compliments

Although there's nothing inherently wrong with clichéd jokes, they often tend to be a self-judgement-caused alternative to genuine intimacy, which requires vulnerability. So a partner/spouse, child or relative who is the subject of jokes tends to go without the shining light of heartfelt, expressed love and appreciation, and the energy and Life Force which that can allow. A compliment is often what many people need and have a yearning desire for, above all else. Meeting that need can be a priceless gift beyond measure. (../compliments)

Christmas

> "One of the things that I do not understand is grown people who sit around complaining that they have to go somewhere for Christmas, they have to go to someone's house that they don't want to. I don't care who it is, I don't care if it's your mother, your mother-in-law, whatever it is, if you are over 21 and you don't want to go then you *don't go*." – Jenni Trent Hughes

Sensible people celebrate Christmas and other occasions on their own terms, if at all. I like the magical, romantic qualities of Christmas, and I back myself to create them without having to have that be interrupted by the commercialism, and the lack of authenticity and genuine fulfilment that almost inevitably comes with it.

As it's Christmas it's not so much a self-judgement as it is an Elf-judgement. (Pantomime audience groans). So shall we clear all those pesky Elf-judgements out of the way, and have an authentic, fulfilling Christmas that's what we want – or not? Who you *have* to see, that you *have* to buy presents, what you *have* to eat or drink, the games you *have* to play, the clothes you *have* to wear, the traditions you *have* to follow, the office party you *have* to attend – it all can go if you choose. And what you want can stay. If you were to 'invite in a *Christmas* beyond self-judgement', what would that look like for you?

And employers, what self-judgements are stopping you from being okay with the fact that some of your staff may not want to attend a Christmas party? (../christmas)

www.KissingConsciousness.com/relationships

Chapter Eight

Being an Unofficial Facilitator

Everyone is giving everyone else advice in the pubs and clubs, at coffee mornings and in the workplace already anyway, so we might as well all do that:

a. Effectively
b. With the use of question-based tools to actually invite the Choice of change in, rather than just intellectualise around the matter

This is a simple but also quite profound process. You're literally giving people their Life Force back, and giving them back parts of themselves. The only qualifier to that statement is that it is their will and Choice which is doing it.

As with all personal development work, this is not intended to be a replacement for appropriate medical or professional help. Always consult your General Practitioner or Mental Health Professional.

Being The Space of Non-Judgement

All that is required for us to effectively support others in finding themselves and being themselves is first for us to be the 'space' of non-judgement. Our role is to *be* Love Consciousness, to hold the space for that. Then we simply use the letting go questions as appropriate.

Being The Space vs Filling The Space

You can't 'be the space of non-judgement' or 'hold the space' if you're 'filling the space' with your own opinions, conclusions, Fear Consciousness and judgements at the same time. Facilitation is about helping the other person to find *their* truth, not yours. This means:

- No Conclusion (a mind almost as if you have never formed an opinion in your life)
- No Pressure (to have them gain results at your speed, or even at all)
- No Judgement (of what arises, or how they are)
- No Agenda (for what they should or shouldn't be choosing)

All of these are different forms of conclusion and judgement.

"You've got this!" or "You can do this!"

"You can do this!" or "You've got this!" is generally mediocre advice. If someone is doubting themselves, I would rather facilitate them and invite Awareness in. Otherwise we're just burying people's doubts. People's doubts are trying to tell us/them something; they are informative, so why would we want to bury them?! They are the very thing we want to facilitate. What Awareness is being blocked out that if you faced it would remove your or their self-doubt? It's impossible to give people Confidence, but you can invite them to choose it.

Again, as a Facilitator, you're not there to give people your truth (which might even be Neediness by the way), you're there to help them remove the blocks to being fully and confidently in touch with their own truth. And even then, that is provided that's what they choose. "You've got this!" usually encourages people to be External Referral, not Self-Referral. That's Fear Consciousness. It's an example of Filling The Space, rather than Being The Space.

"It'll be okay!" and "Don't worry"

For the same reason, I would almost certainly not say, "It's okay", "It's going to be okay", "Don't worry." These phrases are often quite unhelpful and possibly even dangerous things to say, if they result in people shutting down their Awareness. If you're worried I'd want to know what Awareness you have underneath that.

Radical Non-Assumption

aka: Infinite Non-Assumption

To engage effectively in Kissing Consciousness Facilitation we require a 'position' – an attitude – of Radical Non-Assumption, or Infinite Non-Assumption, about how the world should be, about how the person should be, about anything. This allows the freedom for truth to arise. Attachment to conventional thinking and limitation is also dropped. Without Non-Assumption, we're doing people a disservice by imposing our own conclusion limitations upon them.

Infinite Non-Instruction

As part of this we are also declining giving any kind of instructions. If and when our Awareness suggests it, we may offer insights or suggestions, but we do that while acknowledging the person's right to make up their own mind in the final instance, and choose their own path. We generally meet questions such as "Should I do this, or should I do that?" with a question in reply, such as, "What does your Awareness say?", or "What would you like to choose?", rather than giving people advice.

Powerful Gifting

Radical Non-Assumption and Infinite Non-Instruction are not about limiting the help and value we as Facilitators can give to others; rather, they are about ensuring the value we give is not undermined by our own judgement. In no way does not giving advice or instruction stop us from gifting people with our insights and Awareness, including those in this book. For example, if someone relates being controlled, instead of telling them not to put up with that, we can ask them, "Do you enjoy being told what to do?", "Is it your choice to allow that to continue?", "If not, is it safe for you to choose something else?" Radical Non-Assumption actually facilitates the incredibly effective and powerful Facilitator within you.

The Caveat for Facilitating Couples or Relationships

The moment we start working with more than one person, or on something that involves more than one person, such as a relationship, there arises the possibility that facilitation may surface the truth that people want different things and might want to end a relationship. Facilitation helps move people into the right relationships or relationship statuses *for them* – which might not be welcome to everyone's expectations and attachments. So we need to mention **The Facilitating Conscious Relationship Caveat** to people, as mentioned in Chapter Seven.

Facilitation as a 'Plugin' for Specific Expertise Coaches

Because Kissing Consciousness Facilitation deals with *general* blocks to a person's 'Permissions', it is a different thing to the *specific* knowledge and skills taught by teachers and coaches in their own particular fields of specialism, and can therefore be used to complement them. Here's the A-Z of just some of the specialised areas it can help with:

- Acting Coach
- Book Writing Coach
- Business Coach
- Cookery Coach
- Dance Coach
- Music Teacher
- Sports Coach
- Zookeeping Trainer

(How else was I going to get a 'Z' example!) If you're an acting coach, business mentor, sports coach or any other, you will have expertise related to your specific industry and subject. Kissing Consciousness Facilitation can be used to add another dimension entirely. What's the point in mentoring the founder of a new business startup about the mechanics of business, if they also have an Unconscious self-judgement that they're not allowed to be successful, or happy in their work?! Or if they're uncomfortable speaking to people?! Those things need clearing first if people are to be effective. If you're an acting coach, and you notice your student is not 'owning it', you can invite them to let go of whatever is preventing that: "Anything that isn't allowing you to own this performance, would you like to let that go?" And, of course, you can do clearings on yourself as a coach or teacher, wherever you may have blocks. You can even do these *during* the sessions of teaching others. They don't even have to know if you don't want them to – it can be a mere 'Flick of the Consciousness'. (../plugin)

Chapter Nine

Being an Official Facilitator

Facilitator Training

"Consciousness Facilitation is easy: You just stand in the middle of a room and love people." – James Blacker

For those who wish to, the option is there to become an official Kissing Consciousness Facilitator and officially facilitate others, either on a full-time or part-time basis, at group gatherings or one-to-ones, or both. You can find out more via this link below:

www.KissingConsciousness.com/training

It may give you a buzz to help others, and you may find it fulfilling to work on something that is deeply pragmatic, ethical and positive for society. Consciousness Facilitation is like life 'coaching' activity (specifically, life 'liberating' activity) that is simultaneously social and humanitarian activity. Any time you move yourself, or anyone else, from a point of self-judgement, to self-love; whilst the individual benefits, the collective whole also benefits. We all share the same whole energy, and one same Universe, as well as the same cultural memes and collective psychological 'centres of gravity' in society. By doing a clearing, by becoming more Conscious, we're increasing the amount of love and Awareness in the world. The movement from Fear Consciousness into Love Consciousness is the salvation of everyone.

Facilitating others will also almost certainly make you more effective at facilitating yourself. Doing that as a professional is about as good a support for your own personal Success and life as you can possibly get.

And whilst Volume II on 'Co-creating a World Beyond System Failure' addresses a series of complex social and global issues, as a Kissing

Consciousness Facilitator you don't have to. That's an unofficial contribution, not part of the 'job description'. That said, Kissing Consciousness has taken a rather rare and pioneering step by intertwining collective and systemic global-social solutions with a personal development methodology, and this offers additional strength as a foundation. For one thing, we can move beyond the stress and soul-destroying 'hustle' of 'them vs us' marketing, and instead step into the Consciousness of new, efficient, more rewarding and integrated ways of generating prosperity, where personal Success and social prosperity run side by side.

Expanding Your Permissions, Expanding Your Capabilities

As a Facilitator, the typical reality is that the more you facilitate yourself to be in greater allowance of yourself, the more effective you'll be at facilitating others. This is a profession whereby the more Happiness and freedom you allow in for yourself, the more valuable you are to other people. That includes economic value. You might well become the very energy of self-acceptance that people pick up on, the very energy of Love Consciousness that they lack, and it is this energy you reflect which gives others the sense that they can be that also. When you're the energy of Love Consciousness, in one sense it doesn't much matter what else you actually *do*. It's often the quality of that Consciousness itself which you ignite in others which provides the benefit, so expanding your own Permissions may very much expand your contribution and your capabilities as a Facilitator. Let's look at four further areas in which we can potentially increase our value and abilities:

Inviting in Awareness: One skill you can develop with experience as an official Facilitator is getting a sense of where common self-judgements tend to hide, what kind of self-judgements are common to us all as a result of our society, and what judgements tend to arise in specific areas of life.

"If you can't explain it simply, you don't understand it well enough." – Albert Einstein

Mastery of The Insights: Repeated reading of this book offers the chance to become fluent in its wisdom and the insights and dynamics shared.

Combined with The Kissing Consciousness Tool itself, this ought to allow you to become very useful to anyone wishing to break free of false limitation.

Getting a Feel for Facilitating: The formal Kissing Consciousness Tool and Structures will give you more than enough to effectively facilitate others. On top of that, as you both release your own Permissions, and become more familiar with the processes, you can *get a feel* for Consciousness Facilitation.

Declining Conflicting Philosophies: There was an advert during my childhood: "It's the fish John West rejects that makes John West the best." Similarly, the effectiveness of Kissing Consciousness is found, in part, by not confusing it with other approaches. It's very easy to jump online, see a personal development quote that sounds good and buy into it, without realising that it's locking in a limitation, a Subconscious sense of obligation or a conclusion. If it conflicts with the approaches and philosophies here, it could actually inhibit rather than enhance your own empowerment, and prevent you from seeing the world in a way that gives you clarity. There's a purity and simplicity to Kissing Consciousness which could be *weakened* by diluting it.

Hosting Workshops and Gatherings

In addition to private one-to-one sessions – either in person or online – working with people in groups can range from formal seminars of a day or more, to small gatherings of an hour or two. Kissing Consciousness events may also include Intuitive Loving Touch, or even The Boundaries Exercise. In fact, if you want to do nothing other than host Intuitive Loving Touch, you may do that.

The Value of 'Showing Up'

If you are travelling to host an event and aren't feeling like you're in the zone or Confident, or even if you're doubting that you have anything to offer, that may be great news. "Wait, what?" You can acknowledge to yourself that if you allow that to be okay, i.e. don't judge it – or even if you do judge it – you may still be doing a great service to people merely by your Willingness to be that, and show up. If you treated your guests as unconditionally as you treated yourself, that's an event I'd feel good about being at. You're offering the gift of the invitation to authenticity. In this day and age, anyone who's Willing to show up authentically is an extremely wonderful gift to the world. Of course, if your genuine Awareness is you'd rather do something else, or you need to cancel, then you want to listen to that.

Beyond 'Polished' Presentations

Love Consciousness is beyond the need for 'polished' presentations, which people have already started to see through anyway. It's not about being smooth or polished or a 'star turn', it's about Being. And that is what it is. If that happens to be smooth and polished, then fine. If we're not sharing that invitation to authentic Being and Freedom, we're not sharing Love Consciousness. This is why I'm advocating totally redefining what Success is, and what a 'success coach' may look like, or how they may behave – not just for us, but for the whole of society and the world.

"Erm, You Know!"

After a radio interview I gave, a presenter from an adjoining room commented on how well I spoke. That was mainly because 20 years previously I'd had field training whilst working as a window salesman (indeed) – from a man called Bill Window, of all things (double indeed) – and he gave me a nice, sarcastic, embarrassing but valuable debriefing after my pitch, caricaturing my repeated "erm"-ing and "ah"-ing and making me aware of them. Without judging ourselves for saying "erm" or "you know", and even though the point above about not needing to be polished remains true, we can still appreciate the possible benefit of dropping the habit of being Unconscious to our own discomfort and filling the space with 'white noise'. There are sports World Cup winners who say "you know" four, five, six times in a 20 word answer to a question. People do this in all other walks of life, too. They speak lots without ever actually *saying* anything, or very little of any substance. If you practice silence in the face of the temptation to say "You know", then you may sharpen your grasp on genuine, useful capabilities and insights, and then share them more effectively. You may find you start to get really clear on what it is you *are* saying, what it is that has value that you are seeking to convey. "You know" doesn't add value to a personal development event or one-to-one. Utilising 'empty space' is 'what we do' as Kissing Consciousness Facilitators; filling it with white noise potentially takes us in the opposite direction, away from the gift of Consciousness and holding Presence. If we're Unwilling to allow uncomfortable silences, we're offering our audience our Fear Consciousness.

Anywhere you feel pushed to fill empty space with 'white noise', would you like to let that go?

And would you like to ask your body if it would like to let that go?

'Let The Wave Meet The Shore'

The Kissing Consciousness way is generally to have no agenda as to what will arise and what to allow the space and time to be for. We're simply offering facilitation, plus a background understanding of the dynamics involved.

Rather than needing a fixed agenda for a Kissing Consciousness event or session, and certainly instead of planning what we're going to say in any great detail, the default approach to KC group sessions is to allow the space to fill itself, and to let people identify what is a priority for them from their Awareness, but ultimately steered by the host's own Awareness. If people find, on a given day, that they are focused on money, it might not be the most effective thing to start inviting clearings on, say, parenting or diet. I call this approach 'letting the wave meet the shore'. It can also accommodate those whose current priority is in the minority, by assuring they get some time to address that.

> "As a teacher, I insist that anyone who has been told by their professor that they have to be here … leaves now. I will not speak to captive audiences. (Laughter; nobody moves.) … That's good then, alright." – Christopher Hitchens

We also want to be responsive to the flow and feel of the group. Massage/therapy tables may be available for pre-arranged – or spontaneous – Intuitive Loving Touch processes. Some people might want to break out from being formally facilitated to make use of them and rest, or, if the host is cool with it, exchange ad hoc Intuitive Loving Touch. We're going to need a *lot* of massage tables. Providing it doesn't disturb too much, I would allow people to come and go, and change their sitting, standing, lying down state according to their Awareness. If they clear a major block and their Awareness says to follow it up immediately with action elsewhere, I wouldn't want them to stay, I'd say go, do what calls you. This is the flexibility of world we require. We've been standing on attention for too long.

The main thrust of the work is inviting people's Consciousnesses, bodies and nervous systems to get used to self-acceptance beyond self-judgement, so a host can respond to where people are with that, both individually and collectively. You don't even need an event title, you can just say, "Hey, we're going to do a Kissing Consciousness session. Feel free to show up with whatever you've got and whatever's vital for you right now."

Demand-Led, Commitment-Based Event Scheduling

It might be worth taking a demand-led approach to choosing if and when to run events. Deciding to run an event and then seeing if there is demand, or trying to get people to attend might be old school. Why give Facebook or Google good money? And as a host you have to hire a venue, or at least put yourself out plans-wise if you're hosting at your home, so why allow people to decide on the day, or to cancel and expect a refund? I always find it's better to establish demand first, then let people commit if they're committed. Then if they cancel it doesn't matter, you've still got their payment to cover your bottom line. You have to appreciate your own position, otherwise nobody else will. You can also do clearings for charging what the event is worth, of course, and what price you're willing to do it for: 'Pricing by Awareness'.

Participant Code of Conduct

There is one main requirement of attending a Kissing Consciousness event, which is that if participants don't wish to be actively supportive of other participants, and of the host, they are at least of a neutral attitude towards them, both in energy and in behaviour. It is essential that this is observed, because of course the environment needs to be a safe space for everyone. (../code)

You can find out about current Kissing Consciousness events and find a Facilitator at:

www.KissingConsciousness.com/facilitators

www.KissingConciousness.com/events

Spirit vs Shadow: A Cautionary Tale

Since this book became too big to fit into a single volume, the section on spiritual wisdom, spiritual teaching and enlightenment has been separated from this volume on personal success and development.

There is a word of caution I must raise here as a result, which is that I have heard from several people who have invested many years, sometimes decades, in some form of spiritual path, perhaps with a spiritual group or a spiritual teacher, only to find that they are no closer to the happiness they sought from when they started. As I discuss this with people, we often arrive at the Awareness that they would have been better off engaging in some form of psychodynamic practice – Shadow Work – such as this volume presents, instead. I'd hate to think I could have prevented you from losing decades to this potential pitfall and had not done so – hence this additional note.

Spirituality and enlightenment has its value, and may be timely for some people, but there's nothing inherent to its practice of transcendence which actively addresses the blocks to our true personalities, truths and choices, or as we've called them here, our 'No' Permissions. To put it bluntly, while it may be beneficial not to identify with the weeds in your garden, you might simply want to pull the buggers up. This is all fully explained in Volume II.

"The purpose of spiritual practice is to awaken from the dream. And the purpose of psychodynamic practice is to stop the dream from turning into a nightmare." – Ken Wilber

Personal Development Alone is Not Enough

Contrary to what some of us may think – and what I certainly thought in the past – **Personal Development** on its own has never been enough to maximise a person's quality of life. Nor can it always guarantee that our quality of life will increase overall. We have always been an interdependent species.

Teamwork is crucial to our survival, and our 'thrival': Our potential to thrive.

The False Self also creates a false sense of separation which prevents us from living life effectively. There are many ways in which we falsely separate ourselves: Believing we are separate from the world or from nature, believing we have to earn a living, believing we are independent.

For every two steps forward we take, improving our lot in life through personal endeavour and enterprise, the world around us can drag us back three steps or more. You have probably noticed society getting strained in all directions. Wealth inequality is always increasing. Our systems are breaking apart. The worst case scenario is that any of the existential challenges we face – from economic collapse to environmental breakdown – could wipe us out. At the very least, the combined effect of a dozen such factors, even if mitigated, could drastically change our experience of life as we know it.

The upside is that we, as humanity, also have a huge opportunity to build an unimaginably good life on earth with properly functioning systems. Is the breakdown of our systems adversity, or is it opportunity? It may be both.

Personal Development is something that only you can do for yourself. This has been the focus of Volume I. However, just as we as individuals can have Stuckness due to Fear Consciousness, as humanity we also have many elements of *Collective* Fear Consciousness. There is much (global) cultural Stuckness. Added to that, we also have other forms of social and global 'Stuckness', such as limiting or unhelpful rules or laws, or blocked access to resources.

And so we need **Collective Development** *alongside* our Personal Development drives to maximise the quality of life that's possible for us, and avoid disaster. My Integral Philosophy colleagues and I have some creative ideas as to how we might co-create a world beyond this current system failure, plus deep insights to help us understand what is going on. All that is the subject of Volume II of this book, and is very much a necessary part of the Kissing Consciousness Handbook and movement.

For now, I hope you have found something of use in this volume. I'm thrilled to have been able to share all of this with you, and intrigued as to what Awarenesses, benefits or outcomes may arise from it.

I offer you my best wishes and most powerful benevolent energies, care and compassion for whatever comes next. If you would like to have a one to one private session with a Kissing Consciousness Facilitator, or attend a Kissing Consciousness event, you can do so via these links.

With love,

James

www.KissingConsciousness.com/1-to-1

www.KissingConsciousness.com/events

www.KissingConsciousness.com

Index

C

D

F

M

T

U

CPSIA information can be obtained
at www.ICGtesting.com
Printed in the USA
LVHW080400170920
666201LV00010B/289

9 781916 258709